Elegance in Flight

A Comprehensive History of the F-16XL Experimental Prototype and its Role in NASA Flight Research

Albert C. Piccirillo

Library of Congress Cataloging-in-Publication Data

Piccirillo, Albert C.
  Elegance in flight : a comprehensive history of the F-16XL experimental prototype and its role in NASA flight research / Albert C. Piccirillo.
    pages cm
  Includes bibliographical references and index.
1. F-16 (Jet fighter plane) 2. Fighter planes--United States. 3. Airplanes, Military--United States--Prototypes. 4. United States. National Aeronautics and Space Administration--Research. I. Title.
  UG1242.F5P53 2015
  623.74'64--dc23
                                        2014039182

This publication is available as a free download at
http://www.nasa.gov/ebooks

ISBN 978-1-62683-022-6

9 781626 830226

National Aeronautics and Space Administration
Washington, DC

Table of Contents

Dedication

To the memory of my mother,
Eva Potter Piccirillo,
For her unwavering love and support.

The first F-16XL cruising over the Texas countryside on its first test flight, piloted by General Dynamics test pilot James A. McKinney. (Lockheed Martin)

Foreword

One of the most elegant American fighters ever built took to the skies over Fort Worth, TX, on July 3, 1982. Based on the combination of a stretched F-16 fuselage and a highly tailored cranked-arrow wing, the F-16XL began as an initiative of the General Dynamics Corporation (GD). GD recognized that the standard F-16 increasingly was being committed by the Air Force to a multirole mission that the aircraft had never been intended for. Originally designed as a lightweight air combat fighter, the aircraft was more and more often being tasked to perform ground attack missions. The F-16 was far from optimal for that role. Weight and drag penalties, imposed by air-to-ground ordnance and related targeting sensors, severely reduced its speed and range capabilities. The aircraft was also seriously limited in the number of weapons that it could carry compared to a larger aircraft. Initially known as Supersonic Cruise and Maneuver Prototype (SCAMP), the GD initiative was also intended to address emerging Air Force interest in supersonic combat capability. By independently developing an experimental prototype that would inexpensively validate the concept of transonic/supersonic cruise and maneuverability along with improved air-to-ground capabilities, GD hoped to interest the Air Force in supporting development and production of what was essentially a new aircraft, but one that shared much in common with the basic F-16.

GD was well aware of the National Aeronautics and Space Administration (NASA) supersonic transport and fighter research efforts based on the use of cranked-arrow wing planforms. During both the YF-16 Lightweight Fighter technology demonstrator program and the follow-on F-16 full-scale development programs, GD and NASA had established a highly productive working relationship. That arrangement had proven immensely effective in quickly and effectively resolving a number of very difficult technical issues related to the F-16. Based on those successes, GD established an arrangement with NASA for SCAMP research that was so effective that it can truly be stated that the F-16XL prototype configurations were in many significant ways the direct result of the joint research effort with NASA. At the same time, the company was able to obtain Air Force support and partial funding for a flight demonstration program. Early on, this evolved into a competitive evaluation with the aircraft that the senior leadership within the Air Force really wanted—an air-to-ground version of the F-15 Eagle air superiority fighter known as the F-15E. General Dynamics attempted to convince the Air Force that a production variant of the F-16XL was complementary to the standard F-16 and did not need to be in competition with the larger F-15. However, Congress directed that only one of these aircraft was to be funded for production as what the Air Force termed its Dual-Role Fighter (DRF). Additional complicating factors were the ongoing and covert development and production of the F-117 stealth attack aircraft and the emerging Advanced Tactical Fighter (ATF) program, first funded in fiscal year 1983. The ATF was focused on developing a supersonic cruise–capable air superiority fighter with both high maneuverability *and* all-aspect stealth. Both the F-117 and the ATF enjoyed extremely high priorities within the Air Force.

The Air Force flight-test evaluation of the F-16XL was conducted during the 1982–1983 timeframe. It was based on a Combined Test Force (CTF) approach that was similar to what had been used very successfully during the YF-16 evaluation. Under this concept, a combination of developmental- and operational-utility-type testing was conducted by a flight-test team that included both military and contractor participation in nearly all aspects of the test effort. The F-16XL flight-test program at Edwards Air Force Base, CA, progressed at a very rapid pace, with 369 flights accomplished by the end of Phase I testing on May 15, 1983. During the evaluation, the F-16XL had demonstrated many outstanding capabilities. Its range, payload, and supersonic performance were superior to those of the standard F-16, but it was unable to cruise supersonically without the use of afterburner. Also, takeoff and landing distances were longer than desired, and although the aircraft exhibited outstanding spin resistance and recovery characteristics, there were a large number of flight control issues that remained to be resolved at the conclusion of testing. Additionally, the relatively low thrust-to-weight ratio combined with the high induced drag produced by the low aspect ratio highly swept wing resulted in rapid loss of airspeed during sustained subsonic high–acceleration of gravity (g) maneuvering flight. Flight-test evaluation results for both competing aircraft and other sources of information, including the outcomes of computerized war games, were used in the Air Force DRF source selection. The F-15E was selected for production in January 1984. Based on competing programmatic and budgetary choices, the Air Force rationally had elected to fund the F-15E, the F-117, and the ATF, finally terminating the F-16XL development in mid-1985. Funding was provided for limited continuing flight testing, much of it oriented to evaluation of the General Electric F110 turbofan engine, which lasted until October 1985. By that time, both F-16XL prototypes had accumulated a total of nearly 800 sorties between them.

During the 1990s, NASA was pursuing a complex High-Speed Research (HSR) program that involved many facets. One of these was the potential application of a supersonic laminar flow control (SLFC) capability to a highly swept, cranked-arrow wing. The concept was to come up with a flight demonstration that would reduce the technical risk of using SLFC technology in the design, development, and production of a High-Speed Civil Transport (HSCT). The F-16XL, with its cranked-arrow wing planform that closely resembled candidates for the HSCT, provided a unique opportunity as an SLFC test bed. Thus, NASA arranged for the two aircraft to be transferred from storage at the General Dynamics facility in Fort Worth, TX, to the Dryden Flight Research Center. The F-16XLs would be used for a series of HSR-related test projects during the 1990s, with the SLFC research being the most challenging and high-visibility. The F-16XL-2 was highly modified for the purposes of SLFC research, during which it demonstrated that the concept was technically feasible. However, there were technical and practical operational issues related to operational use of laminar flow technology on a large civil airliner. For example, manufacturing the active suction wing panels, which incorporated millions of laser-drilled holes, was considered impractical and economically infeasible by the aircraft industry. The NASA F-16XL program ended even prior to the demise of the entire HSCT program in 1999. Follow-on NASA experiments with the F-16XLs produced a very large volume of technical data and reports that were very effectively used to further the state of the art in computer modeling of aerodynamic, acoustic, and sonic boom phenomenology. In particular, the F-16XL Cranked-Arrow Wing Aerodynamics Program (CAWAP) was a major contributor to understanding the vortex flows over highly swept wings. CAWAP and the SLFC project made major contributions to the development and validation of Computational Fluid Dynamics (CFD) capabilities and related design tools and methodologies across the aerospace community, both in the United States and internationally.

The intent of this book is to discuss comprehensively both the F-16XL development and its flight testing. In many ways, the development of the F-16XL is as much a NASA story as it is an Air Force and General Dynamics/ Lockheed Martin story. The author has chosen to address the F-16XL story in the light of the technical, programmatic, budgetary, and political considerations that shaped its development and subsequent use as a research aircraft. Thus, the book is essentially a comprehensive case study covering all aspects of the F-16XL saga from its early conceptual design—including wind tunnel and ground testing, computer simulations, and program advocacy—through construction of the two prototypes and their use in both the Air Force flight demonstration effort and NASA aeronautical research.

General Dynamics YF-16 prototype over the Mojave during the Lightweight Fighter (LWF) competitive fly-off. (USAF)

CHAPTER 1

Experimental Prototyping and Supersonic Combat

On January 13, 1975 Air Force Secretary John McLucas announced the YF-16 as the winner of the LWF competition, justifying Harry Hillaker's belief in a small, high performance jet that flies circles around "bigger is better" fighters then in vogue. A revolutionary design, the F-16 combines internal avionics, Fly-By-Wire, low cost and provisions for growth.

—Inscription in the Legacy Hall of Building 200, Lockheed Martin, Fort Worth, TX.

Both the standard F-16 and its F-16XL derivative trace their lineage to the experimental prototyping program of the 1970s. The Department of Defense (DoD) had implemented an Advanced Prototype Development Program in early 1971 in direct response to the release of a Presidential Blue Ribbon Defense Panel report in July 1970. That special commission had been chartered by President Richard M. Nixon to examine the DoD weapons system acquisition process in response to strong congressional and public criticism of several major defense weapon system programs.[1] The Blue Ribbon Panel report was highly critical of the defense acquisition process, which had a history of moving major weapons systems into full-scale development without any prior validation of their capability to achieve specified operational requirements. The panel strongly recommended competitive prototyping as a key element of its package of proposed defense acquisition reforms.

Prototyping and the Onset of the Lightweight Fighter Program

Even prior to release of the Blue Ribbon Panel report, Deputy Secretary of Defense David Packard had issued a memo on weapons system acquisition in which he announced that the DoD would be moving to a "Fly-Before-Buy" approach. The Advanced Prototype Development Program was formally implemented by the DoD in early 1971. In May of that year, the secretary of the U.S. Air Force (USAF) proposed that the USAF develop a plan that would identify new candidates for prototyping. These candidates would focus on initiatives that were important to meeting future Air Force operational needs.[2]

The DoD strongly supported the Air Force initiative and urged that one or two candidates be selected to start development in 1972. An Air Force Prototyping Study Group was formed, and it recommended several candidates for prototyping. These included two efforts that were highly significant in light of subsequent aircraft developments. One proposed prototyping effort was for a low-radar-cross-section (RCS) technology demonstrator aircraft. This evolved into a highly classified "special project" that would become known as "Have Blue." It developed a small experimental prototype aircraft that used a concept of faceted airframe shaping to achieve a very low RCS. The Have Blue demonstrator (covertly developed by a Lockheed Skunk Works team) flew for the first time in December 1977 and proved that a true low-RCS stealth aircraft was feasible. Have Blue led to the successful F-117A program.

Another of the rapid prototyping programs that had been recommended by the Air Force was a Lightweight Fighter (LWF). It was officially approved to begin in 1972 by a DoD Program Decision Memorandum released on August 25, 1971. Two days later, the Air Force established the Prototype Program Office within the Aeronautical Systems Division (ASD) at Wright-Patterson Air Force Base (AFB), OH.[3] Out of this program would spring two LWF prototypes—the single-engine, single-fin General Dynamics YF-16 and the twin-engine, twin-fin Northrop YF-17. Both were extraordinary aircraft, and both led to widely produced production derivatives—the General Dynamics (later Lockheed Martin) F-16 and the McDonnell-Douglas (later Boeing) F/A-18.

The Air Force Prototyping Study Group had recommended that streamlined management processes be implemented to facilitate successful prototype programs. A new DoD directive (DoDD 5000.1) formalized the new approach. It stated that "the advanced technology effort includes prototyping, preferably using small, efficient design teams and a minimum of documentation. The objective is to obtain significant advances in technology at minimum cost."[4] This new DoD approach to prototyping was intended to provide the benefits of risk reduction and increased confidence in new technologies without the necessity of having to commit to a specific weapon system design. In August 1971, the new prototyping approach was presented to industry by senior DoD and Service acquisition officials. They highlighted that future DoD prototype programs were to meet the following guidelines. (As will be seen later, these guidelines were closely followed in structuring and executing the F-16XL effort as well as the associated Air Force Dual-Role Fighter [DRF] competition that would result in the selection of the McDonnell-Douglas F-15E for follow-on full-scale development and production.)

- Prototypes were to be experimental systems. They were to precede detail engineering development of any new weapon system.
- Prototypes were intended to support future military needs.
- Prototypes were to be focused on reducing risk to future development programs. In this context, they were to address not only technical risk but also cost and schedule risk, as well as uncertainties in operational requirements.
- Prototype programs were expected to include some degree of technology uncertainty and risk, but they should also have a reasonable chance of success.
- Prototypes were to have low relative cost compared to potential follow-on development and production programs.
- Prototypes were intended to help achieve lower-cost alternative solutions.
- Finally, experimental prototypes were not intended to form the sole basis for system procurement decisions.

From Lightweight Fighter to F-16

As mentioned earlier, a Lightweight Fighter program was one of the recommendations of the Air Force Prototyping Study Group. An LWF Request for Proposals (RFP) was released to industry in early January 1972 with responses due in mid-February. The purpose of the LWF program was to determine the feasibility of developing a small, lightweight, low-cost fighter; to establish what such an aircraft can do; and to evaluate its possible operational utility. The Prototyping Study Group had defined a set of general objectives for an LWF that are very interesting in light of the results of the subsequent F-16 and F-16XL development programs. The LWF aircraft was to have a gross weight at takeoff of less than 20,000 pounds; possess superior performance and maneuvering in the transonic, high-g flight regime; and be capable of operating in a 225 nautical mile (nm) radius on internal fuel and out to a 700 nm radius with external fuel. It was to be capable of Mach 1–1.2 speeds at sea level and Mach 2.0 at altitude. Armament and avionics were to be limited to those elements that were absolutely mission-essential for within visual range (WVR) air combat. In addition, the LWF was to have excellent visibility and handling qualities with an emphasis on close-in air combat capabilities. Nine companies responded to the LWF RFP, with the Air Force selecting the proposals submitted by General Dynamics and Northrop. These would be built as the GD YF-16 and the Northrop YF-17, with two prototypes of each design being constructed for a 1-year flight-test program. Each contractor would pick the starting date for its respective 1-year flight-test program. The separate flight-test programs were to be two independent evaluations of the performance and combat potential offered by the advanced technology and design innovations that were implemented in each of the alternative LWF designs. Each LWF design would be evaluated by a Joint Test Team (JTT) consisting of contractor, Air Force Flight Test Center (AFFTC), Tactical Air Command (TAC), and Air Force Test and Evaluation Center (AFTEC) representatives. From the program's inception, it was intended that NASA technical expertise and facilities would be used by the aircraft development contractors to facilitate the implementation of advanced aeronautical technologies into their LWF designs. Since the LWF concept was so oriented to close-in maneuvering combat capability, the results of NASA research into so-called vortex lift was a technology area of high interest to the industry design teams.

On left: General Dynamics YF-16 prototype over the Mojave during the Lightweight Fighter (LWF) competitive fly-off. On right: The Northrop YF-17, which, despite losing the LWF competition, evolved into the subsequent F/A-18 naval strike fighter. (Both images USAF)

General Dynamics had begun to develop the aerodynamic configuration of what eventually became the YF-16 as far back as 1968. They had been testing wide forebody strakes for increased lift and were exploiting the results of NASA research in this area, as was Northrop with their YF-17 design, which also incorporated forebody strakes. NASA aerodynamicists had pointed out that at high angles of attack (AoA), flow separation from sharply swept wings and forebody strakes was inevitable and rather than attempting to avoid separated flow, it was better to control and exploit it. NASA wind tunnel testing had showed that sharp-edged forebody strakes produced a more stable flow pattern that generated lift, improved directional stability, and shed vortices over the wings, which delayed wing stall by continually mixing boundary-layer air with free-stream air. These qualities became known as controlled vortex lift and were highly important to both the F-16 and the F-16XL designs. NASA Langley's

Edward C. Polhamus had been a leader in vortex lift research, and his reports and technical publications were widely disseminated throughout the aircraft industry in the late 1960s continuing into the 1980s.[5]

By mid-1973, General Dynamics had finalized the YF-16 design. The first experimental prototype rolled out on December 13 of that year at the GD Fort Worth, TX, facility. On January 20, 1974, the prototype had an unscheduled first flight that occurred during a high-speed taxi test. As it raced down the runway, it began a lateral pilot-induced oscillation (PIO) at a rate of one roll cycle every 1.4 seconds (due to excessively high gain scheduling in the flight control system [FCS] when weight came off the wheels). The rolling motion caused the left wingtip and right horizontal tail to contact the ground, and the plane veered off the runway centerline. Test pilot Phil Oestricher wisely elected to take off rather than remain on the ground. Thus, before the startled eyes of onlookers, he added power and the little YF-16 thundered into the air, climbing into the Mojave sky. Afterward, Oestricher reflected,

> At that point, I had little choice of actions, since the airplane was beginning to drift to the left side of the runway. I powered it up and just sort of let go and the airplane just flew off the runway very smoothly once I quit irritating it. I stayed in the landing pattern and came around and made a relatively uneventful landing. We hadn't intended to fly in a noticeable way that day, but we did. Incidentally, I was impressed with the way the marketing/public relations people got around our UNOFFICIAL first flight. They just called it "flight zero," and that made the next one number one![6]

The inadvertent flight lasted 6 minutes. Oestricher had masterfully averted potential disaster, and afterward, technicians swiftly adjusted the FCS gains.

The first officially scheduled flight took place in February. Within a few days, the aircraft was conducting high-g maneuvers at supersonic speeds. By March 1974, Mach 2.0 had been reached. The flight-test program progressed at an impressive pace and was completed by January 31, 1975, with a total of 439 flight hours accomplished on 347 test sorties using the two experimental prototypes.

The YF-16 proved to be outstandingly successful as both an experimental prototype and a technology demonstrator. The combination of technologies and innovations incorporated in its innovative design produced a significant advance in fighter performance. (In addition to its advanced aerodynamic features, these included a quadruple-redundant fly-by-wire [FBW] flight control system; a high visibility, high-g cockpit with a reclined ejection seat; a sidestick controller; and a high thrust-to-weight afterburning turbofan engine.) The

Two General Dynamics (now Lockheed Martin) F-16A Fighting Falcons. Fighter pilots swiftly dubbed the little jet the "Viper," by which name it is now more popularly known. (USAF)

YF-16 flight-test effort reduced the risk of successfully incorporating this set of advanced technologies into production from the earlier high-risk rating to an assessment of low risk for a Full-Scale Development (FSD) program. Three main factors contributed to this outstanding achievement: the success of the Joint Test Team concept; careful planning of the flight-test program; and the quality of design, engineering, and construction of the YF-16, which exhibited high reliability in addition to its high performance. A fourth factor that is worthy of note was the exceptional quality of the technical support that had been provided to the Air Force and General Dynamics by NASA throughout the YF-16 and F-16 conceptual and detail design efforts. This support included a variety of wind tunnel and spin tunnel testing, drop model tests, and simulator tests in support of flight control system development. NASA provided especially important contributions to the final F-16 design by helping to resolve flutter issues associated with the carriage of external weapons.[7]

The YF-16 was selected as the winner of the Air Combat Fighter (ACF) competition, in which it competed with the Northrop YF-17, in January 1975. The subsequent Full-Scale Development effort proceeded at an extremely rapid rate. The first of eight preproduction F-16s flew in December 1976, followed by the first production F-16A in August 1978. The production F-16 featured many changes from the YF-16 prototype. These included increases in fuselage length and wing and tail sizes, internal structural revisions, and avionics and flight control system changes needed to enhance mission capabilities.

The F-16A became operational with the USAF and several European air forces during the 1979–1980 timeframe. To date, over 4,500 F-16s have been produced, and the aircraft is operational with the air forces of over 25 nations. The F-16 has undergone an amazing series of upgrades and modifications in the years since its first flight in January 1974. These have kept the latest versions of the F-16 remarkably competitive with more recent foreign fighter designs that have generally adopted most of the innovations first pioneered by the YF-16, and it has fought in numerous wars over the Balkans, the Middle East, and Southwest Asia, proving to be both a redoubtable air-to-air and air-to-surface fighter.[8]

F-16 Derivative Investigations

Almost immediately after General Dynamics had been declared the winner of the ACF program, David Lewis, chairman of the board of directors and chief executive officer, directed the Fort Worth Division to evaluate F-16 upgrades and derivatives to help guarantee its future success. Harry J. Hillaker, who had served as the YF-16 deputy chief engineer and then as the F-16 director of marketing, was selected to lead GD efforts involving concept formulation and preliminary design of new F-16 derivatives. This effort eventually evolved into the F-16XL via the Supersonic Cruise and Maneuver Prototype (SCAMP) project. The XL suffix that was used to informally identify the F-16XL came from Hillaker's pastime as an avid golfer. At the time, the newly introduced Top Flite XL golf ball was advertised for its aerodynamic refinements that provided maximum range performance. Hillaker proposed physical and aerodynamic refinements to increase the range and aerodynamic performance of the F-16. Under his lead, F-16 upgrades, improvements, and derivative design studies were conducted. These were oriented to extending range and payload, expanding basic missions, and developing advanced versions or derivative configurations of the aircraft. Importantly, these were intended to enhance both air-to-air and air-to-ground capabilities while retaining the maximum possible commonality with the basic F-16 design.[9]

During most of 1976, a GD team examined operational capabilities and characteristics of fighters in the Air Force inventory as well as those then being introduced into service. The assessment focused on the limitations of these aircraft in likely future combat scenarios. An important aspect of the assessment was evaluation of improvements in system characteristics and capabilities that would have a critical effect on successful mission outcomes. Improvements examined included enhanced weapons carriage, increased fuel capacity, better range and payload, greater maneuvering performance, reduced takeoff and landing distances, and survivability considerations. In their preliminary assessments, GD included several F-16 derivative designs. These used different wing configurations that were designed to mate with the F-16 fuselage. The F-16 fuselages were lengthened as necessary for proper integration with each wing configuration. For comparative purposes, the existing F-16A was used as a reference. Wing planforms evaluated in these studies included what GD referred to as an equal weight composite (EWC) wing, a forward-swept wing (FSW), a "cranked-arrow" wing, and a design that featured a standard 60-degree delta wing with a forward fuselage-mounted canard.[10] The EWC wing configuration used a redesigned and somewhat larger version of the existing F-16 wing with the increased size achieved by use of lightweight composite materials. It retained the 40-degree leading-edge wing-sweep angle of the standard F-16 wing. Although geometrically similar to the F-16's trapezoidal wing, the EWC wing had an increased

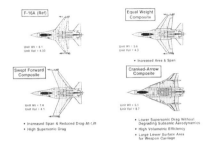

General Dynamics investigated various wing planforms integrated with appropriately modified F-16 fuselages. (Lockheed Martin)

wingspan and a larger aspect ratio and wing area, and it contained a 7-percent-larger internal volume.[11]

The physical characteristics of the candidate wing planforms are shown in Table 1. The table also includes the characteristics of the conceptual aircraft design with the forward-mounted canard surface used in conjunction with a standard 60-degree delta wing. In the table, unit weights and volumes are referenced to those of the standard F-16, which was used as the comparison baseline. For example, the EWC design has the same unit weight and a 7-percent increase in internal wing volume compared to the standard F-16 wing. The forward-swept wing, despite its much greater wing area, had an internal volume that was essentially the same as that of the F-16. The cranked-arrow composite wing had the best volumetric efficiency of the four candidates. It was 15 percent lighter and had an internal volume 2.16 times greater than the standard F-16 wing. The next best candidate, from the perspective of volumetric efficiency, was the 60-degree delta-wing/canard combination.[12]

Table 1

Characteristics of various candidate wing planforms evaluated by General Dynamics during early conceptual design efforts

Wing Planform	Aspect Ratio	Area (sq. ft.)	Sweep Angle (degrees)	Unit Weight	Unit Volume
Baseline F-16	3.0	300	40	1.00	1.00
Equal Wt. Composite	3.28	338	40	1.00	1.07
Forward Swept	4.15	800	−15	1.21	1.02
Cranked Arrow	1.62	646	70/50	0.85	2.16
60-deg. Delta Canard	1.87	414	60	0.92	1.61

Relative to one another, the various wing planforms showed advantages and disadvantages. At subsonic speeds, both the equal weight composite and the forward-swept wing had improved lift-to-drag (L/D) ratios at moderate- and high-lift conditions compared to the other designs. This enabled better takeoff and landing performance and sustained maneuvering capabilities. But while the L/D ratios of the cranked-arrow, canard-delta, and baseline F-16 were essentially equal at subsonic speeds, at supersonic speeds, the so-called "cranked-arrow" planform showed pronounced advantages that encouraged its adaptation.

While the conventional delta originated in German and American work, the cranked arrow had its origins in Sweden, home to a small but vibrant aircraft industry. In the late 1940s, Saab began development of a supersonic delta-wing jet fighter, the J 35 Draken (Dragon). The design requirements demanded a high climb rate, supersonic speed, excellent maneuverability and good handling qualities at both high and low speeds, and the ability to operate from a dispersed network of highway strips with minimal maintenance. Various wing configurations were explored, with designers favoring a delta with a very long root chord running almost to the nose of the aircraft. But instead of a classic triangular shape, it had a sharply swept inner wing section that "broke" at midspan, with the wing-sweep angle reducing markedly so that the span of the delta increased significantly. This distinctive planform was swiftly dubbed a "double delta."

First flown by Saab test pilot Bengt Olow in 1954, the J 35 proved to be a great success in Flygvapnet (the Swedish Air Force) service despite its having a deep stall issue and a tendency to encounter PIOs when its stability augmentation system was not engaged. The Mach 2.0–capable J 35 had excellent performance and very good instantaneous turn rates but, as with all delta-winged aircraft, airspeed and energy bled off rapidly during tight sustained turns, something encountered by the later F-16XL as well. The Draken became one of the most distinctive and successful of the early supersonic jet fighters, serving in the Swedish, Danish, Finnish, and Austrian air forces and, after its retirement from combat service, as a test-pilot and flight-test-engineer trainer with the National Test Pilot School at Mojave Air and Space Port, CA. (The National Test Pilot School, a remarkable and unique civilian educational institution staffed by veteran leaders in flight-test operations, practice, and methodology, trains test pilots and flight-test engineers from around the world using a variety of other fixed- and rotary-wing aircraft.) Not surprisingly, during early thinking for the XL, General Dynamics engineers studied and discussed the Draken, recognizing its general similarity in design and relevance to their studies.[13]

At supersonic speeds, and especially as Mach number increased beyond 1.2, the cranked-arrow wing offered improved lift to drag characteristics at both

A two-place Saab Sk 35C Draken trainer of the National Test Pilot School cruising over the Sierra Nevada range on a training flight from Mojave Air and Space Port, Mojave, CA. Its "cranked-arrow" double-delta wing is readily apparent; the configuration anticipated by over a quarter century the cranked-arrow planform of the General Dynamics F-16XL. (National Test Pilot School photograph, courtesy Gregory V. Lewis and Russ Stewart)

cruise and moderate angles of attack compared to the others. At supersonic speeds and at higher lift conditions, the cranked-arrow wing was equal to the other candidates in the improvements it offered compared to the baseline F-16. Drag with the cranked-arrow wing during wings-level acceleration in 1-g flight was comparable to that of the baseline F-16, the equal weight composite, and the canard-delta, and it was significantly better than that of the forward-swept wing. At Mach 2.0, only the canard-delta and cranked-arrow planforms showed the potential to provide increased L/D. Both of these planforms were comparable in terms of cruise efficiency at all speeds from Mach 0.9 to Mach 2.0. The canard-delta and the cranked arrow were equal to the baseline F-16 at Mach 0.9, and their L/D ratios were better across the entire supersonic speed range.

GD studies also indicated that the spanwise location of the wing crank had a significant effect on subsonic and transonic lift-to-drag ratios. The cranked-arrow wing could be optimized to retain a subsonic efficiency (as measured by L/D) that was closely comparable to that of the F-16. An additional advantage was its very significant design and integration advantages. These included a greatly increased wing area that provided much more volume for additional fuel and an increased wing chord that allowed for efficient conformal weapons carriage. However, studies and analyses of the competing wing planforms conclusively showed that the cranked-arrow wing traded off sustained maneuver capability for decreased drag during 1-g acceleration, better L/D at supersonic speed, and improved cruise efficiency. This reduction in sustained subsonic maneuvering capability when compared to the basic F-16 proved to be a very significant factor in the later Air Force flight-test program and would eventually influence the Air Force's decision not to select a variant of the F-16XL for full-scale development and production.[14]

General Dynamics had been one of the companies responding to a Request for Proposals jointly issued by the Defense Advanced Research Projects Agency (DARPA) and the Air Force Flight Dynamics Laboratory in 1977. The RFP called for industry to respond with their design concepts for an experimental aircraft with a forward-swept wing. The GD FSW design was tested in the Unitary Plan Wind Tunnel at the NASA Langley Research

A wind tunnel test model of a modified F-16 fuselage fitted with a forward-swept wing mounted in the NASA Langley Unitary Plan Wind Tunnel in 1980. (NASA)

Center (LaRC) in 1980. However, Grumman's FSW technology demonstrator concept was selected instead in December 1981. Designated the X-29A, Grumman built two demonstrators that were flight-tested by the Air Force and NASA from December 1984 through late 1991. Several NASA pilots who participated in the X-29 flight research effort—including William H. Dana, Dana D. Purifoy, and James W. Smolka—would also fly the F-16XL.[15]

Supersonic Cruise Studies: First Steps on the Path to the F-16XL

Also during the mid-to-late 1970s, the U.S. Air Force was expressing increasing interest in the possibilities offered by advanced fighters. This was being driven by the improving lethality of modern integrated air defense systems along with the prospective fielding of new Soviet fighters and advanced surface-to-air missile (SAM) systems. In particular, efficient supersonic performance over significant operational ranges was now considered a highly desirable feature. Other attributes important to success in modern air combat (to include high maneuverability and good payload, along with advanced sensors and weapons) were also receiving increasing emphasis. The Air Force Flight Dynamics Laboratory issued many contracts to the aircraft industry, including General Dynamics, for studies of advanced fighter designs and related technologies needed to deal with emerging military requirements and potential enemy threats. Results from these studies were presented to the Air Force and NASA in the form of detailed reports and presentations at specialist technology conferences. These included the 1976 Technology for Supersonic Cruise Military Aircraft conference and a follow-on conference in 1977 titled Operational Utility of Supersonic Cruise. Both conferences were held at Wright-Patterson AFB, home of the USAF Aeronautical Systems Division. In these and other similar venues, a strong consensus affirmed that supersonic cruise performance was not only achievable but that such a capability would greatly enhance military mission success.[16]

Supersonic Cruise Integrated Fighter Concept Investigation

The NASA Langley Research Center had been heavily involved in most aspects of the abortive U.S. Supersonic Transport (SST) program of the 1960s (which had been cancelled in 1971). In conjunction with the SST program, cranked-arrow wing designs had been heavily studied during NASA's Supersonic Commercial Air Transport (SCAT) effort. The ultimate embodiment of SCAT research was SCAT-15F, with its huge cranked-arrow wing, tested in the NASA LaRC High-Speed 7- by 10-foot Wind Tunnel in mid-1969.

After the U.S. SST program had been cancelled, Langley's supersonic research efforts were refocused under the Supersonic Cruise Research (SCR) program.[17] A number of research areas important to achieving economical supersonic flight were assessed in the SCR effort. Among these were major investigations intended to optimize highly swept wing configurations for efficient supersonic performance and to advance knowledge in the area of vortex flow technology. These vortex flow technology investigations were intended to enhance aerodynamic performance of highly swept wings at the higher lift conditions associated with transonic maneuvering and on final approach to landing—both areas of serious concern. Langley had also initiated a focused research program known as the Supersonic Cruise Integrated Fighter (SCIF) program. Its overall goal was to foster the use of supercruise technologies in military fighter aircraft. The SCIF effort, led by Langley's Roy V. Harris, Jr., was oriented to studying the feasibility of supersonic cruise aircraft fighter concepts. Under the SCIF effort, NASA Langley's resources and aerodynamic and flight dynamic test capabilities were focused on investigations that used a variety of fighter aircraft configurations. Developed in-house at Langley, these designs were highly oriented toward supercruise

A SCAT-15F model during Langley testing in June 1969. (NASA)

capability. At the same time, Langley also coordinated its research activities with industry teams involved in similar supersonic cruise studies. In cooperation with the Air Force and various industry focus groups, the Langley research staff designed and tested supersonic cruise fighter concepts across the Mach number ranges that were available using Langley's wind tunnels. Six different SCIF design concepts were developed. These provided coverage of anticipated military requirements for supercruise. Concepts ranged from a design that cruised at Mach 1.4 while also having good maneuverability to a Mach 2.6 design that strongly emphasized supersonic cruise performance.

The SCIF configurations were based on highly swept cranked-arrow wing planforms. They featured wing twist and camber approaches that were tailored to minimize supersonic drag. The outer wing panels on the SCIF wings had reduced sweep, a feature that increased wingspan, improved subsonic and transonic aerodynamic efficiency, and provided improved aircraft handling qualities. At higher angles of attack, these highly swept wing planforms created powerful vortices over the wing leading edges. These vortices produced so-called vortex lift while also reducing drag. Vortex lift provided possibilities for improved maneuverability. It was the subject of many investigations at NASA Langley over a period of many years. Following supersonic wind tunnel testing, two of the SCIF designs, designated SCIF-4 and SCIF-5, were selected for extensive testing over a wide Mach number range. These wind tunnel tests generated extensive data for use in follow-on supersonic design and performance studies. SCIF-4 was oriented to the air superiority mission and had a cruise Mach number of 1.8. The other design (SCIF-5) had a higher fineness ratio with primary emphasis placed on achieving a very high supersonic cruise speed of Mach 2.6. Both SCIF designs were based on tailless cranked-arrow wing planforms that featured highly swept inboard wing segments to meet supersonic cruise requirements.[18]

In 1977, Langley research engineer Barrett L. Shrout reported on the results of the NASA Langley investigation of the supersonic cruise point design known as SCIF-4. This represented a supersonic fighter optimized for sustained cruise at a Mach number of 1.8. Its cranked-arrow wing configuration featured twin vertical tailfins mounted at the intersection of the inner and outer wing segments. A SCIF-4 force model was tested across the Mach number range from 0.6 to 2.16 using NASA Langley's 8-foot transonic pressure tunnel and the Unitary Plan Wind Tunnel. A large, captive free-flight model demonstrated flight to higher angles of attack in Langley's 30- by 60-foot Full-Scale Tunnel. The SCIF-4 configuration had limited maneuvering capabilities at higher angles of attack. Shrout noted that this concept was aerodynamically very similar to that of a supersonic transport. It was based on the technical knowledge and design methodology that had evolved from the SST program and was supplemented by subsequent NASA supersonic research efforts. In fact, the knowledge base and analytical methodologies that derived from the earlier supersonic transport effort heavily influenced the entire SCIF effort.[19]

That same year, Langley's O.A. Morris reported on a wind tunnel investigation of subsonic and supersonic aerodynamics that included

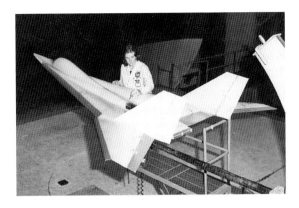

A wind tunnel force model of the NASA SCIF-4 supersonic cruise fighter configuration being prepared for testing at NASA Langley in 1977. (NASA)

longitudinal and lateral stability. This wind tunnel investigation used a model of the SCIF-5 fighter design concept. It featured a highly swept cranked-arrow wing designed for a cruise Mach number of 2.6. Leading-edge sweep angle was 74 degrees on the inboard wing segments and 65 degrees on the outer wing panels. SCIF-5 incorporated sophisticated wing twist and camber, features that were intended to minimize supersonic drag due to lift. Twin vertical tailfins were located outboard on the wing. During the SCIF-5 investigation, the configuration was modified with larger outboard vertical tailfins. Small nose-mounted strakes were also tested with this model.[20] Results from the SCIF program and related NASA efforts were presented at the supersonic cruise conferences held at Wright-Patterson AFB in 1976 and 1977. Published in a number of Air Force and NASA Technical Memoranda, the results were widely distributed across the aircraft industry, the military services, and academia.[21]

NASA/GD Supercruise Cooperative Efforts

Efficient supercruise performance was seen by most experts in NASA and the aerospace industry as being a primary driver in future fighter designs. It was generally believed that very highly swept wing platforms would be needed to achieve efficient supercruise performance. These supersonic cruise wing planforms were visualized as being similar to those used on the Anglo-French Concorde, the Soviet Tupolev Tu-144, and the cancelled U.S. SST program. However, subtle modifications and adaptations of supersonic cruise wing designs to meet fighter maneuverability requirements would be needed if a fighter with both supercruise capability and high transonic/supersonic maneuverability was to be viable. Coming up with these technological adaptations was a strong motivation for aircraft industry interaction with the NASA

Langley staff. Industry was looking to benefit from Langley's expertise, design methods, and experience with highly swept wing designs gained during efforts oriented to a civil supersonic transport such as the SCAT effort as well as the SCIF effort.[22] Subsequent to the SCIF program, Langley joined with several industry partners in cooperative, nonproprietary studies of supercruise configurations that were intended to be applicable to future advanced fighter designs.[23] General Dynamics had initiated supercruise fighter conceptual design efforts in 1976. That year, the first conceptual supercruise fighter layout was completed under the supervision of GD aeronautical engineer Gordon F. Gibson, who had also done the layout work on the YF-16 Lightweight Fighter. During discussions with NASA, GD highlighted the fact that the modular construction approach successfully used in the YF-16 Lightweight Fighter prototype and the production F-16 aircraft could be adapted quickly and inexpensively to create a supercruise fighter technology demonstrator. This technology demonstrator aircraft would use an F-16 fuselage mated with a highly swept supersonic wing. This was intended to be derived from a cooperative research effort with NASA. This new wing concept would be optimized for both good transonic/supersonic cruise capability and good transonic/supersonic maneuvering performance. General Dynamics was confident that a supersonic cruise fighter demonstrator aircraft would attract interest and support from the Air Force. However, a strong corporate commitment along with a significant financial investment would be needed.[24]

One of the earliest meetings to promote a cooperative supersonic wing design effort between General Dynamics and NASA occurred in March 1977. Discussions focused on a joint project involving advanced supersonic wings to be designed in conjunction with NASA. Testing was to be accomplished in the supersonic Langley Unitary Plan Wind Tunnel and the transonic Langley High-Speed 7- by 10-Foot Wind Tunnel. In order to be considered, candidate wing concepts had to be capable of being integrated with the basic F-16 fuselage. The goal was to create an advanced version of the F-16 with longer range, heavier payload, generally enhanced performance, and the potential for supersonic cruise capability. As part of the cooperative effort, General Dynamics would assign several engineers to temporary duty at the Langley Research Center. Their initial efforts would focus on supercruise wing design methodology. Project leader for supersonic design efforts at NASA Langley at the time was David S. Miller. GD engineering personnel were periodically collocated with the Langley research staff, where NASA's Charles M. Jackson served as overall manager of the collaborative effort. General Dynamics's Roy T. Schemensky, in cooperation with Miller and Langley researchers John E. Lamar and C. Subba Reddy, coauthored a number of professional papers and technical reports. These were published over the next several years, and they detailed technical aspects and results from the NASA/GD collaboration.[25] Wind tunnel testing and analytical studies continued to validate earlier assumptions that many of the conflicting demands of efficient supersonic cruise and transonic maneuver could be met with a properly designed and tailored wing.

Based on these highly promising results, General Dynamics initiated a company-funded development intended to produce a derivative of the F-16 with supersonic cruise and maneuver capabilities and made this a high priority within the corporation. A cooperative agreement with NASA covering mutual efforts that could lead to development of a new flight demonstrator aircraft was developed and approved. GD soon began to refer to this flight demonstrator aircraft as the Supersonic Cruise and Maneuver Prototype. By 1978, wind tunnel testing of new wing designs integrated with a modified F-16 fuselage was indicating a supersonic performance improvement of about 30 percent compared with the basic F-16. At subsonic speeds, performance was generally similar to that of the standard F-16. Encouraged by these positive results, General Dynamics committed to development of the SCAMP concept. It used a highly swept "cranked" (double delta) wing planform to achieve enhanced supersonic cruise efficiency and transonic maneuvering capabilities. Refinement of the SCAMP concept would eventually lead to the development of the F-16XL design. Several cooperative research projects with NASA would use the SCAMP/F-16XL configuration in follow-on studies covering a wide range of important topics. These included supersonic conformal store carriage concepts, low-speed stability and control of highly swept wing configurations, and determination of spin characteristics.[26] In the longer term, the F-16XL prototypes would be transferred from the Air Force to NASA, and they would be used for a number of research efforts related to high-speed research into technology risk reduction for a prospective high-speed civil transport. Foremost among these was the Supersonic Laminar Flow Control project. The range of NASA F-16XL research efforts will be discussed in depth later in this book.

Endnotes

1. See, for instance, Robert J. Art, *The TFX Decision: McNamara and the Military* (Boston, MA: Little, Brown and Company, 1968); Robert F. Coulam, *Illusions of Choice: The F-111 and the Problem of Weapons Acquisition Reform* (Princeton, NJ: Princeton University Press, 1977). The highly controversial Tactical Fighter Experimental (TFX) program eventually led to the development and production of the General Dynamics F-111. Intended to become the basis of a standard multipurpose fighter for joint service use by both the Air Force and the Navy, the very large, heavy aircraft ended up being used solely for the long-range strike mission by the Air Force after the Navy withdrew from the program.
2. Richard P. Hallion, "A Troubling Past: Air Force Fighter Acquisition since 1945," presented at the Triangle Universities' *Security Seminar on Changing Technologies and New Weapons Systems*, Durham, NC, February 2–3, 1990, and published in *Airpower Journal* 4, no. 4 (winter 1990).
3. David C. Aronstein and Albert C. Piccirillo, *Have Blue and the F-117A: Evolution of the Stealth Fighter* (Reston, VA: American Institute of Aeronautics and Astronautics [AIAA], 1997); David C. Aronstein and Albert C. Piccirillo, *The Lightweight Fighter Program: A Successful Approach to Fighter Technology Transition* (Reston, Virginia: AIAA, 1996). The latter reference was based heavily on a report of the same title that the authors prepared for the Joint Advanced Strike Technology (JAST) Program Office in March 1995.
4. David C. Aronstein and Albert C. Piccirillo, "The F-16 Lightweight Fighter: A Case Study in Technology Transition," in *Technology and the Air Force: A Retrospective Assessment*, ed. Jacob Neufeld et al. (Washington, DC: Air Force History and Museums Program, 1997).
5. J.K. Buckner, D.B. Benepe, and P.W. Hill, "Aerodynamic Design Evolution of the YF-16," AIAA Paper 74-935 (1974); Edward C. Polhamus, "A Concept of the Vortex Lift of Sharp-Edge Delta Wings Based On A Leading-Edge-Suction Analogy," NASA Technical Note (TN) D-3767 (December 1966); Edward C. Polhamus, "Vortex Lift Research: Early Contributions and Some Current Challenges," in *Vortex Flow Aerodynamics—Volume I, Proceedings of Conference held October 8–10, 1986 at Langley Research Center*, NASA Conference Publication (CP) 2416, Paper No. 1 (1986), pp. 1–30.
6. Quoted in Lou Drendel, *F-16 Fighting Falcon in Action—Aircraft No. 53* (Carrollton, TX: Squadron/Signal Publications, 1982), p. 31.

7. Joseph R. Chambers, *Partners in Freedom: Contributions of the Langley Research Center to U.S. Military Aircraft of the 1990's*, Monographs in Aerospace History Number 19 (Washington, DC: NASA Special Publication (SP) 2000-4519, 2000).

8. Aronstein, Piccirillo, *The Lightweight Fighter Program*; Michael Ennis, "The Plane the Pentagon Couldn't Stop," *Texas Monthly* (June 1981): pp. 132–151.

9. Hillaker had worked at the Convair division of General Dynamics and then at the Fort Worth Division of GD since 1942. During that time, he was involved in the development of every operational aircraft that emerged from the Fort Worth facility. These included the World War II B-24 Liberator bomber (produced in greater quantity than any U.S. combat aircraft), the 10-engine Strategic Air Command (SAC) B-36 intercontinental bomber, SAC's Mach 2.0-capable B-58 Hustler, and the controversial swing-wing F-111. For information on these Convair/GD aircraft, see John Wegg, *General Dynamics Aircraft and Their Predecessors* (Annapolis, MD: Naval Institute Press, 1990); Eric Hehs, "Harry Hillaker: Father of the F-16," *Code One Magazine* (April 15, 1991).

10. Harry J. Hillaker, F-16XL presentation to the Lone Star Aero Club, Arlington, TX, September 3, 1998.

11. The average distance from a wing's leading edge to its trailing edge is known as the chord, denoted by the symbol c. The distance from one wingtip to the other is the wingspan, given the symbol b. The shape of the wing, when viewed from above, is called its planform. For most wing planforms, the chord length varies along the span. The wing area, S, is bounded by the leading and trailing edges and the wingtips. Aspect ratio (AR) is a measure of how long and slender a wing is from tip to tip, or simply the ratio of its wingspan to average chord. The AR of a wing is most easily calculated as the square of its wingspan divided by its wing area. In simple mathematical terms, $AR=b^2/S$. High aspect ratio wings have long wingspans while low aspect ratio wings have short spans (like the F-16 fighter) and/or long chords (like the Space Shuttle and the F-16XL). An important component of overall drag is induced drag, which varies inversely to the aspect ratio of the wing. Thus, a high aspect ratio wing has lower induced drag than a low aspect ratio wing. Because the long-range efficiency of an airliner or a bomber depends on the ratio of the lift to the drag (or the L/D), these aircraft are designed with high aspect ratio wings. Conversely, high-speed aircraft and highly maneuverable fighters have lower aspect ratio wings. NASA Glenn Research

Center, *Beginner's Guide to Aerodynamics* (hereafter BGA), Wing Geometry Definitions, at *http://www.grc.nasa.gov.*

12. Major Patrick K. Talty, USAF, "F-16XL Demonstrates New Capabilities in its Flight Test Program at Edwards AFB, California," Air Command and Staff College, USAF Air University, Report Number 86-2490, April 1986; Patrick K. Talty and Donald J. Caughlin, "F-16XL Demonstrates New Capabilities in Flight Test at Edwards Air Force Base," *Journal of Aircraft* 25, no. 3 (March 1988): 206–215.

13. A total of 644 J 35s were built in six primary variants at the Saab Linköping factory. Surplus ex–Danish Air Force two-place Sk 35 Draken were subsequently employed in support of both flight-test and dissimilar air combat training programs conducted by U.S. military services. As many as six surplus Sk 35s were operated by the National Test Pilot School (NTPS) in Mojave, CA, and some were still flying as recently as the fall of 2012. They were used for both test pilot training and in support of systems test and evaluation efforts conducted by U.S. Government agencies as well as aerospace contractors. The NTPS Sk 35s were sometimes leased by military test pilot schools for use in their training syllabi. A particularly interesting aspect of their use in the NTPS syllabus was for high-angle-of-attack, deep stall, and spin recovery training. Roger Bacon, "Straight and Level," *Flight International* (July 31, 1982): p. 269; Hans G. Andersson, *Saab Aircraft Since 1937* (Washington: Smithsonian Institution Press, 1989), pp. 125–136; Walter J. Boyne, "Airpower Classics: J 35 Draken," *Air Force Magazine* (December 2011): 68; Robert Wetherall, e-mail communication with author, December 25. 2012; Wetherall noted, "We studied and discussed what we could about the aircraft [the Saab J 35] during the XL development, so it is relevant if only from that point."

14. Talty, "F-16XL Demonstrates New Capabilities."

15. Jay Miller, *The X-Planes: X-1 to X-45* (London, UK: Ian Allen Publishing, Ltd., 2005).

16. David S. Miller and Roy T. Schemensky, "Design Study Results of a Supersonic Cruise Fighter Wing," presented at the AIAA 17th Aerospace Sciences Meeting, New Orleans, LA, January 15–17, 1979, AIAA Paper 79-0062 (January 1979); David C. Aronstein, Michael J. Hirschberg, and Albert C. Piccirillo, *Advanced Tactical Fighter to F-22 Raptor: Origins of the 21st Century Air Dominance Fighter* (Reston, VA: AIAA, 1998).

17. Erik M. Conway, *High Speed Dreams: NASA and the Technopolitics of Supersonic Transportation, 1945–1999* (Baltimore, MD: Johns Hopkins University Press, 2005).

18. E.C. Polhamus, "Applying Slender Wing Benefits to Military Aircraft," presented at the AIAA/AHA Aircraft Design, Systems and Technology Meeting, Fort Worth, TX, October 17–19, 1983, AIAA Paper 83-2566 in *Journal of Aircraft* 21, no. 8 (August 1984): 545–559.

19. B.L. Shrout, "Aerodynamic Characteristics at Mach Numbers from 0.6 to 2.16 of a Supersonic Cruise Fighter Configuration with a Design Mach Number of 1.8," NASA Technical Memorandum (TM) X-3559 (September 1977).

20. O.A. Morris, "Subsonic and Supersonic Aerodynamic Characteristics of a Supersonic Cruise Fighter with a Twisted and Cambered Wing with 74° Sweep," NASA TM X-3530 (August 1977).

21. USAF, "Technology for Supersonic Cruise Military Aircraft—Design Conference Proceedings," Air Force Flight Dynamics Laboratory, Wright-Patterson AFB, 1976.

22. John E. Lamar, Roy T. Schemensky, and C. Subba Reddy, "Development of a Vortex-Lift-Design Method and Application to a Slender Maneuver-Wing Configuration," presented at the AIAA 18th Aerospace Sciences Meeting, Pasadena, CA, January 14–16, 1980, AIAA Paper 80-0327 (January 1980).

23. The SCAT-15F design served as the initial baseline for the NASA High-Speed Civil Transport (HSCT) research effort that would start in the late 1980s. Joseph R. Chambers, *Innovation in Flight: Research of the NASA Langley Research Center on Revolutionary Advanced Concepts for Aeronautics*, Monograph in Aerospace History Number 39 (Washington, DC: NASA SP-2005-4539, 2005); Chambers, *Partners in Freedom.*

24. In fact, the Air Force interest in a fighter with supercruise performance would coalesce into the entirely new Advanced Tactical Fighter (ATF) program by the early 1980s. This bold concept attempted to balance a variety of highly conflicting design characteristics in a totally new air superiority fighter design. ATF was to be capable of supercruise without use of afterburning at high Mach numbers over long ranges, was to possess exceptional maneuverability, and was to carry a large payload of ordnance. Most significantly, ATF was to be designed from the beginning to achieve exceptionally demanding all-aspect radar "stealth" requirements. The ATF program would eventually lead to development and fielding of the

Lockheed F-22A Raptor; see Aronstein, Hirschberg, and Piccirillo, *Advanced Tactical Fighter to F-22 Raptor*.

25. For example: Lamar et al., "Development of a Vortex-Lift-Design Method"; Miller and Schemensky, "Design Study Results of a Supersonic Cruise Fighter Wing."

26. Chambers, *Partners in Freedom*.

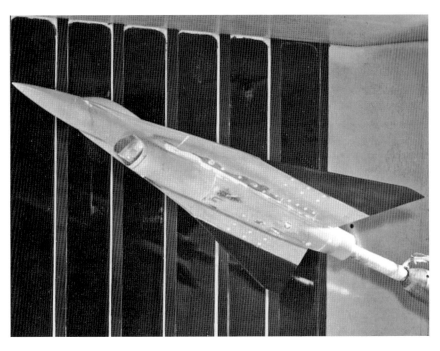

Test model of an interim SCAMP concept mounted in the NASA Langley Unitary Plan Wind Tunnel in 1978. (NASA)

CHAPTER 2

From SCAMP to F-16XL: A Collaborative Development

By 1976–1977, General Dynamic's Harry Hillaker, often referred to as the "Father of the F-16," was strongly advocating the development of what GD initially termed the Supersonic Combat and Maneuvering Prototype program.[1] The concept envisioned a flight demonstrator aircraft that used a modified F-16 fuselage fitted with a highly refined cranked-arrow delta wing.[2] The initiative very quickly was renamed the Supersonic Cruise and Maneuver Prototype (still SCAMP but with the emphasis on cruise capability) to take advantage of the rapidly emerging Air Force interest in supercruise fighter capability. The rationale behind the SCAMP concept was based on several characteristics important to air combat outcomes. Supersonic cruise capability would provide a faster reaction time along with a lower exposure time to enemy air defenses. This would lead to improved combat outcomes and better survivability. Improved maneuverability, as evidenced by the ability to rapidly gain or lose energy, coupled with high turn rates and tight turn radii would allow opponents to be rapidly defeated in close-in air combat.

This rationale echoed nearly word for word the concepts fostered by the informal but influential "fighter mafia." This small but well-connected group of military officers and civilians operating from within the Department of Defense had been instrumental in lobbying for an alternative to what they saw as the overly large and complex F-15. Their efforts had seen fruition in the Lightweight Fighter program that evolved into the F-16 production program via the General Dynamics YF-16 LWF prototypes.[3] Using statements that could have come directly from USAF Col. John Boyd (widely acknowledged as the unofficial leader of the "fighter mafia"), Harry Hillaker boldly proclaimed that SCAMP would go even further than the basic F-16 in "enhancing air combat by incorporating 'fast transient' concepts that would provide a faster, more fluid tempo that would act inside enemy space and time capability," enabling its pilots to "generate a rapidly changing air combat environment" and "be as non-predictable as possible."[4]

Conceptualizing SCAMP

From the start, SCAMP had been visualized by General Dynamics as an F-16 derivative that would utilize a newly designed delta wing tailored to improve supersonic efficiency and retain good maneuvering performance. In designing this wing, GD intended to capitalize on the latest techniques emerging from NASA aeronautical research efforts. The design would focus on improving both supersonic flight performance and aerodynamic efficiency compared to the standard F-16. In this context, the NASA Langley–GD cooperative effort would be heavily oriented toward the development of a transonic/supersonic fighter wing design using an extensive wind tunnel test program. The cooperative program would develop and expand the existing design and technology base to significantly improve the benefits of wing camber as applied to a highly swept delta-wing planform. An important consideration was risk reduction. The new aerodynamic technologies and capabilities needed to be successfully integrated into a technology demonstrator or prototype fighter design. In order to reach these goals, a wide variety of wind tunnel models and NASA test facilities would be used during the cooperative development effort and follow-on detail design work. To this end, some of these subscale models (the so-called matrix models) were designed to be capable of rapid modification. This allowed the rapid investigation of a wide variety of aerodynamic refinements. These included different wing-camber and wing-twist concepts as well as detail design changes to the basic aircraft configuration. The matrix model concept turned out to be very useful in efficiently testing the full matrix of design test points and configurations during the wind tunnel test effort at NASA Langley.[5]

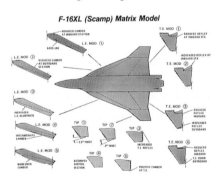

The matrix model could be rapidly modified using a variety of removable leading edges, wingtips, and trailing edges to efficiently assess their effects on aerodynamic characteristics. (Lockheed Martin)

The cooperative test concept called for the potential benefits of transonic vortex wing camber to be evaluated using four wing configurations. These different configurations would be used to explore the effectiveness of various wing-camber approaches in providing properly tailored leading-edge vortices. These tailored vortices would improve lift as well as provide some thrust in the direction of flight. Achieving favorably tailored vortex lift would reduce the drag penalties associated with maneuvering at higher angles of attack. Two of the test wings would have cranked-arrow leading-edge planforms with sweep angles of 76.6 and 66.6 degrees. One of these cranked-arrow wings would use a fixed vortex camber while the other was fitted with leading- and trailing-edge movable flaps. The other two wings used in the investigation were delta shapes that were used in transonic vortex camber assessments. Both of these delta wings had leading-edge sweep angles of 71.6 degrees. One of the delta wings would be designed with leading-edge vortex camber while the other was a basic noncambered delta wing used as a baseline for comparison purposes. Eventually, five other wing concepts would be used to investigate various approaches to improve supersonic drag performance, both at cruise conditions and in maneuvering flight. A major constraint was that all of these wing planforms needed to be capable of being mated with a lengthened F-16 fuselage. During the cooperative design and test effort, various fore and aft fuselage-plug concepts would be considered to increase the fuselage length and fineness ratio.[6]

Another aspect of the SCAMP studies was an investigation of various conformal weapons carriage concepts that were intended to reduce aerodynamic drag and improve mission performance. Although not a totally new concept, conformal carriage increasingly was being seen as a way to reduce the drag penalties associated with external weapons carriage.[7] Conformal carriage of both air-to-ground and air-to-air munitions was to be addressed with a focus on efficient aerodynamic integration of external stores oriented toward enhancing both volume and cross-sectional area distribution. A number of other areas for future NASA-GD cooperative work were identified in September 1977. These included assessing various leading-edge crank angles and different leading-edge-flap concepts to further enhance vortex lift/thrust and evaluations of the benefits of various canard concepts to further increase lift. Canard concepts that were identified at the time included fixed, movable, and fully retractable possibilities. Other areas that were seen as possibilities for cooperation with NASA were research into the effects of strake and wing-camber integration, variations in fuselage camber, and lower fuselage surface and internal volume distribution studies. Another possibility investigated by GD involved incorporation of variable geometry anhedral (e.g., angled-down) wingtips into the SCAMP configuration (à la the North American XB-70A Valkyrie Mach 3 bomber of the early 1960s).[8] The use of variable geometry anhedral wingtips on supersonic fighter designs had also been investigated by NASA Langley during the earlier SCIF design and wind tunnel test efforts.

GD laid out a very aggressive validation plan for the proposed SCAMP collaborative effort with NASA Langley. This preliminary SCAMP Validation Plan of early 1977 included a provision for a cooperative NASA-GD team approach to model design and fabrication.[9] Low- and high-speed wind tunnel tests were oriented toward investigating the effects of various wing-camber approaches using a number of different delta-wing planform shapes. This portion of the effort was to be completed in February 1978 with the results used to refine the SCAMP configuration. This refined configuration would then form the basis for computer simulations. These simulations were to include computer modeling of an integrated fire and flight control system (IFFCS) incorporated into the SCAMP concept. GD's subcontractor, Ling-Temco-Vought (LTV), would support the air-to-air aspects of this modeling effort with Martin Marietta providing air-to-ground simulation expertise. The NASA Langley pilot-in-the-loop Differential Maneuvering Simulator (DMS) facility would be used during this portion of the collaborative effort. Effects of fast transient maneuvers and the use of various advanced weapons delivery solutions, including IFFCS approaches, would be investigated using the DMS.[10] The results, as well as those derived from the vortex lift and camber studies, stability and control assessments, and conformal carriage investigations, would then be used to further refine the SCAMP design.

The goal was delivery of a well-defined aircraft configuration along with a detailed technical description of its aerodynamic parameters and stability characteristics by late 1978. Also noteworthy was the investigation of a variable-geometry inlet (VGI) design. Wind tunnel testing of a 1/15-scale model fitted with a VGI was planned with results to be factored into the SCAMP conceptual design. GD would go on to prepare a fully functional, full-scale VGI (including actuators and control hardware) for the F-16XL design. A VGI was included in the flight demonstration proposal to the Air Force as a possible option for incorporation into the full-scale F-16XL flight demonstrators. However, the additional cost and weight (estimated at 224 pounds) associated with the variable-geometry inlet did not offset its performance benefits and it was not included in the final design.[11]

As it transpired, the cooperative effort that eventually culminated in the F-16XL continued well into 1982. During the joint SCAMP-F-16XL effort, NASA Langley's High Speed Aerodynamic Division was the focal point from 1976 through 1979 with the Dynamic Stability Branch coming onboard in early 1978

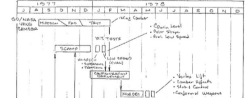

This early 1977 GD chart lays out the collaborative effort with NASA. Joint efforts actually continued even after first flight of the F-16XL, in July 1982. (Lockheed Martin)

and being increasingly active into 1982 as the first flight dates of the actual F-16XL aircraft approached. Even after that date, NASA representatives participated in activities related to monitoring and advising the Air Force F-16XL flight-test program. As an example, Marilyn E. Ogburn of Langley's Dynamic Stability Branch served as a NASA observer during the Air Force Flight Test Center evaluation of the F-16XL at Edwards Air Force Base.[12]

SCAMP Configuration Evolution

General Dynamics began the SCAMP effort by evaluating the performance potential of cranked-arrow wings. These derived from concepts that had been evaluated earlier during the NASA Langley Supersonic Cruise Aerodynamics Research (SCAR) effort. Analytical and experimental data from the SCAR work was considered for potential application to a modified F-16 to provide supersonic cruise capability as well as improvements in the areas of subsonic performance, maneuverability, and aircraft handling qualities. GD proposed to, with NASA assistance, conduct wing optimization studies that would consider various aspects of wing design that could be important to improving F-16 performance. These included determination of the effects of noncranked and cranked leading edges, assessments of various leading-edge sweep combi-

nations, variations in wing aspect ratio and wing area, and determination of the resultant internal wing fuel volumes. Issues associated with adequate aircraft control, including methods to provide effective pitch and roll control on very highly swept wings, were to be evaluated. An important concern was dealing with rapidly varying trim requirements resulting from the aft movement of the center of lift as speed increased from subsonic to supersonic.

By late 1977, the combined NASA-GD effort led to a configuration based on

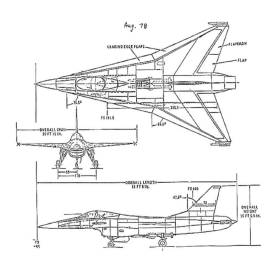

This SCAMP concept featured an all-moving vertical tail and full-span leading-edge flaps on both the inboard and outboard wing segments of its highly swept cranked-arrow wing. (Lockheed Martin)

an F-16 stretched fuselage mated with a cranked-arrow wing. Two 20-inch plugs, one aft of the cockpit and one just forward of the lower vertical fin, increased fuselage length by 40 inches. The new extended fuselage was 51.8 feet long. The highly swept cranked-arrow wing had a span of 30 feet 10 inches and an aspect ratio of 1.38. Total wing area was 600 square feet, double the area of the standard F-16 wing. Leading-edge sweep angles were 76.6 degrees (inboard) and 66.6 degrees (outboard). To provide good maneuverability and handling qualities, full-span leading-edge flaps, capable of being deflected up to 60 degrees, were mounted on both inboard and outboard wing segments. Trailing-edge flaps were mounted on the aft inboard wing segments with additional flap power provided by outboard elevons (essentially, combination elevators and ailerons). These served as elevators for pitch control and ailerons for roll control. Other characteristics of this design concept were an all-moving vertical tail and a variable-geometry single-ramp engine inlet. This would be used to control the airflow entering the engine out to speeds of Mach 2.2 (the standard F-16 used a fixed-geometry inlet). This design concept was also intended to be used to evaluate additional performance enhancements that might be possible by incorporating a two-dimensional thrust-vectoring nozzle. A modified version of this arrow-wing concept was tested in the NASA Langley Unitary Plan Wind Tunnel. This ¹⁄₁₅-scale model had leading-edge wing-sweep angles of 71 degrees on the inboard wing segments and 57 degrees on the outboard segments.

By 1978, the NASA-GD collaboration had resulted in a refined cranked-arrow-wing configuration with the fuselage now lengthened by 52 inches. Leading-edge sweep angles were revised to 70 degrees on the inboard section and 50 degrees on the outboard (cranked) section of the wing. The wing crank was relocated from its earlier 63 percent outboard position (measured from the aircraft centerline) to 70 percent outboard. The trailing edge of the wing now featured a uniform sweep angle of –8.6 degrees. This was somewhat reduced from that of the earlier SCAR-derived arrow-wing planform discussed above. This new wing proved to be a better choice than

Test model of an interim SCAMP concept mounted in the NASA Langley Unitary Plan Wind Tunnel in 1978. (NASA)

the earlier arrow-wing configuration. The smaller aft movement of its mean aerodynamic center (MAC) as the Mach number changed from subsonic to supersonic minimized flight control issues.[13] This aft shift in mean aerodynamic center was reduced to a much more manageable 10.5 percent. This compared to a rearward shift in MAC of as much as 26 percent during transition from subsonic to supersonic flight for the standard F-16. This was due largely to the reduced leading-edge sweep angle on the cranked outboard portions of the wing. The revised wing also provided major improvements in low-speed roll control as well as significant supersonic rolling capabilities. GD claimed this newer wing design would provide a 9-g instantaneous maneuvering capability at Mach 2.0 at an altitude of 50,000 feet using the maximum available up-elevon deflection angle of 20 degrees.[14]

As initially conceived, this configuration began with hand-drawn illustrations, typical of those commonly seen in conceptual design efforts in the aircraft industry in the era before computer-based graphics and computer-aided design. This SCAMP configuration incorporated an aeroelastically tailored composite wing fitted with full-span leading-edge flaps and a VGI. Other features included an all-movable

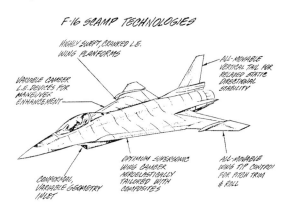

Although bearing a general resemblance, this SCAMP design concept, circa September 1977, was still somewhat removed from the eventual F-16XL configuration in a number of significant respects. (Lockheed Martin)

vertical tail (that would have provided relaxed static directional stability) as well as all-movable wingtips for both pitch trim and roll control.[15]

The existing horizontal tail surfaces from the production F-16A were studied for possible use as both an all-movable tailfin and as all-moveable wingtips. The all-movable vertical tailfin and all-movable wingtips would be dropped from the final SCAMP–F-16XL configuration. This reportedly resulted after negative feedback during discussions between GD engineering and Air Force engineers from the Aeronautical Systems Division who perceived these items as creating unnecessarily high technical risk.[16] This negative position was reinforced by subsequent NASA wind tunnel testing in the 30- by 60-foot Full-Scale Tunnel with a matrix model fitted with these features. This revealed that the all-movable wingtip control surfaces did not provide adequate aircraft

Key members of the GD SCAMP development team with a matrix model circa late 1977. From the left: Harry J. Hillaker, program manager; Andrew Lewis, aerodynamics; Kenny Barnes, stability and control lead; and Jim Gordon, lead program engineer. (Lockheed Martin)

control during low-speed, high-angle-of-attack maneuvering. Another important negative consideration was that all-movable wingtips prevented the use of wingtip-mounted AIM-9 Sidewinder infrared guided air-to-air missiles, as used on the standard F-16. The all-moving vertical fin was eliminated due to reduced effectiveness at higher angles of attack due to its low height as well as the risk of stall at high deflections in sideslip conditions.

Key members of the General Dynamics SCAMP design team at this time (1977) were Harry J. Hillaker, program manager; Roger Marquardt, chief aerodynamicist; Kenneth H. Barnes, stability and control lead; and James A. Gordon, SCAMP lead engineer. Kenny Barnes was a very key player on the GD SCAMP team, effectively leading efforts focused on modifying the F-16 fly-by-wire flight control system to adapt to the requirements of the radically different SCAMP–F-16XL configuration. These cooperative efforts would eventually provide effective flight control at much higher angles of attack than were ever possible with the basic F-16 configuration. During the SCAMP cooperative effort, Andrew Lewis and the General Dynamics aerodynamics group worked closely and effectively with NASA Langley researchers in evolving major aspects of the SCAMP aerodynamic configuration and its associated wing planform. These included selection of the eventual airfoil, the wing twist, and the highly sophisticated camber that reduced transonic and supersonic drag while providing enhanced lift. The final wing camber and twist combination used on the F-16XL aircraft prototypes showed superior performance compared to the standard F-16. Drag was reduced during 1-g flight and in maneuvering flight at both high subsonic (Mach 0.9) and supersonic (Mach 1.6) flight conditions.[17]

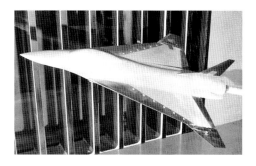

SCAMP matrix model seen during 1978 tests in the NASA Langley Unitary Plan Wind Tunnel. (NASA)

NASA Wind Tunnel Testing

Extensive wind tunnel testing was accomplished on a SCAMP model with an 8.6-degree trailing-edge sweep angle. But during testing in the Langley Unitary Plan Wind Tunnel during early 1978, this configuration exhibited a serious increase in nose-up pitching moment as angle of attack was increased. Pitching moment characteristics were determined to be nonlinear with increasing angle of attack—a sudden pitch-up was the result. Such an increased nose-up pitching moment with increasing angle of attack is a highly undesirable aerodynamic characteristic indicative of longitudinal instability. Such pitch axis instability can easily result in the nose suddenly pitching up during slow-speed or maneuvering flight with a high potential for total loss of aircraft control.

A NASA Langley team led by Joseph L. Johnson, Jr., of the Dynamic Stability Branch identified low-speed stability and control issues with the SCAMP configuration. They worked closely with GD engineers on wing-planform revisions that led to a much more stable configuration. This intense work was accomplished in the Langley Full-Scale Tunnel and tunnels at General Dynamics. The forward wing shape was truncated and smoothly blended into the forward fuselage. Other modifications resulting from NASA wing camber/twist/reflex tradeoff studies were incorporated into the design. The wing trailing edge was also changed to improve pitch stability. This modification involved a rearward extension of the aft inner wing segments. Overall wing area increased from 600 to 643 square feet. The new aft inner trailing-edge wing segment was swept forward at an 8-degree angle. The rounded and blended forward wing and the extended trailing edge created the wing planform that would become familiar on the F-16XL aircraft. This configuration featured elevons mounted on the inner trailing edge of the wing and ailerons on the outboard wing segments. Finally, the full-span leading-edge flaps on the inner wing segments, previously under consideration, were deleted, as were the movable wingtips. Leading-edge maneuvering flaps were fitted on the outboard wing segments of the cranked-arrow wing. These enhanced airflow over the ailerons and provided resistance to yaw divergence at higher angles of attack. As eventually implemented, the leading-edge flaps would be automatically scheduled by the F-16XL flight control system in response to actual flight conditions.[18]

In summation, the cooperative NASA Langley–General Dynamics research effort led to significant modifications in the final SCAMP configuration. This was especially the case in the important area of aircraft stability and control. Pitch and yaw instability had been encountered during wind tunnel testing of earlier SCAMP configurations and became an area of special emphasis. This led to the apex of the wing, at the point where it merged into the forward fuselage, being reshaped to incorporate an S-curve blend. This S-shaped apex would subsequently become a distinctive feature of the F-16XL's cranked-arrow wing. In addition, prominent fairings were incorporated at the trailing edge of the wing. Positioned at the intersection of the inner and outer wing segments, these fairings housed the hydraulic actuators that activated the ailerons. They also provided volume for aft-facing electronic sensors and chaff and flare dispensers—capabilities that would have been incorporated into a production version of the aircraft. In conjunction with what NASA termed "air dams," the wing fairings helped to control spanwise airflow over the outer portions of the cranked-arrow wing at higher angles of attack, significantly improving lateral stability and enhancing controllability.[19] The penultimate SCAMP configuration incorporated the S-curved wing apex, the aft wing trailing-edge extension, the wing fairings, and the outer wing dams or fences, but it did not yet include the larger vertical fin and the large drag chute fairing that would be featured in the final SCAMP/F-16XL configuration.

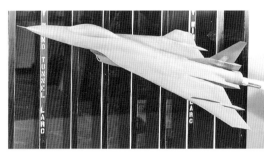

A near-final SCAMP–F-16XL configuration mounted in the LaRC Unitary Plan Wind Tunnel. The vertical tailfin was returned to the original F-16 production tail for improved lateral stability at higher angles of attack. (NASA)

NASA Langley research engineer Sue B. Grafton produced an excellent professional report summarizing the significant results of the wind tunnel testing accomplished at Langley to resolve the low-speed, high AoA issues associated with earlier SCAMP configurations.[20] In the report, she noted that earlier NASA research efforts had determined that highly swept arrow wings typically experienced pitch-up tendencies along with both directional and roll instability at higher angles of attack. These tendencies were determined to be caused by leading-edge vortex breakdown over the wing that resulted in severe lateral and directional instabilities. The Langley wind tunnel investigation of SCAMP stability used a 0.15-scale wind tunnel model of the configuration that was intensively tested in the Langley 30- by 60-foot Full-Scale Tunnel. This rather large model, constructed mainly of wood and molded fiberglass, incorporated a flow-through inlet duct and had a length of 7.34 feet, a wingspan of 4.86 feet, an aspect ratio of 1.75, and a wing area of 13.5 square feet. Using the 15-percent scale model, aerodynamic forces were measured and the resultant pitching moments on the aircraft were determined for a baseline SCAMP configuration as well as for several alternative configurations. The baseline configuration had been modified to incorporate a notched-wing apex, an extended-wing trailing edge, wing fences, and combinations of all of these fixes. The wind tunnel test program covered the angle of attack range from –4 degrees to +41 degrees, with sideslip angles as high as 13.5 degrees being investigated. Smoke-flow investigations were used to assist in documenting wing vortex flow behavior and to establish the relationship between vortex flow breakdown as a function of angle of attack and angle of sideslip. Results for all tested configurations were comprehensively documented in the form of detailed graphs and tables that provided aerodynamic coefficients and stability factors related to pitch, yaw, and roll for each tested configuration as a function of variations in angle of attack and angle of sideslip.[21]

The successful F-16XL design evolution was heavily dependent on experimental aerodynamic research efforts conducted in Langley wind tunnel facilities. As it unfolded, the NASA-GD cooperative test program demonstrated that the earlier SCAMP configurations exhibited high levels of maximum lift but also displayed unstable longitudinal and lateral-directional stability characteristics at moderate to high angles of attack. Longitudinal- and lateral-directional stability characteristics were significantly improved by the combination of the aforementioned wing-apex notch, the wing trailing-edge extension, and the addition of wing fences. However, these features were also noted by Langley researchers as causing some reduction in achievable maximum lift coefficient, a factor that pales in relation to the fact that without these critical aerodynamic fixes, any practical fighter derived from the earlier SCAMP concepts would have been unacceptable to test pilots from an aircraft handling qualities perspective. In addition, the use of fly-by-wire flight controls also made XL feasible where the pure SCAMP configurations with conventional controls would not have been. The lateral-directional control from the outboard leading-edge flaps and the rudder-aileron interconnect from the basic F-16 flight control logic also helped make the aircraft controllable.[22]

By mid-1980, SCAMP had converged on the aerodynamic layout that would soon materialize in the actual F-16XL design. This progression in aerodynamic and geometric configuration depicts the design evolution that occurred during the cooperative test program. The Greek symbol η denotes the geometrical location of the wing crank measured outboard from the fuselage centerline of the aircraft. For example, η=0.63 indicates that the wing crank is located 63 percent of the distance from the aircraft centerline to the wingtip. During the F-16XL design evolution, the location of the wing crank moved from its initial 63-percent position to one that was 70 percent of the distance to the wingtip. Although the inner wing's leading-edge sweep angle remained little changed (going from 71 degrees to 70 degrees), the sweep angle of the outboard wing sections were decreased from 57 degrees to 50 degrees to provide better lateral control. As discussed earlier, to improve pitch stability, the trailing-edge sweep angle on the inner section of the wing was revised from the earlier 8.6-degree aft sweep to a forward (negative) sweep angle of –8 degrees. This, along with the S-shaped curvature implemented on the forward portion of the wing, gave the F-16XL its final distinctive wing planform.

General Dynamics had spent $15.9 million of corporate funding on the SCAMP effort by the time that the jointly developed SCAMP–F-16XL configuration was selected in late 1980. Up until that time, somewhat over 1,397

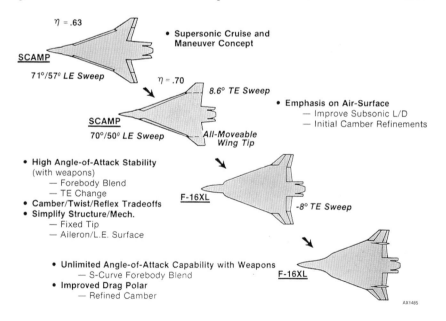

During the course of the cooperative program, the early SCAMP concept evolved to the cranked-arrow-wing configuration eventually adapted for the F-16XL. (Lockheed Martin)

hours of wind tunnel testing had been accomplished. This included 611 hours of low-speed testing, 419 hours at transonic speeds, and 367 hours at supersonic conditions. On December 1, 1980, GD corporate management approved initiation of the next phase of the F-16XL effort. This would focus on detail design and construction of two flight-test prototypes. During this phase, General Dynamics would expend $41.7 million of corporate Independent Research and Development (IRAD) funding with an additional $7.8 million provided by their vendors and suppliers. Additional wind tunnel tests, focused on detailed aerodynamic refinements and technical issues important to the flight-test program, would continue well into 1982. GD continued to use NASA Langley facilities on an as-required contract basis and also used facilities located at the NASA Ames Research Laboratory at Moffett Field near San Francisco, CA. Other wind tunnel testing related to the F-16XL was accomplished in cooperation with Calspan Corporation (previously Cornell Aeronautical Laboratories) and at GD's Convair Division in San Diego, CA.[23]

Follow-On Flutter, Spin, Drop Model, and Weapons Carriage Tests

During follow-on phases of the F-16XL wind tunnel test effort, a number of specialized F-16XL test models were designed, built, and tested. These models were used to explore important aerodynamic issues that needed to be resolved before detailed aircraft design and flight-testing could begin. In 1981, a 0.18-scale wind tunnel free-flight model of the F-16XL, equipped with fully functional flight control surfaces and important elements of the full-scale control system, was built and flown at angles of attack up to and greater than 50 degrees in the Langley Full-Scale Tunnel. The captive free-flight model was remotely

On left: NASA Langley's Sue Grafton is shown with the 0.18-scale captive free-flight wind tunnel model used to validate F-16XL aerodynamic and flight control modifications. On right: the 0.18-scale F-16XL model is seen during free-flight testing in the NASA Langley Full-Scale Tunnel. (Both images NASA)

flown from pilot stations located in the wind tunnel control room. Powered by high-pressure compressed air, it was used to explore aircraft controllability and handling qualities at high angles of attack. This model also played a vital role in the determination of the aircraft's maneuvering boundary and supported refinements to the final flight control configuration.

Flutter Model Tests

The F-16XL flutter envelope was successfully cleared in the NASA Langley 16-Foot Transonic Dynamic Tunnel using a large 0.25-scale model of the F-16XL. The Transonic Dynamic Tunnel had previously been used to clear the flutter envelope of the standard F-16, also using a 0.25-scale test model. To produce flutter test results that were representative of the full-scale aircraft, the flutter model had to replicate not only the geometry of the full-scale aircraft but its mass and structural elasticity characteristics. This was essential because flutter is a synchronized vibration that occurs in flexible aircraft structures moving through the atmosphere. Flutter occurs when rhythmic motions within the various elements of the airframe structure coincide and amplify one another. As the structural vibrations increase in magnitude and the airframe distorts, the surrounding airflow acts to further amplify the structural distortions. Flutter can lead the airframe to bend and twist in a divergent manner, potentially leading to structural failure.[24]

Since the free-flight dynamic characteristics of the actual aircraft are a critical aspect of flutter, the model tests in the wind tunnel needed to simulate the aircraft in free flight. NASA Langley research staff members had previously devised a cable-mounting system for flutter testing that securely suspended the model in the center of the wind tunnel. The suspension system was designed to allow enough flexibility to simulate the real aircraft as it responded to aeroelastic stresses. The F-16XL wind tunnel flutter model was fitted with remotely controlled pitch and roll controls that were operated by a "pilot" operator who was a member of the NASA Langley wind tunnel test staff. He used a miniature control stick to keep the model positioned in the center of the wind tunnel as measurements were taken. F-16XL flutter model testing was conducted under the supervision of NASA Langley research engineer Charles L. Ruhlin. Processed data from the NASA Langley wind tunnel flutter tests was analyzed and published in a report prepared by General Dynamics engineer J.A. Ellis. These data were used in conjunction with the results from ground vibration tests with the full-scale F-16XL aircraft to ensure that structural vibration modes and frequency responses were identified prior to the start of the flight-test program.[25]

Spin Tests

Data from spin tunnel and drop model tests conducted at NASA Langley were used to further refine the F-16XL flight control system software and validate automatic antispin features and the characteristics of the spin recovery parachute design and installation. The inherent value of these NASA efforts was evident in the exceptional resistance of the F-16XL to inadvertent loss of control during high-AoA maneuvering—capabilities that would be conclusively demonstrated during the subsequent Air Force flight-test program.

Spin Tunnel Testing: In conjunction with the ongoing cooperative program with General Dynamics, the Langley Vertical Spin Tunnel was used to determine the spin characteristics of the definitive F-16XL design. For these tests, NASA research engineers Raymond D. Whipple and William L. White used a ¹⁄₂₅-scale model that was ballasted to obtain dynamic similarity of motions with the characteristics of the full-scale F-16XL aircraft design. The spin model's mass, center of gravity (cg), and moment of inertia characteristics were fully representative of those of the full-scale aircraft. The spin tunnel test model was 2.1 feet long. It was fitted with a mechanism that actuated the flight control surfaces on remote radio command from an operator in the control room during spin recovery attempts. The control surface deflection angles used in these recovery attempts were fully representative of the flight control surface capabilities that were intended to be available on the actual aircraft. In addition to spin testing with the clean aircraft configuration (no external stores), the test model was configured with various external stores combinations in a series of comprehensive spin tunnel tests that began at NASA Langley in 1981 and continued into 1983.

Detailed subscale models of munitions and external fuel tanks were used to evaluate the large variety, quantities, and combinations of munitions and external fuel tanks that would be carried on the actual aircraft for their effects on spin entry and recovery characteristics. Both symmetric and asymmetric stores combinations were evaluated during the test program. The tests with asymmetric loads were especially important in understanding the ability of the F-16XL's flight control system to cope with the forces and moments on the aircraft during potential out-of-control situations. The external stores loads that were evaluated during the NASA spin tunnel test effort are shown in Table 2. Details related to the F-16XL's weapons and stores carriage and management systems and the associated NASA and Air Force wind tunnel and flight-test efforts, which were exceptionally comprehensive, are discussed in a number of follow-on sections of this document.

Table 2.

A variety of F-16XL external stores loadings (both symmetric and asymmetric) were evaluated during spin tunnel testing at NASA Langley from 1981 to 1983. NASA

Load	Description	WT Launchers	Symmetry
1	Clean Aircraft—Mid cg (x/c = 0.460) (x/c = the location of the aircraft's cg on the wing chord line)	Off	Symmetric
2	4 AMRAAM (2 pylon, 2 wingtip)	On	Symmetric
2a	1 AMRAAM (pylon mounted)	On	Asymmetric
2b	1 AMRAAM (wingtip mounted)	On	Asymmetric
2c	2 AMRAAM (1 wingtip, 1 pylon on same side)	On	Asymmetric
3	6 AGM-65 missiles (3 on each wing, single pylons)	On	Symmetric
3a	5 AGM-65 missiles (3 on one wing, 2 on the other)	On	Asymmetric
3b	1 AGM-65 missile on outboard pylon)	On	Asymmetric
4	6 AGM-65 missiles (on 2 TER racks)	On	Symmetric
4a	3 AGM-65 missiles (on 1 TER rack)	On	Asymmetric
5	10 SUU-65 stores on 10 single pylons	On	Symmetric
5a	9 SUU-65 stores (outboard rear pylon empty)	On	Asymmetric
6	Clean Aircraft—Forward cg (x/c = 0.430)	Off	Symmetric
7	Clean Aircraft—Aft cg (x/c = 0.491)	Off	Symmetric
8	2,370-gallon drop tanks	On	Symmetric
8a	1,370-gallon drop tank	On	Asymmetric

During the NASA Langley spin test program, the center of gravity of the F-16XL model was varied between its allowable forward and aft locations to determine the effect of cg location on spin recovery. The allowable cg range as a percentage of the mean aerodynamic chord for the F-16XL aircraft was determined to lie between 46 percent (forward cg) to slightly over 49 percent (aft cg). Different spin recovery flight control approaches were evaluated for their relative effectiveness during both erect and inverted spins. Spin test results showed that an automatic spin prevention system, integrated into the F-16XL flight control system, could eliminate the development of erect spins. Without an automatic spin prevention system, two flat erect spin modes—one fast and steady, one slower and oscillatory—were shown to be possible. In addition, testing showed that the potential existed for a moderately steep, relatively slow inverted spin mode. Recovery from this inverted spin mode was easily achieved by neutralization of the flight control surfaces.

The NASA spin tests determined the appropriate piloting techniques for acceptable recoveries from the different spin modes of the aircraft. The F-16XL's spin prevention system, as integrated into its fly-by-wire flight control system, was refined as a result of the spin tunnel testing. The ability of this spin prevention system to automatically prevent spins from fully developing was completely validated through a rigorous combination of test techniques. These included the spin tunnel tests, NASA Langley drop model testing, and follow-on Air Force flight testing with the full-scale aircraft. Additionally, a considerable effort was made in the development of the antispin system using the Langley Differential Maneuvering Simulator.[26] The NASA drop model tests are described in the following section while the Air Force flight-test effort is described in detail in a separate chapter.

The emergency spin recovery parachute installation, designed for use on the F-16XL during high-AoA maneuvering, was evaluated in conjunction with tests of the spin recovery system. The aerodynamic effects of the so-called "Quadra Pod" spin recovery chute installation on the F-16XL's flight characteristics were determined using the 0.18-scale captive free-flight model. During these tests, sizing requirements for the anti-spin parachute were investigated using a variety of miniature spin recovery parachutes with different towline lengths. The spin chutes were deployed by remote command from a Quadra Pod spin

F-16XL model fitted with the "Quadra Pod" spin recovery parachute installation during wind tunnel testing at NASA Langley in May 1982. (NASA)

chute installation mounted on the ⅕₅-scale spin model during tests in the Langley 20-foot Vertical Spin Tunnel. Testing showed that for the full-scale F-16XL, a 34.2-foot-diameter parachute with a drag coefficient of 0.50 on a 100-foot towline, deployed in conjunction with spin recovery rudder and aileron control deflections, produced the best results on the full-scale F-16XL. This spin chute–towline combination was designed to provide emergency recovery from all potential spin modes, even with very large lateral weight asymmetries. Based on the NASA recommendation, this spin chute configuration was adopted for the flight demonstration program, but it never had to be used to recover the aircraft from an inadvertent out-of-control or spin situation.

In addition to the tests described above, other potential flight control surface deflection combinations and optional/alternative design approaches were evaluated in the NASA Langley spin tunnel using the appropriately modified F-16XL spin model. These included all-moving wingtips, an all-moving vertical tail, and inboard-mounted leading-edge vortex flaps. These flight control approaches had been included as possible options in the early SCAMP conceptual layout, and they were evaluated by NASA Langley at GD's request. NASA testing showed that these alternative control surface approaches had limited to negligible effects on F-16XL spin recovery characteristics.[27]

High-Angle-of-Attack Drop Model Tests

A large, radio-controlled 0.18-scale drop model of the single-seat F-16XL was used in remotely controlled high-AoA investigations conducted by NASA Langley. The configuration of this model was similar to that of the 18-percent captive free-flight wind tunnel model used in earlier Langley testing. It was

constructed mainly of composite materials in order to better represent the actual flight characteristics of the full-scale aircraft, with appropriate beefing up to withstand landing impact loads. The drop model tests were conducted at NASA Langley's Plum Tree Island satellite test facility, located about 5 miles from the Langley AFB runway complex. The 0.18-scale model was released from a specially configured launch rack mounted on the right-hand side of a NASA-operated Bell UH-1

A radio-controlled 0.18-scale drop model is prepared for release from a NASA Bell HU-1 helicopter at the Plum Tree Island test facility in 1983. (NASA) helicopter. The NASA Langley lead researcher for the drop model test effort was Mark A. Croom.[28]

After checkout and release, the drop model was maneuvered to high-AoA flight conditions to test its aerodynamic response to a variety of potential out-of-control situations. A high-resolution video camera was used to track the model after release. Telemetry uplink and downlink capabilities were provided via a flight operations computer located in the control center. Graphic displays, including images of the model in flight and its location within the geographic confines of the test range, were presented at the remote pilot control station at the Plum Tree Island test complex. A video image of the view from the model was presented to the pilot along with digital displays that included parameters of interest such as angle of attack, sideslip angle, altitude, yaw rate, and normal acceleration level. A ground-based flight control computer located at the Plum Tree Island test complex was capable of being reprogrammed with revised flight control laws between test missions. Proposed control system refinements could be programmed into the ground-based computer using the drop model as a validation tool. An all-terrain vehicle was used to retrieve the drop model from the soft marshy terrain on Plum Tree Island following its parachute landing.[29]

The 0.18-scale drop model being recovered after a successful drop model test at the Plum Tree Island test facility in Virginia. (NASA)

Weapons Carriage and Separation Tests

General Dynamics conducted an F-16XL weapons carriage study in conjunction with the USAF Armament Division at Eglin AFB, FL. Results from the study supported the development of the conformal weapons carriage system that was successfully used on the F-16XL. Additional wind tunnel testing was dedicated to examining both air-to-air and air-to-ground weapons in various combinations using low-drag conformal carriage concepts that emerged from the study. F-16XL conformal weapons carriage wind tunnel tests were conducted at NASA Langley in the Unitary Plan Wind Tunnel with detailed weapons separation tests accomplished at the Air Force's Arnold Engineering Development Center (AEDC) in Tullahoma, TN. During weapons carriage testing at NASA Langley, the 4-foot wind tunnel was used to investigate supersonic F-16XL conformal carriage weapons integration issues. These tests determined the F-16XL's aerodynamic drag character-istics with various conformal weapons carriage configu-rations over the supersonic speed range from Mach 1.6 to Mach 2.16. The F-16XL wind tunnel model carried various combinations of external wing tanks and con-formally carried munitions during wind tunnel testing at NASA Langley.[30]

F-16XL wind tunnel test model fitted with six CBU-58 sub-munitions dispensers, two 370-gallon fuel tanks, and two wingtip-mounted AIM-9L missiles in the Langley Unitary Plan Wind Tunnel in 1982. (NASA)

Wind tunnel testing at the AEDC addressed the aero-dynamic characteristics of a number of air-to-air missiles and air-to-ground weapons during release and separation from the F-16XL. These separation tests were conducted over the speed range from moderate subsonic to high supersonic. A team of engineers representing the Air Force and General Dynamics played key roles in the F-16XL weapons separation test effort. These included AEDC's Alex Money, Bob Bigi from the F-16 Systems Program Office, Bruce Frantz from GD, and R.A. Paulk of Calspan Engineering Services. A ¹⁄₁₅-scale model of the F-16XL— along with an array of ¹⁄₁₅-scale models of air-to-air and air-to-ground weapons; external stores, such as drop tanks and sensor pods; and weapons launchers and pylons—were specially fabricated for the weapons separation tests at AEDC. The subscale stores models were both geometrically and dynamically scaled to represent their full-scale counterparts and included the AGM-65 Maverick air-to-ground guided missile (AGM), the AIM-9L Sidewinder and AIM-120 advanced medium-range air-to-air missiles (AMRAAM), the 370-gallon exter-nal fuel tank, CBU-58/B and SUU-65 sub-munitions dispensers, and Mk-82 500-pound and Mk-84 2,000-pound bombs in both conventional unguided free-fall and laser-guided configurations.[31]

Subscale weapons and stores separation tests were conducted in Aerodynamic Wind Tunnel (4T), located in the Propulsion Wind Tunnel (PWT) facility at AEDC, from May 21 through June 8, 1982.[32] Separation trajectories were obtained at a variety of Mach numbers, angles of attack, simulated altitudes, and simulated load factors. During the subscale-model separation tests, aero-dynamic loads on the stores were obtained using the captive trajectory sup-port system. This technique involved attaching the subscale weapon or store model to a stinger that then was moved through the aerodynamic flow field surrounding the F-16XL model as aerodynamic force data were collected. Postrelease trajectory data were collected using both captive trajectory and dynamic drop techniques. During dynamic drop testing, the scale weapons and external stores models were photographed with two high-speed cameras (400 frames per second) as they were released from the F-16XL model using scaled ejection forces produced by springs. The cameras were installed such that their sight lines intersected orthogonally at the wind tunnel centerline. Special screens installed in the wind tunnel for this purpose were used to catch the models for subsequent reuse. Data from the motion picture cameras were reduced using a film reader that projected each frame onto a screen. Positions of the stores' reference points, relative to the same point on each frame of data film, were measured along two orthogonal axes by manually positioning horizontal and vertical crosshairs located on the surface of the screen. Digital output from the film reader was input into a computer that then calculated full-trajectory positions and attitudes. Following the separation tests, force, moment, and trajectory data for each weapon evaluated at AEDC were provided to General Dynamics for use in refining the design and developing the weapons carriage and release system and the stores management system.[33]

NASA Vortex Flap Research and the F-16XL

Highly swept wings produce strong vortices over their upper-wing surfaces at higher-AoA flight conditions, such as those associated with takeoff, landing, or aggressive maneuvering. These vortices can result in greater lift for takeoff and maneuvering, better control of the aerodynamic center of lift, and improved airflow over a wide range of angle of attack and Mach number. Unfortunately, the vortex flows created by flow separation from the wing leading edge result in a large drag increase for a highly swept wing. The leading-edge vortex flap is specially designed to control the airflow over highly swept wing leading edges. Properly designed vortex flaps can enable the aircraft designer to reorient part of the vortex force vector in the forward direction instead of directly normal to the wing-chord plane without compromising other aerodynamic characteristics such as stability and control.[34]

Although not adopted on the final F-16XL configuration, the potential application of full-span leading-edge vortex flaps on the highly swept wing inboard segments of supercruise fighters like SCAMP was a major area of investigation during NASA Langley research efforts. If additional reductions in transonic drag were attainable by the proper formation of leading-edge vortices to improve low-speed and transonic maneuvering capabilities, increased lift-to-drag ratios were possible. Edward C. Polhamus led the Langley vortex research program with his research group concentrated in the Transonic Aerodynamics Division, led by Percy J. Bobbitt. This team had previously made many significant contributions in the area of vortex lift during earlier NASA-industry research programs as well as in direct support of important military aircraft programs. These included the Air Force's F-16 and the Navy F/A-18. The F-16 and the F/A-18 had evolved from the Air Force's LWF program of the 1970s, a program that highlighted the importance of tailored vortex lift to improve fighter maneuverability and also indirectly led to the F-16XL. John E. Lamar and James F. Campbell, along with other members of the NASA Langley vortex lift research team, would be heavily involved in the cooperative SCAMP effort with General Dynamics as well as later research efforts involving NASA's use of the F-16XL to better understand and predict the aerodynamics of cranked-arrow wings at higher angles of attack.[35] Follow-on NASA F-16XL efforts oriented toward vortical airflow research are discussed in detail in a later chapter.

During wind tunnel tests in the Langley 7- by 10-foot High-Speed Tunnel and associated analysis efforts, the NASA-GD team focused on achieving a 4-g transonic turning maneuver using a cranked-arrow wing planform with a highly swept leading edge similar to that used on the SCAMP configuration. Langley's John Lamar, in collaboration with GD engineers, conducted wind tunnel and computational analyses in an attempt to optimize SCAMP wing camber and shape to best meet the conflicting demands of supersonic efficiency and acceptable transonic maneuverability. Langley's earlier experience with vortex flow research suggested that emerging vortex control concepts could be effectively applied to the SCAMP configuration. One of these concepts was the vortex flap. This concept involves using specially designed leading-edge flaps to modify undesirable leading-edge flow separation behavior. Vortex flaps could enable highly swept wings to recover lost leading-edge thrust without compromising other aerodynamic characteristics, such as stability and control. With the vortex flap concept, the vortex force vector can be reoriented in the forward direction instead of directly normal to the wing-chord plane. In exploratory testing, certain combinations of deflected full-span leading-edge and trailing-edge flaps on a zero-camber wing produced almost the same drag improvements at transonic speeds as the highly refined cambered wing implemented on SCAMP.

NASA wind tunnel test results with vortex flaps showed great promise. Well-designed leading-edge vortex flaps provided nearly the same supersonic efficiency as a highly tailored wing designed purely for supersonic flight during NASA Langley wind tunnel testing. Lift-to-drag ratio during subsonic cruise using the vortex flap concept was nearly as good as that of the standard F-16 and better than that of the supersonic wing design. L/D ratio during transonic maneuvering flight was midway between that of the standard F-16 and the wing tailored for supersonic flight. Issues associated with vortex flap design, fabrication, and testing generated many in-house and NASA contractor studies. These focused on refining and validating vortex flap design methodologies as well as investigating innovative applications of vortex control with deflected flaps. NASA vortex flap research would lead to the publication of a large number of professional papers and technical reports that were widely disseminated throughout the aerospace industry and the aircraft design community.[36]

Neal T. Frink led a NASA Langley team assessing the effects of varying wing leading-edge sweep angles and the geometric characteristics of various leading-edge vortex flap approaches. The overall effectiveness of vortex flaps was evaluated in an extensive series of wind tunnel tests that resulted in performance information for highly swept delta wings with constant-chord leading-edge vortex flaps. This formed the basis for development of an analytical approach to the vortex flap design process. As a result, forces and moments on highly swept wings equipped with vortex flaps, as well as detailed pressures for different vortex flap configurations, could be predicted. Frink's work resulted in the development of a leading-edge vortex flap design procedure in 1982.[37] Separately, Dhanvada M. Rao determined that reducing inboard flap length actually improved the efficiency of leading-edge vortex flaps on very highly swept wings. Tailoring the shape of the flap in the spanwise direction also improved vortex flap efficiency and favorable vortex formation over wing leading edges. Rao and a separate independent team led by W. Elliott Schoonover, Jr., of NASA Langley and W.E. Ohlson of Boeing determined that increasing the geometrical area of the vortex flap delayed the movement of the vortex inboard with some reduction in overall drag. The use of differentially deflected vortex flaps to improve aircraft roll control was also evaluated with some promise.[38]

During 1981, NASA Langley researchers Long P. Yip and Daniel G. Murri investigated the effects of vortex flaps on the low-speed stability and control characteristics of generic arrow-wing configurations in the 12-foot Low-Speed Tunnel at Langley. Test results showed improvements in both lateral stability and lift-to-drag ratio; however, an unacceptable nose-up pitching moment was produced by the flaps. Geometric modifications to the vortex flap configuration, including adjusting spanwise flap length and leading-edge geometry, were evaluated in the wind tunnel. A vortex flap concept that incorporated a deflected tab on its leading edge was shown to moderate the nose-up pitching moment. The tabbed leading-edge vortex flap was installed on a 0.18-scale captive free-flight wind tunnel model of a later SCAMP configuration, which had been transformed into the F-16XL configuration. Captive free-flight tests with this model were conducted in the Langley 30- by 60-Foot (Full-Scale) Tunnel in 1982. The tabbed vortex flap was also evaluated on a 1/25-scale model of the

F-16XL in the NASA Langley spin tunnel. The vortex flap did not produce adverse effects on aircraft spin recovery characteristics.

NASA vortex flap research with the F-16XL would eventually continue well into the 1990s, especially driven by the High-Speed Research program with its focus on technical risk reduction for the High-Speed Civil Transport. This program is described in "Chapter Test" results reported by General Dynamics' Dennis B. Finley and Langley researcher W. Elliot Schoonover in 1986; the results indicated that F-16XL maneuvering performance could be enhanced with vortex flaps with no adverse effects on configuration aerodynamics.[39] Later, during the NASA flight research effort with the F-16XL, there was a plan to install and test leading-edge vortex flaps to support risk reduction activities associated with the High-Speed Civil Transport. However, that effort was terminated before the vortex flap modification to F-16XL-1 was accomplished, despite the fact that the necessary tooling had already been delivered to Dryden.

The F-16XL's Wind Tunnel Test Summary

Approximately 3,550 hours of wind tunnel testing were accomplished by the time the first F-16XL took to the air on July 3, 1982. During the entire wind tunnel test program, a total of 149 configuration variables were evaluated. These included 11 wing planforms, 12 vertical tails, 15 leading-edge flaps, 40 vortex fences, 7 wingtips, 7 spoilers, 6 different fuselage stretches, 13 forebody strake designs, 21 camber variations, 3 different airfoils, and 14 canard arrangements.[40]

The F-16XL, with its long-chord cranked-arrow wing extending virtually to the radome, allowed few possibilities for proper geometric positioning of movable canard surfaces without a major redesign of the forward fuselage. In addition to various canard approaches, GD also reportedly briefly considered the possibility of incorporating a horizontal tail on the aircraft. The potential use of canards, a horizontal tail, or vortex flaps were driven by the desire to improve takeoff and landing performance and sustained maneuverability. Takeoff and landing speeds of delta-wing aircraft are typically high and their controllability is somewhat limited during approach to landing, which has to be flown at a steep pitch attitude to achieve the higher angles of attack necessary for adequate lift. Also, delta-winged fighters have high levels of induced drag (sometimes called "drag due to lift") at higher angles of attack and during sustained maneuvering due to the aerodynamic influence of their low-aspect-ratio wings. This high induced drag causes a rapid loss of available energy (both potential and kinetic energy as characterized by altitude and airspeed), putting pure deltas somewhat at a disadvantage in hard maneuvering combat against fighters with more conventional wing-tail configurations.[41]

Separately, geometrically and dynamically scaled models of six different weapons, four external stores, and three guided missiles were evaluated in joint GD–Air Force F-16XL weapons separation tests conducted at AEDC wind tunnels in Tullahoma, TN. By the end of the Air Force F-16XL program in 1985, over 4,000 wind tunnel test hours had been logged in a variety of test facilities. Dealing with and assimilating the mass of data generated by the diverse wind tunnel test program was a huge challenge to the GD design team.

A contemporary cartoon by GD graphics artist F. Brubaker illustrates the dilemma of the conceptual design engineer as he attempts to converge on the "best" and final aircraft configuration. The cartoon graphically depicts why conceptual aircraft design is sometimes referred to as the rubber airplane phase of the engineering development process.

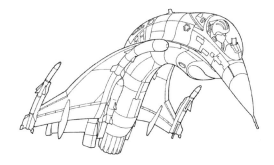

Many F-16XL variations were evaluated during the "rubber airplane" conceptual design phase, as shown in this drawing by General Dynamics' graphic artist F. Brubaker. (Lockheed Martin)

Endnotes

1. Hehs, "Harry Hillaker: Father of the F-16."
2. Harry J. Hillaker, "SCAMP: Supersonic Combat and Maneuvering Prototype Program Presentation," General Dynamics Corporation, Fort Worth Division, September 1977.
3. Aronstein and Piccirillo, *The Lightweight Fighter Program*.
4. Harry J. Hillaker, "F-16XL Flight Test Program Overview," presented at the Second AHS, IES, SETP, SFTE, and DGLR Flight Testing Conference, Las Vegas, NV, November 16–18, 1983, AIAA Paper 83-2730 (November 1, 1983).
5. Robert Wetherall, "F-16XL First Flight Anniversary Celebration: The GD Years," presentation at the F-16XL First Flight 25th Anniversary Celebration, July 3, 2007.
6. Ibid.
7. The McDonnell-Douglas F-4 Phantom II and the later F-15 Eagle carried four conformally mounted AIM-7 Sparrow radar-guided air-to-air missiles in semisubmerged cavities under the fuselage; Charles Epstein, "Taking the Drag Out of Bombs," *Flight International* (August 21, 1982) pp. 418–420.
8. Hillaker, "SCAMP."
9. Ibid.
10. The DMS had originally been developed by NASA to simulate two spacecraft or aircraft maneuvering together.
11. Hillaker, "SCAMP."
12. Chambers, *Partners in Freedom*.
13. The location on the wing where the aerodynamic pitching moment remains constant is known as the aerodynamic center (ac). Using the aerodynamic center as the location where the aerodynamic lifting force is applied eliminates the problem of the movement of the center of pressure with angle of attack during design analyses. For a wing with a positive-cambered airfoil, the pitching moment on the wing results in a counterclockwise (pitch up) rotation of the wing. For wings with nonrectangular planforms (like the F-16 and the F-16XL), the location of the mean aerodynamic center (MAC) depends on the planform shape of the wing. Source: NASA Glenn, *BGA*.
14. As the aerodynamic center of lift on the wing shifts aft during the transition from subsonic to supersonic flight, the aircraft's pitch control surfaces must compensate for the increase in nose-down pitching moment on the aircraft. The resultant control surface deflection

results in increased supersonic trim drag. Harry J. Hillaker, "F-16XL Presentation to the Lone Star Aero Club," Arlington, TX, September 3, 1998.

15. Ibid.
16. Robert Wetherall, interview with the author, August 13, 2012.
17. Ibid.
18. Ibid.; Chambers, *Partners in Freedom.*
19. Similar devices, more commonly referred to as wing fences, had been used on many earlier swept- and delta-wing jet aircraft developed in a number of countries including the United States, France, the United Kingdom, Sweden, and the Soviet Union. Examples include the MiG-15 Fagot, MiG-17 Fresco, MiG-19 Farmer, MiG-21 Fishbed, MiG-23 Flogger, Sukhoi Su-7 Fitter, Douglas D-558-2 Skyrocket, Convair XF-92A Dart, Republic RF-84F Thunderflash, Convair F-102A Delta Dagger, Grumman F9F-6 Cougar, Grumman F11F-1 Tiger, de Havilland Venom FB 1, de Havilland Sea Vixen FAW 1, and Saab J 29 Tunnen and J 32 Lansen. These earlier wing-fence applications were intended to cure tip stall and resulting pitch-up tendencies. As noted in the text, the air dams, as implemented on the F-16XL, were to ensure lateral stability. Correspondence with Joseph R. Chambers, November 27, 2012.
20. Sue B. Grafton, "Low-Speed Wind-Tunnel Study of the High-Angle-of-Attack Stability and Control Characteristics of a Cranked-Arrow-Wing Fighter Configuration," NASA TM 85776 (May 1984).
21. The technical material contained in the Grafton report was widely disseminated throughout the U.S. and international aerospace industries. It was also used for teaching purposes in formal aerospace engineering courses and related research projects; see for example W.H. Mason, "Some High Alpha Aerodynamics" (lecture, Virginia Polytechnic Institute and State University, Blacksburg, VA, 2010; Alexander M. Benoliel, "Aerodynamic Pitch-Up of Cranked Arrow Wings: Estimation, Trim, and Configuration Design" (master's thesis, Virginia Polytechnic Institute & State University, Blacksburg, VA, May 1994).
22. Grafton, "Low-Speed Wind-Tunnel Study"; Wetherall, "F-16XL First Flight Anniversary Celebration."
23. Wetherall, "F-16XL First Flight Anniversary Celebration."
24. A recent example of structural failure related to flutter occurred during the 2011 Reno Air Races when the highly modified P-51 Mustang "Galloping Ghost" lost its elevator trim tab at a speed

estimated as 40 miles per hour (mph) higher than the aircraft was ever tested. The resulting crash killed the pilot and 10 spectators on the ground and injured 64 others, 16 seriously. The final National Transportation Safety Board (NTSB) accident report determined that the "probable cause of this accident was the reduced stiffness of the elevator trim tab system that allowed aerodynamic flutter to occur at racing speeds. The reduced stiffness was the result of deteriorated locknut inserts that allowed the trim tab attachment screws to become loose and to initiate fatigue cracking in one screw sometime before the accident flight. Aerodynamic flutter of the trim tabs resulted in a failure of the left trim tab link assembly, elevator movement, high flight loads, and a loss of control." NTSB, "NTSB Accident Brief: Pilot/Race 177, *The Galloping Ghost*, North American P-51D N79111, Reno, Nevada, September 16, 2001," NTSB/AAB-12/01, PB2012-916203 (August 27, 2012).

25. Peter Garrison, "The Hammer: For Every Airplane, There's a Region of the Flight Envelope into Which it Dare not Fly," *Air & Space Magazine* (March 2001); Chambers, *Partners in Freedom*; Wilmer H. Reed III, "Aeroelasticity Matters: Some Reflections on Two Decades of Testing in the NASA Langley Transonic Dynamics Tunnel," NASA TM 83210 (September 1981); J.A. Ellis, "Flutter Analysis of F-16XL Air-to-Air Configurations," General Dynamics Corporation Report 400PR062 (June 28, 1982); R.S. Adams and J.C. Elrod, "F-16XL Ground Vibration Test No. 1 (Air-to-Air)," General Dynamics Corporation Report 400PR066 (July 9, 1982); R.S. Adams and J.C. Elrod, "F-16XL Ground Vibration Test No. 2 (Air-to-Ground)," General Dynamics Corporation Report 400PR083 (December 20, 1982).

26. Marilyn E. Ogburn, T. Luat, and Phillip W. Brown, "Simulation Study of a Cranked-Arrow Wing Fighter Configuration at High Angles of Attack," NASA TM 85800 (November 1984).

27. R.D. Whipple and W.L. White, "Spin-Tunnel Investigation of a 1/25th Scale Model of the General Dynamics F-16XL Airplane," NASA TM 85660 (October 1, 1984).

28. Joseph R. Chambers, *Modeling Flight: The Role of Dynamically Scaled Free-Flight Models in Support of NASA's Aerospace Programs* (Washington, DC: NASA SP-2009-575, 2009).

29. Ibid.

30. GD, "F-16XL Flight Test Program—Final Report."

31. The 800-pound CBU-58 cluster bomb unit (CBU) consisted of the standard Air Force SUU-30 submunitions dispenser loaded with

650 spherical bomblets. The clamshell-like SUU-30 was 7 feet 9 inches long and 16 inches in diameter. Four fins were attached at a 90-degree angle to the aft end of the dispenser and were canted at an angle of 1.25 degrees to impart spin-stabilized flight after release. An arming wire-lanyard initiated the fuse arming and delay cycle after release. After fuse functioning, the forward end of the dispenser was unlocked. Ram air action forced the two halves apart, releasing the submunitions, and allowing the individual bomblets to spin-arm and self-dispense. Fluted fins on the outer surface of each spherical bomblet caused them to disperse over a very wide area. The some-what similar SUU-65 Tactical Munitions Dispenser (TMD) was 7 feet 2 inches long and 16 inches in diameter. After release, three panels were released from the TMD, allowing submunitions of various types to be dispensed.

32. Calspan provided major engineering support to AEDC, and they were also responsible for operating the AEDC Aerodynamic Wind Tunnel (4T) during the F-16XL weapons separation test conducted by AEDC's director of aerospace flight dynamics. Wind tunnel 4T was a closed-loop, continuous-flow, variable-density tunnel. Mach number could be varied over the range from 0.2 to 1.3 and set at discrete Mach numbers of 1.6 and 1.96. Its test section was 4 feet square and 12.5 feet long.

33. R.A. Paulk, "A Wind Tunnel Test to Determine the Separation Characteristics of Several Stores from the F-16XL Aircraft at Mach Numbers from 0.5 to 1.96," Arnold Engineering Development Center Report AEDC-TSR-82-P20 (July 1982).

34. J.E. Lamar and J.F. Campbell, "Vortex Flaps—Advanced Control Devices for Supercruise Fighters," *Aerospace America* (January 1984): 95–99.

35. Edward C. Polhamus, "Vortex Lift Research: Early Contributions and Some Current Challenges," in *Vortex Flow Aerodynamics—Volume I, Proceedings of Conference held October 8–10, 1986 at Langley Research Center*, NASA CP-2416, Paper No. 1 (1986), pp. 1–30; C.W. Smith, J.F. Campbell, and J.K. Huffman, "Experimental Results of a Leading-Edge Vortex Flap on a Highly Swept Cranked Wing," *Tactical Aircraft Research and Technology*, NASA CP-2162 (1980), pp. 563–580; Chambers, *Innovation in Flight*.

36. J.E. Lamar, "Subsonic Vortex Flow Design Study for Slender Wings," presented at the AIAA 16th Aerospace Sciences Meeting, Huntsville, AL, January 16–18, 1978, AIAA Paper 78-154 (January 1978); John E. Lamar, Roy T. Schemensky, and C. Subba Reddy,

"Development of a Vortex-Lift-Design Method and Application to a Slender Maneuver-Wing Configuration," presented at the AIAA 18th Aerospace Sciences Meeting, Pasadena, CA, January 14–16, 1980, AIAA Paper 80-0327 (January 1980); J.E. Lamar, R.T. Schemensky, and C.S. Reddy, "Development of a Vortex Lift Design Procedure and Application to a Slender-Maneuver-Wing Configuration," *Journal of Aircraft* 18, no. 4 (April 1981): 259–266; David S. Miller and Roy T. Schemensky, "Design Study Results of a Supersonic Cruise Fighter Wing," presented at the AIAA 17th Aerospace Sciences Meeting, New Orleans, LA, January 15–17, 1979, AIAA Paper 79-0062 (January 1979).

37. James F. Campbell and Russell F. Osborn, "Leading-Edge Vortex Research: Some Nonplanar Concepts and Current Challenges," NASA CP-2108 (November 1979), pp. 31–63; H.W. Carlson, and D.S. Miller, "The Influence of Leading-Edge Thrust on Twisted and Cambered Wing Design for Supersonic Cruise," presented at the AIAA Aircraft Systems and Technology Conference, August 11–13, 1981, Dayton, OH, AIAA Paper 81-1656 (August 1981); N.T. Frink, "A Concept for Designing Vortex Flap Geometries," NASA TP-2233 (December 1983).

38. D.M. Rao, "Leading-Edge Vortex Flaps for Enhanced Subsonic Aerodynamics of Slender Wings," *Proceedings of the 7th Congress of the International Council of the Aeronautical Sciences*, ICAS Paper 80-13.5 (1980); D.M. Rao, "Low-Speed Wind Tunnel Study of Longitudinal Stability and Usable-Lift Improvement of a Cranked Wing," NASA CR-178204 (1987); D.M. Rao, "Vortical Flow Management for Improved Configuration Aerodynamics—Recent Experiences," *Proceedings of the AGARD Symposium on Aerodynamics of Vortical Type Flows in Three Dimensions*, Rotterdam, The Netherlands, April 25–28, 1983, AGARD CP-342 (1983).

39. Dennis B. Finley and W. Elliott Schoonover, Jr., "Design and Wind Tunnel Evaluation of Vortex Flaps for the F-16XL," in *Vortex Flow Aerodynamics—Volume II*, NASA CP-2417, Paper No. 13 (1986), pp. 249–276.

40. Hillaker, "F-16XL Presentation to the Lone Star Aero Club."

41. For these reasons, the very successful Soviet MiG-21 and the equally successful U.S. Navy Douglas A-4, both originally designed in the 1950s, featured tailed-delta approaches that provided them with superior sustained maneuvering capabilities. In the years since these entered service, virtually all high-performance fighters with delta-type wings have also used either conventional tails or canards. See

Richard P. Hallion, "Sweep and Swing: Reshaping the Wing for the Jet and Rocket Age," in *NASA's Contributions to Aeronautics* Vol. 1, ed. Richard P. Hallion (Washington: NASA SP-2010-570-Vol 1, 2010); Ray Whitford, *Design for Air Combat* (London: Jane's Publishing Company, Ltd., 1987).

The F-16XL-2 during radar signature testing conducted by General Dynamics. (Lockheed Martin)

CHAPTER 3

Flight Demonstration Program Planning

Early in 1980, General Dynamics held initial discussions with the Air Force F-16 System Program Office (SPO) related to their intent to submit an unsolicited proposal for what they termed a SCAMP flight demonstration program. If acceptable to the Air Force, this proposal was intended to lead to the design, manufacture, and flight test of two F-16XL flight demonstrator aircraft. The flight-test program that GD proposed was based on the three major elements listed below. Successful execution of the proposed program would require the full cooperation of the Air Force along with a commitment of both resources and funding.[1]

1. As a GD Corporate initiative, the company would design, manufacture, and provide safety of flight certificates for two F-16XL demonstrator aircraft.
2. The Air Force would provide two F-16 aircraft and the associated Government-furnished equipment (GFE) necessary for GD to manufacture two prototypes. GD would use Independent Research and Development funding to design and manufacture the two prototypes.[2]
3. Finally, the Government (U.S. Air Force) would fund the F-16XL flight-test program and any additional wind tunnel time required to certify the aircraft for flight testing (such as flutter and weapons separation testing).

The General Dynamics F-16XL Proposal

On February 22, 1980, GD submitted their F-16XL proposal directly to Lt. Gen. Lawrence A. Skantze, the commander of the Aeronautical Systems Division at Wright-Paterson AFB, OH. Skantze assigned the F-16 SPO the responsibility for evaluating the GD proposal for the F-16XL flight-test program. GD had proposed to use a management approach similar to what they and the Air Force used during the YF-16 Lightweight Fighter prototype effort.[3] This included collocation of the entire development team, the formal preparation of minimum essential documentation only, full and open program participation by major subcontractors, and cost and schedule tracking by individual work breakdown structure (WBS) element; and in order to speed development and control cost, the F-16XL design would be based on a firm configuration definition and specific capability goals. Air Force participation was to begin as soon as possible, starting with coordinating the lease of selected F-16 assets needed for the program, and it would include continuous F-16 SPO coordination with the GD F-16XL program manager as the program unfolded. Both the design and flight-test effort were intended to facilitate a smooth transition to an F-16XL-derived production program—if that option was selected by the Air Force. However, many technical, cost, and schedule issues associated with the F-16XL design were still being addressed throughout 1980. These included concerns over excessive wingtip flexibility, leading-edge flap and aileron actuation provisions, final vertical tail size and shape, environmental cooling system (ECS) capacity, external wing fuel tank location, electrical generation capacity, and the producibility of the composite wing skin design.[4]

In its evaluation of the preliminary F-16XL proposal, the Air Force F-16 System Program Office concluded that the aircraft was feasible and the proposed cost of the flight-test effort proposed by GD was realistic. The SPO also noted that the proposed schedule was challenging but feasible. Proposed costs for both the F-16XL Full Scale Development effort and the production program were considered to be somewhat optimistic. However, on May 1, 1980, the F-16 SPO informed GD that the Air Force did not have a requirement for the F-16XL at that time. They recommended that GD examine the possibility of initiating an F-16XL flight demonstration using company Independent Research and Development funding with the possibility of some assistance being provided from the Air Force. Such assistance was noted as potentially including various items of GFE and flight-test support.[5]

General Dynamics undertook an extensive program of briefings on their proposed F-16XL flight demonstration effort in an attempt to gain Air Force support for the program. Meetings and briefings were arranged, and detailed presentations on the flight-test concept were given at all levels of the Air Force covering both systems development agencies and operational commands, including the Air Staff. However, GD was unsuccessful in obtaining Air Force funding to start the effort in 1981 or in convincing the Air Force to incorporate the F-16XL into the fiscal year (FY) 1982 Program Objective Memorandum (POM).[6] After the Air Force had submitted their FY 1982 POM to the Office of the Secretary of Defense (OSD) for review, GD and their supporters within the Air Force were able to convince the Undersecretary of Defense for Research and Engineering (USDR&E) within the OSD to direct the Air Force to initiate a new Combat Aircraft Prototype (CAP) program. This was to be focused on design, construction, and flight test of the F-16XL. The Air Force objected to the USDR&E direction on the basis that commercial competition was required in order to initiate such an effort and also because OSD should not specifically direct what the Air Force should test to best accomplish its mission. In discussions with OSD, the Air Force noted that the F-15E was also a candidate for a flight-test demonstration along with the F-16XL. In a breakthrough for the program, the Air Force did agree to add necessary funding for a competitive prototype program that would involve both the F-16XL and the F-15E. This competitive prototyping effort would begin in FY 1982 and continue through 1983 and 1984. The Air Force budget request was then modified to provide funding for an F-16XL flight demonstration effort with $22.5 million provided in FY 1982, $25 million in 1983, and $10.2 million in 1984. These numbers closely corresponded to the General Dynamics estimate of funding required to execute the F-16XL flight demonstration program.[7]

On August 27, 1980, General Dynamics submitted its proposal for a USAF-sponsored development and flight-test program to the Air Force F-16 Systems Program Office (usually simply referred to as the F-16 SPO).[8] In keeping with the streamlined program approach that GD advocated, the proposal was very concise, being only 40 pages long. GD referred to the flight demonstrator aircraft as "SCAMP" in their proposal. The actual company designation was Model 400, but the aircraft rapidly became known by the designation created by Harry Hillaker—the F-16XL. GD stated that they intended to initiate the development effort on October 1, 1980, using internal company IRAD funds. This approach would continue through September 30, 1981, at which time Air Force funding would be used for the balance of the prototyping and flight demonstration program. Air Force support for the GD approach was soon forthcoming. In a October 15, 1980, letter to General Dynamics, Lt. Gen. Lawrence A. Skantze, commander of the USAF Aeronautical Systems Division, stated, "I support your plan to conduct the F-16XL program using IRAD...."[9] He also committed the Air Force to providing necessary material support for the project as laid out by GD in their proposal: "We can respond favorably to your request to provide GFE [Government Furnished Equipment] requirements...." These GFE items were listed as "two F-16 aircraft (A-3 and A-5), three F100-PW-200 engines, and one two-place forward fuselage, equipments and assets available under the F-16 contract at no cost on a non-interference basis." The two F-16A aircraft identified in the Skantze letter would be built as the F-16XL-1 (the single-seat prototype) and F-16XL-2 (the two-seat flight demonstrator).[10]

Shortly after GD submitted their proposal to the Air Force, articles describing the anticipated capabilities of the F-16XL began to appear in the aviation press, reportedly based on interviews with company representatives. Numerous claims, including one that stated that the F-16XL maximum sustained cruise speed was Mach 2.2—as compared to Mach 0.93 for the F-16A—were circulated in print. Others stated that air-to-air mission radius would be increased 125 percent and supersonic radius of action doubled. In the air-to-ground role, mission radius was reportedly increased by 120 percent. Sea level penetration speed was indicated as being 90 knots higher than the F-16A while carrying 2.5 times the weapons payload. Takeoff and landing distances were reported as being decreased by about 33 percent. Takeoff distance in the air-to-air configuration was claimed to be 1,640 feet versus 2,425 feet for the F-16A. Landing distance was claimed to be as low as 1,180 feet with the use of the F-16XL's drag chute, as compared to the landing roll of 2,480 feet for the standard F-16A, which did not have a drag chute.[11] As often is the case during the early stages of a nascent aircraft program, some of these early flight performance estimations subsequently did not match actual flight-test results. In particular, supercruise, takeoff and landing performance, and subsonic maneuvering capability all fell short.

The F-16XL Gets Under Way

On December 1, 1980, the chairman and chief executive officer of the General Dynamics Corporation, David S. Lewis, gave the go-ahead to build the aircraft, reportedly committing over $53 million of GD funding to the effort. Referring to the F-16XL as "a bright star," Lewis said, "We aren't about to sit on our laurels and risk the F-16 becoming obsolescent."[12] From then on, progress was very rapid, with the first engineering design release occurring only 17 days later on December 18, 1980. Such an impressive achievement was in large part due to the fact that GD had already begun F-16XL detail design work in anticipation of favorable Air Force and corporate decisions to proceed.[13] In line with the streamlined program management approach that GD had used on the YF-16 effort, key members of the XL design team were colocated in a single closed area referred to as the "green room" to facilitate communications and coordination across all engineering and management disciplines. The team was not constrained by nonessential requirements and specifications and had the design freedom to concentrate on achieving performance objectives; as Harry Hillaker later said of the F-16XL, "Every piece on this aircraft earned its way on."[14]

In December 1980, Harry Hillaker met with NASA executives at the Agency's headquarters in Washington, DC, to review the status of the evolving F-16XL effort. During the meeting, the NASA officials affirmed that the

Agency was committed to participation in the F-16XL program and might even be interested in sponsoring construction of a third aircraft fitted with a wing that was fully optimized for supersonic cruise. Hillaker was asked if GD had identified a specific role for NASA in the prototype flight demonstration program. The GD engineer responded by noting that a vectorable, two-dimensional thrust-reversing nozzle and leading-edge vortex flaps were worthwhile areas for NASA investigation and that these technologies could be incorporated into subsequent phases of the F-16XL flight demonstrator program.[15] The meeting concluded with a NASA Headquarters commitment to support F-16XL requirements for NASA wind tunnels as long as these wind tunnel requirements were agreeable with the NASA research Centers to be involved.[16]

On January 7, 1981, General Dynamics Program Director D. Randall "Randy" Kent wrote to Brig. Gen. George L. Monahan, the F-16 SPO director, to coordinate details of the development effort. In his letter, Kent noted that the corporation had formally initiated the F-16XL program in December 1980. The GD management team had been selected, project personnel had been collocated to the mezzanine area of Hangar 8 overlooking where the aircraft would be built, and the release of engineering drawings had already started.[17] Program milestones and performance indicators that would lead to a first flight in July 1982 had been established.[18] The approved F-16XL program schedule called for 240 flights to be completed with the two demonstrator aircraft by May 15, 1983, during the Air Force–funded flight-test portion of the program. Engineering, design, and fabrication efforts initially were focused on producing the tooling and designing the components needed to manufacture the two prototypes. This aspect of the effort was complete in December 1981, by which time 1,400 design and manufacturing drawings had been produced. Almost exactly 1 year after the first detailed design drawings were released, a small "first chips" ceremony attended by key GD program officials was held at the Fort Worth factory. This January 21, 1981, event marked the start of component fabrication, an activity that would continue until late in January 1982. Key members of the General Dynamics F-16XL team at the end of 1980 included Randy Kent, F-16XL vice president and program director; Harry J. Hillaker, deputy program director; Clarence E. Hart, chief engineer; James A. Gordon, aerodynamics lead; Charles F. Crabtree, propulsion lead; Kenneth H. Barnes, flight control system lead; and G.H. Hayward, airframe design.[19]

In April 1981, Chief Engineer Clarence Hart forwarded an interesting GD internal memorandum to all members of the F-16XL engineering team. He noted that the program was proceeding in a very satisfactory manner with the aircraft configuration yielding encouraging results in wind tunnel tests. However, Hart highlighted the one major problem that demanded the attention of the entire team. The problem was excessive weight, an issue that is

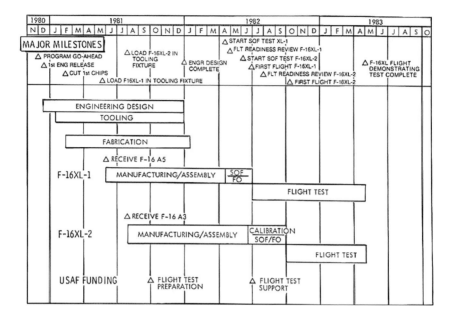

The F-16XL flight demonstrator design, fabrication, assembly, and flight-test program schedule, as depicted on a GD chart circa 1980. (Lockheed Martin)

commonplace with most high performance fighter aircraft at this stage of their development cycle, both before and since the F-16XL. Hart noted that

> The wing is currently estimated to be 547 lb. over proposal weight. Additionally weight increases in flight controls, electrical and fuel system have added another 287 lb. If this condition is not corrected, our weapons loading could be reduced by two 500 lb. bombs and our acceleration time from 0.9 to 1.6 Mach would be increased significantly. We must take steps to correct this problem.
>
> I am asking each of you to give this problem your serious consideration and send me your ideas concerning possible weight savings. Do not limit your thoughts to just your area of responsibility and do not hesitate to propose an idea for weight savings because it is unusual or unorthodox. We need your help in solving this most difficult problem.[20]

By mid-1981, the wing's weight problem was under control and manufacturing efforts were well underway on both aircraft. As manufactured, the empty weight of F-16XL-1 would end up at 19,690 pounds as compared to

15,586 pounds for the basic F-16A, a difference of about 4,100 pounds. The two-seat F-16XL-2 would have an empty weight of 21,157 pounds. This extra weight combined with the same engine thrust meant that the F-16XL had a lower thrust-to-weight (T/W) ratio compared to that of the F-16. Thrust-to-weight ratio, along with wing loading and high lift-to-drag ratio, are important components that define the overall energy maneuverability capability of any fighter. (The relatively low thrust-to-weight ratio of the F-16XL and its effects on takeoff distance and sustained maneuvering capability would later be highlighted by the Air Force as a significant factor in determining the eventual outcome of the dual-role fighter source selection, which chose the McDonnell-Douglas F-15E Strike Eagle.)[21]

In the F-16XL manufacturing process, the single-seat XL-1 was somewhat in the lead, its fuselage having been installed in the assembly tooling fixture in May. The two-seat aircraft, the F-16XL-2, was in its assembly fixture by the end of July 1981.[22] Both aircraft would retain their original F-16A serial numbers when they returned to flight status as F-16XLs equipped with F-16 Block 10 avionics. Their airframes were designed for a minimum service life of 8,000 hours based on a structural design that provided 9-g capability at an aircraft weight of 35,000 pounds with full internal fuel and 6.5-g capability at the maximum aircraft takeoff gross weight of 48,000 pounds. Both prototypes were intended to carry four AIM-120 AMRAAM missiles in semi-submerged mountings under the aircraft plus two wingtip-mounted AIM-9 Sidewinders. In reality, dummy AIM-120s, fabricated from wood and sheet metal, were scabbed onto the undersurfaces of the F-16XL flight demonstrators as the AIM-120 missile was yet to be integrated onto the standard F-16, and incorporation of the semisubmerged missile housing with its associated ejector launcher would have required a separate development and integration effort. A large variety of air-to-ground weapons and drop tanks could be carried on as many as 16 wing stations.

As the General Dynamics F-16XL effort ramped up at Fort Worth, a wide variety of specialized personnel would be assigned to the project. At the peak, these included a total of 540 people. Of these, 13 were staff and managers, 205 were from the various engineering disciplines, 260 were directly involved in production/manufacturing, 20 were dedicated to material/supply, 10 were focused on preparation for test and evaluation, 20 were dedicated to quality assurance, and 12 were Production Planning and Control (PPC) types. Air Force personnel assigned to the F-16XL effort at Fort Worth and Edwards AFB brought the total project staffing level up to about the 600 people. During the course of the F-16XL design and fabrication effort, over 1,000,000 work hours would be expended. The manufacturing effort to build the two flight demonstrators ran on a two-shift basis and ended up costing GD $41.7 million between late 1980 and June 1982. This was in addition to the $15.9 million expended by GD during the cooperative NASA-GD configuration definition effort between 1976 and 1980. GD vendors and suppliers helped fund the flight demonstrator design and fabrication effort to the tune of an additional $7.8 million. Thus, the contractor cost of the F-16XL effort up to the July 1982 first flight was $65.4 million.[23]

F-16XL Performance Pluses and Minuses

In articles in military journals, in professional society papers and presentations, and during interviews with the aviation press, General Dynamics strongly advocated the improved capabilities incorporated into the F-16XL. In particular, they emphasized that the cranked-arrow design chosen for their aircraft would lead to significant improvements in range and payload compared to the standard F-16 while also addressing other aspects of fighter mission success. The cranked-arrow wing was said to retain the advantages of the conventional delta wing for high-speed flight while overcoming its disadvantages. These advantages partially resulted from the cranked-arrow wing's less highly swept outboard wing panels, which provided excellent low-speed characteristics while minimizing the trim drag penalties of a more conventional tailless delta design. Although the wing area of the F-16XL was more than double that of the standard F-16, GD showed that the overall drag on the aircraft was actually reduced. Despite the fact that the F-16XL's skin friction drag was larger than the standard F-16 (due to its much greater surface area), the other components of total drag (supersonic wave drag, interference drag, and trim drag) were actually lower. This resulted from the F-16XLs streamlined aerodynamic configuration and the geometrical arrangement and semiconformal carriage of its external stores. Thus, while the larger F-16XL in a clean configuration had an overall drag that was slightly lower than that of a standard F-16 at high subsonic speeds, its drag was 40 percent lower when comparing each type carrying bombs and missiles. Although, because of weight gain (as previously discussed), the thrust-to-weight ratio of the F-16XL was lower than that of the F-16, its excess thrust was actually greater due to the F-16XL's lower total drag, especially at higher subsonic and supersonic speeds.[24]

But in actuality, this only held true for 1-g (straight and level) flight, and it partially accounted for the improved range and payload capabilities of the F-16XL. For example, on an air-to-surface mission, the F-16XL could carry twice the payload of the F-16 up to 40 percent farther without having to carry eternal tanks. With equal payloads and carrying external tanks, the XL mission radius was nearly double that of the F-16. A fully loaded F-16XL had a speed advantage of up to 80 knots calibrated airspeed (KCAS) in military power at sea level over the F-16 with a similar payload.[25] However, during high-AoA sustained subsonic maneuvering, the F-16XL (like delta configurations generally) had a much higher induced drag penalty. This was a natural result of the aerodynamics of its very-low-aspect-ratio cranked-arrow wing. During the latter Air Force flight-test program, this higher induced drag would prove to cause a rapid loss of excess energy. This, in turn, was manifested by a rapid loss of airspeed and altitude during sustained subsonic high-g turns as compared to the standard F-16. In the "real world" of fighter-versus-fighter combat, this constituted a major performance deficit, given potential opponents such as the powerful and highly agile Soviet Mikoyan MiG-29 Fulcrum and Sukhoi Su-27 Flanker.[26]

In their briefings and marketing literature, General Dynamics emphasized that the F-16XL had two additional advantages that would contribute to increased overall effectiveness and survivability in combat situations. These were its improved instantaneous maneuvering capability and its reduced radar cross section, as compared to the standard F-16.

In an attempt to offset the reduced performance capabilities of the F-16XL during sustained hard-maneuvering combat, GD highlighted its excellent instantaneous turning performance. This, they claimed, would enable an F-16XL pilot to quickly change direction and get his missiles off before an enemy was able to react and adjust his tactics. In this regard, the F-16XL with its much lower wing loading did have a distinct instantaneous turning advantage, for it was able to reach 5 g's in less than 1 second and 9 g's in about 2 seconds. Both times were less than half those of the standard F-16A. Also, then-recent advances in infrared guided missile target seekers provided the capability to engage enemy aircraft from all aspect angles, rather than just the aft quartering region where infrared energy was strongest. This reduced the dependence on sus-

tained high-g maneuvering to gain an effective firing position on an enemy aircraft in fighter-versus-fighter combat. This was certainly true for the AIM-9L version of the classic Sidewinder infrared-guided missile then being carried on USAF F-15s and F-16s. The United States had rapidly supplied the AIM-9L to the British during the spring 1982 Falkland Islands

The F-16XL-2 during radar signature testing conducted by General Dynamics. (Lockheed Martin)

conflict with Argentina. The all-aspect target engagement capabilities of the AIM-9L were widely acknowledged as a major factor in Britain successfully regaining control over the Falklands.[27]

The F-16XL's radar signature (usually termed its RCS) was somewhat lower than that of the standard F-16 when measured head on without air-to-ground ordnance, drop tanks, and Low Altitude Navigation Targeting Infra-Red Night (LANTIRN) navigation and targeting pods. RCS was reported as being 50 percent lower than that of the standard F-16 during testing conducted by GD.[28] Since the detection range of an enemy radar varies with the forth root of its target's radar cross section, halving the radar signature of the target aircraft reduces its detectability (detection range) to enemy radars by about 16 percent.[29] However, frontal signature reduction would have been negligible when the aircraft was loaded with the external stores mentioned above for the air-to-ground mission.

Endnotes

1. D.R. Kent, vice president and program director, F-16XL program, General Dynamics Fort Worth Division, letter to Brig. Gen. G.L. Monahan, ASD, Aeronautical Systems Division, January 7, 1981.

2. Under U.S. Federal Acquisition Regulations (FARs), IRAD efforts must fall within one of the following four categories: Basic Research, Applied Research, Development, or Systems/Concept Formulation Studies. Allowable IRAD costs are limited to those projects determined to be of potential interest to the DoD based on their contributions to the criteria listed below.
   - Enable superior performance of future U.S. weapon system and components.
   - Reduce acquisition costs and life-cycle costs of military systems.
   - Strengthen the defense industrial and technology base of the United States.
   - Enhance the industrial competitiveness of the United States.
   - Promote the development of technologies identified as critical.
   - Increase the development and promotion of efficient and effective applications of dual-use technologies.
   - Provide efficient and effective technologies for achieving environmental benefits.

   In various ways, the F-16XL initiative clearly met all of these criteria.

3. Harry J. Hillaker, "F-16XL Flight Test Program Overview"; Aronstein and Piccirillo, "The Lightweight Fighter Program: A Successful Approach to Fighter Technology Transition."

4. K.R. Hinman, "F-16E Point Paper," General Dynamics Corporation, July 27, 1981.

5. Kent, letter.

6. The Program Objective Memorandum is the primary document used by the military services within the Department of Defense to submit their programming proposals. The POM includes an analysis of missions, objectives, alternative methods to accomplish objectives, and allocation of resources. It presents planned activities and the personnel and budget obligation authority required over a 5-year period to build, operate, and maintain the proposed program.

7. Harry J. Hillaker, "F-16XL Presentation to the Lone Star Aero Club," Arlington, TX, September 3, 1998.

8. Wetherall, "F-16XL First Flight Anniversary Celebration."

9. Lt. Gen. Lawrence A. Skantze, USAF, Headquarters Aeronautical Systems Division (AFSC), letter to Richard E. Adams, vice president

and general manager, General Dynamics Corporation, October 15, 1980; Hinman, "F-16E Point Paper."

10. Skantze, "Letter to Richard E. Adams."
11. Mark J. Bulban, "Mach 2.2 F-16 Development Underway," *Aviation Week & Space Technology* (July 21,1980): pp. 20–22.
12. David P. Garino, "General Dynamics to Spend $53 Million on Two Versions of its F16 Fighter Plane," *The Wall Street Journal*, December 8, 1980.
13. Author not identified, "General Dynamics Developing F-16XL Hardware," *Aviation Week & Space Technology* (April 6, 1981): 57.
14. F. Clifton Berry, Jr., "The Revolutionary Evolution of the F-16XL," *Air Force Magazine* 66, no. 11 (November 1983); Wetherall interview.
15. Both of these technology areas would later be investigated by NASA using suitably modified F-16XL subscale wind tunnel models, but they never became part of the full-scale flight-test program with the aircraft.
16. H.J. Hillaker, vice president and deputy program manager, F-16XL, memo to D.R. Kent, December 15, 1980.
17. The initial release of F-16XL engineering drawings occurred on December 18, 1980, only 17 days after program go-ahead. These drawings were released quickly because they were relatively straight-forward changes to the existing engine installation in the F-16. Robert Wetherall, correspondence with author, July 14, 2012.
18. Kent, letter to Monahan.
19. Wetherall, "F-16XL First Flight Anniversary Celebration"; D.R. Kent, "F-16XL Program Organization," General Dynamics Fort Worth Division, F-16XL Program Directive Memorandum No. 2, November 25, 1980; C.E. Hart, "F-16XL Fighter Engineering Organization Assignment of Responsibilities," General Dynamics Fort Worth Division, Project Engineering Memorandum (PEM) No. 19-1.1, November 20, 1980, Revision A, December 30, 1980.
20. C.E. Hart, chief engineer, F-16XL program, "Memo to F-16XL Engineering Personnel: F-16XL Weight Saving," General Dynamics, Fort Worth Division, F-16XL-ENG-48, April 10, 1981.
21. "A source of some frustration to GD was the fact that "the Air Force would not allow us to use the GE F110 engine in our pro-posal even though the No. 2 XL, the 2-place version, was powered by a F110 engine and provided better performance than the P&W F100 engine." Robert Wetherall correspondence with the author, December 20, 2012.
22. Wetherall, "F-16XL First Flight Anniversary Celebration."
23. Ibid.

24. Hillaker, "F-16XL Presentation to the Lone Star Aero Club"; "General Dynamics F-16XLC/D MULTIROLE FIGHTER"; General Dynamics Corporation Marketing Brochure, Fort Worth Division (undated, circa 1983).

25. Hillaker, "General Dynamics F-16XLC/D MULTIROLE FIGHTER."

26. Talty, "F-16XL Demonstrates New Capabilities."

27. During the relatively brief Falklands conflict, Royal Navy British Aerospace Sea Harrier FRS 1 fighters launched AIM-9L Sidewinder missiles during 23 air-to-air engagements with Argentine aircraft. The AIM-9L accounted for 19 confirmed kills for an overall success rate of 82 percent. See Jeffrey Ethell and Alfred Price, *Air War South Atlantic* (New York: Macmillan Publishing Company, 1983).

28. Wetherall, "F-16XL First Flight Anniversary Celebration"; C.A. Robinson, Jr., "USAF Studies Fighters for Dual-Role, All-Weather Operations," *Aviation Week & Space Technology* (January 3, 1983) p. 39.

29. Eugene F. Knott, John F. Schaeffer, and Michael T. Tulley, *Radar Cross Section: Its Prediction Measurement and Reduction* (Norwood, MA: ARTECH House, Inc., 1985), p. 35.

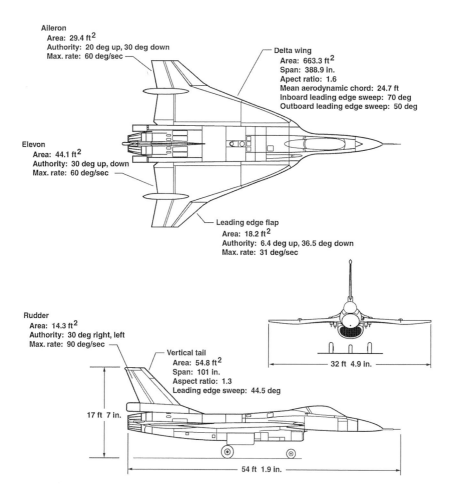

Aileron
Area: 29.4 ft^2
Authority: 20 deg up, 30 deg down
Max. rate: 60 deg/sec

Delta wing
Area: 663.3 ft^2
Span: 388.9 in.
Apect ratio: 1.6
Mean aerodynamic chord: 24.7 ft
Inboard leading edge sweep: 70 deg
Outboard leading edge sweep: 50 deg

Elevon
Area: 44.1 ft^2
Authority: 30 deg up, down
Max. rate: 60 deg/sec

Leading edge flap
Area: 18.2 ft^2
Authority: 6.4 deg up, 36.5 deg down
Max. rate: 31 deg/sec

Rudder
Area: 14.3 ft^2
Authority: 30 deg right, left
Max. rate: 90 deg/sec

Vertical tail
Area: 54.8 ft^2
Span: 101 in.
Aspect ratio: 1.3
Leading edge sweep: 44.5 deg

32 ft 4.9 in.

17 ft 7 in.

54 ft 1.9 in.

The physical and geometric properties of the F-6XL aircraft are illustrated in this NASA drawing. The effects of conical camber and twist on the wing are evident in the front view of the aircraft. (NASA)

CHAPTER 4

Design and Construction Details

By the early 1980s, General Dynamics released detailed illustrations and descriptions of the F-16XL configuration. They noted that the cranked-arrow-wing design had both aerodynamic and configuration benefits and significant potential for increased combat range. The cranked F-16XL arrow wing had an area that was 115 percent larger than that of the standard F-16A wing. The resulting larger internal wing volume enabled much more fuel to be carried—5,000 pounds as compared to about 1,150 pounds in the standard F-16 wing. The two fuselage plugs resulted in a new fuselage that was 56 inches longer than that of the standard F-16. This enabled the F-16XL to carry over 7,600 pounds of fuel inside its fuselage compared to slightly over 5,800 pounds carried in the standard F-16's fuselage.[1] Wing camber and twist were optimized to minimize drag during high-speed cruise and level acceleration. Supersonic wave drag was

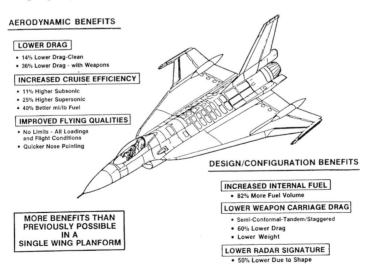

AERODYNAMIC BENEFITS

LOWER DRAG
- 14% Lower Drag-Clean
- 36% Lower Drag - with Weapons

INCREASED CRUISE EFFICIENCY
- 11% Higher Subsonic
- 25% Higher Supersonic
- 40% Better mi/lb Fuel

IMPROVED FLYING QUALITIES
- No Limits - All Loadings and Flight Conditions
- Quicker Nose Pointing

MORE BENEFITS THAN PREVIOUSLY POSSIBLE IN A SINGLE WING PLANFORM

DESIGN/CONFIGURATION BENEFITS

INCREASED INTERNAL FUEL
- 82% More Fuel Volume

LOWER WEAPON CARRIAGE DRAG
- Semi-Conformal-Tandem/Staggered
- 60% Lower Drag
- Lower Weight

LOWER RADAR SIGNATURE
- 50% Lower Due to Shape

A General Dynamics perspective on the range of benefits that was possible by integrating the cranked-arrow wing in the F-16XL design. (Lockheed Martin)

reportedly reduced by 17 percent, and any low-speed pitch-up tendency was eliminated. In press releases and interviews with the aerospace media, GD stated that the extensive wind tunnel test program with NASA had shown that the F-16XL's cranked-arrow wing, with its sophisticated tailored twist and camber features, did not display the high induced drag at high lift and the adverse tail-trim characteristics that were usually associated with tailless delta-wing aircraft.

NASA continued to provide extensive support to General Dynamics during engineering development and subsequent refinement of the F-16XL design, leading up to its first flight in July 1982. This support included wind tunnel model development and testing, wing design methodology and analytical procedures, performance predictions based on wind tunnel test results, and inputs into the design of the tailored flight control system. The latter item was based in part on successful pilot-in-the-loop testing in the Differential Maneuvering Simulator at NASA Langley. All of these efforts proved to be very important as the GD engineering team converged on the final F-16XL detailed design and moved forward

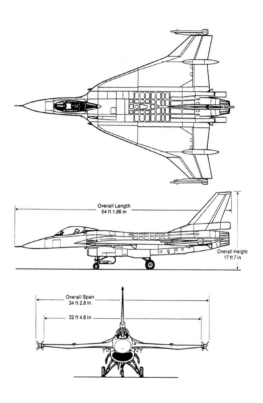

The single-seat F-16XL is illustrated with four semi-submerged AIM-120 AMRAAM radar-guided missiles and two wingtip-mounted AIM-9L infrared-guided Sidewinder missiles. (Air Force)

with construction of the prototype flight demonstrator aircraft.[2] Data from Langley research efforts on automatic spin prevention were factored into the detail hardware design of the F-16XL's leading-edge flaps (LEFs) and the programming of the software used in its computerized fly-by-wire flight control system. These flight control system features provided a significant contribution to the aircraft's carefree handling qualities. The F-16XL's very high resistance to inadvertent loss of control or spin development would be convincingly demonstrated during the subsequent Air Force flight-test program.

Wing Geometry and Structural Design

The F-16XL zero-dihedral cranked-arrow wing had an overall span of 32 feet 5 inches. When the wingtip-mounted AIM-9 missiles and their launchers were installed, wingspan was increased to 34 feet 3 inches. Wing area was a little over 663 square feet compared to 300 square feet for the F-16's trapezoidal wing. The aspect ratio of the wing was a very low 1.6 as compared to the F-16 aspect ratio of 3.0. Leading-edge sweep angles were 70 degrees on the inboard segments of the wing and 50 degrees on the outboard segments. The long-chord wing had a thickness-to-chord ratio of 4.5 percent. The mean aerodynamic chord of the cranked-arrow wing was 24.7 feet.[3]

A modified National Advisory Committee for Aeronautics (NACA) 64A airfoil was used on the inboard portion of the cranked-arrow wing. This portion of the wing had its camber conically tailored from the root outward. This feature was designed to reduce drag at transonic and supersonic speeds and improve the acceleration characteristics of the aircraft. The outer wing panels used a modified biconvex airfoil. The angle of incidence of the wing was –0.65 degrees over the inboard wing segment and then varied as the wingtip was approached, reaching a negative incidence of 4.1 degrees at the tip.[4] This conical camber resulted in a distinctive twisted effect when the wing was viewed from the front. This can be seen in the three-view drawing of the aircraft.

Elevons were mounted on the aft inner wing segments. Ailerons and leading-edge flaps were installed on the outboard wing panels. Hydraulically operated aileron actuators were located in large pods on the aft portion of the wings between the ailerons and the elevons. These pods were also intended to house electronic warfare equipment including chaff and flare dispensers. The hydraulically operated elevon actuators were contained inside the wing structure close to the root on each side. The leading-edge-flap rotary actuators—electrically commanded but hydraulically operated—were mounted on the forward spars of the outer wing panels.[5] Further details concerning the F-16XL's elevon, flap, and aileron design and their functional modes of operation are contained in the flight control section.

Computer-aided design (CAD) and computer-aided manufacturing (CAM) systems were extensively used in both the design and manufacture of the F-16XL. The use of computer-based structural analysis, design, and manufacturing systems in aerospace applications was greatly influenced by a major NASA initiative known as the NASA Structural Analysis System (or NASTRAN for short). NASTRAN had been developed under NASA Langley Research Center management leadership. NASTRAN led to the development and use of many commercially developed CAD/CAM systems, with various tailored capabilities, that were subsequently used in the aerospace industry and many other design and manufacturing industries.[6]

General Dynamics purchased a CAD/CAM system that had been developed by Lockheed called CADAM. It used an IBM mainframe computer that served interconnected CADAM terminals. During engineering design of the F-16XL, it was quickly found that these terminals had to be carefully prioritized and scheduled because there were not enough of them to go around for every member of the engineering team to have full-time access. In fact, the fuselage parts were drawn mostly on paper for this reason. The CADAM system played a major role in the design, manufacture, and smooth integration of the complex cranked-arrow wing into the prototypes. The two segments of the F-16XL's cranked-arrow wing were designed with new wing attachment fittings. These fittings mated with the stretched fuselage at the existing F-16 wing attachment points and at additional attachment points located on the aft fuselage extension. The greater physical depth of this wing over the standard F-16 wing led to the need to "invert" the wing attachment fittings by introducing an angle into the inboard portion of the wing skins.[7] Later, during stability and control flight tests involving very high roll rate maneuvers, structural loads instrumentation indicated that the stress in the wing-fuselage shear tie at Fuselage Station (FS) 463.1 could exceed the flight-test limit.[8] This led to the design and installation of a reinforced shear tie in both aircraft.

The robust internal structure of the F-16XL wing was designed to handle the stresses associated with aerodynamic loads including loads created during operation of the independently actuated elevons, ailerons, and leading-edge

flaps. Loads on the wing hard points produced when external stores were carried and forcefully ejected from the aircraft also had to be accommodated in the wing structural design. Not long after the July 1982 first flight of the F-16XL-1, data from the inflight structural loads instrumentation system led structural engineers to conclude that the aft wing spar could fail at 86 percent of its design load limit. To deal with this issue, GD engineers developed a structural fix that resulted in the replacement of a 22-inch-long section of the aluminum rear spar with

The robust internal structure of the F-16XL's cranked-arrow wing viewed looking outboard from the wing root toward the wingtip. (Lockheed Martin)

a strengthened part made of high-strength steel. The new steel part also incorporated a flange with increased depth for even further strength. The wing on F-16XL-1 was modified with the new component at Fort Worth. Inflight stress measurements validated the adequacy of the aft wing spar structural fix. The strengthened aft wing spar modification was incorporated into the wing on F-16XL-2 prior to its first flight at Fort Worth in October 1982.

Specially tailored upper and lower composite wing skins were developed for use on the F-16XL. These composite skins were mechanically attached to the aluminum understructure of each wing using special fasteners. The composite wing skins covered most of the surface area of each wing segment. The skin design was based on the use of aeroelastically tailored graphite-bismaleimide laminates (composed of T300 fiber with a V378-A matrix) that were intended to save structural weight. The F-16 had used a graphite-epoxy composite material (T300 fiber/3501-6 matrix), but GD moved to the polyimide-based family (of which bismaleimide is a subset) for their superior high-temperature properties. The skins were tailored to deform favorably under load while meeting the strength requirements of a minimum weight, damage-tolerant structure. They ranged in thickness from 0.25 to 0.75 inches. By the time of the F-16XL development, graphite-polyimide composites were being increasingly used in aerospace applications, including on the Space Shuttle. The development and widespread use of graphite-polyimide composite structures in the aerospace industry

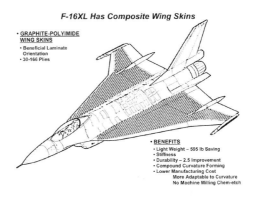

Composite wing skins increased structural strength, saved weight, reduced manufacturing cost, and improved durability. (Lockheed Martin)

had been heavily influenced by NASA-sponsored research conducted with many companies including General Dynamics. In addition, GD had more than a decade of development experience with composite materials, sponsored in large part by the USAF Materials Laboratory at Wright-Patterson AFB.

The graphite-bismaleimide composite material had excellent mechanical strength, being able to handle stresses of up to 50,000 pounds per square inch (psi), as well as good heat-resistance properties. For the F-16XL application, the composite wing skins were built up of laminated layers of graphite-bismaleimide material in which its thickness consisted of anywhere from 30 to 166 plies. The individual layers used to build up the laminates had been laid-up over a mold by hand as automatic tape-laying equipment was still in development. The specific number of plies used in an individual laminated layer was dependent on the highest computed local structural load and stress levels likely

Graphite-bismaleimide laminates were used in various combinations and orientations to build up the composite wing skins. (Lockheed Martin)

to be encountered across the F-16XL's aerodynamic flight envelope. During assembly of the skins, the laminates were carefully laid down in a precisely planned geometric orientation intended to optimize the distribution of stresses across the wing skins to reduce structural weight. The process had to be done in a time-critical way, as the bismaleimide resin in the graphite tape would slowly begin to cure as it warmed up after removal from refrigerated storage. Following the room temperature lay-down process, the skins were placed on a mold that replicated the required curvature of the outer wing surfaces. The skins were then cured under high pressures and high temperatures in a special autoclave. This resulted in the formation of permanently hardened graphite-bismaleimide composite wing skins with the proper compound curvature. Following final manufacturing details, such as insuring an exact fit and drilling the fastener mounting holes, the skins were ready for installation onto the basic metallic wing substructure.[9]

The graphite-bismaleimide composite wing skins not only saved weight (a savings GD claimed was 595 pounds), but they also reduced manufacturing and production costs. This was due to the fact that the composite materials used to build up the wing skins were more adaptable to being formed into the compound curvature surfaces that were features of the F-16XL arrow-wing design. The compound curvature of the wing skin surface was due to its complex combination of wing camber and twist. Composite wing skins did not require machine milling or chemical etching as metallic skins did. Other benefits were increased stiffness and better rigidity compared to metallic counterparts and an anticipated 2.5 times improvement in durability in operational service.[10]

Vertical Fin and Rudder

The two distinctive ventral fins located under the aft fuselage on the standard F-16 were deleted on the F-16XL. The ventral fins would not have had sufficient ground clearance during takeoff or on landing. This was due to two factors: the lengthened F-16XL aft fuselage and the GD decision to use standard F-16 landing gear and wheel well locations. The dorsal fin measured 101 inches from its base to the tip. The F-16XL's height measured to the tip of its fin was 11 inches greater than that of the standard F-16. Fin aspect ratio was about 1.3, leading-edge sweep angle was 44.5 degrees, and surface area was 54.8 square feet. A biconvex airfoil, varying in thickness-to-chord ratio from 5.3 percent at the root to 3 percent at the tip, was used. Increased rudder hinge moment capability was required to deal with the higher stresses resulting from the changed aerodynamics of the F-16XL. The rudder was also strengthened to provide a 50-percent increase in its capability to handle the higher hinge moments. The rudder had a surface area of 14.3 square feet. Maximum deflection was 30 degrees in either direction.[11]

Later, during the Air Force flight-test program, the F-16XL-2 was ferried back to Fort Worth from Edwards AFB, on January 28, 1985, for several planned structural modifications. In conjunction with this effort, a Large Normal Shock Inlet (LNSI), discussed under the propulsion section, replaced the standard inlet. A structural inspection of the entire airframe was conducted during the structural modification effort. During this comprehensive inspection, cracks were discovered at the base of the fin rear spar. The corrective engineering modification developed by GD engineers required the removal of the entire vertical tail. This was necessary to enable a bathtub-shaped fitting doubler to be added to the rear fin spar. The fin modification was completed on F-16XL-2 at Fort Worth before it was flown back to Edwards in June 1985. The fin doubler modification was installed on F-16XL-1 at Edwards AFB by a GD onsite modification team.[12]

A drag chute system was housed in a prominent dorsal fairing mounted at the base of the tailfin. At the time of the F-16XL development, standard F-16s did not have a drag chute installation. The exception was the F-16 configuration for the Royal Norwegian Air Force. Norwegian pilots had to operate from remote strips, many of which were short and endangered by ice and snow, where drag chutes literally could make the difference between life and death. On the larger, heavier F-16XL with its increased landing speeds, the drag chute provided several operational advantages. It allowed the aircraft to land safely with heavy payloads or to operate from runways that had been shortened by enemy action. The drag chute also enabled F-16XL operations at higher gross weights from the shorter runways that existed on many North Atlantic Treaty Organization (NATO) airfields. With the drag chute, an aborted takeoff could be accomplished safely on a standard 8,000-foot-long NATO airfield at a maximum takeoff gross weight (TOGW) of 48,000 pounds with a wet runway at warm-day conditions. The F-16XL drag chute was based on the pattern used on the Norwegian F-16; however, it was manufactured with an even larger canopy area for use on the F-16XL.[13]

Fuselage

The F-16XL fuselage was a lengthened and modified version of the standard F-16 fuselage. In response to a request from GD, the Air Force had allocated two F-16 fuselages for the F-16XL program. The first fuselage came from F-16A serial number 75-0749. This was the fifth Full-Scale Development aircraft, and it had accumulated 401.5 hours of flying time in support of the FSD program. Powered by a Pratt & Whitney F100-PW-200 turbofan engine with 24,000 pounds of sea level static thrust (SLST), its primary role had

been climatic and environmental testing, much of which had been conducted in the huge McKinley Climatic Laboratory at Eglin AFB, in northwest Florida.[14] The fuselage was delivered to the GD Fort Worth factory for conversion into the single-seat F-16XL on May 4, 1981, arriving on a large commercial flatbed truck that had been chartered from the Leonard Brothers Trucking Company of Miami, FL.[15]

The damaged fuselage of the third Full-Scale Development F-16A (75-0747) following its emergency landing and nose gear collapse on Rogers Dry Lake, October 5, 1980. (NASA photograph via Tom Grindle)

The second fuselage assigned to the F-16XL program came

from the third F-16 Full-Scale Development aircraft (serial number 75-0747). It had a rather interesting background. Originally built as a single-seat F-16, it was powered by a General Electric F110-GE-100 turbofan engine that produced 29,000 pounds of sea level static thrust. This aircraft had primarily been used to test the F-16's avionics and environmental control system and for vibration and acoustics testing. On October 5, 1980, after accumulating 1,212.2 hours of flying

The fuselage from F-16A 75-0747 was allocated to General Dynamics by the Air Force for conversion into the single-seat F-16XL. It is seen on arrival at the Fort Worth plant on May 4, 1981. (Lockheed Martin)

time, it was severely damaged in an accident at Edwards AFB during an airshow associated with the Edwards Open House. The nose landing gear tire had blown on takeoff.[16] The pilot wisely chose to land on Runway 18, etched out on the hard dry lakebed on Rogers Dry Lake. As the pilot lowered the nose to the ground after landing, the forward landing gear snapped off and the fuselage dropped to the ground. The radome, the leading edge of the equipment bay, and the inlet were dragged across the lakebed. Major damage to the fuselage resulted, and the engine was ruined by sand ingestion. In August 1981, the damaged fuselage was delivered to the Fort Worth factory by an Air Force Lockheed C-5A transport. During the subsequent conversion process at GD, the damaged fuselage would be rebuilt using a newly manufactured two-seat

forward fuselage. The original Air Force serial number was retained after the fuselage was lengthened, converted from the original single-seat into a two-seat configuration, and then integrated with the cranked-arrow wing to become F-16XL-2.[17]

The modified fuselages of both the single-seat and the two-seat F-16XL aircraft incorporated a 30-inch forward extension added at fuselage station 189. This forward fuselage plug provided 11.6 cubic feet of additional internal

The fuselage from the single-seat F-16A 75-0747 was delivered to GD Fort Worth in August 1981, for conversion to the two-seat F-16XL-2. (Lockheed Martin)

fuselage volume, and it moved the cockpit forward. It did not, however, increase the length of the engine intake, only the upper fuselage. The forward fuselage extension housed specialized flight-test instrumentation on the two F-16XL flight demonstrators, while on production aircraft it was intended that this extension would house additional mission avionics. A second 26-inch "Z" plug fuselage extension was added at midfuselage. The upper part of the Z ran aft for 26 inches from FS 373.8, increasing internal fuel. The lower leg of the Z started at FS 343.12 (the landing gear bulkhead) and likewise ran aft, increasing the intake length.[18] Other changes to the F-16XL fuselage included removal of the F-16 leading-edge-flap drive used on the standard F-16 (this enabled additional fuel to be carried) and modifications to both the engine inlet diverter and the ram inlet for the environmental cooling system. These modifications were required to match the forward fuselage stretch. Recontoured forebody strakes matched the new wing shape and allowed its smooth aerodynamic integration into the stretched forward fuselage. Finally, the aft fuselage was canted upward by an angle of 3.16 degrees. The upward cant was necessary to prevent the lengthened aft fuselage from dragging on the runway during take-off and landing since GD had decided not to lengthen or relocate the landing gear despite the lengthened aft fuselage. This decision eased detail design and kept aircraft gross weight down but resulted in other problems, which will be discussed later. Other aft fuselage modifications were necessary to enable dummy AIM-120 AMRAAM missiles to be carried.[19]

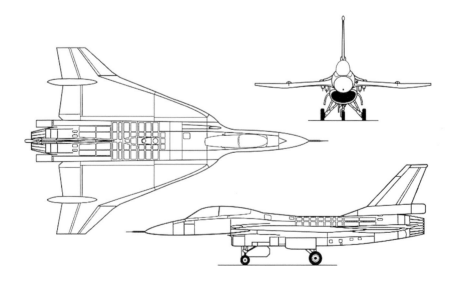

Three-view drawing of the two-seat F-16XL. (NASA)

As initially delivered, the two F-16XL prototypes retained the standard F-16A landing gear. This limited the aircraft to a maximum takeoff gross weight of 37,500 pounds. Later on in the flight-test program, both aircraft were modified to incorporate an increased capacity landing gear that was being developed for production F-16s. This modification required strengthening the main landing gear wheel-well bulkheads and adding new wheel well doors to accommodate the somewhat wider tires. With the strengthened landing gear, the F-16XL maximum takeoff gross weight was increased to 48,000 pounds, compared to the 37,500-pound limitation with the standard F-16A landing gear originally fitted.

Flight Control System

The F-16XL's primary flight control system was a four-channel, analog-computer-based fly-by-wire flight control system. It was similar to the FBW flight control system used in the standard F-16, but it was modified to function with the XL's unique flight control surfaces.[20] Changes were also made to the air data system that determined the various parameters needed by the flight control system, such as static and dynamic air pressures and angles of attack and yaw. The flight control computers were modified to incorporate new control laws necessitated by the radically different aerodynamic configuration. The air data sensor installation was modified from that used on the standard F-16. A third conical angle-of-attack transmitter was added on the left side of the forward fuselage with an L-shaped probe on the right side providing the third source of total and static air pressure needed by the four independent flight control computers.

The cockpits installed in both F-16XL prototypes were configured with the same flight controls, displays, avionics, and sensors used in early production F-16A and F-16B aircraft. However, a significant new feature was installed in the F-16XL; this was the microprocessor-based self-test function for the flight control system. Following engine start, a button push activated the self-test function that evaluated the functionality of the entire fly-by-wire flight control system. This resulted in the complete flight control system, from controller inputs to rate sensors to actual servoactuator operations, being automatically checked—a process that took about 90 seconds. During the self-testing process, the pilot could detect the chatter of the flight control surface movements over the nose of the idling engine as the system went through its preprogrammed series of very-high-frequency control surface actuations.[21]

On the F-16XL, aircraft pitch attitude was controlled by symmetric deflection of the two elevons mounted on the trailing edges of each inner wing segment. Elevon area was about 44 square feet. The elevons were capable of deflection over the angular range between 30 degrees up and 30 degrees down. Additional pitch control was provided by symmetrically deflecting the outboard ailerons. The ailerons had a total surface area of 29.45 square feet. Each aileron was capable of movement through an arc that ranged from 20 degrees up to 30 degrees down. Roll was controlled by asymmetric deflection of the ailerons assisted by elevon deflection. The roll axis of the flight control system was based on roll rate command and used roll rate feedback. The maximum available roll rate was 308 degrees per second. The actual allowable roll rate was scheduled as a function of aircraft angle of attack to prevent overstressing the aircraft or encountering potential out of control situations. The rudder provided yaw control. It was interconnected to the ailerons via the FBW flight control system. This ensured smooth aileron-rudder coordination during rolling maneuvers, especially at higher angles of attack. The yaw axis of the flight control system used rudder position commands based on yaw rate and lateral acceleration feedback along with inputs from the aileron-rudder interconnect.[22]

Secondary flight control surfaces included the leading-edge flaps, installed on the outer wing panels, and standard F-16 speed brakes (though recontoured on their outer mold-line for use on the XL) were mounted one on each side of the aft fuselage adjacent to the engine exhaust nozzle. Total surface area of the leading-edge flaps was about 18.2 square feet. The LEFs were capable of being deflected through an arc ranging from 6.4 degrees up to 36.5 degrees down. The leading-edge flaps were automatically scheduled by the flight control system to optimize maneuvering performance and assist the elevons in providing adequate pitch control at higher speeds and dynamic pressures. The leading-edge flaps were automatically deflected upward at higher Mach numbers to minimize aerodynamic drag. In addition, asymmetric leading-edge-flap deflection was used to assist the rudder and ailerons in ensuring lateral-directional stability at higher angles of attack. Aircraft spin recovery was automatically assisted by the FBW flight control system, which differentially deflected the leading-edge flaps when the angle of attack was greater than 35 degrees. The differential deflection capability of the LEFs ranged up to an angle of 40 degrees. Two clamshell-type speed

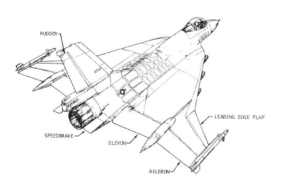

A combination of flight control surfaces provided pitch, roll, and yaw control across the entire F-16XL flight envelope. (NASA)

brakes were located on each side of the engine nozzle. They functioned simultaneously when actuated by the pilot and opened symmetrically, with each segment deflecting 60 degrees.[23]

During flight operations, the pilot commanded normal load factor (aircraft g-level) throughout most of the flight envelope using the standard F-16 sidestick controller. The pitch axis of the FCS was essentially a g-command system that utilized g-level, AoA, and pitch rate as feedback. During the powered landing approach configuration, with landing gear and flaps down, and at angles of attack above 19 degrees in the cruise configuration, the FBW flight control system automatically provided blended g-level (load factor) and AoA commands to ensure speed stability. An AoA limiter was incorporated in the F-16XL flight control system to minimize opportunities for out-of-control situations during maneuvering flight. This limiter was similar to that used in the standard F-16A, but the allowable AoA envelope was expanded to 29 degrees at low speeds (up from the

The F-16XL used the force-displacement sidestick controller adopted from the standard F-16. (NASA)

25-degree limit in the basic F-16). At speeds above Mach 0.9, the allowable AoA was restricted to a maximum of 26 degrees. The allowable angle of attack when the landing gear was extended was automatically limited to 16 degrees.

In the event of a departure from controlled flight, the leading-edge flaps were automatically used to augment the rudder in limiting high yaw rates from developing at angles of attack between 35 and 50 degrees. If a stabilized deep stall condition was encountered, the flight control system featured a manual pitch override (MPO) capability. MPO allowed the pilot to bypass the AoA limiter, providing him or her with full pitch command authority to initiate a pitch-rocking maneuver and break the deep stall. Pitch-rocking was successfully used on the F-16 to break deep stalls, and it also was fitted with an MPO capability.[24] NASA Langley had played a significant role in the development of the F-16 deep stall recovery system. The flight control systems installed in the two F-16XL prototypes were fitted with an automatic pitch override system intended to break any deep stall that might be encountered. This automated system provided pitch-rocking commands to the flight control system in the event of a stabilized deep stall.[25] F-16XL flight control system functionality and effectiveness were evaluated during extensive wind tunnel, spin tunnel, and drop model test efforts at NASA Langley.

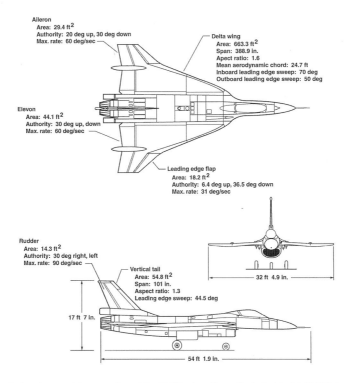

Aileron
Area: 29.4 ft^2
Authority: 20 deg up, 30 deg down
Max. rate: 60 deg/sec

Delta wing
Area: 663.3 ft^2
Span: 388.9 in.
Apect ratio: 1.6
Mean aerodynamic chord: 24.7 ft
Inboard leading edge sweep: 70 deg
Outboard leading edge sweep: 50 deg

Elevon
Area: 44.1 ft^2
Authority: 30 deg up, down
Max. rate: 60 deg/sec

Leading edge flap
Area: 18.2 ft^2
Authority: 6.4 deg up, 36.5 deg down
Max. rate: 31 deg/sec

Rudder
Area: 14.3 ft^2
Authority: 30 deg right, left
Max. rate: 90 deg/sec

Vertical tail
Area: 54.8 ft^2
Span: 101 in.
Aspect ratio: 1.3
Leading edge sweep: 44.5 deg

32 ft 4.9 in.

17 ft 7 in.

54 ft 1.9 in.

The physical and geometric properties of the F-6XL aircraft are illustrated in this NASA drawing. The effects of conical camber and twist on the wing are evident in the front view of the aircraft. (NASA)

Avionics

Both F-16XL flight demonstrator aircraft were equipped with standard F-16A avionics suites. If the F-16XL had been selected for full-scale development as the USAF dual-role fighter, GD planned on incorporating the avionics suite developed under the F-16C/D Multi-Stage Improvement Program (MSIP) into production aircraft. These aircraft would have been equipped with an improved APG-66 fire control radar; the AN/ALR-74 threat warning system; the LANTIRN auto navigation, terrain avoidance, and targeting system; an airborne self-protection jammer; the ALE-40 chaff/flare dispensing system; both an inertial navigation system (INS) and a global positioning system (GPS); and MIL-STD-1760 data interface capability with advanced weapons, including the AIM-120 AMRAAM air-to-air guided missile. In addition, an Identification, Friend or Foe (IFF) subsystem with air-to-air IFF capability would have been provided as would provision for HAVE QUICK secure ultra-high frequency (UHF) communications capability. When fully implemented, the MSIP would have provided night, under-the-weather, navigation, and air-to-ground weapon delivery and beyond-visual-range (BVR) air-to-air missile engagement capabilities. The front cockpit would have retained the features and capabilities of the F-16C. The LANTIRN wide-angle, improved-video Head-Up Display (HUD) incorporated a forward-looking infrared (FLIR) navigation video display at night. Two 4-inch high-resolution multifunction displays (MFDs) would have been available for both sensor and weapon-video and interactive control of the weapon system. An optional 5-inch color MFD was available for integration into the center console. This display was to provide moving presentations with overlaid navigation information, color-coded electronic flight instruments, and other color-coded aircraft pilot-selectable information. Integrated upfront Communications, Navigation, and Identification (CNI) controls were to be provided along with a dedicated threat warning system. The rear cockpit in the dual-role fighter version of the F-16XL was to have the controls and displays, including a color-moving map, to accomplish a full range of day/night/all-weather missions.[26]

Engine and Inlet

The single-seat F-16XL was fitted with a Pratt & Whitney F100-PW-200 afterburning turbofan engine, the same engine used in the basic F-16A. This engine had a SLST of 14,370 pounds at 100 percent revolutions per minute (rpm) in dry (nonafterburner) power and 23,770 pounds in full afterburner. The Pratt & Whitney F100-PW-200 engine was installed in F-16XL-1 for the entire duration of the flight-test program. The two-seat F-16XL was initially fitted with a General Electric F101 Derivative Fighter Engine (DFE) that produced nearly 29,000 pounds of static thrust at sea level in full afterburner. Later in the Air Force test program (in mid-1984), F-16XL-2 was returned to Fort Worth for installation of a General Electric F110-GE-100 "Slimline" engine. The particular engine installed in F-16XL-2 was a prototype version of the production F110 engine configured with hardware designed for the production engine's performance envelope. As installed in the F-16XL, this prototype engine was essentially equivalent to the production F110-GE-100 engine. It produced 28,000 pounds of afterburning thrust at full rpm at SLST conditions. At military thrust conditions (100-percent throttle setting without afterburner), the F110-GE-100 engine provided 17,530 pounds of thrust at SLST conditions.

The General Electric F110-GE-100 engine, developed under the Air Force Alternate Fighter Engine (AFE) program, had a diameter of 46.5 inches (this was the same diameter as that of the less powerful Pratt & Whitney F100 engine). The F110 engine used the same engine core as the earlier GE F101 engine developed for the B-1 bomber.[27] The F110-GE-100 produced something over 4,000 pounds more thrust in afterburning power at sea level than the F100-PW-200 engine. Thus, for optimum performance, the F110 engine required a larger inlet capture area for increased airflow.[28] This resulted in a revised inlet design and development effort that led to what GD referred to as the Large Normal Shock Inlet. The LNSI had slightly different geometric proportions than the standard F-16 inlet. Its larger capture area of 778 square inches compared to the 714-square-inch capture area of the inlet that was used with the Pratt & Whitney F100 engine. The larger capture area successfully accommodated the greater airflow needs of the more powerful General Electric F110 engine. This inlet subsequently went into production on C-

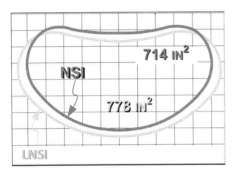

The Large Normal Shock Inlet compared to the smaller normal shock inlet. (Lockheed Martin)

and D-model F-16s equipped with the GE engine. The larger inlet was installed in F-16XL-2 at the GD factory in Fort Worth in conjunction with other structural modifications and maintenance actions. The LNSI installation was completed by late June 1985, in time for the aircraft to participate in the final phase of the Air Force flight-test evaluation at Edwards AFB.[29]

Fuel and Hydraulic Systems

The F-16XL fuel tank system consisted of six fuselage fuel compartments and four wing compartments. The single-seat F-16XL carried 11,273 pounds of fuel internally, while the two-seat aircraft had a slightly lower capacity (10,258 pounds). Internal fuel fraction, an important measure of mission capability in a fighter aircraft, was 0.32 as compared to 0.28 for the basic F-16A.[30] In this context, fuel fraction is the ratio of internal fuel to takeoff gross weight with both aircraft in the same basic mission configuration. For this comparison, both aircraft carried six MK-82 bombs and two AIM-9L missiles without any external fuel tanks. Electrical and hydraulic boost pumps were used to support fuel transfer with a hydraulically driven fuel flow proportioner and an electrical fuel trimmer system automatically controlling aircraft center-of-gravity location and proper tank feeding sequence. As with the standard F-16, hydraulic power was provided by separate 3,000-psi primary and secondary systems that supplied the flight control surfaces and the landing gear and brakes. However, on the F-16XL, increased-capacity hydraulic pumps and greater hydraulic fluid reservoir and accumulator volumes were provided to supply the increased hydraulic power needs of the flight control surfaces on the larger and heavier aircraft. To prevent excessive hydraulic flow demand when the landing gear was lowered, the electronic flight control system automatically commanded the elevons to the 5-degree trailing-edge-down position.[31]

Weapons Carriage and Stores Management System

The F-16XL's cranked-arrow wing, with its very long chord, allowed weapons to be carried in a semiconformal manner. A low-profile, tandem, staggered arrangement of the weapons under the lower wing surfaces improved the fore and aft weight distribution relative to the aircraft center of gravity, reducing trim effects during multiple weapon releases. Semiconformal carriage also provided significant drag reduction, resulting in increased speed capability when compared to the standard F-16 with an equivalent external payload. Twelve Mk-82s individually carried in LODE-14 vertical ejector bomb racks had the same drag as six Mk-82s mounted on the two triple ejector racks (TERs) carried on the F-16A. When equal numbers of bombs were carried on both the F-16XL and the F-16A, carriage drag was 60 percent lower at Mach 0.9 and total drag was reduced by 36 percent. A significant contribution to this overall drag reduction was the fact that external wing tanks were not routinely required on the F-16XL due to its larger internal fuel volume.

Similarly, four AIM-120 AMRAAM missiles carried in semisubmerged fashion on ejector-launchers under the F-16XL fuselage produced a carriage drag reduction of 70 percent when compared to the drag produced by the same number of AMRAAMs mounted on conventional underwing pylons. Conformal weapons carriage also saved weight. The two multiple ejector racks (MERs) and the associated pylons needed to carry 12 Mk-82 bombs on the F-16A weighed 1,039 pounds compared to 516 pounds for the LODE-14 ejector racks used for semiconformal, low-profile carriage of the same number of bombs on the F-16XL.[32]

Other conformal carriage advantages included reduced aerodynamic interference during near-simultaneous weapons releases, since the individual conformal stores stations were horizontally separated, and improved individual weapon delivery accuracy. The latter resulted from both the reduction in aerodynamic interference between individual bombs during multiple releases and the fact that all bombs were ejected vertically rather than with the lateral forces that were imparted on ejection from TER ejectors. Additionally, the structural loads on the wing hard points were reduced with the elimination of MER and TER carriage of heavy clusters of bombs. The better distribution of weapons allowed higher aircraft roll rates and maneuvering limits than were possible with conventional

MER or TER carriage of ordnance. With heavy external weapons loads, the F-16XL was authorized for maneuvering up to 7.33 g's compared with 5.58 g's in the F-16A. When external fuel tanks were carried, maneuvering was limited to less than 5.86 g's. The F-16XL maneuvering envelope was cleared to the full 9-g capability with a full load of air-to-air missiles and a full internal fuel load (aircraft gross weight of 36,000 pounds).[33]

A large number of strengthened hard points at various locations enabled bombs, missiles, external fuel tanks and sensor pods to be carried. There were 5 2,000-pound underwing hard points, 16 1,000-pound hard points, 2 LANTIRN stations for the separate navigation and targeting pods associated with that system, 4 AMRAAM stations, and wingtip missile launcher mountings for 2 AIM-9L Sidewinder missiles. Additionally, there was a tandem pylon system for carrying two Mk-84s, which could be attached to stations 5A, 5C, and

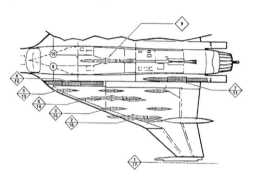

A complex hard-point arrangement was developed for the F-16XL to enable external stores to be mounted in dense conformal arrangements. (Lockheed Martin)

5F (and the corresponding 13A, 13C, and 13F). "These were XL-unique," Thomas Grindle recalled, "and once mounted became a single unit and placed both weapons close to the wing, much like the LODE-14 pylons, and in tandem to reduce drag."[34]

The integrated electronic stores management system in the F-16XL was modified from that used in the F-16 to accommodate the added store locations. Release and jettison capability was provided at 10 underwing store stations on each wing. In addition, provisions were incorporated for carriage and fuel transfer from up to four 370-gallon wing-mounted fuel tanks as well as a 300-gallon centerline drop tank. For long-range ferry purposes, two 600-gallon fuel tanks could be mounted on special heavyweight pylons under the wings. However, each of the inboard "heavy/wet" fuel tank pylons was mounted at essentially the same butt-line distance (as measured from the centerline of the fuselage) as two of the underwing weapons pylons. These weapons pylons had to be removed in order to mount the inboard heavy/wet fuel tank pylon under each wing. This meant that if the special pylons for the two 600-gallon fuel tanks were carried, four air-to-ground munitions could not be loaded onto the aircraft. Furthermore, if this heavy/wet wing station was used for external fuel, the fuel tank physically blocked an additional wing station, preventing the loading of a store on that station. Practically, this meant that if external fuel tanks were mounted on the inboard heavyweight pylon, the maximum number of air-to-ground weapons that could be carried under each wing was five instead of the normal eight. If underwing fuel tanks were not used, the F-16XL could carry up to 16 500-pound class weapons under the wings. Two more 500-pound weapons could be carried on a special fuselage centerline adaptor. Alternatively, the 300-gallon fuel tank could be mounted under the fuselage centerline in place of the centerline weapons adaptor.[35]

Two sensor stations located under the engine inlet were used to carry the pods associated with the LANTIRN system. These were mounted on ordnance stations 8 and 10. The two LANTIRN stations were not enabled until the LNSI was later installed on the F-16XL as the attachment points and wiring for the LANTIRN system was not originally on the two FSD F-16 fuselages used to create the prototypes. Interface and control provisions were incorporated for AGM-65 Maverick air-to-ground missiles and AIM-9 Sidewinder infrared guided air-to-air missiles. Electrical and fire control provisions as well as the recessed missile launchers for the four AIM-120 AMRAAM missiles, intended to be carried on a production version of the F-16XL, were not installed in the prototypes as this weapon had yet to be integrated into the basic F-16 aircraft. The F-16XL would have also been capable of carrying and delivering B61 nuclear weapons. Up to five of these weapons potentially could be carried. In reality, for various practical reasons associated with the control of nuclear weapons, the actual operational load would likely have been one or two B61s. For peacetime training missions, the 715-pound BDU-38 practice bomb, available in either free-fall or parachute-retarded versions, was used to simulate the employment options available with the B61 nuclear weapon. These consisted of either a surface burst or an air burst option. The BDU-38 had the same weight, physical, and aerodynamic characteristics as the actual B61 bomb. The 20-millimeter (mm), hydraulically driven, electrically fired, six-barreled M61A1 rotary cannon, mounted in the left side of the F-16 fuselage, was retained in the same location on the F-16XL along with the large drum magazine that had a capacity of 510 rounds of ammunition.[36]

Flight-Test Instrumentation

Both F-16XL aircraft had relatively large volumes of internal space available below and behind the cockpit to house flight-test instrumentation-related equipment, with F-16XL-1 having approximately 9.5 cubic feet while F-16XL-2 had roughly 10 cubic feet that could be used. The Air Force–developed Airborne Test Instrumentation System (ATIS) was installed in both test aircraft. ATIS had been developed by the Air Force Flight Test Center and was provided to GD for use during the F-16XL evaluation. Other instrumentation was designed and incorporated into each aircraft based on the specific data-collection tasks assigned to that aircraft. The ATIS was combined with General Dynamics–developed hardware and provided telemetry and recording capability for both frequency modulation (FM) and pulse code modulation (PCM) data. The PCM portion of the ATIS system had the capability of recording parameters where frequency characteristics ranged from static to about 200 Hertz (Hz). It was the main source of data measurement used during F-16XL flight testing. The FM subsystem could measure up to 20 high-response parameters. It was used for measurements of phenomena such as vibrations or for obtaining acoustic data at frequencies in excess of 200 Hz, where PCM capabilities were inadequate. Each aircraft was equipped with a 14-track magnetic tape recorder with up to 90 minutes of recording time. The recording system capacity was 200 PCM and 20 FM multiplexed data items. Data telemetry capabilities were provided by a system developed by GD that included transmitters and power supply. It was able to transmit all PCM and up to 15 FM multiplexed channels. For the operational evaluation phase, a video recorder was also available to record Head-Up Display and radar/electro-optical scope images. The instrumentation system could record a relatively large number of flight-test parameters. These are listed by flight-test objective and individual aircraft in Table 3.[37]

Test instrumentation parameters were tailored to the data requirements and individual test objectives assigned to each aircraft. F-16XL-2 was primarily

Table 3.
F-16XL test instrumentation capability by test aircraft (number of parameters)

Flight Test Area	F-16XL-1	F-16XL-2
Stability and Control	42	23
Flutter	28	—
Structural Loads	—	27
Performance	38	38
Propulsion	12	20
Weapons Separation	—	12
Operational Utility Evaluation	Video Recorder	Video Recorder

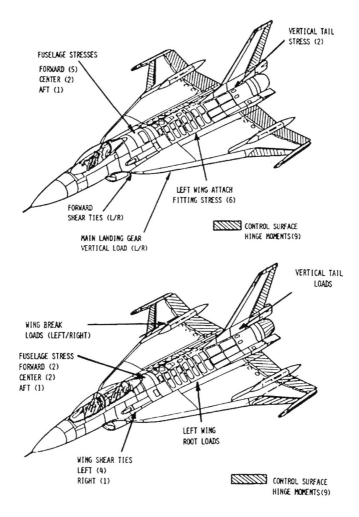

Sensors for determining structural loads on the airframe were positioned at different locations on F-16XL-1 and F-16XL-2 as shown in these GD drawings. (Lockheed Martin)

assigned duties involving structural loads and propulsion testing while F-16XL-1 focused on stability and control (including at high AoA), flutter testing, and flight control system evaluations. Both aircraft were to participate in aircraft performance and stores separation testing as well as the Operational Utility Evaluation (OUE) that would be conducted by the Air Force Operational Test and Evaluation Center (AFOTEC). In addition, F-16XL-2 carried six high-speed film cameras. Mounted externally under the wings, the cameras were focused on the external weapons and stores. Separation characteristics following weapons release from the aircraft would be filmed for subsequent postflight analysis. Sensors to record different structural loads were mounted at various locations on each airframe. Each aircraft was used to record structural loads in various parts of the airframe; for instance, F-16XL-1 recorded main landing gear vertical loads while XL-2 determined the loads at the left and right wing break locations. Later in the flight-test program, individual aircraft instrumentation would be revised relative to the first phases of the flight-test effort to account for specific test objectives that were assigned to each aircraft.[38]

Endnotes

1. Author not identified, "SCAMP Cuts Drag, Increases Fuel Load," *Aviation Week & Space Technology* (August 18, 1980): p. 96.
2. The dual-dome Differential Maneuvering Simulator provided a means of simulating two fighter aircraft or spacecraft maneuvering with respect to each other. Each 40-foot-diameter dome contained a generic cockpit with glass instrumentation, programmable control inceptors, a 360-degree field-of-view visual system, a target image generator system, and a high-resolution area-of-interest visual system.
3. The chord on most wing planforms varies at different positions along the span, growing narrower toward the wingtips. For this reason, a characteristic reference figure that can be compared among various wing shapes is used. This is known as the mean aerodynamic chord, or mac (sometimes the notation MAC is also used). With the F-16XL, the overall cranked-arrow wing planform is composed of two different planforms on the inner and outer segments of the wing, thus its MAC is a composite of both segments. NASA Glenn Research Center, "Beginner's Guide to Aerodynamics," *http://www.grc.nasa.gov/WWW/k-12/airplane/bga.html*, accessed May 17, 2012.
4. The angle of incidence is the angle formed by the wing chord line and the aircraft longitudinal axis. The wing chord line extends from the leading edge of the wing to the trailing edge of the wing. The longitudinal axis is an imaginary line that extends from the nose of the aircraft to the tail. NASA Glenn Research Center, "Beginner's Guide to Aerodynamics," *http://www.grc.nasa.gov/WWW/k-12/airplane/bga.html*, accessed May 19, 2012.
5. General Dynamics Corporation, "Preliminary Design Drawing: Internal Arrangement, Dual Role Fighter Aircraft," General Dynamics Corporation, Fort Worth Division, F-16 DRF Proposal, April 22, 1983.
6. David C. Aronstein, "NASA and Computational Structural Analysis," Case 8 in Hallion, *NASA's Contributions to Aeronautics*, vol. 1.
7. Robert Wetherall, correspondence dated December 20, 2012.
8. Fuselage stations are numbered according to their position relative to the length of the fuselage, measured from the nose. Thus, FS 463.1 was located 463.1 inches along the fuselage as measured from a reference point located forward of the nose of the aircraft. The aircraft station coordinate system is based on an XYZ coordinate system originally developed for nautical engineering purposes and commonly used in ship and boat design. The X-axis of this system (usually referred to as the fuselage station, or FS) is positive pointing aft from a reference

point located forward of the nose of the aircraft. The Y-axis (the so-called butt-line distance) is measured from the centerline of the fuselage (zero butt line) with the positive direction measured outboard on the right wing. The Z-axis is positive pointing upward from a reference line located approximately along the centerline of the fuselage when seen from the side. Distances measured from the waterline (WL) are known as WL distance.

9. Jane's editorial staff, *Jane's All The World's Aircraft*, F-16XL entries in various annual volumes (London: Jane's Information Group, Inc., 1981–82, 1982–83, 1983–84, 1985–86, 1995–96).
10. Hillaker, presentation to the Lone Star Aero Club.
11. GD, "F-16XL Flight Test Program—Final Report."
12. Ibid.
13. Ibid.; Talty, "F-16XL Demonstrates New Capabilities."
14. Conceived during WWII and completed in 1947, McKinley Climatic Laboratory provides facilities for all-weather testing of aircraft, weapons, and support equipment. The laboratory can accommodate the largest bombers and transports. Nearly every weather condition can be created, with temperatures ranging from –70 to +180 degrees Fahrenheit. Every aircraft in the current DoD inventory has been tested inside the McKinley Climatic Laboratory.
15. GD, "Flight Test Program—Final Report."
16. Hillaker, "F-16XL Flight Test Program Overview."
17. GD, "F-16XL Flight Test Program—Final Report."
18. Thomas J. Grindle, NASA DFRC, correspondence with author, January 1, 2013.
19. Dummy AMRAAM missiles were carried on the four AMRAAM missile stations during the F-16XL flight-test program. The two in the front bays were ballasted, but the aft ones were made of wood and fitted with metallic nosecones and fins.
20. Aronstein and Piccirillo, *The Lightweight Fighter Program*.
21. Robert R. Ropelewski, "F-16XL Shows Advances in Range, Ride and Flying Qualities," *Aviation Week & Space Technology* (September 26, 1983): pp. 62–71; GD, "F-16XL Flight Test Program—Final Report."
22. Talty, "F-16XL Demonstrates New Capabilities."
23. James O. Young, *History of the Air Force Flight Test Center, 1 January 1982–31 December 1982*, Vol. I (Edwards AFB, CA: Air Force Flight Test Center, 1983).
24. Aronstein and Piccirillo, *Lightweight Fighter*; Chambers, *Partners in Freedom*. Interestingly, the Swedish Saab J 35, with its cranked-arrow wing planform, was also susceptible to a serious deep stall condition,

and its pilots were specially trained in both stall avoidance and recovery techniques; see Walter J. Boyne, "Airpower Classics: J35 Draken," *Air Force Magazine* 94, no. 12 (December 2011).

25. Talty, "F-16XL Demonstrates New Capabilities"; Sheryl Scott Tierney, "Inflight Excitation of the F-16XL," presented at the Third AHS, CASI, DGLR, IES, ISA, ITEA, SETP, and SFTE Flight Testing Conference, Las Vegas, NV, April 2–4, 1986, AIAA Paper 86-9782 (1986).

26. F. Clifton Berry, Jr., "The Revolutionary Evolution of the F-16XL," *Air Force Magazine* 66, no. 11 (November 1983); Low Altitude Navigation and Targeting Infrared for Night, or LANTIRN, is a combined system that uses two externally mounted pods carried under the F-16's engine inlet. One pod is used for navigational purposes while the other is employed for targeting air-to-ground weapons. LANTIRN significantly increased combat effectiveness, allowing flight at low altitudes, at night, and under-the-weather, and it enabled ground targets to be attacked with a variety of precision-guided weapons; GD, "General Dynamics F-16XLC/D MULTIROLE FIGHTER," General Dynamics Corporation, Fort Worth Division (undated, circa 1983).

27. Jane's editorial staff, *Jane's Aero Engines*, Issue 30 (Alexandria, VA: Jane's Information Group, Inc., 2011).

28. Later, during the NASA supersonic laminar flow control flight-test program, a GE F110-GE-129 engine capable of producing 29,500 pounds SLST in full afterburner was installed in F-16XL-2. The fully developed F110 engine eventually produced over 32,000 pounds SLST in the F110-GE-132 version.

29. GD, "F-16XL Flight Test Program—Final Report"; Talty, "F-16XL Demonstrates New Capabilities."

30. Ibid.

31. GD, "F-16XL Final Flight Test Report."

32. Ibid. The Low Aerodynamic Drag Ejector (LODE-14) bomb rack was fitted with shackles spaced 14 inches apart, enabling standard U.S. Mark 80- series general purpose bombs to be carried.

33. Talty, "F-16XL Demonstrates New Capabilities"; GD, "F-16XL Flight Test Program—Final Report."

34. Grindle correspondence.

35. Ibid.

36. Ibid.

37. Hillaker, "F-16XL Flight Test Program Overview"; GD, "F-16XL Flight Test Program—Final Report."

38. Hillaker, "F-16XL Flight Test Program Overview."

F-16XL-1 photographed at the rollout ceremony at the GD Fort Worth factory on July 2, 1982. (Lockheed Martin)

CHAPTER 5

First Flight and Initial Testing

Preparations for First Flight

In April 1982, F-16XL-1 was removed from its assembly fixture and towed to an area of the Fort Worth factory where static testing was accomplished. Internal subsystems and equipment, to include flight-test instrumentation, were installed. Intensive systems testing and final preparations for flight testing now began. The flight control system was thoroughly checked out, the fuel system was checked and calibrated, and a program consisting of comprehensive structure coupling, aeroservoelastic, and ground vibration tests was accomplished. Finally, engine, electronics, avionics systems, and test instruments were determined to be in proper order. A series of safety of flight and flight readiness reviews—attended by the Air Force, GD, its subcontractors, and NASA representatives—culminated with the aircraft being declared ready for flight in late June. The next step before the first flight was the formal rollout ceremony, scheduled for 11 a.m. on July 2, 1982.

On left: The first F-16XL, 75-0749, is seen in April 1982 after its removal from its assembly fixture. The composite wing skins and wing-fuselage mounting bolt locations are evident. On right: The F-16XL-1 is seen being prepared for static structural proof testing in the spring of 1982. (Both images Lockheed Martin)

Rollout Ceremony

The eagerly awaited F-16XL rollout ceremony began exactly on time, at 11 a.m. on July 2, 1982, at General Dynamics' Fort Worth facility.[1] The large function was well attended by political dignitaries, senior corporate and Government officials, and high-ranking military officers. Chairman of the Board and Chief Executive Officer David S. Lewis and GD President Oliver C. Boileau cohosted the event. Congressional attendees included such defense and aerospace stalwarts as Senators Barry Goldwater of Arizona, John G. Tower of Texas, and Howard W. Cannon of New Mexico, along with Representatives Jim Wright and Martin Frost, both of Texas.[2]

For the Air Force, Chief of Staff Gen. Charles Gabriel, along with senior officers and representatives from key Air Force agencies and organizations involved in various aspects of research, development, acquisition, and management, were present. These included Dr. Alton G. Keel, assistant secretary of the Air Force for Research, Development, and Acquisition; Lt. Gen. Lawrence A. Skantze, commander of the Aeronautical Systems Division; Lt. Gen. Kelly Burke, deputy chief of staff for Research, Development, and Acquisition; Lt. Gen. Thomas H. McMullen, vice commander of the Tactical Air Command; and Brig. Gen. George L. Monahan, of the F-16 Systems Program Office. In recognition of NASA's significant contributions to the F-16XL, NASA Administrator James M. Beggs represented NASA scientists and engineers who rendered invaluable assistance in development and refinement of the cranked-arrow wing and other important F-16XL design and flight safety features over a period of several years.[3]

During the ceremony, GD Chairman Lewis commented that the F-16XL "combines the best technology of the 1980s with a proven design that enabled us to make only a minimum number of changes."[4] Herbert F. Rogers, vice president and general manager of the General Dynamics Fort Worth Division, added, "while the F-16XL looks drastically different, it really is not. The major differences are that the wings and tails have been removed and replaced by the cranked arrow wing, and two fuselage plugs totaling 56 inches have been added." Rogers went on to note that General Dynamics was urging the Air Force to consider procurement of an F-16 variant based on the F-16XL design. "The F-16XL represents a truly dramatic increase in fighter capability, and because it shares a substantial commonality with the F-16, it could easily be phased into production with the F-16."[5]

In his comments, Skantze observed, "The F-16 is rapidly becoming the backbone of Tactical Air Command. It is being produced in a superb fashion, on schedule and at cost. It has well acquitted itself as a combat aircraft," the latter a passing reference to its success in Israeli hands during combat against the Syrian air force that was unfolding even then over Lebanon's Bekaa Valley.

He called the rollout "a very exciting event. It is a great tribute to the management of General Dynamics and a far greater tribute to the work force and designer team of this great aircraft."[6]

In his prepared remarks, Tower also noted the success of the F-16 program, and he added, "I am proud of what General Dynamics has done, and it has been consistent with the Department of Defense's goal of improving existing systems, rather than developing new systems."[7] Tower's remarks may also have been a pointed commentary on the fact that the Air Force had committed to embark on a totally new air superiority fighter to be developed under the Advanced Tactical Fighter program. Featuring true supercruise performance (that is, the ability to cruise at supersonic speeds without using afterburner),

A Lockheed Martin F-22A Raptor of the USAF Air Combat Command's 27th Tactical Fighter Squadron, 1st Fighter Wing, over Okinawa. (USAF)

sensor fusion, thrust-vectoring, and advanced extremely high stealth capabilities, the ATF evolved to create the superlative Lockheed Martin F-22A Raptor, the world's most advanced air dominance fighter.

Just prior to the highlight of the ceremony—the debut of the F-16XL— two armed F-16s taxied out in front of the assembled audience. One was loaded for an air-to-air mission with four AIM-9 Sidewinder missiles and a 300-gallon centerline fuel tank. The other was in an air-to-ground mission configuration with six 500-pound Mk-82 bombs, two 370-gallon underwing drop tanks, an electronic countermeasures pod, and two AIM-9 missiles mounted on the wingtips. The F-16XL then taxied out and parked between the two F-16s. To graphically demonstrate its multimission capabilities, GD had configured the F-16XL to fly either an air-to-air or an air-to-ground mission on the same sortie without having to carry external fuel tanks. To emphasize its dual-role mission capabilities, the aircraft was loaded with AIM-9L missiles on wingtip launchers with four dummy AIM-120 AMRAAM missiles conformally carried at the location where actual missiles would have been attached in semisubmerged mountings. Additionally, 16 Mk-82 general-purpose bombs were mounted on individual low-drag bomb racks under the wings. Fort Worth General Manager Herb Rogers concluded the rollout ceremony by telling the audience that the first flight of the F-16XL was imminent, noting, "Just nineteen months ago, this was a paper airplane. Now it is a reality."[8]

On left: F-16XL-1 photographed at the rollout ceremony at the GD Fort Worth factory on July 2, 1982. On right: Aft view of F-16XL-1 as photographed at the Fort Worth rollout ceremony on July 2, 1982. (Both images Lockheed Martin)

Harry Hillaker (front row, standing hands on hips) and members of the F-16XL design and flight-test team with the first F-16XL, at General Dynamics' Fort Worth plant. (Lockheed Martin photograph via Robert Wetherall)

First Flight: July 3, 1982

Less than 24 hours after conclusion of the rollout ceremony, F-16XL-1 (75-0749), piloted by General Dynamics F-16XL Project Pilot James A. "Spider" McKinney, started up and taxied to the Carswell AFB main runway, adjacent to the GD factory.[9] For the first flight, only full internal fuselage fuel (6,700 pounds) was carried. Two AIM-9L missiles were mounted on the wingtips (store stations 1 and 17) and four dummy AIM-120 AMRAAM missiles were carried on stations 6, 7, 11, and 12. At 10:47 a.m. local time on a sunny Texas day, after successfully completing functional checks of the aircraft subsystems and the special test instrumentation system, McKinney executed a maximum power afterburner takeoff. During the 65-minute first flight, the aircraft reached a maximum Mach

The first flight of the F-16XL-1. This flight photograph was subsequently autographed by GD test pilot James McKinney. (Lockheed Martin)

number of 0.9 at 30,000 feet, a maximum load factor of 3 g's, and an angle of attack of 20 degrees. McKinney was reported as saying that the aircraft had a solid ride and performed as predicted, but its flight characteristics were very different from those of the standard F-16.[10]

During the postflight debriefing and subsequent exuberant celebration festivities, an enthusiastic McKinney said that the F-16XL met or exceeded all expectations on the first flight with excellent aircraft handling qualities and systems operations. He reported that the aircraft had a solid feel and was comfortable to fly after only a few minutes. Shortly after the 65-minute first flight, Jim McKinney forwarded the following memo to the F-16XL development team (somewhat, but understandably, understating any issues that had been encountered).

> We had an outstanding first flight of the F-16XL on Saturday, 3 July 1982. The aircraft flew like a dream and met or exceeded our goals for the first flight. The systems on the aircraft performed flawlessly and the handling qualities were superb. The F-16XL reflects a tremendous effort by everyone and especially during the past few weeks as everything started coming together. I wanted to congratulate and thank you for your efforts during this program. The aircraft you have developed and built is a new generation of fighter aircraft and is at the forefront of aviation today. I am honored to be associated with you and am confident we can succeed in the challenges ahead.[11]

General Dynamics Vice President and F-16XL Program Director D. Randal "Randy" Kent quickly issued an attractive first flight certificate to all members of the F-16XL development and flight-test team. It complemented the entire development team with these inspiring words:

> These are dates I'm sure we will all long remember. They represent the culmination of an extraordinary achievement by all of you who participated in the birth of this beautiful aircraft.
>
> When we started the project in November 1980, we knew that to fly 19 months later represented a most ambitious and difficult undertaking. But, because of your dedication and personal sacrifices and those of your family, the challenge was met—indeed, we beat the schedule! I am sure you shared with me the thrill and sense of pride when F-16XL-1 took to the air on Saturday morning, 3 July.
>
> As a result of your skill and efforts, we can now offer our country an important new defense weapon—the F-16XL Fighting Falcon.[12]

First Flight Pilot Report

Jim McKinney's first flight pilot report, quoted verbatim below, provides excellent insight into the initial flight of what would eventually become a significant second career for the F-16XL as a NASA supersonic research test bed.

Objectives:

> This was the first flight of the F-16XL. The flight was devoted to functional verification of the aerodynamic design, the checkout of existing/modified/new F-16 systems, and checkout of aircraft instrumentation.

Ground Operations:

> All ground operations are straightforward and easily accomplished with minimal pilot workload. Pilot involvement in FLCS [flight control system] is minimal and requires only turning on and then off the test to accomplish a thorough checkout.
>
> Aircraft handling during ground operations was smooth and easy to control. During the taxi test, improper nose strut servicing resulted in excessive nose bounce when taxiing over seams in the concrete

ramp. Proper servicing between the taxi test and first flight significantly reduced this tendency.

Takeoff:

Aircraft acceleration during the max A/B [afterburner] takeoff was brisk. Aircraft rotation was initiated at approximately 150 KCAS (predicted takeoff 165 KCAS). The pitch attitude changed quickly in response to the slight amount of aft stick applied, indicating a pitch sensitivity with weight on the landing gear (gains will be changed for flight 2). While pitch attitude was definitely controllable, judicious pitch inputs were required to avoid excessive attitude changes. As a result, a less than optimum takeoff attitude was established and resulted in a 170-175 KCAS liftoff.

Once airborne, the initial pitch sensitivity disappeared and smooth and precise aircraft control was easily achieved. A landing gear down climb to 15,000 ft. was performed during which time this pilot gently started to get the feel of this new aircraft. Handling was pleasant and confidence in the FLCS was quickly gained.

Enroute:

A mild and brief PA [pitch axis] handling qualities evaluation was conducted prior to raising the landing gear and verified the positive impressions experienced during the climb. The landing gear was cycled twice; the JFS [jet fuel starter] started and shut down, ECS [environmental control system] and instrumentation checked prior to departing overhead Carswell [Air Force Base] for the high altitude checks.

A mil [military] power climb to 30,000 feet was initiated at 350 KCAS. Climb rates were good and precise airspeed control was easily achieved. Once at 30,000 ft., stability and control blocks were performed at 0.8M [Mach] and 0.9M. Aircraft response was smooth and quick, and showed excellent handling qualities. During ½ stick rolls, handling was pleasant; however, an obvious side slip was evident after approximately 180 deg. of roll (post-flight examination of TM [telemetry] traces shows that roll is a bit "overcoordinated" in the current control implementation. This will be corrected later in the flight test program.). At roll termination, the sideslip immediately went to zero without an obvious overshoot. During a slow down to 20 alpha [degrees of angle of attack], a light high frequency low amplitude airframe buffet was noted. The aircraft was very solid in all axes during the deceleration to 20 alpha which occurred at 110 KCAS. A mil power sustained turn was completed at 0.9M/30K [Mach 0.9 at an altitude of 30,000 feet] with results that corresponded exactly to the predictions.

An idle power descent from 30K to 10K was performed to allow for a brief photo session prior to conducting a PA maneuver block. Aircraft feel in PA was solid and the aircraft could be quickly and easily trimmed at the desired AOA. During 45 deg. bank-to-bank rolls, a sideslip buildup was evident, but was not uncomfortable. Aircraft reactions to raising and lowering the landing gear were minimal. The final two times the gear was cycled prior to landing, the leading edge flap servo light illuminated and reset on the first attempt.

Landing:

A straight-in approach to landing was performed to a full stop landing. The aircraft was trimmed to 12-13 deg. AOA (155 KCAS) for the approach and provided a solid platform to perform the landing. At one mile from landing some turbulence was experienced and AOA decreased intentionally to approximately 11 deg. (165 KCAS approx.) for the final phase. A constant pitch attitude with no flare landing was performed which resulted in a smooth but faster than optimum touchdown. Concern for the pitch sensitivity noted on takeoff rotation prevented any significant aerodynamic braking attempt. Once the nose wheel was lowered to the runway, aircraft deceleration without wheel braking was not appreciable and the drag chute was deployed to keep from overheating the brakes. Deceleration from the drag chute was excellent. Aircraft directional control with the drag chute deployed (no crosswind) was no problem.[13]

Pitch Oscillation "Gallop" Issue

A longitudinal oscillation in the pitch axis had been briefly observed by Jim McKinney on the first flight of F-16XL-1. Its impact on aircraft flying qualities would result in an interim fix in the form of a notch-type filter that was inserted in the pitch path of the flight control computer. The notch filter reduced available pitch gain by 25 percent. A prolonged investigation by the Air Force and

GD into the engineering root cause of the pitch oscillation continued well into 1985. This eventually revealed a disagreement between the analytical model of the flight control system and the actual flight control system hardware installed in the aircraft. Flight testing conducted by the Combined Test Force at Edwards AFB determined that a 2.5 Hz pitch oscillation existed in the aircraft longitudinal axis. This oscillation was encountered in the 0.9 to 0.95 Mach number range at all altitudes during 1-g flight. The amplitude or severity of the pitch oscillation increased as altitude decreased (and air density increased). The amplitude of the pitch oscillation was dependent on the specified FCS gain in the longitudinal axis. The gain turned out to be 180 degrees out of phase in the frequency range where the longitudinal oscillation existed. Pilots came to refer to this oscillation as "pitch gallop," or "lope." It was considered a general nuisance in 1-g flight. However, as g-level was increased during simulated combat maneuvers, the severity of the oscillation also increased to the degree that it was impossible to adequately track a maneuvering target with the lead computing optical gun sight. The pitch oscillation issue led to a dedicated CTF flight-test evaluation of the F-16XL's FCS. An inflight excitation test procedure was developed that obtained actual aircraft frequency responses using actual aircraft hardware and aerodynamics at any condition within the flight envelope. As this interesting aspect of the Air Force F-16XL flight evaluation was not completed until much later in the test program (in 1985, well after the Dual-Role Fighter source selection was complete), it will be discussed in more technical detail in a later section.[14]

Transference of Flight Testing from Texas to Edwards

Insofar as continuing flight testing at Fort Worth was concerned, the daily status/pilot flight report for July 6, 1982, noted that future flights at Fort Worth would be spaced to reflect SPO limitations on the number of flights to be conducted at Fort Worth and their duration awaiting a decision on the readiness of the CTF at Edwards AFB to receive the aircraft.[15] GD publicly announced shortly after the first flight that F-16XL-1 was to be ferried to Edwards by the end of July to begin an extensive 250-flight, 9-month evaluation by Air Force and GD test pilots.[16] F-16XL-1 would fly three more times at Fort Worth to expand the flight envelope in preparation for ferrying to Edwards AFB. On July 9, on its second flight, the aircraft exceeded Mach 1. On July 18, 1982, F-16XL-1 flew twice. Following a 1.3-hour local test flight, it was flown on a 2.3-hour cross-country flight and delivered to the F-16XL Combined Test Force at Edwards. Delivery to the Air Force was several weeks ahead of the earlier scheduled delivery date in mid-August. Two days later, on July 20, 1982, Lt. Col. Marty H. Bushnell, director of the F-16XL Combined Test Force, became the first Air Force pilot to fly the aircraft.

Endnotes

1. This was less than 2 weeks later than the planned rollout date of June 22 contained in the "F-16XL No. 1 Ground, Flight Test and Delivery schedule, Revision A-1, of April 1, 1982." As it unfolded, first flight would take place 3 days earlier than the scheduled July 6 date.

2. GD, "F-16XL Rollout and First Flight," *Division Log*, Bulletin 1098, General Dynamics Corporation, Fort Worth Division, July 22, 1982.

3. "Evolutionary F-16XL Makes Its First Flight One Day After Its Rollout at Fort Worth," *General Dynamics World* 12, no. 7 (July 7, 1982).

4. Ibid.

5. Ibid.

6. Ibid.

7. Ibid.

8. Ibid.

9. A former Navy test pilot and 1967 U.S. Naval Academy graduate, Jim McKinney served two combat tours flying F-4 Phantoms from aircraft carriers during the Vietnam War. After leaving GD, he was a vice president with FEDEX and then president of his own moving company. McKinney died suddenly on January 4, 2011, while playing golf in Atlanta, GA.

10. Author not identified, "First Flight for F-16XL," *Flight International* (July 17, 1982): p. 118.

11. Jim McKinney, "Memorandum to F-16XL Development Team, Subject: F-16XL First Flight," General Dynamics Corporation, Fort Worth Division, July 6, 1982.

12. D.R. Kent, vice president and program director, F-16XL Program, "F-16XL Fighting Falcon First Flight Certificate," General Dynamics Corporation, Fort Worth Division, July 3, 1982. The certificate was signed by Kent and is reproduced in its original format in Appendix A.

13. Jim McKinney, "F-16XL Flight No. 1 Pilot Report," General Dynamics Corporation, Fort Worth Division, July 3, 1982.

14. Tierney, "Inflight Excitation of the F-16XL."

15. J.D. Korstian, "F-16XL-1 Daily Status/Pilot Flight Report," General Dynamics Corporation, Fort Worth Division, July 6, 1982.

16. As stated in "F-16XL Rollout and First Flight," *Division Log*, Bulletin 1098, General Dynamics Corporation, Fort Worth Division, July 22, 1982. However, "F-16XL No. 1 Ground, Flight

Test and Delivery schedule, Revision A-1, April 1, 1982" showed XL-1 delivery to Edwards AFB scheduled for August 14.

Each F-16XL had an individualized, multitone grey camouflage scheme. (National Museum of the USAF)

CHAPTER 6

The Integrated Flight-Test Organization, Objectives, and Program

The F-16E Combined Test Force

The F-16E Combined Test Force was established at the Air Force Flight Test Center at Edwards Air Force Base in July 1981, well in advance of the first flight of the F-16XL aircraft in July 1982.[1] Lt. Col. Marty H. Bushnell was the first CTF director (a position which he would hold until November 1, 1983, when Lt. Col. Edwin "Ed" A. Thomas, who had been his deputy, became the CTF director). The F-16E flight demonstration program was accomplished as an integrated effort by the Air Force and General Dynamics. A dedicated team made up of pilots and maintenance personnel from the Air Force Flight Test Center, the Air Force Operational Test and Evaluation Center, the Air Force Tactical Air Command, and General Dynamics was formed and located within the existing F-16E Combined Test Force at the AFFTC. Most of the flying would be accomplished by six project pilots: two each from the AFFTC, AFOTEC, and General Dynamics. The key players on the dedicated CTF team by assigned organization were:

AFFTC:
>Lt. Col. Marty H. Bushnell, F-16XL CTF director
>Lt. Col. Edwin A. Thomas, F-16XL CTF deputy director

AFOTEC:
>Lt. Col. P.C. Burnett
>Maj. John Cary

TAC:
>Lt. Col. Joe Bill Dryden, liaison pilot

General Dynamics:

    G.K. Smith, manager, test and evaluation
    James McKinney, project pilot
    Alex Wolfe, project pilot

Flight Test Phases and Objectives

The flight-test effort was divided into three phases, with basic test objectives varying according to individual phase. These test phases were known as Phase I, Development Flight Test; Phase II, Development (Extended) Flight Test; and Phase III, Pre–Full-Scale Engineering Development (FSED) Flight Test.[2] F-16XL flight testing eventually extended from the July 3, 1982, first flight of F-16XL-1 to October 1, 1985, when the two-seat F-16XL-2 was delivered to GD in Fort Worth following termination of the Air Force–funded program. The Air Force portion of the flight-test effort was funded at $15.3 million dollars in fiscal year 1982 with $11.0 million more authorized in fiscal year 1983.

F-16XL Phase I, Development Flight Test

Phase I was originally scheduled to extend over a 10½ month period starting in July of 1982 with the two prototypes programmed for a total of 270 test flights (157 for XL-1 and 113 for XL-2). Of these 270 missions, 36 were specifically dedicated to an AFOTEC evaluation of the F-16XL's operational potential for the Dual-Role Fighter mission with an emphasis on its air-to-ground capabilities. During this phase of flight testing, the CTF was comprised of test pilots and engineers from General Dynamics and the AFFTC with additional members from the AFOTEC, TAC, and ASD. Phase I testing would evaluate key design and basic airworthiness features of the aircraft with a focus on demonstrating performance and maneuver capabilities as compared to the basic F-16. As Phase I unfolded, program goals were modified to provide detailed data for the USAF Aeronautical Systems Division Derivative Fighter Steering Group (DFSG). The DFSG used data from Phase I testing to support selection of a derivative fighter design for further development as a Dual-Role Fighter. Derivatives of the McDonnell-Douglas F-15 (specifically, the F-15E Strike Eagle) and the F-16E were contenders in the DRF source selection.

The Phase I test program included both Development Test and Evaluation (DT&E) missions and an Operational Utility Evaluation. A wide variety of weapons and stores would be demonstrated and adequate weapon employment envelopes defined for use in the OUE. The OUE would assess the F-16XL's potential combat utility, suitability, and effectiveness, and it would be conducted by AFOTEC. OUE missions were dedicated to operational utility and suitability testing using the facilities and resources of Tactical Air Command's Nellis AFB near Las Vegas, NV. During the OUE, the F-16XLs would be flown in both air-to-air and air-to-ground configurations against Air Force McDonnell-Douglas F-4s flown by operational squadrons, Northrop F-5s from the dedicated Air Force aggressor squadron, and standard F-16s. The Derivative Fighter Evaluation program had planned for 270 flights to be completed by May 15, 1983, using the two F-16XL aircraft, of which 36 were to be allocated to the OUE. In fact, within the time and funding provided, a total of 369 test flights were accomplished during Phase I, which was actually not completed until June 15, 1983. This included 90 OUE flights.[3]

Phase II, Development (Extended) Flight Test

Phase II, Development (Extended) Flight Test followed the completion of Phase I testing that had also supported the Dual-Role Fighter source selection evaluation process. AFOTEC did not participate in Phase II testing. The Air Force DRF source selection decision, announced in January 1984, had resulted in the F-15E being selected for Full-Scale Engineering Development, leading to its eventual production. F-16XL Phase II consisted of additional development testing to expand the demonstrated capabilities of the F-16XL using remaining authorized, but unexpended, flight-test funding. The test plan for the Phase II, Development (Extended) Flight Test effort called for an additional 72 flights. These would evaluate performance and flying qualities with additional weapons and store loadings. Phase II, Development (Extended) Flight Test efforts were conducted from June 15, 1983, to February 1, 1985.[4]

Phase III, Pre-FSED Flight Test

Phase III, Pre-FSED Flight Test was structured to continue development of the F-16XL. The intent of Phase III was to reduce risk for a possible Full-Scale Engineering Development effort that would lead to a production version of the single-seat F-16XL. This aircraft would have been designated F-16F. Phase III was intended to continue flight control system development, weapons separation testing, and flight clearance of additional stores/weapon combinations and load configurations. Another objective of this test phase involved a flight-test evaluation of the General Electric F110 engine installed in F-16XL-2. During this phase of testing, XL-2 was also modified with the installation of a so-called Large Normal Shock Inlet. The LNSI provided increased mass airflow. This would enable the General Electric F110-GE-100 engine in F-16XL-2 to provide its maximum thrust and full acceleration capabilities. Phase III flight testing began on February 1, 1985, and continued until October 1, 1985. On that day, F-16XL-2 was ferried to the General Dynamics factory in Fort Worth and placed in flyable storage along with F-16XL-1.[5]

Edwards AFB Flight-Testing Highlights

On July 18, 1982, Jim McKinney ferried F-16XL-1 from Fort Worth to Edwards AFB on a flight that lasted 2.3 hours. Less than 3 days later, the CTF commander, Lt. Col. Marty Bushnell, flew the aircraft on its first test mission with the CTF. Performance, stability and control, and flight envelope expansion began immediately. Two external payload configurations were initially used in the combined test program. These were the air-to-air configuration, with 6 missiles, and an air-to-ground configuration carrying 12 Mk-82 bombs along with the 6 air-to-air missiles. A maximum Mach number of 1.95 was achieved on flight number 19 on July 28, 1982. This was the highest Mach number ever attained by the Pratt & Whitney F100-powered F-16XL-1 during the course of the entire Air Force test program. Later the same day, the maximum 9-g capability of the aircraft was reached during structural loads testing with F-16XL-1 in the air-to-air configuration.

Speed Brake Actuator Failure

On August 3, 1982, during Ed Thomas's initial checkout flight, a speed brake actuator failed. This was F-16XL-1 flight number 22. The failure happened when the speed brakes were deployed at Mach 1.6 at 30,000 feet. The left-hand speed brake actuator experienced a structural failure, resulting in the loss of the speed brake system's hydraulic supply. Following the incident, Thomas made an uneventful emergency landing on the lakebed runway at Edwards AFB. Subsequent investigation determined that the speed brake design criteria used by GD was based on an assumption that the air loads on both the upper and lower speed brake surfaces were the same when the speed brakes were extended. However, this assumption failed to take into account the aerodynamic effects created by the aft AIM-120 missiles, which were mounted immediately ahead of the lower speed brake surfaces. At higher airspeeds and dynamic pressures, the load asymmetry between the upper and lower surfaces of each speed brake exceeded the structural design capability of the actuators leading to the failure. Corrective action involved incorporation of an electric override into the pilot's speed brake switch that precluded speed brake operation at indicated airspeeds above 525 KCAS. With this relatively simple change to the speed brake opening logic, speed brake actuator loads were kept at acceptable levels with minimal impact to the subsequent flight-test program.

Testing Accelerates

During August 1982, the first aerial refueling from a USAF KC-135 tanker was accomplished. In late August 1982, the CTF reported, "Initial qualitative comparisons with T-38s, F-4s, and the F-16A indicate that the XL is very stable and comfortable at low altitude and indeed may be less susceptible to turbulence upset."[6] In this context, the normally adverse effects of lower wing loading on ride quality appeared to be offset by the ability of the F-16XL's low-aspect-ratio, highly swept cranked-arrow wing to compensate for the effects of gusts and turbulence. Twelve Mk-82 500-pound bombs were successfully released at minimum intervals on August 24. Release conditions were 1-g level flight at an altitude of 13,000 feet and a speed of Mach 0.75. The bombs were ripple-released at 15 millisecond intervals.[7] A single Mk-82 bomb was released from a lateral bomb toss maneuver on flight number 72, flown on October 22. Basic F-16 weapons delivery software was used on the realistic tactical weapons delivery profile. Flight conditions at bomb release were airspeed 540 KCAS at an altitude of 500 feet above ground level during a 4-g turn. The bomb hit within 70 feet of its intended target, well inside the Air Force accuracy criteria of 140 feet for unguided bomb deliveries.

On left: The F-16XL-1 flying a test mission on August 18, 1982, with 12 500-pound Mk-82 bombs, 4 fuselage-mounted AIM-120 AMRAAMs, and 2 wingtip-mounted AIM-9 Sidewinder missiles. On right: On August 24, 1982, the F-16XL-1 successfully released 12 500 pound Mk-82 bombs from individual low-drag ejector bomb racks. (Both images USAF)

On October 27, Joe Bill Dryden ferried F-16XL-1 back to Fort Worth, just in time for the first flight of the two-seat F-16XL-2. Although the overall external dimensions of both aircraft were the same, the empty weight of the two-seat aircraft was nearly 2,000 pounds heavier than the single-seat F-16XL-1 (21,623 pounds as compared to 19,690 pounds). As a consequence of the second cockpit, XL-2 carried about 1,000 pounds less internal fuel than the single seat aircraft. After being removed from its assembly tooling in June 1982, subsystems were installed and checked out. Following final safety of flight reviews, F-16XL-2 flew for the first time on October 29, 1982. General Dynamics Project Pilot Alex Wolfe was at the front seat controls with Jim McKinney in the aft seat. On this occasion, F-16XL-2 easily exceeded Mach 1.0. On November 8, both F-16XL aircraft were ferried together in close formation from Fort Worth to Edwards AFB, where they would undergo a series of intensive flight-test evaluations that would continue until the end of June

1985. For the 2.5-hour formation ferry flight, Tactical Air Command's Joe Bill Dryden and GD Project Pilot Alex Wolfe joined up to crew F-16XL-2.[8] P.C. Burnett, one of the AFOTEC members of the Combined Test Force, flew F-16XL-1. The nonstop formation flight to Edwards was made on internal fuel and without en route aerial refueling. In spite of 90-knot headwinds, both aircraft arrived with normal fuel reserves.

In-Flight Elevon Actuation Horn Failure

During F-16XL-1 flight number 79, on November 9, 1982, Jim McKinney was conducting a stability and control evaluation with the aircraft in the air-to-air configuration. An elevon actuation horn failed while the aircraft was in a rolling maneuver at Mach 0.95 at 10,000 feet altitude. The resultant high-transient structural loads produced on the airframe caused the right-hand AIM-9L missile, along with its launcher, to separate from the aircraft. The vertical fin-tip fairing was also lost, possibly due to a glancing impact by the missile and launcher after they separated from the aircraft. Aerodynamic loads on the elevons under these rolling flight conditions and high dynamic pressures pro-

duced stresses that were near the limit hinge-moment capability. Inadequate material properties in the elevon control horn were determined to have been the cause of the failure. The automatic flight control system immediately retrimmed the aircraft to compensate for the changed aerodynamic configuration of the aircraft. Following engineering investigation and analysis, the elevon actuator horn was redesigned with increased thickness and stronger aluminum alloys. Extensive test-

The F-16XL-1 photograph, which McKinney autographed while recovering to Edwards, November 9, 1982. (Lockheed Martin)

ing subsequently validated the adequacy of the redesign.[9] Jim McKinney had carried an inflight photo of the F-16XL-1 taken earlier in the test program aloft with him on this test flight that he autographed during his recovery to an emergency landing at Edwards AFB.

Pace of Flight Testing Increases

The pace of the combined flight-test effort began to really ramp up, with *Flight International* magazine reporting in early December 1982 that the two aircraft had passed 100 flight hours. By that time, F-16XL-1 had flown 79 times and reached 50,000 feet, and the two-seat XL-2 had flown 17 times, reaching an altitude of 45,000 feet. According to press reports, both aircraft had achieved Mach 2.0 speeds. (This is somewhat of an exaggeration as XL-1 never exceeded Mach 1.95 during the Air Force test program, while XL-2's maximum demonstrated Mach number was 1.6.) General Dynamics released publicity photos showing F-16XL-1 dropping a load of 12 Mk-82 500 pound bombs from its conformal underwing stations while also carrying a full air-to-air missile payload. By the end of the year, nearly 130 F-16XL flights had been accumulated with both aircraft.[10]

After arrival at Edwards in November 1982, F-16XL-2 was used for a 10-flight-test program that examined elevon loads. This was accomplished in conjunction with other testing that included performance, loads, propulsion, and flutter. These combined tests continued through flight number 27, when the strengthened landing gear and improved elevons were installed. These modifications were completed at the GD factory in Fort Worth between November 10, 1982, and January 10, 1983. The new strengthened landing gear allowed aircraft takeoff gross weight to be increased up to 48,000 pounds from the previous limit of 37,500 pounds. Throughout Phase I, both F-16XL aircraft would be used to expand the allowable flight envelope with respect to airspeed, Mach number, load factor, and maneuvering g-limits for various store loadings. The test force reported at this time that "[p]reliminary testing of the aircraft has shown significant performance advantages as a result of using the XL configuration instead of external tanks and multiple store racks to the basic F-16 to achieve a desired range payload combination."[11]

Gun firing tests of the F-16XL's M61 Vulcan 20-millimeter (mm) rotary cannon began on January 10, 1983, with vibration levels being reported as similar to those experienced on the F-16. An antispin chute was installed on XL-1 in late January 1983, and high-alpha test missions were flown with the aircraft both in the air-to-air (missiles-only) configuration and with up to 12 Mk-82 bombs in the air-to-ground configuration. Generally, aircraft characteristics were found to be excellent under the flight conditions evaluated in the first phase of the planned flight-test program, regardless of store configuration tested. Results from Phase I high-alpha testing were used to formulate the next phase of high-AoA testing, during which additional store loadings and configurations would be evaluated.

Additional weapons separation testing was used to determine safe and reliable weapons employment capabilities for the subsequent Operational Utility Evaluation. The OUE would assess F-16XL combat utility and its potential effectiveness as an operational Air Force weapons system. The OUE was conducted during Phase I testing, with some Phase II test missions used to collect additional data as requested by the USAF ASD DFSG for use during the

Dual-Role Fighter evaluation. Pilot comments for all configurations flown during Phase I were largely positive, with the aircraft displaying generally favorable qualities in the areas of performance, flutter, and stability and control. One major area of concern that was quickly highlighted by CTF pilots was the significantly lower thrust-to-weight ratio of the aircraft as compared to the F-16A and F-16B. The implications of this issue under a variety of flight conditions and store loadings were identified as an area for additional careful evaluation as the test program progressed.[12]

Operational Utility Evaluation

A total of 90 test missions, or approximately 25 percent of all Phase I flights, were eventually dedicated to the Operational Utility Evaluation. During the course of the OUE, both F-16XL aircraft were evaluated by Tactical Air Command pilots. On missions conducted at Nellis AFB, simulated air combat engagements were flown against Air Force F-4, F-5, and F-16 fighters using the highly instrumented Air Combat Maneuvering Range (ACMR). For these missions, the F-6XLs carried an ACMR pod on one of the wingtip AIM-9 missile launchers. The pod automatically passed critical air combat maneuvering and fire control system parameters to the ACMR ground stations for postmission review, debriefing, and analysis. During the OUE, high pitch and

Each F-16XL had an individualized, multitone grey camouflage scheme. (National Museum of the USAF)

g-onset rate capabilities of the F-16XL were assessed as key factors in the air combat successes achieved; however, this was somewhat offset by very rapid energy loss that was experienced during sustained high-g turning maneuvers. In the air-to-ground portion of the evaluation, handling qualities and tracking during weapons deliveries in conventional, pop-up, and lateral-toss mode were highly rated by the TAC pilots, and the aircraft was rated as quick, solid, and very responsive in pitch and roll. Ride quality at low altitude and high speed (an area of high technical interest for the program) was assessed as excellent—this despite the much lower wing loading of the F-16XL compared to that of the standard F-16.

Quick Combat Turnaround Demonstration

In conjunction with the OUE flight evaluation, the ability of the F-16XL to be quickly armed and refueled was evaluated using an all Air Force maintenance crew that included AFOTEC and TAC personnel. Some concerns had been expressed over the amount of time that could be required to individually load the 12 separate underwing bomb racks. During the quick combat turnaround demonstration, the aircraft was accepted by the maintenance ground crew following its return from a mission. It was then fully refueled and serviced, a drag chute was installed, the bomb racks and missile launchers were loaded with 12 semiconformally mounted Mk-82 bombs and 2 wingtip AIM-9 missiles, the M61 cannon magazine was loaded with 510 rounds of 20-mm dummy ammunition, the aircraft was accepted by the pilot, the engine was started, the flight control and inertial navigation systems were tested and aligned, and the aircraft was launched, all in a little less than 24 minutes. Servicing and launching a standard F-16 during a quick combat turnaround exercise with a similar armament load took about 16 minutes, but the F-16XL's turnaround time was within the TAC criteria of 25 minutes.[13]

Phase I Testing Completed

The original Phase I flight-test program agreement between the Air Force and GD had called for test objectives to be completed by May 15, 1983, with a minimum of 240 missions accomplished. In reality, by the end of Phase I testing, F-16XL-1 had completed 200 flights and XL-2 had flown 169 times, with the two aircraft averaging 36 sorties per month. The CTF commander, Marty Bushnell, commented that the aircraft's demonstrated reliability and maintainability was about the same as that of the F-16, and F-16XL sortie rates in operational USAF service should also be similar to those of the F-16.[14] During the 369 flights completed in Phase I testing, a number of key performance items were demonstrated. These included a maximum speed of Mach 1.95 in full afterburning power while carrying six air-to-air missiles demonstrated using F-16XL-1. In the air-to-ground configuration, F-16XL-1 reached Mach 1.4 using full engine thrust with afterburner with an external weapons payload of 12 Mk-82 bombs plus 4 AIM-120s and 2 AIM-9 missiles. In the same air-to-ground configuration, a maximum airspeed of 600 KCAS was demonstrated using Military Power thrust (defined as 100 engine rpm without use of afterburning) at an altitude of 500 feet. When loaded with two 370-gallon wing tanks, six Mk-82 bombs, and a full load of six air-to-air missiles, F-16XL-1 was 65 knots faster in Military Power than a comparably loaded F-16. In the air-to-air configuration loaded with six air-to-air missiles, F-16XL-1 demonstrated a sustained load factor of 3.6 g's at Mach 1.4 at an altitude of 30,000 feet. During maximum load factor testing, 9.1 g's was achieved with the air-to-air missile load of 6 missiles with 7.2 g's demonstrated while carrying a load of 12 Mk-82 bombs and 6 missiles. The 9.1-g maximum load factor demonstrated in testing was slightly above the maximum design load factor of 9.0 g's; the slightly higher load factor registered was due to the g-overshoot issue that is discussed subsequently. During the flight-test program, missions were flown up to the maximum takeoff gross weight (MTOGW) of 48,000 pounds.[15]

Neither F-16XL flight demonstrator proved to be capable of true super-cruise performance, as was later attained by the Lockheed YF-22A ATF prototype and the production Lockheed Martin F-22A Raptor. As defined by the Air Force, supercruise provided a capability for sustained supersonic flight without the use of afterburner.[16] However, the F-16XL's low-drag design, along with its ability to carry 11,200 pounds of internal fuel, did provide significantly increased range compared to the standard F-16C. Ironically, when both aircraft were configured for the air-to-air mission, the F-16C actually had better subsonic cruise efficiency than the F-16XL. As speed approached Mach 1.0, the F-16XL's comparative cruise efficiency improved, and at Mach 1.4, the F-16XL had a 25-percent-higher lift-to-drag ratio than that of the F-16C. The clean aerodynamic design of the F-16XL is clearly seen in photographs of the type. On the air-to-air mission profile, the XL demonstrated a 53-percent-better range capability when carrying internal fuel only compared to the F-16C. With external fuel tanks, the F-16XL's range capability was 124 percent higher. Similar results were obtained with air-to-ground payloads. For example, with twice the payload, 12 Mk-82 bombs on the F-16XL compared to 6 similar bombs on the F-16A, the XL's range was 44 percent greater. The F-16XL demonstrated a ferry range of 2,245 nautical miles without aerial refueling when carrying two 600-gallon external fuel tanks.[17]

Shortly after the conclusion of Phase I testing, General Dynamics was quoted in the aviation press as saying that the F-16XL had demonstrated maneuverability that was better than expected, with its cranked-arrow wing planform displaying none of the unfavorable drag characteristics of the tail-less delta. At the same time, and perhaps defensively, GD claimed that there was no discernible difference in performance between the Pratt & Whitney F100–powered aircraft and the aircraft powered by the General Electric F110 engine, and it added that extra thrust was not needed.[18] However, the Air Force reported that the F-16XL was purposely designed to have improved instantaneous turn rates rather than high sustained maneuvering capability.[19] In this regard, the F-16XL demonstrated an instantaneous turn rate that was about 30 percent higher than that of the standard F-16 in the air-to-ground configuration, with both aircraft carrying the same payload at 30,000 feet. At the same altitude, the F-16XL's instantaneous turn rate was 14 percent better than that of the standard F-16 when both aircraft were carrying their full

The F-16XL-2 had a fake "canopy" and air refueling receptacle markings painted on its underside to visually disorient opposing fighter pilots as to the true orientation of the aircraft. The circular white markings were intended to represent pilots' helmets when seen from a distance. (USAF)

air-to-air missile payload. In contrast, there was a significant loss of sustained turn capability compared to that of the F-16. For example, at a Mach number of 0.9 at 30,000 feet, the F-16XL's sustained turn rate was 30 percent lower than that of the F-16 in both the air-to-air and the air-to-ground configurations. This poor sustained turning performance compared to the F-16 was identified by the Air Force as resulting from the high induced drag of the F-16XL's cranked-arrow wing and its relatively low thrust-to-weight ratio. Commenting on this specific issue, Maj. Patrick K. Talty, the former deputy for engineering within the F-16E Combined Test Force at the Air Force Flight Test Center, later reported the following:

> Pilot comments generally expressed concern about the loss of energy that resulted during high g maneuvers with the XL. Typically, in a 180 degree heading change turn the XL would lose about 180 knots. The operational utility of the gain in instantaneous turning capability was masked by this loss of energy. The T/W ratio of the F-16XL with half fuel in the air-to-air loading is 0.7. This is below the historical trend that US fighter aircraft have been following.... The exceptional rolling ability of the XL was used to offset this loss of sustained maneuver capability in simulated combat, but the lack of sustained maneuver capability was always raised as a primary concern by the pilots attached to the test program.[20]

Test Results and Lessons Learned

Takeoff and Landing Performance

All takeoffs were accomplished with maximum (full afterburner) power. Aft stick force was applied at about 25 to 30 knots below computed takeoff speed in order to establish a 10- to 14-degree pitch attitude at liftoff, with the higher pitch attitude used at heavier gross weights to minimize takeoff distance. Pilots reported that the commanded pitch rate tended to stop short of achieving the desired pitch attitude prior to liftoff. Liftoff speeds typically approached 180 knots when the aircraft carried a mixed load of air-to-air and air-to-ground ordnance consisting of 4 AIM-120 missiles, 2 AIM-9L missiles, and 12 Mk-82 bombs.[21] Under such heavyweight conditions, the aircraft had a tendency to settle back toward the runway as it left ground effect. If the pilot did not counter this settling tendency with increased back stick pressure to achieve and maintain a precise takeoff attitude at the computed takeoff speed, the aircraft could touch back down on the runway before it could establish and maintain a positive rate of climb. This tendency to skip and touchdown after liftoff under heavyweight conditions required the pilot to be cautious in retracting the landing gear until a positive rate of climb was established. In spite of these issues, pilots reported that takeoffs were generally safe, with a workload comparable to that encountered with other operational fighters under similar conditions.[22]

Not surprisingly, takeoff performance of the Pratt & Whitney F100–powered F-16XL-1 was significantly degraded as its takeoff weight increased. The high desert conditions at Edwards AFB (which is located at an elevation 2,310 feet above sea level) further affected takeoff performance. The effects of the higher operating altitude and hotter temperatures (often well above 100 degrees Fahrenheit) could be accounted for in performance analyses, but the takeoff performance differential between the two aircraft was very pronounced. The more powerful General Electric F110 engine installed in the two-seat F-16XL-2 noticeably improved takeoff performance on hot days. For example, at relatively heavyweight conditions (a takeoff gross weight [TOGW] of 44,000 pounds) on a hot day at Edwards, F-16XL-1's (F100 engine) takeoff distance was 5,500 feet. This was due to its low thrust-to-weight ratio, which, measured under these conditions, was only 0.33. At the same TOGW, the two-seat F-16XL-2 (with its more powerful General Electric F110 engine) was able to takeoff in a distance of 3,800 feet. Although this was significantly better than the takeoff performance of F-16XL-1, it still did not meet the program goal that called for a takeoff distance of less than 2,000 feet under standard sea level conditions.[23]

The CTF rated F-16XL climb performance in military thrust as satisfactory for all munitions and external store loadings tested with the exception of the Tactical Munitions Dispenser (TMD). Rate of climb with the payload of six TMDs, carried three in tandem under each side of the inboard section of the wing, was marginal. This was caused by aerodynamic drag that was much higher than had been predicted from wind tunnel carriage test results. This was reportedly due to inaccuracies between the subscale TMD models used in F-16XL wind tunnel testing and the characteristics of the full-scale TMD. Fin geometry and, hence, store drag of the TMD subscale models was not representative of the actual weapons. Maximum thrust (full afterburner) climb performance was rated satisfactory for all weapons and external store loadings tested.[24]

Approach and Landing

The F-16XL had a very high approach speed under heavyweight conditions of 200 KCAS with touchdown speeds well above 170 knots. During powered approaches to landing, the F-16XL was reported to be "smooth, responsive, and stable."[25] The aircraft had to be flown at a higher angle of attack on final approach than the standard F-16, limiting over-the-nose visibility and increasing pilot workload. It was less sensitive to the effects of gusts than the standard F-16. Approach AoA was restricted to 13 degrees by limited over-the-nose visibility, and they also ensured adequate aft fuselage clearance with the runway at touchdown. A slight airframe buffet at angles of attack greater than 10 degrees provided the pilot with a useful cue, with the aircraft appearing to have a "natural affinity" for the 13-degree approach AoA. At this AoA, instrument approaches were reportedly easy to fly. The Air Force noted a potential for the aircraft to develop a high sink rate on final approach due to the combined effects of the high induced drag of the large cranked-arrow wing and the relatively slow response of the low bypass ratio turbofan engine. This slower engine response required the pilot to anticipate the need for power changes. The Air Force considered this as another factor in increased pilot workload.

As the F-16XL approached the runway, the aerodynamic characteristics of the aircraft changed. This phenomenon is known as ground effect, and it affects all aircraft. Aircraft with low aspect ratio wings, like the F-16XL, are very sensitive to ground effect. The primary effect is an increase in lift coefficient, with the drag coefficient and pitching moment also changing. A nose-down pitching moment generally occurs. Drag coefficient changes may be positive or negative. Flight in very close proximity to the ground can affect air data measurements and may also affect aircraft flying characteristics. In most cases, ground effects are not excessively troublesome and are easily compensated for by an experienced pilot.[26] With the F-16XL, a very noticeable decrease in rate of descent occurred as the aircraft entered the ground effect region within about 10 to 20 feet of the runway, even when the pilot maintained a constant pitch attitude. A normal flared landing usually resulted in a smooth touchdown. Aerodynamic braking was routinely used by the pilots to assist the brakes, and this helped to reduce the landing rollout distance. This technique involved the pilot holding the nose of the aircraft at a pitch angle of 14 degrees immediately after touchdown. That attitude was maintained until the airspeed reached 100 KCAS, at which time the nose gear was lowered to the runway and the brakes applied. Ed Thomas reported: "For every additional degree of fuselage deck angle, we get a huge increase in drag from that big delta wing, greatly improving our landing performance."[27]

The Convair XF-92A Dart, progenitor of all American delta-wing aircraft, on the ramp of the NACA High-Speed Flight Research Station (now the Dryden Flight Research Center) in 1953. The wing and aft fuselage were tufted for flow visualization studies. Despite its "F" for "Fighter" designation, this was strictly a transonic research aircraft. (NASA)

The XL was reported as being more stable than the standard F-16 in the two-point attitude used during aerodynamic braking after touchdown with pitch control reported as more positive. Pilots also reported that the large drag chute was very effective in initially decelerating the aircraft and helping to reduce landing distance.[28] The F-16XL's approach and landing characteristics, and associated piloting techniques, were similar to those used with the classic earlier delta-wing fighter-interceptors produced by the Convair Division of General Dynamics—the supersonic F-102A Delta Dagger and the Mach 2+ F-106A Delta Dart—and their transonic test bed progenitor, the Convair XF-92A Dart.[29]

The F-16XL did not achieve the goal of having a decreased

A Convair YF-102 Delta Dagger, flown by NACA at Edwards in 1954 on drag and aerodynamic pitch-up studies. (NASA)

A Convair QF-106 Delta Dart on takeoff from Mojave Air and Space Port, 1997. (NASA)

landing distance relative to the standard F-16. Indeed, it was significantly greater: with a full internal fuel load (an aircraft gross weight of 35,000 pounds), the F-16XL's landing distance was 6,700 feet without use of the drag chute. But even with the drag chute deployed on landing, landing distance was still 5,100 feet. The standard F-16 with a full internal fuel load had a landing distance of 4,500 feet under the same conditions at Edwards AFB.[30]

The Air Force attributed the long F-16XL landing distance to several factors. These included a very "flat" approach (characteristic of deltas) with a consequent high-speed approach under heavyweight conditions of 200 KCAS. Touchdown speeds were often well above 170 knots. These high approach and touchdown speeds resulted from an approach AoA that was limited to about 13 degrees due to over-the-nose visibility limitations, and they also ensured an adequate aft fuselage clearance with the runway at touchdown. General Dynamics considered several approaches that would increase lift coefficient while holding angle of attack constant in an attempt to reduce the high approach and touchdown speeds.

These included installation of inboard leading-edge vortex flaps. As previously discussed, the application of vortex flaps to highly swept wings had been extensively investigated by NASA Langley researchers. F-16XL wind tunnel models fitted with leading-edge vortex flaps had been evaluated in Langley wing tunnels. Changes to the F-16XL's flight control system were also being investigated. The available pitching moment on the aircraft would have been increased by modifications to the pitch trim capability. Both approaches to improve the available F-16XL lift coefficient during final approach to landing were ongoing at NASA Langley using analytic and wind tunnel test efforts when the program was cancelled by the Air Force in late 1985.[31]

Flying Qualities in Cruise Configuration

The CTF pilots reported that the mid-envelope flying qualities of the F-16XL were generally similar to those of the F-16. Roll acceleration was actually higher. The increased roll capability of the F-16XL was particularly noticeable when external stores were carried. Roll oscillations were encountered by some pilots due to the aircraft's rapid roll-onset rate. This was not considered to be a serious problem by experienced test force pilots who flew the aircraft on a regular basis.[32] In fact, these pilots felt that the high roll-onset and acceleration rates provided the F-16XL with an initial tactical advantage during close-in aerial combat maneuvering, enabling the aircraft to be quickly pointed in the direction of an enemy threat. Test force pilot reports stated that the aircraft's flying qualities were characterized by high agility, excellent visibility, and a cockpit environment equal to or better than those found in the standard F-16.[33]

High-Speed, Low-Altitude Ride Qualities

F-16XL ride qualities were reported to be smooth and comfortable during flights conducted at the low altitudes and high speeds typical of tactical mission profiles. The aircraft was capable of a maximum speed of 600 knots at an altitude of 500 feet while carrying 12 500-pound bombs and 6 missiles. Some pilots commented that the F-16XL exhibited a somewhat distracting irregular, low-amplitude pitching motion that detracted from its otherwise excellent low-altitude handling qualities. Test pilots that regularly flew the aircraft accepted this as an inherent characteristic of the F-16XL and said it had very little effect on overall mission performance or pilot workload.[34]

High-Speed Handling Qualities

The aircraft was capable of rapid acceleration beyond Mach 1 in level flight in the air-to-air configuration and with some air-to-ground loadings. Trim changes were not required when the aircraft transitioned from subsonic to supersonic flight and buffet was not encountered. Acceleration improved as the aircraft moved beyond Mach 1. As the aircraft accelerated to higher Mach numbers and dynamic pressures, elevon hinge-moment capacity limitations prevented the aircraft from being trimmed to maintain level flight. This limited hinge-moment capacity during high-speed flight resulted in a nose-rise tendency. The CTF considered this a major problem that required correction. Aircraft roll rate degraded rapidly to unacceptable levels at high dynamic pressures (above 1,200 pounds per square foot). During maximum command elevated-g rolls at speeds beyond Mach 1.4, a strong roll oscillation was encountered. The CTF reported that the roll oscillation was due to improper implementation of the aileron-rudder interconnect within the flight control system design. During turning maneuvers with heavy loads at Mach numbers in the vicinity of 0.9, a "pitch inflection" was encountered as angle of attack reached 16 degrees. The pitch inflection was characterized as an abrupt change in pitching moment. During slow-down turns at these conditions, the aircraft would "dig-in" with g-forces reaching between 1 and 2 g's above the commanded level. This was rated as a serious problem because the flight control system was incapable of responding quickly enough to control the resultant g-overshoot. On several occasions during flight near the g-limiter, the aircraft limit-load factor was inadvertently exceeded.[35]

Maximum Airspeed/Mach Number

The F-16XL was intended to be capable of achieving Mach 2.2 at high altitude and Mach 1.2 at sea level. However, its maximum airspeed in some military thrust and in all augmented thrust (afterburning) conditions was never determined during the Air Force flight-test demonstration program. This was due to an elevon hinge moment limitation that prevented CTF pilots from reaching the boundaries of the aircraft's high-speed envelope. Maximum Mach number reached during the Air Force test program was Mach 1.95. The aircraft had the excess thrust necessary to enable it to go faster than the speeds that were demonstrated, especially with the higher power General Electric F110 engine. However, the flight control system as implemented in the two F-16XL prototypes did not provide the hinge-moment capability to trim the aircraft for 1-g level flight at higher speeds. This hinge-moment limitation with the prototypes was not resolved prior to conclusion of the Air Force flight-test effort. The flight control system was to be redesigned to correct this and the other control issues previously discussed if the aircraft had been selected for subsequent full-scale development.[36]

Formation and Aerial Refueling

At moderate weights, the F-16XL could be flown precisely in close formation and during aerial refueling, and it generally required a low pilot workload. Pitch sensitivity increased slightly when external stores (including wing fuel tanks) were carried. However, there was a significant degradation in stability at heavy gross weights. This was especially noticeable in the directional axis, where the aircraft had "a tendency to wallow." When refueling while carrying a load of heavy, high-drag stores, full military power was insufficient to maintain position in the center of the refueling envelope when the tanker was turning at its standard 30-degree bank angle at altitudes above 20,000 feet. In order to maintain the proper refueling position under these conditions, pilots had to resort to cycling into and out of afterburner. This increased both fuel consumption and pilot workload, especially at night or in weather conditions. Extensive air refueling tanker support to the F-16XL flight-test program was provided by Boeing KC-135 and McDonnell-Douglas KC-10 tankers assigned to the Strategic Air Command (SAC). In addition to SAC tankers, a KC-135 belonging to the Aeronautical Systems Division at Wright-Patterson AFB sometimes provided refueling support. During the course of the Air Force F-16XL flight-test program, 127 missions involved air refueling with 175 fuel transfers successfully accomplished. F-16XL's performance during aerial refueling was rated

by CTF test force pilots as unsatisfactory under the conditions originally used for air refueling (a refueling airspeed of 200 knots at an altitude of 20,000 feet). Refueling at these conditions required intermittent use of afterburner, as the aircraft gross weight increased during the fuel transfer process. This was especially noticeable when refueling during turns. The F-16XL simply did not have enough excess thrust available to maintain the proper refueling position while attached to the tanker's refueling boom. Follow-on testing determined

The F-16XL-1 while refueling from a Boeing KC-135 Stratotanker on August 12, 1982. (USAF)

that aerial refueling could be accomplished without the use of afterburner, but only if the tanker flew at a lower altitude of 15,000 feet and increased airspeed to 330 knots.[37]

Target Tracking

Pilots reported some pitch sensitivity above Mach 0.9 and also at indicated airspeeds below 300 knots when attempting to track maneuvering targets with the lead computing optical sight or with the standby sighting reticle. The "pitch gallop" phenomena discussed earlier, consisting of a sustained 2.5-cycles-per-second pitch oscillation, was considered to be much more irritating during high workload target tracking exercises against maneuvering targets. Pitch gallop was encountered at all altitudes between 0.90 and 0.94 Mach, becoming more pronounced in amplitude at lower altitudes. This increased the difficulties encountered in accurately tracking maneuvering targets.[38]

Reliability and Maintainability

The reliability and maintainability evaluation of the F-16XL was limited by several factors. Since the Air Force had not established any goals, thresholds, or contractual requirements for either reliability or maintainability, the evaluation was limited to a comparison with standard F-16A/B aircraft in USAF fleet service. An additional issue was created by the fact that both F-16XLs experienced some reliability issues that were the result of their being constructed using fuselages from F-16 full-scale development aircraft that were not equivalent to standard production F-16A/B aircraft. Several of the subsystems on the F-16XL prototypes were also different from those found in the standard F-16A/B, further limiting the validity of the reliability and maintainability evaluation. Another limiting factor in performing a valid quantitative maintainability assessment was that General Dynamics performed all F-16XL maintenance throughout the evaluation using highly skilled company experts. There was a significant difference between the GD maintenance concept and that used by the Air Force. The Air Force also noted that the unique F-16XL configuration produced some excessive maintenance times due to the somewhat restricted access available in the wing root areas of both prototypes. In fact, the Air Force concluded that most of the F-16XL's maintainability problems resulted from structural modifications that had been made during conversion of the original full-scale development F-16A aircraft to the F-16XL prototype configuration.[39]

F-16XL aircraft maintainability was rated as satisfactory by the Air Force, and in many ways, reliability results were actually excellent. F-16XL-1 had a Mean Time Between Maintenance (MTBM) of 1.6 hours over a period covering 224.7 flight hours, with F-16XL-2 demonstrating an MTBM of 1.8 hours during a period that included 172.4 flying hours. This was a significant improvement over the 0.8-hour MTBM demonstrated by F-16A/B test aircraft during FSD testing. In operational service, the MTBM for the F-16A fleet had risen to 2.9 hours by the time of the F-16XL flight-test effort. The basic similarity of most F-16XL subsystems with those of the standard F-16 was a major contributor to its good maintenance record. Overall, the reliability of major subsystems in the F-16XL was considered comparable to those of the F-16A/B fleet. However, the reliability of the higher-gross-weight (48,000 pound) F-16XL landing gear was rated as unsatisfactory because of recurring brake failures. In fact, the search for suitable wheel, brake, and tire configurations required numerous modifications that were ongoing throughout the flight-test program. Although a tire design suitable for use at a TOGW of 48,000 pounds was finally settled upon after several tire designs were tested, its durability was such that it was limited to only 10 flights. The F-16XL flight control system initially demonstrated poor reliability. Although its reliability continued to improve as the test program unfolded, the Air Force believed

Air Force Flight Test Center Vice Commander Col. William J. "Pete" Knight taxis back from an F-16XL-1 familiarization sortie, August 6, 1982. (USAF)

that the flight control system needed further development before any commitment could be made to a production program. The overall sortie rate capability of the F-16XL was assessed to be virtually the same as that of the standard F-16 throughout all phases of the flight-test program.[40]

The General Electric F110 engine flown in F-16XL-2 was substantially more reliable than the Pratt & Whitney F100 installed in F-16XL-1. The F110 engine achieved an MTBM of 57.5 hours with only three minor failures during 172.4 hours of flight. No mission aborts were charged against the F110 engine. The F110 encountered no augmenter blowouts and had no failures to light or engine stalls throughout the flight-test program. Shop maintenance was not required on the F110 during the basic Air Force flight-test program, and its maintainability was rated as a significant improvement over that of the F100 engine. In comparison, reliability of the F100 engine fitted to F-16XL-1 was comparable to the F100 engine installed in the F-16A/B fleet. Its reliability problems were also typical of those encountered in the standard F-16A/B aircraft. These included instances of fan and compressor stall during afterburner transient operations and cracks in the afterburner nozzle support seals and diverter seals. The F110 engine required no shop visits or engine removals during the flight-test program with F-16XL-2. In comparison, the F100 had to be removed for maintenance four times during its 224.7 hours of flight in F-16XL-1. The MTBM for the F100 engine was 37.5 hours.[41]

Phase I Flight-Test Summary

The basic objectives of the Phase I program were to demonstrate the airworthiness of the F-16XL and evaluate its performance. Since the Air Force had not established specific performance thresholds and goals as standards against which to evaluate the aircraft, all findings and test results were compared with performance predictions provided by General Dynamics. This resulted in criticism from the General Accounting Office (GAO), as well as other critics of the Air Force approach to the "comparative flyoff" and its use in the Dual-Role Fighter source selection. These other critics included General Dynamics itself, which formally protested the fact that the F-16XL was being inappropriately compared to the much larger and more expensive F-15E. This controversial aspect of the F-16XL flight demonstration program and the DRF source selection are discussed in more detail in the section on the Dual-Role Fighter Competition. The summary in Table 4 lists specific test categories along with the number of flights dedicated to each category by individual test aircraft through the end of Phase I flight testing.

Table 4.
F-16XL Phase I flight-test summary

Subject	F-16XL-1 Flights	F-16XL-2 Flights	Percent of Total
Stability and Control	33	19	14
High AoA	29	—	8
Flutter	16	4	5
Structural Loads	2	30	9
Performance	60	55	31
Propulsion	1	4	1
Weapon Separation	9	17	7
Operation Ult. Eval.	50	40	25
Total Flights	200	169	100%

Open Issues at the End of Phase I Testing

Some aircraft handling and flying qualities items that were uncovered during Phase I testing were determined to be significant enough to require additional investigation during later phases of the Air Force's F-16XL flight-test program. These included the following items that were still in the process of being addressed when the program was terminated by the Air Force in 1985.

- Excessive nose-down pitch trim was required in order to maintain level flight at transonic and supersonic flight conditions. At high dynamic pressures, limitations on elevator hinge-moment capacity were very restrictive. At lower altitudes, the trim requirements on the elevons exceeded hydraulic system capabilities at speeds in excess of 650 KCAS.
- Roll rates degraded rapidly to unacceptable levels at dynamic pressures above 1,200 pounds per square inch. During maximum-rate rolling maneuvers at higher g-levels at speeds above Mach 1.4, strong roll oscillations were encountered. This was determined to be due to improper aileron-rudder interconnect coordination by the flight control system.
- The 2.5-Hz pitch oscillation, or "pitch gallop" phenomenon, was encountered in the Mach number region from 0.9 to 0.95. The amplitude of the stable pitch gallop varied as a function of both angle of attack and altitude. It prevented accurate air-to-air target tracking during higher-g-level maneuvering, often frustrating the CTF pilots. Pitch gallop was the subject of an extensive follow-on investigation that continued during the remainder of the F-16XL test program. The results are discussed in some detail in a follow-on section.
- G-overshoot, or "pitch inflection," characterized by an unanticipated g-spike when maximum g-level was commanded by the pilot in the 0.95-to-1.05 Mach range. This resulted in the aircraft exceeding the maximum 9-g-load operational limit, resulting in increased structural loads on the airframe when the aircraft was rapidly decelerating through the transonic region.[42]

Follow-On Flight-Test Activities

Initial follow-on testing evaluated F-16XL flutter and performance characteristics with various external store loadings. These payloads are listed in a follow-on section. They included six SUU-65s and wingtip-mounted AIM-9 Sidewinder missiles, flown both with and without 370-gallon fuel tanks. The full load of six air-to-air weapons was carried with two 600-gallon fuel tanks and six AGM-65 Maverick missiles. An AGM-65 was successfully launched from F-16XL-1 during its 375th flight on March 29, 1985. Additional flight-test efforts were focused on resolving the pitch gallop issue and obtaining comprehensive airframe vibration data. Stability and control test maneuvers prepared the way for high-AoA testing at more extreme flight conditions than had been previously evaluated during Phase I. A major aspect of this phase of the flight-test effort was focused on obtaining stability and control and performance data with the leading-edge flaps locked at the zero deflection position. Approximately 40 test flights were conducted to verify the aft cg limit, identify the effects of 370-gallon tanks on high-AoA handling qualities, and evaluate aircraft characteristics with locked leading-edge flaps.

During these tests, the F-16XL was determined to have a relatively unlimited maneuvering envelope for all store configurations tested. Handling qualities were not degraded with any of the external store configurations evaluated. Longitudinal maneuvering characteristics were evaluated using constant Mach number turns and maximum-g slowdown turns. Static stability was assessed using 1-g accelerations and decelerations. In the air-to-air configuration, the cg location varied over a region that extended from 44.7 percent to 46.4 percent of the wing's mean effective chord as fuel was burned. The aircraft was tested over the cg range from 44.7 to 47.5 percent; this allowed flight testing to be conducted with the cg both forward and aft of the neutral point of the F-16XL. With the cg forward of the neutral point, the aircraft was statically stable. When the cg was aft of the neutral point, the aircraft was statically unstable, relying on continuous inputs from the fly-by-wire flight control system to maintain adequate control. At subsonic Mach numbers, external stores did not cause a shift in neutral point. An increase in pitch control surface deflection was required to maintain 1-g trim above 0.95 Mach number. This was due to a decrease in pitch surface control effectiveness and the aft shift of the neutral point as sonic speed was approached. Trim requirements without external tanks were similar with all weapons loads. When external tanks were carried, 2 to 3 degrees of additional trailing-edge-down trim were required for a given cg location. While the F-16XL had positive longitudinal static stability over all Mach numbers tested, its pitch stability was very low at higher angles of attach and low airspeeds.[43]

High-Angle-of-Attack Testing

The high-AoA flying qualities of the F-16XL, both with and without external stores, were rated as outstanding during the Air Force flight-test evaluation. No airspeed or AoA maneuver limitations were identified with the cg as far aft as 47 percent of the wing mean aerodynamic chord. When AoA excursions did occur, the aircraft rapidly recovered to controlled flight without any pilot actions or control inputs being required. Control response was excellent, even at the very low airspeeds that were encountered while the pilot was maneuvering the aircraft to lower angles of attack For follow-on high AoA and departure resistance flight testing conducted during the summer of 1983, F-16XL-1 was again equipped with the Quadra Pod spin recovery parachute installation. The Quadra Pod spin chute installation was mounted on the aft fuselage in the beginning of August 1984 and was removed in early September when the high-AoA portion of the flight-test program was completed. High-AoA test maneuvers included pitch-yaw-roll doublets, sideslips,

1-g and maximum-g decelerations, maximum commanded rolls, and climb reversals. A number of extreme maneuvers were used to "trick" the aircraft into exceeding the programmed maximum AoA limit. Steep, high-pitch-attitude climbs, often reaching an attitude of 90 degrees (vertical to the horizon), were employed. Other techniques included a 180-degree roll followed by a full-aft pitch control input, forward push maneuvers, and maneuvering while holding a full-aft control input.[44]

Using these techniques, uncommanded AoA excursions were obtained at angles of attack above those imposed by the AoA limiter installed in the F-16XL's flight control system. This was achieved by accomplishing both upright and inverted constant pitch attitude climbs to minimum airspeed while conducting repeated roll reversals in the AoA range of known low pitch stability (16 to 24 degrees AoA) and with the aircraft cg near the allowable aft limit. In some cases, a 90-degree pitch attitude (vertical) climb was maintained to zero airspeed. During the subsequent tail slide and recovery to a nose-down pitch attitude, extreme AoA excursions greater than +120 and –90 degrees were encountered. Total recovery time from start of the tail slide to the point where the pilot was able to fly the aircraft was about 20 seconds. These AoA excursions were the only type of departure from controlled flight that was encountered during the F-16XL flight-test program during flight testing both with and without external stores. Pitch recovery maneuvers were illustrated, as adopted from Talty.[45] So-called "deep stall" tendencies (such as existed with both the standard F-16 and the Swedish J 35 Draken fighter at higher angles of attack) were not encountered during the F-16XL test program.[46] This result was in agreement with results from the Langley Differential Maneuvering Simulator, where the same NASA team that had worked the original F-16 deep stall problem had also worked the F-16XL. The aircraft demonstrated high resistance to inadvertent loss of control or spin entry. The F-16XL was tested with its center of gravity located as far aft as 47 percent of the MAC. The planned high-AoA stability investigation at the full-aft cg limit of 47.5 percent MAC was not completed at the time the F-16XL program was cancelled in mid-1985.[47]

The lateral-directional static stability of the F-16XL was evaluated by wings-level sideslips to the maximum rudder deflection or by applying the maximum lateral control surface deflection required to maintain wings-level flight. Lateral-directional stability was not significantly affected by external stores. As angle of attack was increased above 20 degrees, directional stability began to reduce approaching zero at 24 degrees AoA; however, this reduction in directional stability was not noticeable to the pilot. The lateral control power and rolling performance of the aircraft were also rated as excellent, both with and without external stores. Roll accelerations and roll-time constants consistently were better than those of the standard F-16A. During rolling maneuvers with external weapons loads, the automatic flight control system in the F-16XL effectively reduced the maximum allowable roll rate when the air-to-ground mode was selected by the pilot. With the cockpit selector switch in the air-to-ground mode, maximum allowable roll rate was reduced to 230 degrees per second from the 308 degrees per second available in the air-to-air configuration. During maneuvering flight, the actual allowable roll rate was automatically scheduled by the flight control computer as a function of aircraft angle of attack to prevent overstressing the aircraft or encountering potential out-of-control situations. This insured that the flight control computer maintained precise control over roll and nose-pointing maneuvers when the aircraft was carrying heavy external loads. In addition, tendencies to overshoot or lose control during rapid rolls were minimized. CTF pilot comments were very positive when discussing the responsiveness and maneuverability of the aircraft during ground attack profiles.[48]

Weapons Testing and Loading Configurations

A wide variety of weapons and external store combinations were evaluated using both the single-seat and two-seat F-16XL aircraft. The drag characteristics of the aircraft with these payloads and their effects on performance and handling qualities were determined. However, weapons release and separation testing was not accomplished with all of the configurations flown. In most regions of the flight envelope, flight-test results confirmed GD-provided performance predictions. However, in the transonic and supersonic regions of the flight envelope, the contractor's predictions of excess thrust with most store loadings were anywhere from 10 to 20 percent higher (poorer) than what was actually demonstrated during flight test. This discrepancy held true for both military thrust (100 percent power without the use of afterburner) and maximum (full afterburning) thrust. When the aircraft was configured with SUU-65 Tactical Munitions Dispensers (TMDs), drag was as much as 30 percent higher than had been predicted at transonic and supersonic speeds. The payload configurations that were tested included the combinations of weapons and stores listed below. These weapon payloads were carried on the external store stations shown in the illustration.

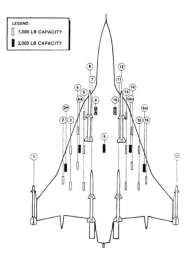

The F-16XL could carry a range of external stores at 29 different locations on the airframe. (USAF)

- Standard air-to-air payload (four AIM-120s plus two AIM-9Ls on wingtip missile launchers)

- Limited air-to-air payload (four AIM-120s only, no wingtip AIM-9Ls, no wingtip missile launchers)

- Standard air-to-air payload plus one 300-gallon centerline fuel tank

- Standard air-to-air payload plus two 370-gallon underwing drop tanks

- Standard air-to-air payload plus six 500-pound Mk-82 bombs

- Standard air-to-air payload plus 12 500-pound Mk-82 bombs

- Standard air-to-air payload plus 12 500-pound Mk-82 bombs and two 370-gallon drop tanks

- Standard air-to-air payload plus two 2,000-pound MK-84 bombs

- Standard air-to-air payload plus four 2,000-pound MK-84 bombs

- Standard air-to-air payload plus six SUU-65 Tactical Munitions Dispensers

- Standard air-to-air payload plus six SUU-65 TMDs and one 300-gallon centerline fuel tank

- Standard air-to-air payload plus six SUU-65 TMDs and two 370-gallon drop tanks

- Standard air-to-air payload plus two BDU-38s and two 370-gallon drop tanks

- Standard air-to-air payload plus six AGM-65 Maverick missiles

Weapons delivery and separation characteristics were rated by the CTF pilots as excellent for those weapons released from the F-16XL during the flight-test program. These included a total of 218 Mk-82 500-pound bombs, dropped on 37 test flights; 18 Mk-84 2,000-pound bombs, released on 7 flights; and 6 800-pound CBU-58 tactical munitions dispensers, ripple released

An unguided AGM-65 Maverick missile was launched from F-16XL-1 store station 3 on March 29, 1985. Weapons carried on this flight included four dummy AIM-120s, two AIM-9Ls, and six AGM-65 missiles. (USAF)

on a single flight. Other ripple releases included 4 Mk-84s and 12 Mk-82s. As mentioned earlier, a single unguided AGM-65 Maverick air-to-surface missile was successfully launched from F-16XL-1 on March 29, 1985. Over the course of the entire flight-test program, 233 F-16XL missions were flown with bombs. This represented about 29 percent of all F-16XL test missions. AGM-65 Maverick missiles were carried on six flights. Fifteen flights were dedicated to investigating the effects of firing the M61 cannon. During these flights, more than 7,300 rounds of 20 mm ammunition were successfully fired.[49] The complete F-16XL Weapon Separation Log listed by specific flight and pilot is reproduced in Appendix B.

F110 Slimline Engine Testing and LNSI Inlet Evaluation

Evaluation of the General Electric F110 Slimline engine was a significant aspect of the F-16XL-2 flight-test program. Airframe, instrumentation, and control modifications were accomplished to enable the aircraft to accommodate the GE F110-GE-100 Slimline engine. These modifications were completed at the GD factory in Fort Worth in mid-July 1984. After two functional check flights from Carswell AFB, F-16XL-2 was flown to Edwards on July 20 to begin the F110 Slimline engine evaluation. Initial testing primarily involved the evaluation of engine transient and air-start capabilities. These objectives were accomplished during F-16XL-2 flights 276 through 281. During flight number 282 on August 17, 1984, telemetered data received in the flight-test control room indicated that an engine compressor stall was imminent. The aircraft was at Mach 0.95 at an altitude of 30,000 feet. GD Project Pilot John Fergione had just switched from the F110 primary engine control mode to the secondary (SEC) control mode. The secondary engine control mode was intended to provide the pilot with a limited "get home" capability in the event of problems with the digital engine control system. When operating in the secondary mode, F110 engine thrust was limited to 70 percent of its full military thrust and afterburner operation was precluded.[50] When Fergione switched over to the secondary mode, the F110 fan duct pressure sensor (known as Pressure Sensor 14, or PS14) had registered an extremely low reading. The engine experts in the test control room believed that the low fan duct pressure reading signaled that an engine stall had occurred.[51] Discussions between the control room and the pilot resulted in a decision to abort the mission. Fergione landed without incident on Lakebed Runway 15 at Edwards AFB. Subsequent investigation determined that the fan duct pressure sensor instrumentation had registered an erroneous value and actual engine operation was in fact normal.

Flight testing resumed on August 20, 1984, with an uneventful flight. However, the next day, during XL-2 flight number 284, the control room received a telemetered engine stall warning indication. This was similar to the one previously encountered and was from the same pressure sensor. The pilot, again GD's John Fergione, switched over to the secondary engine control mode and made a precautionary simulated flameout approach to a landing on Runway 22 at Edwards AFB.[52] This time, a detailed investigation of the F110 engine revealed a crack in a pressure line. Engine operation was being affected even though no abnormal indications were seen by the pilot. In an attempt to resolve the problem, General Electric field representatives reinforced the PS14 sensor manifold fitting locations with an epoxy and fiberglass mixture. This reinforcement added additional mass to the manifold. Perhaps not surprisingly, ground testing of the unsophisticated quick fix showed that the natural vibration frequency of the manifold had been significantly changed. Increased manifold vibration amplitudes were now being encountered, causing the epoxy reinforcement to separate from the fan frame. The next attempt to resolve the issue used bolt-on manifold fittings along with a new "flex-line" manifold. This approach appeared to work during ground tests. The necessary safety of flight paperwork that allowed F-16XL-2 flight testing to resume was signed by the AFFTC commander, Maj. Gen. Peter W. Odgers, on October 8, 1984. The following day, a functional check flight was successful and F110 flight envelope expansion resumed.[53]

Inflight Afterburner Spray Bar Failure

After the F110 test effort resumed, a program of successful air starts, engine/inlet compatibility, and inverted flight demonstrations continued without any problems from F-16XL-2 flight 286 through flight 305. However, on November 20, 1984, during flight 306, the F-16 chase pilot reported seeing a large plume of flame extending about three airplane lengths behind the nozzle. This happened during afterburner operation following a go-around from a simulated flameout landing. John Fergione immediately throttled back to idle and performed an uneventful emergency landing on the lakebed at Edwards. Postflight inspection of the engine revealed that a broken afterburner spray bar had caused the long plume. The resulting abnormal flame pattern had burned through the engine nozzle in the seven to ten o'clock region, when viewed from behind the aircraft. There was also significant fire damage to the left speed brake. A subsequent investigation by General Electric determined that a high fuel-to-air ratio had caused excessive stress levels in the engine, especially in the afterburner section. The fuel-to-air ratio was reduced, and successful ground testing was followed by a spray bar evaluation flight on January 11, 1985. Instrumented spray bar data was collected during flights 307 and 308. These data confirmed that spray bar stress levels were now within the acceptable tolerance range established by GE. One additional F110 envelope expansion flight was conducted following the spray bar stress evaluation before the aircraft was ferried back to Fort Worth on January 28, 1985, for installation of the Large Normal Shock Inlet.[54]

LNSI Testing

F-16XL-2 would be absent from the flight-test program from January 29 until June 25, 1985. During this extended period at the factory, an extensive set of modifications and structural inspections were completed, requiring a total of 105 work days. The Large Normal Shock Inlet was installed, along with additional test instrumentation. Other airframe structural modifications were required based on the results of the inspections. The F110 Slimline test engine that had been in the aircraft was returned to the General Electric factory at Evandale, OH, where it was upgraded to the latest configuration. A functional check flight with the LNSI installation and the upgraded F110 engine was conducted at Fort Worth on June 26, 1985. A second functional check flight on June 28 was followed by a ferry flight to Edwards AFB that afternoon. Once at Edwards, the new spray bar configuration was tested. This was followed by a series of combined structural loads and stability and control evaluations of the aircraft. These included both high-g and elevated-AoA maneuvers to assess the effects of the larger inlet on aircraft performance and handling qualities. Instrumentation verified that structural loads on the airframe with the LNSI installed were not significantly increased. Based on these results, the aircraft was cleared to its original maneuver envelope. During subsequent flight testing of F-16XL-2 with the LNSI, some airframe vibration was encountered. There was insufficient time remaining in the F-16XL flight-test program to address the airframe vibration issue associated with the LNSI. However, it was one of the recommendations for follow-on investigation.[55]

On flight number 324, the F110 engine's fuel-to-air ratio was increased to maximize engine performance with the

F-16XL-2 fitted with the extended air data boom used to measure angle of attack, yaw angle, and static and dynamic pressures. (USAF Photograph courtesy of SMSgt. Norman Taylor, USAF [ret.])

higher mass airflow rate available from the LNSI. The LNSI provided a mass flow rate of 270 pounds of air per second as compared to the 254 pounds per second for the standard inlet. The change in fuel-to-air ratio required another round of spray bar evaluation flights, which were successfully completed. The final F110 test effort consisted of completing a comparative evaluation of engine performance using both JP-4 and JP-8 jet fuels. Additional stability and control and performance testing included data gathered at low altitude on flight 358 over the Pacific Ocean off Vandenberg AFB, CA. After this flight, the engine was removed from the aircraft and replaced with the backup engine that had been held in reserve. Following a successful functional check flight at Edwards, XL-2 was ferried to General Dynamics in Fort Worth on October 1, 1985. Once there, it was placed in flyable storage along with XL-1. This was the final flight of the Air Force F-16XL flight-test program. It marked the 361st test flight for F-16XL-2. The aircraft had logged a total of 407.1 flight hours.[56]

Pitch Gallop Investigation

Preliminary observation of what came to be called pitch gallop had been noted during the very first flight of F-16XL-1 on July 3, 1982. The Air Force flight-test evaluation had confirmed that pitch axis oscillations were generally encountered in the Mach 0.90–0.95 region, becoming more pronounced as altitude decreased and g-level and angle of attack increased. This phenomenon had not been seen when flying the early version of the General Dynamics F-16XL flight simulator. Aircraft characteristics that were modeled in the simulator had been based on aerodynamic data derived from early wind tunnel testing and an analytical model of the F-16XL flight control computer (FCC). Actual flight testing revealed that there was a pronounced increase in F-16XL pitch surface control effectiveness in the high subsonic Mach number range. The magnitude of this pitch effectiveness increase was much greater than had been predicted from wind tunnel–derived data. GD modified the flight simulator using actual flight-test-derived aerodynamic data. However, they still had to incorporate an additional 30-degree phase lag to induce the simulator to create the gallop effect that was observed during actual flight testing. When aerodynamic data derived from actual flight testing was used in conjunction with an actual flight control computer and system hardware instead of the earlier analytical model, the simulator produced a longitudinal pitch oscillation. General characteristics of the pitch oscillation in the modified computer were similar to the pitch gallop encountered in flight testing. Subsequent investigation confirmed that the analytical model of the F-16XL used in the original development of the flight control computer did not accurately represent actual aircraft hardware. Significantly, the aircraft hardware models used in the computer simulation had undergone many independent verification and validation tests prior to and during the test program without the problem having been detected.[57]

The Air Force investigated many possible causes for the pitch gallop phenomenon. Exterior aerodynamics and the pitch axis flight control system were found to be within design specifications. However, flight testing did determine that the autopilot had some effect on the severity of the pitch oscillation, especially at higher altitudes. Changes to the pitch axis gain in the flight control computer were found to have the greatest effect. A notch-type filter was inserted in the pitch control path, and a multiplier of 0.50 or 0.75 was applied after the basic pitch gain was scheduled by the flight control computer. Both multipliers reduced the magnitude of the pitch gallop problem. A pitch gain reduction of 25 percent in the flight control computer was subsequently used as an interim fix for the remainder of the F-16XL flight-test program. However, the Air Force did not consider this interim approach to be a final solution to the pitch oscillation issue as the actual root cause of the problem had yet to be determined. Even the modified flight simulator did not fully replicate the observed pitch oscillation. Therefore, the Flight Test Center decided that a dedicated flight-test effort was needed. This would be focused on determining the frequency response of the total F-16XL system. For this purpose, 11 flight-test missions were dedicated to the pitch gallop evaluation. Actual aircraft hardware and aerodynamics would be used with the pitch gain and phase angle in the flight control computer varied over a range of in-flight conditions. Data obtained using this approach would be used to refine the flight control system to eliminate the gallop problem.

Another goal was to improve the fidelity of the flight simulator at high subsonic Mach numbers.

To determine the system gain and phase angle of the total aircraft, an in-flight excitation system was developed and installed in F-16XL-1. The objective of the in-flight excitation tests was to obtain the system gain and phase angle at specific excitation frequencies and to identify any nonlinearities in gain or phase angle as a function of control surface position based on excitation amplitude. In the test approach developed for the F-16XL, the excitation signals were inserted into the pitch axis control loop, and the system response to pitch inputs from the pilot was measured. The excitation installation was intended to determine the actual FCS pitch channel gain and phase margins with various aircraft configurations and flight conditions. This in-flight excitation approach had been used during flutter and flight control testing with the F-16. In those earlier tests, excitation signals had been sent to the flight control surfaces in order to stimulate the structural modes of the aircraft in various regions of the flight envelope. The excitation system was pilot-activated through a modification to the autopilot panel. When activated, increased levels of aileron/elevon movement would be induced, along with various frequencies of control surface movement. Either a random or one of three sinusoidal control surface movement frequencies could be selected.[58] Maximum signal amplitude was limited to ±1.8-g commands to the pitch control surfaces.

Pitch oscillation investigations conducted during 1985 involved excitation testing throughout the F-16XL's flight envelope. The major focus was on the high subsonic region, known to be the most troublesome area for pitch oscillations. All excitation tests were used the 25 percent gain reduction in the flight control computer pitch path that had been adopted earlier as an interim fix to the pitch oscillation problem. Test results determined that the flight control system installed in the F-16XL prototypes had a high pitch gain with very close to a –180 degrees of phase angle in the high subsonic Mach number region. This was true at all altitudes flown during the excitation tests. A nonlinear effect on system gain as a function of control surface position was apparent from the testing. Ground excitation testing of the system was subsequently used to investigate the nonlinearly of the system in the absence of aerodynamic effects. These ground tests also confirmed the same nonlinearity in gain with neutral pitch trim. This nonlinearity in system gain was found to be a characteristic of the integrated servo-actuators used on the F-16XL prototype pitch control surfaces. The actuator nonlinearity was of sufficient magnitude to drive the aircraft system, consisting of aircraft and aerodynamics, into a limit-cycle oscillation. This was defined as a gain of 1.0 and a phase angle of –180 degrees in the 0.90 to 0.95 Mach range. However, this limit cycle resulted in a stable oscillation that had no tendency to diverge or become unstable. This was due to the fact that as pitch control surface deflection increased in magnitude, system gain got smaller, resulting in a stable system. The pitch oscillation test excitation procedure used on the F-16XL was successful in producing data that correctly defined the aircraft frequency response throughout the flight envelope. These data would have been used to refine the flight control system had the aircraft completed full-scale development.[59]

Refining the F-16XL's Flight Control System: Issues and Resolutions

As earlier discussed, a number of F-16XL flight control–related issues were encountered during the Air Force flight-test program. Many were resolved; however, others remained open when the program ended in 1985. Those flight control issues that were partially or fully resolved included the following items, along with the relevant corrective actions.[60]

Issue	Resolution
Attitude control during aerobraking on landing rollout.	Improved by incorporation of a revised pitch rate command system.
Roll performance at higher dynamic pressures.	Improved by modifications to the aileron roll schedule.
High Mach number, elevated-g oscillatory roll rates.	Eliminated by modifications to the aileron-rudder interconnect.
Longitudinal limit cycle (pitch gallop) encountered in the Mach number range from 0.9 to 0.95.	Partially resolved with a forward pitch loop gain reduction. This modification also improved the low-altitude pitch gallop that was encountered in turbulent conditions.
Low-speed, high-AoA nose-down pitch response.	Improved with a flight control computer software modification.

Some issues associated with the F-16XL control system remained open for possible follow-on investigation when the program ended. The low pitch damping and oscillatory roll rates encountered at higher angles of attack and low airspeeds, identified during Air Force Phase I testing, were still unresolved. Two additional deficiencies resulted from changes to the flight control computer made during the course of the Air Force flight-test program. These were as follows:

1. A tendency for a Pilot Induced Oscillation (PIO) to develop on takeoff and during landing approach. This PIO tendency had been encountered by some CTF pilots following incorporation of the revised pitch rate command system.
2. Larger g-overshoots above the 9g design limit encountered during a maximum command slow down turn through the transonic Mach range. This resulted from the reduction in forward loop gain in the flight control computer that had been incorporated in an attempt to correct the longitudinal limit cycle (pitch gallop) problem.[61]

General Dynamics made the following six recommendations for additional F-16XL flight control system development and flight testing. These were, of course, contingent on the Air Force funding a follow-on F-16E or F-16F full-scale development program, which did not happen.

1. Determine the cause and correct the low speed damping issue that had been encountered at high AoA and low speeds.
2. Optimize the takeoff and landing pitch rate control laws to eliminate the tendency for development of pilot induced oscillations (PIOs).
3. Optimize the pitch control laws to eliminate g-overshoot while at the same time avoiding the longitudinal limit cycle while maintaining the excellent ride and handling capabilities of the aircraft.
4. Evaluate revised a pitch gradient implementation to determine if handling qualities during aerial target tracking are improved.
5. Optimize the aileron-rudder interconnect in the region between Mach 0.9 and Mach 1.2 especially for elevated g rolls.
6. Optimize the rudder fadeout implementation scheme at high angles of attack to eliminate the AoA excursions observed when carrying 370-gallon external fuel tanks.[62]

Air Force Flight-Test Program Summary

The Air Force F-16XL flight demonstration program extended from the first flight of F-16XL-1 on July 3, 1983, to October 1, 1985, when F-16XL-2 was ferried to General Dynamics at Fort Worth. Once there, it was placed in flyable storage along with F-16XL-1, which had been delivered on August 14. The two aircraft had accumulated a total of 939.7 hours on 798 flights. Better than two-thirds of these flights were flown without any system discrepancies being recorded. Specific flight demonstration activities are summarized in Appendix C, with test activities that were presented by engineering objective in Appendix D.[63] Flight Logs for both F-16XL-1 and F-16XL-2 are contained in Appendix E.

Table 5.
F-16XL demonstrator aircraft flight activity
(July 3, 1982, through October 1, 1985)

Flights			
Aircraft	Air-to-Air	Air-to-Ground	Total
F-16XL-1	318	119	437
F-16XL-2	230	131	361
Total	**548**	**250**	**798**

Flight Hours			
Aircraft	Air-to-Air	Air-to-Ground	Total
F-16XL-1	400.0	132.6	532.6
F-16XL-2	283.1	124.0	407.1
Total	**683.1**	**256.6**	**939.7**

Flights Without Discrepancies		
Aircraft	Number of Flights	Percentage
F-16XL-1	336/437	76.9
F-16XL-2	252/361	69.8
Total	**588/798**	**73.7**

Pilots and Sorties			
Source	Air-to-Air	Air-to-Ground	Total
GD (5)	152	51	203
USAF (17)	299	225	524
Other (3)	3	2	5
Total (25)	**454**	**278**	**732**

Aerial Refueling			
Flights and Refueling	Air-to-Air	Air-to-Ground	Total
Total Flights	71	56	127
Wet Refuelings	100	75	175

* Pilot/sorties data valid through June 15, 1985

Fourteen pilots had been fully checked out in the F-16XL during the Air Force flight demonstration program. Of these, five were General Dynamics project pilots and the remainder were Air Force officers. Thirty-six VIPs were given demonstration flights in the two-seat F-16XL-2. Most were senior Air Force officers in command and staff positions involving fighter operations and weapons systems acquisition. In addition, the Israeli Air Force Chief of Staff flew the aircraft, as did NASA experimental test pilot Bill Dana, who flew with Air Force Lt. Col. Joe Bill Dryden on August 12, 1983. Dana would subsequently serve as chief engineer at the NASA Dryden Flight Research Center from 1993 until 1998. During his tenure as chief engineer, both F-16XLs would be based at Dryden, where they would be extensively modified for flight research into supersonic laminar flow.[64] Paul Thayer, then deputy secretary of defense (and reportedly a strong proponent of the F-16XL), flew with Lt. Col. Marty Bushnell on August 17, 1983.[65] In addition, journalists from *Aviation Week & Space Technology* (Clifton Berry) and *Air Force Magazine* (Bob Ropelewski) flew on separate demonstration flights with GD project pilot Jim McKinney during late August and early September 1983. Both Ropelewski and Berry were qualified pilots who were very familiar with the capabilities of the standard F-16. Their in-depth articles, containing interesting and generally accurate assessments of F-16XL performance, were published in these widely read publications prior to the February 1984 Air Force Dual-Role Fighter decision.[66] The F-16XL VIP Flight Log is reproduced in Appendix F.[67]

Endnotes

1. F-16E was the designation that was to be assigned to the two-seat F-16XL had it been selected for further development and production. The two-seat variant would have been the F-16F.

2. Hillaker, "F-16XL Flight Test Program Overview"; Talty, "F-16XL Demonstrates New Capabilities in its Flight Test Program at Edwards AFB, California"; James O. Young, "AFFTC History, 1 Jan 1983–30 Sep 1984." All AFFTC History documents are stored at the AFFTC History Office, Edwards AFB.

3. GD, "F-16XL Flight Test Program—Final Report."

4. Ibid.

5. Ibid.

6. GD, "F-16XL Flight Test Program—Final Report"; "AFFTC History, 1 Jan 1982–30 Dec 1982"; Robert R. Ropelewski, "F-16XL Shows Advances in Range, Ride and Flying Qualities," Aviation Week & Space Technology (September 26, 1983): pp. 62–71; GD, "F-16XL Flight Test Program—Final Report"; Hillaker, F-16XL presentation to the Lone Star Aero Club.

7. "AFFTC History, 1 Jan 1982–30 Sep 1982."

8. An Air Force Academy graduate, a superlative airman, and a gregarious, ever-helpful individual, Joe Bill Dryden had been the lead TAC pilot on the Northrop YF-17 portion of the Lightweight Fighter competition in which the YF-17 was evaluated against the YF-16. After leaving the Air Force, he became a test pilot with GD/Lockheed Martin in Fort Worth, during which time he mentored many airmen from many nations transitioning into the F-16. Sadly, Dryden was killed on May 24, 1993, near Mineral Wells, TX, during a predelivery factory acceptance flight test in an F-16C. His passing was much mourned by the global Viper community, which he had done so much to shape.

9. GD, "F-16XL Flight Test Program—Final Report."

10. Author unlisted, "F-16XLs Pass 100 Hours," Flight International (December 11, 1982): p. 1666; GD, "F-16F (XL) Demonstration Aircraft Flight Activity," foldout chart, General Dynamics Corporation, Fort Worth Division (undated, circa 1985).

11. "AFFTC History, 1 Jan 1982–31 Dec 1982."

12. Ibid.; Talty, "F-16XL Demonstrates New Capabilities in its Flight Test Program at Edwards AFB, California."

13. Ibid.; GD, "F-16XL Flight Test Program—Final Report"; Hillaker, "F-16XL Flight Test Program Overview."

14. F. Clifton Berry, Jr., "The Revolutionary Evolution of the F-16XL," Air Force Magazine 66, no. 11 (November 1983).

15. Talty, "F-16XL Demonstrates New Capabilities in its Flight Test Program"; GD, "F-16XL Flight Test Program—Final Report."

16. Much later, during the NASA flight-test program (with the aircraft totally clean of any external stores, including armament pylons, and powered by the higher-thrust General Electric F110-GE-129 engine, F-16XL-2 demonstrated sustained Mach 1.1 flight in Military (non-afterburning) power at an altitude of 30,000 feet.

17. Talty, "F-16XL Demonstrates New Capabilities in its Flight Test Program."

18. Graham Warwick, "US Fighter Options," Flight International 124, no. 3071 (July 16, 1983): pp. 139–146.

19. Talty, "F-16XL Demonstrates New Capabilities in its Flight Test Program."

20. Ibid. Patrick K. Talty joined the F-16XL CTF as deputy director for engineering in 1984. A Distinguished Graduate of the Air Force Test Pilot School, he later served as an assistant professor of engineering and director of research at the United States Air Force Academy and as deputy director of technology in the Strategic Defense Initiative Office.

21. Ropelewski, "F-16XL Shows Advances in Range, Ride and Flying Qualities."

22. "AFFTC History, 1 Jan 1983–30 Sep 1984"; Talty, "The F-16XL Demonstrates New Capabilities in its Flight Test Program"; GD, "F-16XL Flight Test Program—Final Report."

23. Ibid.

24. Ibid.

25. Ibid.

26. The influence of ground effect on a cranked-arrow wing was of great interest to the HSR program since the proposed High-Speed Civil Transport (HSCT) was intended to have a similar wing. In this context, NASA would later use the F-16XL in a special research project that assessed the influence of ground effect on the aerodynamics of a cranked-arrow wing. This NASA research project is discussed later in this book, based on test results presented in Robert E. Curry, "Dynamic Ground Effect for a Cranked Arrow Wing Airplane," NASA TM 4799 (1997).

27. "AFFTC History, 1 Jan 1983–30 Sep 1984"; Talty, "The F-16XL Demonstrates New Capabilities in its Flight Test Program"; GD, "F-16XL Flight Test Program—Final Report."

28. Ibid.
29. The author checked out in the Convair F-102A in 1962, eventually accumulating about 500 hours in the delta-wing aircraft. For a detailed discussion of both the F-102 and F-106 aircraft and their development programs, see Bill Yenne, Convair Deltas: From Sea Dart to Hustler (North Branch, MN: Specialty Press, 2009).
30. The Edwards AFB runway is located at an elevation of 2,310.5 feet above sea level. This higher elevation somewhat increases both take-off and landing roll distances compared to operations from runways at lower elevations.
31. "AFFTC History, 1 Jan 1983–30 Sep 1984"; Talty, "The F-16XL Demonstrates New Capabilities in its Flight Test Program."
32. During the NASA research effort with the F-16XL, a similar issue was identified during high-rate rolling maneuvers, which NASA pilots referred to as "roll ratcheting." Investigation of this phenomena was the subject of a dedicated NASA research project discussed in depth in John W. Smith and Terry Montgomery, "Biomechanically Induced and Controller Coupled Oscillations Experienced on the F-16XL During Rolling Maneuvers," NASA TM 4752 (1996).
33. "AFFTC History, 1 Jan 1983–30 Sep 1984"; GD, "F-16XL Flight Test Program—Final Report."
34. Ibid.
35. Ibid.
36. Ibid
37. Ibid. For comparison purposes, a combat-loaded F-16 typically refueled from the KC-135 tanker at altitudes approaching 30,000 feet. Higher refueling altitudes are preferable for avoiding weather and for increased fuel efficiency.
38. Ibid.
39. Ibid.
40. "AFFTC History, 1 Jan 1983–30 Sep 1984"; GD, "F-16XL Flight Test Program—Final Report."
41. Ibid.
42. GD, "F-16XL Flight Test Program—Final Report."
43. Talty, "The F-16XL Demonstrates New Capabilities in its Flight Test Program"; GD, "F-16XL Flight Test Program—Final Report."
44. Ibid.
45. Ibid.
46. In a deep stall, an aircraft typically enters a stable, high-AoA descent that becomes progressively steeper and is characterized by

pronounced resistance to conventional stall-recovery techniques. Deep stall has been responsible for several notable aircraft accidents, most memorably an accident to a British BAC 1-11 jetliner that claimed a crack test crew captained by Mike Lithgow, a pioneering British supersonic pilot.

47. Ibid.

48. Ropelewski, "F-16XL Shows Advances in Range, Ride and Flying Qualities"; Talty, "The F-16XL Demonstrates New Capabilities in its Flight Test Program."

49. GD, "F-16XL Flight Test Program—Final Report"; Ropelewski, "F-16XL Shows Advances in Range, Ride and Flying Qualities"; Talty, "The F-16XL Demonstrates New Capabilities in its Flight Test Program."

50. Walter D. Hutto, F110 Fighter Power: F-16/F110-GE-100 Pilot Awareness Program (Cincinnati, OH: General Electric Company, 1987).

51. Alireza R. Behbahani, "Need for Robust Sensors for Inherently Fail-Safe Gas Turbine Engine Controls, Monitoring, and Prognostics," Air Force Research Laboratory, Wright-Patterson AFB, AFRL-PR-WP-TP-2007-217 (November 2006), published in the Proceedings of the 52nd International Instrumentation Symposium, Cleveland, OH, May 7 through May 11, 2006 (2006).

52. Fergione joined General Dynamics, now Lockheed Martin Aeronautics Company, as an experimental test pilot in 1981 after service as a naval aviator and then as an instructor at the U.S. Navy Test Pilot School. He spent 2 years as General Dynamics F-16XL project pilot and conducted the first flights with the General Electric F-110-GE-100 engine, both in the F-16XL and in the F-16C. Assigned to the F-16 Combined Test Force at Edwards AFB from 1985 to 2002, he was also the GD facility manager for much of that time. Fergione was chief test pilot for the F-16 (non-Block 60) programs until late 2002, when he became the F-22A experimental test pilot. A fellow and past president of the Society of Experimental Test Pilots (SETP), Fergione has logged over 6,400 flying hours.

53. GD, "F-16XL Flight Test Program—Final Report."

54. Ibid.

55. Ibid.

56. Ibid.

57. Tierney, S.S., "Inflight Excitation of the F-16XL," AIAA Paper 86-9782, April 1982.

58. GD, "F-16XL Flight Test Program—Final Report."

59. Tierney, "Inflight Excitation of the F-16XL."
60. GD, "F-16XL Flight Test Program—Final Report."
61. Ibid.
62. Ibid.
63. Ibid.
64. Bill Dana, a graduate of the U.S. Military Academy at West Point and a former Air Force fighter pilot, joined the NASA High-Speed Flight Station in 1958. He was a project pilot on the lifting body program, flying the wingless Northrop M2-F1, HL-10, and M2-F3, and the Martin Marietta X-24B lifting body vehicles. Dana flew 16 flights in the rocket-powered hypersonic North American X-15 research aircraft and participated in many other NASA test programs; these included the F-15 Highly Integrated Digital Electronic Control (HIDEC), the F/A-18 High Angle-of-Attack Research Vehicle (HARV), the Mach 3.0 Lockheed YF-12, the Lockheed F-104, General Dynamics AFTI F-16, Piper PA-30 Twin Comanche, and T-38. Dana was Dryden chief engineer from 1993 until 1998, the period when most NASA F-16XL flight research was conducted. He retired in 1998 after 40 years with NASA. NASA Dryden Fact Sheet "Bill Dana—Rocket Pilot," September 4, 2007, *http://www.nasa.gov/vision/earth/improvingflight/rocket_pilot.html*, accessed July 5, 2012.
65. Hon. Thomas P. Christie, interview by the former DoD Director of Operational Test and Evaluation, February 15, 2012. W. Paul Thayer had been a Naval Aviator, a WWII fighter ace, a former chief test pilot at Vought Aircraft, and an ex-president and CEO of LTV Corporation.
66. Berry, "The Revolutionary Evolution of the F-16XL."
67. GD, F-16XL VIP Flight Log, Appendix A to "F-16XL Flight Test Program—Final Report."

A General Dynamics F-111F Aardvark of the 48th Tactical Fighter Wing at the National Museum of the United States Air Force. (USAF)

CHAPTER 7

The Dual-Role Fighter Competition

The comparative evaluation between the F-16XL and the F-15E had its genesis in a need to improve the night and all-weather strike capabilities of U.S. tactical air forces. In 1978, the commander of the Air Force Tactical Air Command, Gen. Wilbur L. "Bill" Creech, directed an analysis of various alternative acquisition approaches for a long-range, all-weather strike aircraft. At that time, this aircraft was being referred to as the Enhanced Tactical Fighter (ETF).[1] As originally conceived, the ETF was intended to supplement or replace the large, heavy General Dynamics F-111F, the outgrowth of Secretary of Defense Robert McNamara's generally disastrous Tactical Fighter Experimental (TFX) development program of the 1960s. Known popularly as the "Aardvark," the F-111F was a long-range, twin-engine supersonic strike aircraft equipped with a sophisticated precision attack system called Pave Tack. But the F-111 family of aircraft were already endangered by newer generations of Warsaw Pact air defense weapons and aircraft and, as well, were not available in significantly large numbers to enable NATO to meet a critical challenge: the ability to conduct long-range strike operations at night and in all-weather conditions against Soviet/Warsaw Pact second-echelon and follow-on armored formations. These forces posed a major threat against the Central Region of NATO. Dealing with critical elements of the integrated air defense system that protected Soviet/Warsaw Pact forces was an important aspect of the ETF requirement.

In some ways, ETF was complementary to the mission conceived for the Lockheed F-117A low-observable fighter then under development. Due to its extremely high security, few in Congress, the Defense Department, or even the Air Force were aware of the existence of this "stealth" strike aircraft development. This undoubtedly was beneficial to the Air Force initiative that evolved from the ETF initiative. This soon became known as the Dual-Role Fighter as its requirements expanded to include air superiority as well as ground attack.[2]

DRF: The Origins

Preliminary Air Force ETF studies had concluded that upgraded versions of the F-111F could satisfy the need for an enhanced deep strike capability in the event of a conflict in Central Europe. However, many Air Force leaders (and especially General Creech) strongly believed that a dual-role variant of an existing fighter was a better all-around alternative to improved F-111Fs. This Dual-Role Fighter was intended to penetrate enemy defenses at very low altitude without having to rely on fighter escorts to deal with enemy interceptors or the need for supporting electronic jamming aircraft. The Air Force's McDonnell-Douglas F-15 Eagle had been conceived as a pure air superiority fighter whose design philosophy was based on the often-quoted phrase "not a pound for air-to-ground." (Indeed, the F-15 became arguably the finest air-to-air fighter in aviation history; "Eagle drivers" of various nations have shot down dozens of opponents without—as of this writing—ever suffering an air-to-air loss themselves.) The relatively large, twin-engine F-15 had tremendous power, surprising agility, and a great deal of internal volume for growth and further development, giving it inherent air-to-ground capability.[3] The F-15 airframe had 15 cubic feet of empty internal volume compared to only 2 cubic feet of empty space in the much smaller F-16. As the large, heavy F-111F was very limited in maneuvering capability and had essentially no capability at all for beyond visual range or in the highly demanding close-in visual combat arena, it was eliminated from further consideration.[4]

Another significant consideration was the strong competition for limited fighter production funding from the lower cost F-16. Many senior leaders within the Air Force were very concerned about the end of F-15 production, for they recognized that it was a remarkably capable aircraft with extraordinary growth potential.[5] "McAir"—the McDonnell-Douglas Corporation (MDC)—was actively promoting the development of a two-seat air-to-ground F-15. It would have longer range made possible by conformal fuel tanks mounted on each side of the fuselage under the wing-fuselage joint. McAir referred to these conformal fuel tanks as "FAST Packs" (*Fuel and Sensor Tactical Pack*ages).

The strike version of the F-15 was to carry FAST Packs along with an extensive array of air-to-ground sensors and advanced munitions. This would provide the capability for all-weather strike missions using precision guided munitions. McDonnell-Douglas and Hughes Aircraft (the company that developed the original F-15 radar) collaborated in a privately funded study that examined the feasibility of adapting the F-15 to the air-to-ground role. They jointly developed a weapon system concept based on using synthetic aperture radar to provide a high-resolution ground-mapping capability.[6] The rear cockpit of the two-seat strike aircraft was to be configured with advanced capabilities for a Weapons System Officer (WSO). The WSO's duties included operating the synthetic-aperture radar (SAR) and other advanced navigation and weapons delivery systems. An external laser designator pod would enable autonomous delivery of laser-guided weapons at night. Weapons carriage and release pylons would be integrated into the FAST Pack conformal fuel tanks, providing the capability for the aircraft to carry a total of 22 air-to-ground weapons on long-range strike missions. The F-15's air superiority systems weapons payload of four AIM-9 Sidewinder infrared-guided missiles and four radar-guided AIM-7 Sparrow missiles would be retained. AIM-7 missiles would be replaced with the far more capable AIM-120 missile as that capability became available and was integrated into the basic F-15.[7]

Creech later recalled how he discussed development of a dual-role mission-capable variant of the F-15 (to be called the F-15E) with George S. Graff, the president of McDonnell-Douglas Aircraft.[8] A strong advocate of the F-15, Creech noted that his and similar efforts by other Air Force leaders "solicited an unsolicited proposal" from McDonnell-Douglas. In Creech's words,

> The Air Force sold McDonnell-Douglas on the idea that the USAF needed the F-15E if it was going to continue buying F-15s into the future. I described to Graff what the F-15E's features needed to be: stretched fuselage, conformal [fuel] tanks for greater range, two-person aircrew, LANTIRN equipped, a radar with great ground map and ground target attack capabilities, modern glass cockpits—all with no diminution in any way in the aircraft's air-to-air weaponry or capabilities…. It's either go dual-role or get out of the F-15 business.[9]

By early 1981, McDonnell-Douglas had (with internal company funding) built what they termed an F-15 Advanced Fighter Capability Demonstrator (AFCD). First flown on July 8, 1980, the F-15 AFCD was modified from F-15B serial number 71-0291, which had been the second two-seat F-15 produced. This aircraft immediately become popularly known as the "Strike Eagle," a name that carried over to the eventual F-15E production aircraft in Air Force service. Demonstrated with conformal fuel tanks and an air-to-ground weapons payload of 22 500-pound-class anti-armor Rockeye munitions dispensers, the AFCD Strike Eagle also carried 4 AIM-9 Sidewinder infrared air-to-air missiles for use in self-defense.[10]

In the summer of 1980, McDonnell-Douglas demonstrated the two-seat Advanced Fighter Capability Demonstrator fitted with conformal fuel tanks and a large payload of weapons at the Farnborough Air Show, where the author of this study was briefed on the capabilities that the aircraft could provide. Numerous Air Force officers were given demonstration flights in the aircraft. They commented very favorably on its capabilities, as exemplified in an enthusiastic report written by Air Force Vietnam fighter ace Steve Ritchie and published in the influential *Air Force Magazine*.[11] Ritchie's impressions were concisely summarized in the article's subtitle: "A fighter ace flies the F-15 dual-role fighter candidate and reports this bird can do it all." It was a statement with ominous implications for the future of General Dynamics' F-16XL, even then gestating at Fort Worth.

At the most senior levels of the Air Force, there was also a consensus on moving forward with an air-to-ground version of the F-15. This aircraft was increasingly seen as providing important capabilities that would be valuable beyond the confines of a Central European conflict. The Strike Eagle clearly incorporated the attributes advocated by Creech, who described the aircraft as a "product improvement concept—for a possible buy of 400 airplanes—for the long-range battlefield interdiction mission, including at night."[12] In testimony to Congress, Creech emphasized the role that the dual-role F-15 could play in operations in the Middle East: "I think it is an outstanding airplane for the Rapid Deployment Force.... In fact, range in the Persian Gulf area takes on a whole new importance that one does not feel in Central Europe.... Saudi Arabia is bigger than the United States east of the Mississippi."[13]

In addition, there was also Air Force support for "building into the F-16 the sophisticated equipment necessary to increase its usefulness and expand its operating window" and for building a prototype and demonstrate advancing technologies in order to be able to respond quickly to changes in threat or mission requirements, to show that "the F-16XL is an example of what could be tested next year."[14]

The Enhanced Tactical Fighter had first been proposed in the Air Force's fiscal year 1980 budget request to Congress, which was submitted in early 1979. Congress refused to fund the program, stating that the requirement was relatively undefined.[15] This led to a complete revision of the concept. Instead of a completely new start, ETF became an evolutionary or derivative development of an existing TAC fighter modified with advanced avionics and weapons delivery capabilities to permit multirole operations in demanding high-intensity combat scenarios. In December 1980, *Air Force Magazine* reported that possible derivative fighter designs included "the enhanced F-15, being funded by McDonnell-Douglas and its associated contractors," but also "in a similar fashion General Dynamics was working on their enhanced F-16XL that used a cranked arrow delta wing."[16]

In March 1981, the Air Force announced its intention to provide a "night, full-adverse-weather weapons delivery capability" (a passing reference to what emerged as the LANTIRN targeting and navigation pod) and that they would "in 1984 begin procuring Strike Eagle ground attack F-15s" for this purpose.[17] At the same time, General Dynamics was claiming that its F-16XL, then in development using company funding, would be capable of Mach 2.2 performance, had reduced aerodynamic drag made possible by conformal weapons carriage, and could carry nearly double the air-to-ground payload of the conventional F-16. With this background, congressional language related to ETF funding was revised to require the Air Force to conduct a competitive evaluation of dual-role variants of both the F-15 and the F-16 before full-scale development and production funding would be provided.

In June 1981, the Air Staff diverted $618 million from planned future funding for the new Advanced Tactical Fighter program to cover the possibility that the F-16XL variant would be selected for full-scale development and eventual production.[18] The term "Enhanced Tactical Fighter," or ETF, now rapidly evolved into the Dual-Role Fighter to better describe the enhanced or derivative nature of the aircraft that the Air Force was seeking in its evaluation of dual-role variants of the F-15 and the F-16. In October 1981, the Office of the Secretary of the Air Force directed the Air Force to conduct a comparative flight-test demonstration program of the two candidate aircraft. The comparative evaluation was intended to provide data to support a decision to proceed with development of either the F-15E or the F-16E as a Dual-Role Fighter. The flight-test program would provide part of the basis for evaluating the forthcoming contractor proposals for full-scale development and production efforts. It would also provide limited Air Force pilot assessments of both F-15 and F-16 derivative fighters. The Air Force emphasized that flight-test data would provide only one of several key sources of data for use in the DRF source selection process. The source selection would consider performance, effectiveness, cost, and operational availability of both candidate aircraft. Their relative contributions to overall mission accomplishment were evaluated based on the results from flight testing, other test efforts, and various mission and logistics analyses.[19]

Thus, the approach used in the DRF source selection called for flight-test data to be supplemented with data from a variety of other sources. These included the results from wind tunnel and high-altitude engine chamber testing, the use

NEEDS	COMPARATIVE FLT DEMONSTRATION	TECHNICAL ANALYSIS	MISSION ANALYSIS	LOGISTICS ANALYSIS	OTHER TESTS	CONTRACTOR INPUTS
PERFORMANCE	✓✓✓	✓✓✓	✓✓	✓	✓✓	✓
EFFECTIVENESS	✓✓	✓	✓✓	✓	✓✓	✓
COST	✓	✓✓	✓	✓✓	✓	✓✓✓
OPERATIONAL AVAILABILITY	✓	✓✓	✓	✓✓	✓	✓

SOURCES

✓ INDICATES RELATIVE CONTRIBUTION TO SELECTION PROCESS FROM EACH SOURCE

The DRF source selection process evaluated performance, effectiveness, cost, and operational availability, weighing their relative contributions, as shown is this extract from an Air Force report. (USAF)

of existing F-15 and F-16 flight-test data, test data from the F-16 Multi-Stage Improvement Program (MSIP), and data from other relevant systems developmental programs. Additionally, insights derived from extensive war-gaming exercises and mission analyses played a significant role in the evaluation, especially in the areas of system performance and combat effectiveness. Results from computer modeling and simulation, as well as operational and logistics support analyses conducted by subject matter experts, were also considered in the final decision. The flight-test programs for each aircraft would be conducted by separate F-15E and F-16E Combined Test Forces at the AFFTC. Personnel from the Flight Test Center would be responsible for the development test and evaluation aspects of the test program, with AFOTEC personnel responsible for operational utility assessments on both aircraft. Flight-test activities and the overall source selection effort would be coordinated by the Aeronautical Systems Division Derivative Fighter Comparison Organization, located at Wright-Patterson AFB.[20]

The Dual-Role Fighter would have to demonstrate superior capabilities for both the air-to-surface mission as well as in the air-to-air role. The aircraft would need to be capable of long-range intercontinental deployment and had to demonstrate high survivability during operations over heavily defended enemy territory. The selected DRF contender would have to possess the best overall combination of the following characteristics:[21]

Table 6.
Desired Dual-Role Fighter operational characteristics

Role	Desired Characteristic
Air-to-Surface	Long range
	Large payload
	Automated, accurate, state-of-the-art avionics and weapons
	High-speed, low-altitude ingress/egress, day/night, within/under weather
	Adequate internal avionics volume
	High combat performance as demonstrated by high speed, high excess thrust, and satisfactory maneuverability/handling qualities
	Two seats with a missionized rear cockpit
Air-to-Air	Long range and endurance
	Long-range, look-down radar
	High combat performance
	Two seats

On January 28, 1982, the Air Force Systems Command (AFSC) directed that its Aeronautical Systems Division form a dedicated organization to evaluate both the F-15 and the F-16 Dual-Role Fighter candidates.[22] The comparative evaluation would examine both candidate aircraft from an analytical perspective as well as in terms of their flying qualities and weapons delivery capabilities. Flight testing was to be conducted at the Flight Test Center at Edwards AFB, where an F-16E Combined Test Force was being formed. It would include test pilots and flight-test engineers from General Dynamics and the AFFTC, with additional personnel being assigned from TAC, ASD, and AFOTEC. The test program also included provision for separate Operational Utility Evaluations (OUEs) of each candidate aircraft's capabilities. These OUEs would be primarily conducted by the Air Force's independent operational test and evaluation organization, AFOTEC, and were oriented to assessing the potential effectiveness and suitability of each aircraft to perform the DRF mission. A Derivative Fighter Steering Group was formed within ASD to provide appropriate senior-level oversight of the overall evaluation effort.

In a Senate Armed Services Committee hearing on the proposed fiscal year 1983 defense budget that was held on February 26, 1982, Creech reported that the Air Force was working on the Dual-Role Fighter, an all-weather attack aircraft based on either a two-seat version of the F-16 (the F-16E) or a two-seat F-15 (the F-15E) and was to be equipped with LANTIRN and the imaging infrared (IIR)–guided version of the air-to-ground Maverick missile.[23] The following week, at another Senate Armed Services Committee hearing, Maj. Gen. Robert D. Russ, chief of Air Force Operational Requirements, stated, "I don't believe it is prudent to have a day, clear weather only fighter force and give the enemy the capability to fight around the clock.... I think the increased capability that it [DRF] gives us is worth the money."[24] The general requirements for the derivative fighter were briefed to the House Armed Services Committee's Research and Development Subcommittee in March 1982. In their testimony at the time, the Air Forces stated that a new dual-role capable fighter was needed by the late 1980s to assist the F-111F in deep interdiction, to complement the F-15 in the air superiority role, and to replace the aging Vietnam-era F-4, which was then the only truly capable dual-role fighter in USAF service. The aircraft was described as being capable of conducting a broad range of air-to-air and air-to-ground missions. Desired Dual-Role Fighter characteristics were long-range and good endurance, a large weapons payload, automatic terrain-following capability at very low altitude, and a rear cockpit for a second crewmember, who would operate the specialized avionics and weapons subsystems needed for day, night, and all-weather operations.[25]

Cost estimates for the F-15E and the F-16E Dual-Role Fighters were completed in conjunction with overall cost analyses conducted by the Air Force in

August 1982 for the F-15 and F-16 programs. These cost estimates included both the incremental costs (defined as the additional costs to add a dual-role fighter capability to each aircraft) and the total cost of the Dual-Role Fighter procurement for each candidate aircraft. These costs are summarized for the F-15E and the F-16E aircraft in Tables 7 and 8.[26]

Table 7.

Incremental Dual-Role Fighter cost breakdown—400 aircraft (Air Force independent cost analyses, August 1982) (then-year dollars)

Costs	F-15E	F-16E
Research and Development	$275 million	$473 million
Incremental Production Cost	$870 million	$2,492 million
Incremental Acquisition Cost	$1,145 million	$2,965 million
Incremental Acquisition Cost per Unit	$2.9 million	$7.4 million
Incremental Recurring Flyaway Cost/Unit	$1.6 million	$5.5 million

Table 8.

Total Dual-Role Fighter cost breakdown—400 aircraft (Air Force independent cost analyses, August 1982) (then-year dollars)

Costs	F-15E	F-16E
Research and Development	$275 million	$473 million
Incremental Production Cost	$14.9 billion	$10.9 billion
Incremental Acquisition Cost	$15.2 billion	$11.4 billion
Incremental Acquisition Cost per Unit	$38.0 million	$28.5 million
Incremental Recurring Flyaway Cost/Unit	$32.6 million	$22.4 million

In its approach to the DRF cost assessment, the Air Force assumed that the dual-role capability would be built into aircraft that were already planned under the existing F-15 or F-16 acquisition programs. Thus, the Air Force viewed Dual-Role Fighter costs as essentially consisting of incremental costs over and above those of existing variants of the F-15 and F-16. The Air Force's view of DRF program costs as being essentially incremental was based on a planning assumption that an adequate quantity of either F-15Es or F-16Es would be bought in future years to satisfy the then-perceived, but still unofficial, Air Force requirement for 400 aircraft Dual-Role Fighters.[27] The Air Force's cost assessment concluded that F-16 E development costs, as well as its incremental costs, were greater than estimated F-15E development and incremental costs. This largely reflected the additional costs of the major airframe design changes required for the radically different F-16E. However, the estimated unit cost of the smaller single-engine F-16E, with its maximum takeoff gross weight of 48,000 pounds, was considerably less than that of the larger, twin-engine F-15E, which has a maximum TOGW of over 80,000 pounds. As seen in Table 7, the unit flyaway cost of the F-15E was about $10 million more per aircraft than the equivalent flyaway cost of the F-16E.[28]

Lt. Gen. Lawrence A. Skantze, the Air Force's deputy chief of staff for research, development, and acquisition, emphasized that the Dual-Role Fighter evaluation would be conducted by a combined team that would include representatives from the Air Force Systems Command and the Tactical Air Command. TAC was responsible for representing the various Air Force overseas operational commands that would operate the aircraft if it was selected for production. Skantze noted that various system upgrades would be examined for each aircraft. He stated that one of the candidates would be selected "for the long range interdictor mission (tailored for the interdiction of the Warsaw Pact's rear echelons), transforming the aircraft in effect into a dual fighter, while the other is earmarked for some lesser upgrading."[29] At the close of 1982, the Air Force was still undecided about the total number of aircraft that would be upgraded for the dual-role mission, but at that time, they expected to select one of the DRF candidates for further development by the summer of 1983.[30]

By late 1982, the original Air Force plan to conduct a competitive fly-off of the two DRF candidates was now being described as consisting of separate independent evaluations of each aircraft's capabilities in accomplishing the dual-role mission.[31] Despite the fact that Congress had restricted the Air Force to buying either the F-15E or the F-16E but not both, General Dynamics spokesmen continued to publicly profess the belief that the Air Force could end up buying both aircraft. In interviews reported in the press, F-16XL Deputy Program Manager Harry Hillaker commented that the two aircraft should not be considered competitive since the F-16 had always been considered to provide a complementary capability to the F-15 in the context of the high/low mix of Air Force fighters. Improving F-15 air-to-ground capabilities, along with enhancing the air superiority performance of the F-16 in the beyond-visual-engagement arena, were both worthwhile ongoing Air Force initiatives. Hillaker emphasized that all forward-based aircraft in Europe, including the F-16, were highly vulnerable to Soviet attack on their airbases. Increased range was the driving requirement behind the development of the F-16XL, and this would greatly enhance its abilities in both European and Middle Eastern operations. Reservations about the restrictive congressional language limiting DRF production procurement to one of the two competing aircraft were reportedly expressed by Richard De Lauer, the Defense Department's director of research and development, and General Charles Gabriel, the USAF chief of staff.[32]

In December 1982, the Congressional Budget Office (CBO) reiterated the congressional guidance that only one of the Dual-Role Fighter candidates was to be selected for full-scale development and eventual production. They also reported that, as of that time, 538 F-16 variants were associated with the DRF program, with potential acquisition of up to 400 dual-role F-15s planned.[33] In the case of the F-16, the total "marginal cost" was reported by the Air Force to be $4.657 billion for the 538 aircraft, or over $8.6 million per aircraft. Marginal costs were defined as those costs associated with modifying an existing F-16 into a derivative F-16 dual-role version, not the total unit cost of an F-16 DRF variant. The GAO also reported that the Air Force had programmed approximately $10 billion to acquire 538 F-16 aircraft for modification into two-seat, dual-role variants of the F-16—if that aircraft were to be selected as the DRF.[34] In early 1983, the Air Force informed Congress that the F-16E would cost more to develop than the F-15E (the estimated development costs that they used were those shown in Table 8: $473 million for the F-16E compared to $275 million for the F-15E). The Air Force also noted that the addition of a two-seat cockpit with new avionics tailored for the DRF mission would add even more development cost to the F-16E. At the same time, the Air Force emphasized that its immediate operational priority was dealing with the serious deficiency in all-weather ground attack capability, with the Dual-Role Fighter providing the means to do so.[35]

During 1982 and into 1983, the Air Force Tactical Air Command worked on evolving a Statement of Operational Need (SON) that included performance thresholds and goals for the Dual-Role Fighter. Separately, individual System Operational Concept documents, one for the F-15 and one for the F-16 Dual-Role Fighter candidates, were being developed. In July 1983, TAC submitted a revised SON to Air Force Headquarters, but this had not been approved by early 1984, when the DRF source selection was essentially complete. At the same time, both the F-15E and the F-16E System Operational Concepts were still in coordination at TAC Headquarters. Performance thresholds and goals incorporated in the earlier draft of the Statement of Operational Need had been withdrawn by the Air Force. The Air Force rationale for this action was that they might influence or predetermine the selection of one candidate aircraft over the other. Thus, specific DRF evaluation criteria were not ranked in order of importance nor were minimum acceptable performance characteristics—such as range and payload—defined. Instead, the F-15E and the F-16E were evaluated separately on the basis of their individual merits and capabilities to perform the Dual-Role Fighter mission.

The separate and independent Air Force evaluation of the F-16XL's ability to accomplish the Dual-Role Fighter mission involved both the single and the two-seat aircraft and began in April 1983. The separate evaluation of the F-15 in this mission role had begun in December 1982 and eventually involved four modified F-15s. These included the two-seat F-15B Advanced Fighter Capability Demonstrator with its rear cockpit upgraded for the air-to-ground mission. It was equipped with a modified version of the Hughes APG-63 radar capable of high-resolution, synthetic-aperture ground mapping. Additionally, two two-seat F-15Ds, delivered directly from the production line, were equipped with modified stores stations to enable a variety of different air-to-surface weapons combinations to be tested from the F-15. Finally, a single-seat F-15C, fitted with the conformal fuel tanks to be used on the proposed F-15E, conducted aerodynamic and handling qualities evaluations with various air-to-ground weapons. The F-15C portion of the F-15 DRF evaluation had begun in August 1982 and continued through September 1983.[36]

The DRF Competition: GAO's Concerns

Shortly before the formal Air Force announcement of the result of the Dual-Role Fighter competition, Frank C. Conahan, director of the National Security Division of the General Accounting Office, in a January 1984 letter to Secretary of Defense Caspar W. Weinberger, expressed concerns about the Air Force's DRF source selection approach.[37] These concerns centered on two major issues: first, the Air Force had not fully defined the operational concept and detailed system requirements for the Dual-Role Fighter, and second, the F-15 and F-16 derivative designs were not being compared against a common set of evaluation criteria that set minimum performance characteristics. Also, the GAO noted that the Air Force intended to select either the F-15E or the F-16E for full-scale development in early 1984, in advance of any congressional hearings on the fiscal year 1985 budget. A separate GAO report elaborated on the GAO's DRF source selection concerns. Of significance, it specifically highlighted the fact that the F-16E required major changes to the basic F-16 airframe. The GAO report noted that these changes included a fuselage stretched by 56 inches, integration of a new cranked-arrow wing that replaced the existing F-16 wing and horizontal tail, and provision for a strengthened landing gear. Changes required for the F-15E were not considered by the GAO to be as great as those needed for the F-16E, and mainly consisted of structural modifications to the wings as well as a strengthened landing gear.[38]

In the GAO's opinion, the Air Force approach used in the Dual-Role Fighter source selection was inappropriate in that the Air Force had not compared the F-l5E and the F-16E against common evaluation criteria to determine how well each candidate aircraft fulfilled these criteria. They noted that procedures for defining and documenting system operational requirements were defined in a formal process that progressed from mission area analyses to definition of a formal Statement of Operational Need.[39] The SON was intended to identify an existing operational deficiency and state the need for a new or improved capability. A System Operational Concept would then be established to describe the intended purpose of the new system, its employment concept, and its intended deployment and support approaches. Finally, quantitative and qualitative levels of system performance—such as range, payload, and maneuvering capabilities—were to be formally established and used for evaluating candidate systems capabilities before a full-scale engineering development decision was made.

The GAO highlighted the fact that there were formally established Air Force policies and procedures for selecting contractors for development, production, or modification of major defense systems.[40] These required that common evaluation criteria be established to assess contractor proposals to fulfill an operational need. These evaluation criteria were to focus on core issues related to the mission of the proposed system and were to be ranked in relative order of importance in the source selection evaluation. Characteristics, such as range and payload, were to be used as measurable objective standards for evaluating contractor proposals. These characteristics, which were intended to flow from the process of refining the system's operational requirements, were to be quantitative where practical and serve as the required minimum acceptable system performance. The GAO cited the primary DoD directive on major systems acquisitions.[41] This required that a formal operational requirement be established to validate or demonstrate the performance of candidate systems in conjunction with the source selection process. They also reported that the Air Force had not followed its own established source selection policies and procedures for "any modification, maintenance, services, and/or other program/project estimated to require $300 million or more."[42] The DRF procurement far exceeded this program guideline.

The Air Force responded that the standard source selection procedures relating to establishing specific performance criteria, as set forth in Air Force Regulation 70-15, did not apply to the Dual-Role Fighter comparison. The Air Force also noted that a normal source selection would have started with a common Request for Proposals to each bidding contractor. In the case of the DRF, separate proposal instructions, respectively tailored to the F-15 and the F-16 candidates, were used to accommodate inherent differences in those aircraft. The Air Force position was that ranking the evaluation criteria and further refining and quantifying them might have predetermined the results of the comparison and defeated their objective of determining the most cost-effective DRF solution.[43] In many ways, the Air Force approach to the DRF source selection mirrored that used during the Lightweight Fighter program, which had conducted separate independent evaluations of the performance and combat potential offered by each candidate design.[44]

The Air Force's DRF Decision

After a series of internal reviews within the Office of the Secretary of Defense, the Air Force's source selection decision was upheld and on February 24, 1984, the F-15E was publicly announced as the winner of the Dual-Role Fighter competition.[45] A contract was issued to McDonnell-Douglas Corporation to develop the necessary modifications to provide enhanced air-to-ground capability to the F-15 for the deep-strike mission. The Air Force stated that it planned on acquiring 392 F-15Es. The incremental acquisition cost of these 392 F-15Es amounted to $1.5 billion—this compared to the $1.145 billion estimate for 400 F-15Es contained in the Air Force's 1982 cost analysis. Delivery of the first production F-15E was scheduled to occur in 1988.[46] In announcing the DRF decision, Air Force Chief of Staff Gen. Charles A. Gabriel stated that the F-15E "is vitally needed to redress our tactical forces' limited ability to operate over long ranges in adverse weather conditions, day or night." He also went on to note, "while the F-15 demonstrated clearly superior dual-role mission capabilities, the modified F-16 with its cranked arrow wing demonstrated high potential for follow-on development."[47]

Had the two-seat version F-16XL won the Dual-Role Fighter competition, the production version of the aircraft would have been assigned the Air Force designation F-16E. Shortly after the DRF announcement in January 1984, reports confirmed that the Air Force would evaluate the F-16XL's potential for continued development but as an advanced single-seat fighter with dual-role capabilities, to

An F-15E Strike Eagle, of Air Combat Command's 391st Fighter Squadron, dropping a 5,000-pound GBU-28 deep-penetrating laser-guided bomb during exercises at the Utah Test and Training Range, August 2010. (USAF)

be designated F-16F. Lt. Gen. Robert D. Russ, Air Force deputy chief of staff for research, development, and acquisition, in a mid-1984 *Air Force Magazine* article on the USAF "Fighter Roadmap," noted the following:

> Another Roadmap feature is a follow-on to the F-16, the F-16F, which will possess an improved air-to-air capability and a significantly enhanced air-to-ground capability.... While we cannot, at this point, define the precise configuration of this aircraft, there are a variety of promising technologies in various states of evaluation that may be incorporated in the F-16F.[48]

As the Air Force Flight Test Center reported in 1986, "To the surprise of few, the F-16XL did not 'win' the comparative fly-off (which, in fact, had been a simulated fly-off conducted at Aeronautical Systems Division)."[49] The CTF director, Lt. Col. Edwin A. Thomas, in an interview conducted for the Flight Test Center history, summarized the strengths and weakness of the aircraft. He noted that the F-16XL represented a "significant improvement" in capability over the standard F-16. Thomas was impressed by the aircraft's increased range and a payload twice that of the standard F-16, as well as the "tremendous speed capability inherent in this design." The aircraft's ride performance and handling qualities, especially at low altitudes, were considered by Thomas to be exceptional, with its increased internal volume providing room for systems growth. He noted that the F-16XL was "tremendous for what it was designed to do" but went on to say, "you don't get any of these things for free."[50] In their attempt to optimize the aircraft for the air-to-ground role, he noted that GD had made certain tradeoffs and compromises. The XL had a very low aspect ratio wing as well as a significantly lower thrust-to-weight ratio than the standard F-16. As a result, it lacked the F-16's aerial combat maneuvering capabilities at lower speeds, where it suffered a significant loss in sustained turning capability. The F-16XL's takeoff and landing speeds were also considered to be too high for a new fighter. Thomas noted that many of the F-16XL's limitations could have been resolved if it had continued into full-scale development although some involved major development and redesign efforts. In particular, the flight control system was identified as requiring redesign to provide the larger hinge-moment capabilities necessary for high-speed operations. Although the F-16XL "lost" the Dual-Role Fighter comparative fly-off, Thomas considered that it was nevertheless far from a failure and had demonstrated tremendous potential.

Maj. Patrick K. Talty, USAF, who had served as deputy for engineering on the F-16E Combined Test Force, described the strengths and areas of deficiency encountered with the F-16XL aircraft during the Air Force flight-test evaluation. Undoubtedly, the strengths and weaknesses (along with cost and full-scale development risks) that he noted were important considerations during the Air Force Dual-Role Fighter source selection process. Talty gave his perspective on the program in an Air University thesis published in the spring of 1986.

> The F-16XL accomplished the air-to-ground mission role better than the F-16A/B.... The XL modification to the F-16 stretched airframe provided increased payload and range. The XL had significant increased speed capability with more than twice the air-to-ground weapon load when compared to the F-16A. The F-16XL provided the capability to economically carry a large air-to-ground weapon load while maintaining a potent air-to-air capability (4 AMRAAMs and 2 AIM-9Ls) for extended ranges.
>
> The XL modification provided many improvements in the air-to-air maneuver region. The XL had outstanding high angle of attack flying qualities and departure resistance characteristics. The pilot could recover from departures with hands-off-control. The high angle of attack flying characteristics were not degraded by air-to-ground weapons. The XL had increased AOA and g capability with external stores. The roll performance both at elevated AOA and with external stores and tanks was improved, including the ability to roll 360 degrees with bombs. Supersonic performance was significantly improved over the F-16A with external stores.
>
> Areas of deficiencies were primarily related to thrust and weight requirements. At low thrust-to-weight ratios the takeoff distance was significantly increased. The F110 engine provided greater thrust on hot day conditions and the takeoff distance is noticeably improved. The low thrust-to-weight ratio negated the advantage of increased instantaneous maneuver potential compared to the F-16 since the increased drag caused the XL to rapidly lose energy during hard maneuvers. The heavyweight approach and landing performance was not acceptable. The heavyweight approach speed of 200 KCAS required a drag chute for routine operations (to minimize brake wear) and resulted in increased landing distances. The requirement to fly 13 degree AOA approaches reduced visibility over the nose of the aircraft. The test program to reduce the approach and landing speed was not completed due to program termination.[51]

Following the Air Force DRF decision, *Flight International* magazine reported, "GD was reluctantly drawn into the dual-role fighter contest, and will continue to offer its arrow-wing F-16XL to the US Air Force in the hope that, later in the F-16 programme, production will switch to this longer-range fighter version."[52] Reflecting the General Dynamics perspective on the DRF outcome, John G. Williams, GD's lead engineer on the XL commented, "The XL is a marvelous airplane, but was a victim of the USAF wanting to continue to produce the F-15, which is understandable. Sometimes you win these political games, sometimes not."[53]

A decade later, Harry Hillaker, by then officially retired from General Dynamics but still serving as a consultant to the corporation, provided a very interesting (if understandably emotional) retrospective perspective on the Air Force approach to the Dual-Role Fighter competition. Hillaker was responding to a December 1994 article published in the Lancaster, CA–based defense journal *Aerotech News and Review*. In the article, the journal quoted McDonnell-Douglas officials who had been interviewed concerning their possible participation in an Air Force–sponsored comparative evaluation of the production F-15E with the proposed Lockheed F-16ES.[54] In reporting the story, *Aerotech News* had summarized the earlier Dual-Role Fighter competition between the F-15E and the F-16XL in the following manner:

> Such an evaluation would follow previous comparisons. In the Dual-role Fighter competition funded by Congress and conducted by the U.S. Air Force in the early 1980s, a prototype of the F-15E decisively beat an F-16 variant called the F-16XL. The prototype F-15E, carrying conformal fuel tanks with tangential weapons carriage, a high-technology "glass" cockpit, high-resolution ground-mapping synthetic aperture radar and an infrared targeting system, was superior to the F-16XL in mission radius, payload, sustained aircraft performance, survivability, automated weapon system performance and cost-effectiveness. As a result, the Air Force procured the F-15E as its dual-role interdiction fighter.[55]

Hillaker's rebuttal to the depiction of the Dual-Role Fighter evaluation as presented in the *Aerotech News and Review* article was forceful, colorful, and insightful. His intimate involvement in development of the F-16XL, as well as his perception of the politics surrounding the Air Force DRF source selection decision, provide an interesting perspective on the final outcome of the program.

As the recognized "Father of the F-16," and Chief Project Engineer during the concept formulation and preliminary design phases of the F-16XL and Vice President and Deputy Program Director during the prototype phase, the article was of considerable interest to me. The disappointment was that only one side of the issue was presented, a highly biased, self-interest input that does not adequately, nor accurately, present the real story of the selection of the F-15E.

First, it should be understood that we (General Dynamics) did not initiate the F-16XL as a competitor to the F-15E, then identified as the F-15 *Strike Eagle*. We stated as unequivocally as possible to the Air Force, that the Dual-Role mission should be given to the F-15: that the F-15 should complement the F-16 in ground strike missions in the same manner that the F-16 complements the F-15 in air-air missions. A fundamental tenet of the F-16, from its inception, has been as an air-air complement to the F-15— no radar missile capability, no M=2.0+ capability, no standoff capability: a multi-mission fighter whose primary mission was air-surface with backup air-air capability.

We proposed the F-16XL as a logical enhancement of its air-to-surface capabilities. The F-16C represented a progressive systems enhancement and the XL would be an airframe enhancement optimized more to its air-surface mission—lower weapons carriage drag and minimum dependence on external fuel tanks.

The statement that "a prototype version of the F-15E decisively beat an F-16 variant called the F-16XL," is misinformation. I don't know what was meant by "beat," it is patently true that McDonnell-Douglas clearly won what was called a "competition." However, by the Air Force's own definition, it was, in reality, an evaluation to determine which airplane would be better suited to the dual-role mission. In a formal competition, each party is evaluated against a common set of requirements and conditions. Such was not the case for the dual-role fighter. The F-15 Strike Eagle and the F-16XL were evaluated and flight tested to different sets of conditions and to different test plans—no common basis for evaluation existed.

The F-15 had only one clear advantage in the evaluation—a "paper" advantage. The weapon loading for one of the missions used in the evaluation precluded the use of external fuel tanks on the F-16XL; the F-15 could carry that particular weapon loading and still carry external fuel tanks, the F-16XL could not. That one mission was the only place the F-15 had a clear advantage. (It should be noted that a fundamental design feature of the XL was the elimination of external fuel tanks with their attendant restrictions on flight limits and their weight and drag penalty.) Further, the Air Force would not allow us to use the GE F110 engine in our proposal even though the No. 2 XL, the 2-place version, was powered by a F110 engine and provided better performance than the P&W F100 engine. And although you would expect the F-16's clear advantage to be cost, the Air Force treated the F-15E as a simple modification to a planned production buy and the F-16XL as a totally new buy. Neither airplane used in the flight test evaluation was a "prototype" of a dual-role fighter. The F-15 was closer systems and cockpit-wise than the F-16XL and the F-16XL was closer, much closer, airframe-wise. The F-16XLs were designed to, and flew, at their maximum design gross weight of 48,000 pounds, whereas the F-15, more than once, blew its tires while taxiing at 73,000 pounds, well below its maximum design gross weight [which was 81,000 pounds], a condition not demonstrated in the flight test program.

In a meeting that I attended with General Creech, then TAC CINC [Commander-in-Chief], the general stated that either airplane was fully satisfactory. When asked why he and his staff only mentioned the F-15 (never the F-16XL) in any dual-role fighter statement or discussion, he gave a reply that was impossible to refute, "We have to do that because the F-16 has a heart and soul of its own and we have to sell the F-15." I'll have to admit that I sat mute upon hearing that statement because there was no possible retort.

We had no allusions as to what the outcome of the Dual-role fighter "competition" would be and debated whether to even respond to the request for information. We did submit, knowing full well that it was a lost cause and that to not submit would be an affront to the Air Force who badly needed the appearance of a competition to justify continued procurement of the F-15—they had patently been unable to sell the F-15 *Strike Eagle* for five years. As is the case with too much in our culture today, the Air Force was more interested in style, in appearances, than in substance.

Even today, I feel that giving the F-15 a precision air-surface capability was proper and badly needed. What continues to disturb me is that the F-16XL had to be a pawn in that decision and had to be so badly denigrated to justify the decision—a selection that could have been made on its own merits.[56]

D. Randall (Randy) Kent, General Dynamics vice president and program director for the F-16XL, had presented his views on the F-16XL's accomplishments in an interview published in *Air Force Magazine* (*AFM*) in late 1983, shortly before the Air Force decision that selected the F-15E as the Air Force Dual-Role Fighter. In the *AFM* article, Kent firmly expressed the GD goal to move the program into full-scale development and eventual production:

The F-16XL flight-test program has conclusively demonstrated that the XL performs as predicted. This performance level represents a significant increase in mission capability for USAF. Coupling this with the affordability and low risk of the F-16XL presents USAF with a viable way to increase mission capability while simultaneously growing to a forty-wing TAC force structure.[57]

F-16F Full-Scale Development Effort

General Dynamics had begun planning for an F-16XL Full-Scale Development program prior to the Air Force decision that selected the F-15E for production in January 1984.[58] Initially, the intent had been to develop the aircraft as a two-seat replacement for the F-111 under the designation F-16E. However, following the DRF decision in February 1984, the Air Force announced its intention to develop the single-seat version of the F-16XL as the F-16F. Before finally terminating the program in August 1985, the Air Force had allocated funding to begin initial FSD efforts on the F-16F. The F-16F design concept was based on using the Multi-Staged Improvement Program avionics from the production F-16C. The production aircraft would have incorporated the fuselage plugs developed for the F-16XL along with its tailored cranked-arrow wing. The production program proposed by General Dynamics would have

resulted in initial F-16F deliveries to the Air Force from the
Fort Worth factory in 1987.
Under GD's proposed FSD
development approach, the
two existing F-16XL aircraft
would have been modified
to F-16F production-repre-
sentative standard. Two more
F-16F test aircraft would be
built for the FSD flight-test
program that was based on
the use of four test aircraft.

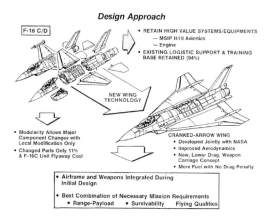

Design Approach

F-16 C/D
• RETAIN HIGH VALUE SYSTEMS/EQUIPMENTS
  — MSIP II/III Avionics
  — Engine
• EXISTING LOGISTIC SUPPORT & TRAINING
  BASE RETAINED (94%)

NEW WING
TECHNOLOGY

• Modularity Allows Major
  Component Changes with
  Local Modification Only
• Changed Parts Only 11%
  & F-16C Unit Flyaway Cost

CRANKED-ARROW WING
• Developed Jointly with NASA
• Improved Aerodynamics
• New, Lower Drag, Weapon
  Carriage Concept
• More Fuel with No Drag Penalty

• Airframe and Weapons Integrated During
  Initial Design

• Best Combination of Necessary Mission Requirements
  • Range-Payload   • Survivability   Flying Qualities

The General Dynamics F-16F design concept was based
on component modularity with the production F-16C
program while also retaining a very high percentage
of the existing F-16 logistic support and training base.
(Lockheed Martin)

Production planning for
the single-seat F-16F aircraft continued into 1985.
However, early on in the Full-
Scale Development effort, it
became evident that a different management approach from that used during
the F-16XL development effort was needed. This had also been the case during
the transition from the YF-16 flight demonstrator effort to the production
F-16 program.[59]

An unsigned internal GD memorandum pleading for better communications
and improved coordination between elements of the F-16F team reflects some
of the difficulties encountered during this transition from what was essentially a
prototyping effort to a full-scale development program.[60]

> An important aspect of design productivity is effective communica-
> tion among the various design disciplines so that design changes
> can be evaluated and incorporated in the most efficient and pro-
> ductive manner. This is doubly important in a program such as
> the F-16XL where the configuration continues to undergo devel-
> opment, and changes occur daily. On the XL prototype program,
> collocation of aero, structures, loads, materials, mass properties,
> manufacturing, systems and management kept all groups informed
> of design changes, and kept the system flexible enough to react to
> such changes with little duplication of effort or wasted manpower.
> In contrast, the XL FSD program has been almost entirely segre-
> gated with virtually no effective means of communications between
> groups, in a phase of the aircraft's life where changes are even more
> critical and have a much greater impact downstream. There have

been many instances of "oh, by the way, we need to incorporate this…" type of after the fact design changes, which serve only to duplicate effort and reduce the productivity of the engineer. I spend a great deal of my time marching back and forth between buildings chasing down engineers from various design disciplines to exchange information not readily conveyed via phone or mail, or replanning daily events due to the unavailability of the 'unscheduled' CYBER or VAX terminals or the too-rigidly-scheduled CADAM terminals.[61]

The F-16F Full-Scale Development effort ended when the Air Force terminated the program in the summer of 1985, although some ongoing flight-test efforts continued for a few months longer. These supplemental efforts were completed by the end of September. On October 1, 1985, F-16XL-2 was flown to Fort Worth and placed in storage. This marked the last flight of the Air Force F-16XL program, which had completed a total of 798 flight-test missions. The wide variety of objectives accomplished during the Air Force flight-test program is shown in Table 9. During the course of the program, F-16XL-1 flew 437 times and F-16XL-2 accomplished 361 flight-test sorties. The two-seat F-16XL-2 aircraft was painted in the so-called "Ferris" camouflage scheme, which was being evaluated for possible adoption by the Air Force.[62]

Both F-16XLs are seen in close formation with the full air-to-air missile payload of four AMRAAMs and two Sidewinders. The two-seat F-16XL-2 in the lead is painted in the so-called "Ferris" deceptive camouflage scheme. (USAF)

Table 9.
F-16XL Activity Through October 1, 1985

Event	F-16XL-1	F-16XL-2	Total
Milestones			
1st Flight–Last Flight	7/3/82–8/14/85	10/29/82–10/1/85	—
1st Supersonic Flight	Flt #2 (7/9/82)	Flt #1 (10/29/82)	—
Maximum "G" Flight	9.0 (Flt #20 7/28/82)	—	—
Max Mach Number	1.95 (Flt #19 7/28/82)	1.6 (Flt #25 12/7/82)	—
Maximum Altitude	50K Feet (Flt #11 7/24/82)	50K Feet (Flt #212 9/13/83)	—
Longest Range Demo	1,985 NM (Flt #224 9/23/83)	—	—
1st Flight with GE F110 Slim-Line Engine	—	Flt #274 (7/19/84)	—
1st Flight with Large Normal Shock Inlet	—	Flt #311 (6/26/85)	—
Flights			
Total Number of Flights	437	361	798
Air-to-Air Flights	318 (72.8%)	230 (63.7%)	548 (68.7%)
Air-to-Ground Flights	119 (27.2%)	131 (36.3%)	250 (31.3%)
Flight Hours			
Total Flight Hours	532.6	407.1	939.7
Air-to-Air Flight Hours	400.0 (75.1%)	283.1 (69.5%)	683.1 (62.7%)
Air-to-Ground Flight Hours	132.6 (24.9%)	124.0 (30.5%)	256.6 (27.3%)
Average Hours Per Flight	1.22	1.13	1.18

Program Cancellation: General Dynamics' Perspective

Many years later, Randy Kent presented his perspective on the fate of the F-16XL program. This was in conjunction with the 25th anniversary celebration of the first flight of the F-16XL, held in Fort Worth in July 2007. Kent stated that the F-16XL program had been going well, it was on schedule and on cost, performance predictions were being verified by flight-test results, and reasonable production costs had been established. He noted that the USAF budget contained funding for a preliminary F-16XL production plan and, in his opinion, there was strong military and congressional support. However, the Air Force had raised several technical issues. Kent said that their main complaint was that the F-16XL was too heavy for the available engine thrust. He countered that this resulted in "a small loss in subsonic turn capability" compared to the basic F-16 and, besides, "a growth engine [the GE F110] was in the works."[63] The Air Force also noted that the F-16XL flyaway cost was three million dollars higher than the flyaway cost of a standard F-16. Kent retorted that this still "was much lower than the competing F-15E."[64] His presentation also highlighted the programmatic issues that, in Kent's opinion, influenced the Air Force decision to terminate the program.

Kent stated that the Air Force at the time had significant budget problems and major debates were under way concerning F-16 versus F-15 procurement. There were serious concerns that the F-15 production line would be closed down as delivery of the last of the planned air superiority variant of the F-15 fighter was imminent. Finally, "a new program—the Advanced Tactical Fighter (that would evolve into the Lockheed F-22 Raptor)—was becoming a major focus at the USAF senior staff level."[65] Randy Kent concluded his presentation to the audience, made up largely of Lockheed Fort Worth representatives, with a chart that accurately summarized the decisions taken by the Air Force leadership in the 1984–85 timeframe. Using the following statements, Kent reported that the USAF senior staff had concluded that there were more programs upcoming than the budget could support, the F-15 line must be kept open, the F-15E (an air-to-ground version of the F-15) would be funded, the Advanced Tactical Fighter program must proceed immediately, the F-16XL program must be eliminated, and the F-16XL was a great idea at the wrong time.

End of the Air Force F-16XL Flight-Test Program

On October 1, 1985, F-6XL Program Manager Randy Kent forwarded a memo titled "End of the F-16XL Flight Test Program" to David S. Lewis, chairman of the board of General Dynamics. Kent reported, "F-16XL No. 2 ferried to Fort Worth from Edwards Air Force Base today, arriving 10 minutes ahead of schedule and on prediction for fuel usage. This marks the end of the F-16XL program under USAF contract.... To all of you who worked so hard to make the program a success, please accept my thanks for a job well done. Perhaps fortune will smile on F-16XL at a later date but for now it is a sad day."[66] Responding the very next day, Lewis stated, "It is a sad day. But all of those who worked on the F-16XL should take pride in the fact that their work resulted in a superb aircraft which under normal circumstances would be going into production instead of into the barn.... It has been rewarding to read the highly complementary comments on the quality of the XL volunteered by the USAF and GD pilots who had the opportunity to work on a real winner, even though no prize was awarded!"[67]

Even today, 30 years after its first flight, the F-16XL continues to have a dedicated and enthusiastic following among many former General Dynamics employees who participated in the engineering development and flight testing of the aircraft. Robert J. Wetherall, who as a newly hired young structural engineer at GD Fort Worth in the early 1980s worked on the development of the F-16XL, summarized why he liked the aircraft in these words: "It was beautiful, cool, had elements of *The Six Million Dollar Man* in it, and I was building something!"[68] Unfortunately, the ranks of former F-16XL team members continue to decrease as age takes its toll: Harry Hillaker, who played such a significant role in the original YF-16 Lightweight Fighter program and the subsequent F-16XL effort, passed away in 2009, and Jim McKinney, who piloted the aircraft on its first flight in 1982, died suddenly while playing golf in Atlanta in early 2011. Randy Kent, former F-16XL Program Manager, passed away after a long illness in 2014.

Endnotes

1. James C. Slife, *Creech Blue: Gen Bill Creech and the Reformation of the Tactical Air Forces, 1978–1984* (Maxwell Air Force Base, AL: Air University Press, 2004).
2. Aronstein and Piccirillo, *Have Blue and the F-117A.*
3. Hallion, "A Troubling Past: Air Force Fighter Acquisition since 1945."
4. Slife, "Creech Blue."
5. As of late 2012, the F-15 was still in production. Over 1,500 F-15s have been delivered or are on firm order. Production is anticipated to continue for foreign military sales through at least 2015.
6. Synthetic-Aperture Radar (SAR) was developed to address the limitations of conventional radars in imaging surface targets. SAR systems achieve good azimuth resolution independent of the slant range to the target. A synthetic aperture is produced by using the forward motion of the radar. As the aircraft moves toward a surface target, the target reflects radar pulses in rapid sequence. The SAR system in the aircraft processes these returns and creates a so-called "synthetic aperture" in the computer, providing much improved azimuth resolution and, hence, greater bombing accuracy.
7. Slife, "Creech Blue."
8. In addition to his role as president of McDonnell-Douglas Aircraft Corporation, Graff had been selected to serve on the McDonnell-Douglas Board of Directors in 1973; "People and Posts," *Flight International* (May 10, 1973).
9. Slife, "Creech Blue."
10. Clarence A. Robinson, "USAF Pushes Production, Performance," *Aviation Week & Space Technology* 114, no. 11 (March 16, 1981): pp. 48–53.
11. Steve Ritchie, "An Eagle for All Arenas," *Air Force Magazine* (November 1983).
12. Slife, "Creech Blue."
13. Ibid.
14. Robert D. Russ, USAF, "Tactical Fighter Development: We Have Debated Long Enough," *Air Force Magazine* 64, no. 4 (April 1981).
15. U.S. Congress, Senate, Committee on Armed Services, *Department of Defense Authorization for Fiscal Year 1980*, Hearings, 96th Cong. 1st Session (April 2, 1979), p. 2,213.
16. Edgar Ulsamer, "In Aeronautics Affordability is King," *Air Force Magazine* 63, no. 12 (December 1980).

17. Robinson, "USAF Pushes Production, Performance," pp. 48–53.

18. David C. Aronstein, Michael J. Hirschberg, and Albert C. Piccirillo, *Advanced Tactical Fighter to F-22 Raptor: Origins of the 21st Century Air Dominance Fighter* (Reston, VA: AIAA, 1998).

19. Young, "History of the Air Force Flight Test Center, 1 January 1983–30 September 1984."

20. Ibid.

21. Ibid.

22. John Pike, "Dual Role Fighter," *GlobalSecurity.org*, updated July 7, 2011, *http://www.globalsecurity.org/military/systems/aircraft/drf.htm*, accessed December 11, 2011.

23. Marshall L. Michel, *The Revolt of the Majors: How the Air Force Changed After Vietnam* (Ph.D. diss., Auburn University, 2006).

24. U.S. Congress, Senate Armed Services Committee, *Tactical Air Warfare*, 97th Cong. 2nd Session (March 2, 1982), p. 312.

25. USAF, "TACAIR Dual Role Fighter Requirement Briefing for the House Armed Services Committee, Research and Development Subcommittee," U.S. Air Force Tactical Air Command (March 24, 1982).

26. Both tables are from Enclosure I in Frank J. Conahan's letter to Casper W. Weinberger, "Concerns About the Air Force Approach to the Dual Role Fighter Comparison," GAO/NSAID-84-49 (January 19, 1984).

27. Conahan, "Concerns About the Air Force Approach to the Dual Role Fighter Comparison." In this document, the GAO also noted that "if F-15 production were stabilized at 36 aircraft per year, as intended by the conferees on the 1984 Congressional Authorization Act, annual F-15 production would have to be considerably greater than 36 aircraft to meet the Air Force's DRF fielding schedule."

28. Unit flyaway cost is a measure of the cost of a military aircraft. It includes the cost of the airframe, engines, avionics, weapons carriage and delivery systems, and other hardware and software installed in the aircraft. Unit flyaway cost does not include prior program costs such as research, development, test and evaluation (which are treated as sunk costs); the cost of support equipment; or future costs such as fuel, spares, and maintenance. Unit acquisition cost is the total price of an individual aircraft. It includes not only the airframe, avionics, and engine costs, but also auxiliary equipment costs, initial spares, technical data, support and training equipment costs, as well as one-time, nonrecurring contract costs such as Research, Development, Test and Evaluation (RDT&E), and program-related military construction costs. J. Richard Nelson, "F/A-22 Independent Cost

Estimate," Institute for Defense Analyses, Report P-4029 (August 2005). As an illustrative example of the very wide range that can exist between flyaway cost and total program unit acquisition cost, in 2012, the Air Force reported that the F-22A unit flyaway cost was $143 million while the GAO reported the F-22A program unit acquisition cost as $412 million.

29. Edgar Ulsamer, "Scoping the Technology Baseline," *Air Force Magazine* 65, no. 12, (December 1982).

30. Ulsamer, "Scoping the Technology Baseline."

31. Author unidentified, "USAF Wants Both F-15E and F-16E," *Flight International* (November 13, 1982): p. 1,426.

32. Ibid.

33. CBO, "A Review of the Department of Defense June 30, 1982 Selected Acquisition Report," Congress of the United States, CBO Special Study (September 1982).

34. Based on a comparative analysis by the author, the respective procurement quantities contained in the CBO report (538 F-16 DRFs vs. 400 DRF F-15s) apparently resulted from an assumption that the total derivative fighter modification cost would be held constant regardless of which variant was selected. The anticipated unit cost differential between the two variants, as determined by the Air Force in its August 1982 program cost analysis, was used to determine the potential F-16 DRF procurement quantity based on the procurement cost of 400 F-15 DRFs.

35. Graham Warwick, "US Fighter Options," *Flight International* 124, no. 3071 (July 16, 1983): pp. 139–146.

36. Dennis R. Jenkins, *McDonnell Douglas F-15 Eagle, Supreme Heavy-Weight Fighter* (Arlington, TX: Aerofax, 1998).

37. Conahan, "Concerns About the Air Force Approach to the Dual Role Fighter Comparison."

38. Ibid., Enclosure I.

39. USAF, Air Force Regulation (AFR) 57-1, Operational Requirements, Statement of Operational Need.

40. USAF, AFR 70-15, Source Selection Policy and Procedures.

41. DoD, Department of Defense Directive 5000.1, Major System Acquisitions.

42. USAF, AFR 70-15.

43. Conahan, "Concerns About the Air Force Approach to the Dual Role Fighter Comparison," Enclosure I.

44. Aronstein, *The Lightweight Fighter Program.*

45. Eugene Kozicharow, "USAF Selects F-15 as Dual-Role Fighter," *Aviation Week & Space Technology* 120, no. 10, (March 5, 1984): pp. 18–19; Edgar Ulsamer, "In Focus: The Dual Role Eagle—USAF Chooses the F-15E as Derivative Fighter," *Air Force Magazine* 67, no. 4 (April 1984).

46. First flight of the first Full-Scale Development F-15E occurred on December 11, 1986, with the first production aircraft (serial number 86-0183) delivered to the Air Force in April 1988. The first F-15E unit was operational in October 1989 at Seymour Johnson Air Force Base in North Carolina. Production of the F-15E for the U.S. Air Force ended in 1991 with 236 aircraft delivered. Additional variants of the basic F-15E design were tailored for the needs of Israel (25 aircraft), Saudi Arabia (72), South Korea (40), and Singapore (12). In a deal that was announced in December 2011, Saudi Arabia stated its intent to buy an additional 84 F-15Es. This will bring total F-15E production up to 469 aircraft.

47. Ulsamer, "In Focus: The Dual Role Eagle."

48. Robert D. Russ, Lt. Gen. USAF, "The Fighter Roadmap," *Air Force Magazine* 67, no. 6 (June 1984).

49. Young, "AFFTC History."

50. Lt. Colonel Edwin A. Thomas, Director, F-16XL CTF, interview by Dr. Richard P. Hallion, AFFTC History Office, June 1985. Quoted in Young, "AFFTC History."

51. Talty, "The F-16XL Demonstrates New Capabilities."

52. Author unidentified, "F-15 Wins US Fighter Contest," *Flight International* (March 3, 1984): p. 550.

53. Ibid.

54. The F-16 Enhanced Strategic (ES) was a variant of the F-16C/D fitted with conformal fuel tanks that provided it with 40 percent greater range. It had an internal forward-looking infrared (FLIR) system with the capabilities of the LANTIRN navigation and targeting system but without the drag associated with external pods. The F-16ES was unsuccessfully offered to Israel as an alternative to the F-15I Strike Eagle in late 1993. It was one of several F-16 options offered to the United Arab Emirates (UAE) and led to development of the F-16E/F for the UAE. An F-16C was modified to ES configuration to test the conformal tanks with simulated FLIR sensor turrets fitted above and below the nose of the aircraft. The F-16ES test aircraft first flew on November 5, 1994, with flight testing completed in January 1995.

55. Author unidentified, "McDonnell Douglas Prepared to Compare F-15E and F-15ES," *Aerotech News and Review* 9, no. 24 (December 9, 1994).

56. Harry J. Hillaker, "Personal letter to Paul J. Kinson, Publisher/Editor, *Aerotech News and Review*," January 24, 1995.

57. Berry, "The Revolutionary Evolution of the F-16XL."

58. GD, "Manufacturing/Project Planning Chart: F-16XL Production Flow (Two Place Aircraft)," General Dynamics Corporation, Fort Worth Division, January 26, 1983.

59. Aronstein, *The Lightweight Fighter Program*.

60. This internal, undated, unsigned GD memo was provided courtesy of Robert Wetherall, Lockheed Martin.

61. The CDC Cyber mainframe-class supercomputers were the primary products of Control Data Corporation (CDC) during the 1970s and 1980s. In their day, they were the computer architecture of choice for mathematically intensive computing such as modeling fluid flow, stress analysis, electrochemical machining analysis, and other applications. Virtual Address eXtension (VAX) was an instruction set architecture (ISA) developed by Digital Equipment Corporation (DEC) in the mid-1970s. The VAX name was also used by DEC for a family of computer systems based on this processor architecture.

62. This disruptive camouflage scheme was named after the brilliant and highly influential aviation artist Keith Ferris, who proposed its use on combat aircraft. Reminiscent of the dazzle schemes that had been successfully used on warships and merchant shipping as far back as the First World War, Ferris camouflage schemes were evaluated on a number of aircraft, including the F-14 and F-15, but test results were inconclusive and it was not adopted for service use.

63. Randy Kent, "Perspectives on the F-16XL Program," presentation to the F-16XL First Flight 25th Anniversary Celebration, Lockheed Martin Corporation, Fort Worth, TX, July 3, 2007.

64. Ibid.

65. Ibid.

66. Ibid.

67. Ibid.

68. *The Six Million Dollar Man* was a popular TV series in the late 1970s about a test pilot who survived the crash of an experimental lifting body reentry vehicle with severe injuries. After undergoing extensive surgery and receiving bionic implants, he went on to work on highly classified special projects. The show, based on the novel *Cyborg* by Martin Caidin, appeared on the ABC TV network from 1973 to 1978 with the actor Lee Majors playing the title role.

F-16XL-2 flying with a supersonic laminar flow control suction glove leading edge, April 1996. (NASA)

CHAPTER 8

NASA Supersonic Laminar Flow Research

After remaining in storage for several years, both F-16XLs were subsequently transferred to NASA for flight research into a number of areas relevant to the development of a high-speed commercial transport aircraft. These included investigations into supersonic laminar flow, noise abatement, and acoustic signatures. In addition, the aircraft were employed to study pitch-and-roll oscillation phenomenology, for flutter research, and in the evaluation of a digital flight control system upgrade to the aircraft.

NASA use of the F-16XL as an experimental research aircraft had its genesis in the High-Speed Research program that began in the late 1980s. The HSR program was NASA's highest aeronautical priority during the 1990s. This was in large part driven by the commercial aircraft and engine companies. They believed that NASA could make its most useful contribution to development of a future High-Speed Civil Transport by focusing the HSR program on demonstrating and maturing the basic technologies that could lead to a practical supersonic transport. Boeing, in particular, highlighted the fact that there were major technical risks inherent to successful development of a supersonic transport aircraft. These were so great that the aircraft and engine industries were unwilling to invest in an HSCT effort unless NASA reduced the known technical risks by defining a well-focused HSR program.[1] As a result of such industry concerns, the HSR program was restructured in 1992 to emphasize those technologies that best addressed critical issues related to the economic viability of commercial supersonic travel. The restructuring effort was headed by Cecil C. Rosen, the NASA director of aeronautics. Phase I had concentrated on proving that the environmental concerns of daily SST operations could be overcome. The goal of the restructured program, now referred to as HSR Phase II, was to mature the technologies necessary for a post-2000 HSCT to be economically competitive with subsonic civil transports. Economic competitiveness was defined as a ticket surcharge of no more than 20 to 30 percent for supersonic travel. Following extensive analytical studies and economic market analyses, both Boeing and McDonnell-Douglas concluded that this goal drove the maximum takeoff gross weight of a future HSCT to an upper limit of not greater than 750,000 pounds. The conceptual HSCT was intended to carry 300 passengers while cruising at Mach 2.4 over intercontinental ranges of up to 5,000 nautical miles. The takeoff gross weight limitation drove the HSR program to emphasize the set of technologies that would have the most impact on achieving the HSCT takeoff gross weight goal.

The HSR Phase II program was led by the HSR Program Office at Langley and was supported by the Dryden Flight Research Center, the Ames Research Center, and the Lewis (now Glenn) Research Center. Major industry partners in the HSR program were Boeing Commercial Airplane Group, McDonnell-Douglas Aerospace, Rockwell Corporation's North American Aviation Division, General Electric Aircraft Engines, and Pratt & Whitney. Research tasks were accomplished by a joint NASA-industry team, with personnel divided into integrated work units. Boeing was designated overall industry manager for HSR activities. The HSR Program Office established management offices that were focused on critical HSCT-related technology topics. These included technology integration (under William P. Gilbert), aerodynamic performance (Robert L. Calloway), materials and structures (Rodney H. Ricketts), environmental impact (Allen H. Whitehead, Jr.), and flight deck technology (Daniel G. Baize). Major decisions in the program were made by a team comprised of one member from each of the four prime contractors representing the two airframe companies and the two engine developers (Boeing, McDonnell-Douglas, General Electric, and Pratt & Whitney) and two from NASA. This team, known as the Integrated Planning Team (IPT), oversaw the efforts of the Airframe Management Team (AMT) and the Propulsion Management Team (PMT). Subordinate to the airframe and propulsion management teams were a series of Technology Management Teams (TMTs). The TMTs, in turn, supervised the efforts of Government and industry researchers organized into a variety of Integrated Technology Development (ITD) teams. In addition to the prime contractors, more than 40 major subcontractors were also on the integrated HSR team. The NASA Glenn Research Center (formerly known as the Lewis Research Center) oversaw the efforts of the Propulsion Management Team. The PMT was organizationally similar to the Airframe Management Team, and its efforts also came under the oversight of the High-Speed Research program IPT.

As it continued to evolve, the HSR program was focused on developing the critical technologies that would enable a future supersonic transport to achieve its performance goals at an economical cost. A clear consensus emerged within NASA and the aircraft industry that strong technology development efforts were needed in the areas of airframe and composite structures and advanced propulsion if this vision was to be feasible. To this end, a small supersonic laminar flow flight research effort that was originally part of the NASA

Aircraft Energy Efficiency (ACEE) program was transferred under the HSR program. This was not an easy sell, and supersonic laminar flow control just squeaked into the program. ACEE had supported flight research into laminar flow control and had sponsored a number of flight-test efforts using various types of subsonic civil and military aircraft.[2] After the ACEE program had been terminated in 1986, Langley continued its support of laminar flow research through a Laminar Flow Control (LFC) Project Office. Studies conducted prior to the formal start of the HSR program had led the LFC Project Office to consider an aircraft flight research program focused on SLFC. Many members of the Langley research staff felt strongly that SLFC was a critical ingredient to the success of a future supersonic transport, especially if such an aircraft was intended to be economically viable.[3]

The NASA Langley LFC Project Office, under Richard D. Wagner, had issued contracts to both Boeing and McDonnell-Douglas Corporation in 1988. The purpose of these studies was to determine the potential benefits that might be achieved through the use of SLFC on a supersonic civil transport. In their study, Boeing used their Boeing Model 2707-300 SST configuration that had originally been conceived as the U.S. contender to the Anglo-French Concorde before it was cancelled. They determined that if SLFC could be successfully integrated into this design, its fuel consumption could be reduced by 12.5 percent, and the maximum takeoff gross weight of the aircraft could be reduced by 8.5 percent. The payload of the basic Boeing supersonic transport design was calculated to be only 7 percent of its takeoff gross weight. The MDC study indicated that SLFC was feasible for their 308-passenger Mach 2.2 conceptual design that featured a cranked-arrow wing and rear-mounted tail surfaces. MDC had concluded that fuel consumption could be reduced by 17 percent if both the wing and tail surfaces could be made *fully laminar back to the control surface hinge lines*.[4] The savings in fuel consumption and gross weight that potentially could be achieved using SLFC represented major improvements in the capability of an HSCT. However, SLFC technology was considered risky and its payoffs problematic at best. It had to be proven to be both feasible and practical for commercial airline use. In summary, both Boeing and McDonnell-Douglas highlighted the major issues and risks related to incorporating SLFC technology into future supersonic transports.[5]

Laminar flow had been the subject of extensive research efforts since the 1930s, and the technology potentially offered very significant reductions in fuel consumption. However, practical applications of the technology to production aircraft (especially large aircraft) had eluded engineers despite a long series of attempts over the years. Laminar flow technology, especially as it related to the supersonic flight regime, had significant risks involving airframe design, system integration, production engineering, and manufacturing.

Another major unknown area with perceived high risk was the operations and maintenance of HSCT aircraft fitted with supersonic laminar flow control systems in widespread airline service. Overall, the risks associated with laminar flow control technology were known to be high. Most experts believed that a practical, low- to moderate-risk SLFC approach was unlikely to be ready in time to be integrated into an HSCT design on the planned schedule that called for initiation of airframe and engine full-scale development in the year 2000 without a major risk-reduction initiative.

The general belief in the aircraft industry in the late 1980s was that selection of supersonic laminar flow technology for use in an HSCT development was a high-risk challenge. They strongly urged that supersonic laminar flow control technology be demonstrated and matured via a Government-funded flight demonstration program. NASA agreed that a flight research program was needed to validate the benefits that could be achieved from the use of SLFC. Without such a Government-sponsored program, industry would be unwilling to adopt the concept. Obtaining an appropriate high-speed aircraft that could be readily modified for a NASA SLFC research program was considered a mandatory requirement for the demonstration. MDC had already addressed the possible use of the F-16XL for an SLFC technology demonstration in their NASA-sponsored study. Langley's Jerry N. Hefner was familiar with NASA's role in the F-16XL development effort and recognized that its cranked-arrow wing design was similar to that envisioned for use on a future HSCT. Hefner recommended using the two Air Force F-16XLs, then in storage at the GD factory in Fort Worth, as test platforms for a NASA research program. Theodore G. Ayers, the deputy director at NASA Dryden, strongly supported the F-16XL initiative, as did James W. Smolka and Joe Bill Dryden; both were GD F-16 project pilots in Fort Worth at the time.[6] Hefner and Wallace C. Sawyer, who headed the HSR program at Langley, worked with NASA Headquarters to establish an SLFC program based on the F-16XLs as test aircraft. Cecil C. Rosen, the director of aeronautics at NASA Headquarters, agreed that these aircraft would be important to a NASA flight research effort. Arrangements were then made with the Air Force for the transfer of the two F-16XL prototypes for NASA use in support of the HSR program.[7]

As Jerry Hefner subsequently recalled,

> My interest in the F-16XL came after a Director's tour to GD when I was Branch Head of the Civil Aircraft Branch. I saw the airplanes and wondered out loud to those around me whether we might use them for laminar flow research. A year or two later, one of the individuals that showed us the airplanes called me and said the USAF was going to destroy them by live fire. He thought if I (NASA) would like them for research that now was the time to act.

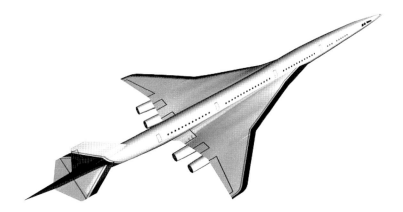

NASA's conceptual HSCT design featured a cranked-arrow wing similar to that of the F-16XL. (NASA)

Wally [Wallace C. Sawyer] and I talked about my desire to get the airplanes for SLFC. Jan Tulinius (at Rockwell), who had been talking to me about using SLFC to cool supersonic fighters' leading edges to reduce their signature, was very interested and he wanted to conduct a quick experiment on the F-16XL ship 1 to see if LF could be achieved back to the front spar.[8] With this information Wally agreed to approach Cecil Rosen about getting the two aircraft. Wally felt that Cecil would not approve getting the aircraft for SLFC, but if he thought Rockwell wanted us to have the aircraft to conduct experiments to improve the stealth characteristics of supersonic aircraft, then Cecil might approve the transfer. Wally was right and GD transferred the aircraft to NASA and avoided their being destroyed in live fire. The rest is history.[9]

The F-16XL Transfer to NASA and a Research Synopsis

Final arrangements for the transfer of the F-16XLs were completed in 1988. Later that year, F-16XL-1 was removed from storage and prepared for flight. On March 9, 1989, GD test pilot Joe Bill Dryden flew the aircraft on its first functional check flight since it had been in long-term storage. This was the first time that it had flown since August 14, 1985. Earlier in his career, Dryden had been one of the original project pilots assigned to the F-16XL combined test force at Edwards AFB. The actual transfer of the aircraft to NASA officially occurred on March 10, 1989, when David McCarthy of General Dynamics

The F-16XL-1 photographed on the ramp of the NASA Langley Research Center in Hampton, VA, during its brief deployment to the East Coast in 1994. (NASA)

signed the Department of Defense DD Form 250, titled *Material Inspection and Receiving Report*.[10] Assigned NASA aircraft identification number 849 (the "8" prefix indicating a Dryden aircraft), the F-16XL-1 would be modified for passive (shape and profile effects) and active (inflight-suction) laminar flow research studies. Its first flight with a highly instrumented laminar flow wing glove occurred on May 3, 1990, when it was flown by NASA Dryden test pilot Steven D. Ishmael. The single-seat F-16XL-1 was briefly assigned to the NASA Langley Research Center in Virginia from April to November 1994, where it was to be used to determine takeoff performance and engine noise as part of a project to evaluate a future HSCT configuration. After a short stay at Langley, F-16XL-1 departed for the Ames-Dryden Flight Research Facility in November 1994. In 1995, after being returned to its original aerodynamic configuration and fitted with acoustic pressure sensors, F-16XL-1 was used with a NASA Lockheed SR-71 and a propeller-driven Lockheed YO-3A in a research project intended to further quantify sonic boom phenomenology. In 1997, F-16XL-1 was modified with a digital fly-by-wire flight control system (DFCS) that replaced the original analog FBW flight control system.

On February 12, 1991, Joe Bill Dryden, who had retired from the Air Force to become a company test pilot with General Dynamics, flew the F-16XL-2 from Fort Worth to Dryden, where it was formally transferred to NASA. Prior to its delivery to NASA, the more powerful General Electric F110-GE-129 turbofan engine had been installed in the aircraft, replacing the F110-GE-100 engine that was been used during the Air Force flight-test program. The two-seat

F-16XL-2 carried the NASA identification number 848. At Dryden, F-16XL-2 was fitted with an experimental titanium wing glove section installed on its extended left wing for use in a NASA project involving supersonic laminar flow control investigations. The glove, designed by Rockwell, was fitted with an active laminar flow suction system. This system was used to siphon off a portion of the aerodynamic boundary layer over the leading edge of the wing. Suction was applied through 10 million extremely small holes drilled through the wing glove. These holes had been precisely cut by a special laser. The active suction was intended to maintain smooth airflow within the boundary layer during supersonic flight conditions. A wind tunnel model of the aircraft fitted with the active suction control modification was subjected to about 2,800 hours of testing to validate its aerodynamics with the wing glove. In addition to wind tunnel testing, a computer model of the aircraft with the glove modification was evaluated at NASA Dryden to ensure that its handling qualities were not adversely affected. Since the objectives of the SLFC project were oriented to application of the technology to an HSCT, high-g, high-AoA maneuvering was not required. This had led to a decision to design the SLFC glove modification for 3-g flight conditions. This restriction was imposed on the subsequent SLFC flight-test program. F-16XL-2 was flown 45 times on the NASA SLFC project between October 13, 1995, and November 26, 1996.

Dryden had initially used F-16XL-1 for exploratory investigations of laminar flow technology in 1992, during which time a small, perforated-titanium active-suction wing glove with a turbocompressor was installed on the aircraft. This initial research effort with F-16XL-1 was followed by a more ambitious program of supersonic laminar flow control testing with the two-seat F-16XL-2. This effort would use of a larger active suction glove mounted on the left wing of the aircraft. In the spring of 1992, Boeing had begun working with NASA Langley and Dryden, as well as with Rockwell and McDonnell-Douglas, in an HSR-sponsored project for design and testing of this larger active suction wing glove on F-16XL-2. Boeing and Rockwell were responsible for the fabrication and installation of the highly complex titanium glove, which reportedly cost about $14 million and required three attempts to produce.[11] Boeing and McDonnell-Douglas were responsible for assisting NASA in analyzing flight-test data. Michael C. Fischer, from NASA Langley's LFCPO, was the NASA technical principal investigator, with Lisa J. Bjarke serving as Dryden principal investigator. The NASA F-16XL flight project office was located at the NASA Dryden Flight Research Center at Edwards, CA. Marta R. Bohn-Meyer was the Dryden F-16XL-2 SLFC flight-test project manager.[12] Carol A. Reukauf later became the Dryden project manager after Bohn-Meyer was promoted to Dryden chief engineer. Dana D. Purifoy and Mark P. Stuckey were the Dryden project research pilots for the F-16XL-2 SLFC project.[13]

F-16XL-2 flying with a supersonic laminar flow control suction glove leading edge, April 1996. (NASA)

F-16XL-2 Supersonic Laminar Flow Control Flight-Test Synopsis

Flight measurements were obtained for the airflow on the leading-edge passive glove installed on the F-16XL-2's right wing during the 1991 to 1992 timeframe. The passive glove had been designed by McDonnell-Douglas Corporation and built at the NASA Dryden Flight Research Center. The goal of the initial SLFC flight tests with XL-2 was to obtain surface pressure data needed to calibrate computer software design codes, particularly in the leading-edge boundary layer attachment-line region. In the first phase of flight tests, the program addressed the major technical issue of preventing the fuselage turbulent boundary layer from contaminating the attachment-line region of the wing. Characterizing the acoustic disturbance field and the disturbances from the fuselage boundary layer was another objective. The pressure and laminar flow data from this initial flight-test phase provided valuable information for use in designing the active suction glove that would be mounted on F-16XL-2's left wing in the next phase of the SLFC test effort.

The perforated active suction glove used on F-16XL-2 had been designed in a collaborative effort between Boeing, McDonnell-Douglas, Rockwell, and NASA. The glove covered about 75-percent of the upper-wing surface and 60-percent of the wing's leading edge. It was constructed of inner and outer titanium skins and aluminum stringers. A turbocompressor in the aircraft's fuselage provided suction to draw air through nearly 12 million holes. These were positioned in 20 individual suction regions on the glove surface. Air was drawn through the millions of individual holes in the glove via a highly complex manifold system that employed 20 valves. The glove was instrumented to determine the extent of laminar flow and to measure other variables, such as the acoustic environment that affected laminar flow at various flight conditions. Suction was provided by a modified Boeing 707 turbocompressor installed in what had previously been the M61 Vulcan cannon's 20-mm ammunition bay located aft of the cockpit on F-16XL-2. The SLFC flight research effort with F-16XL-2 was intended to achieve laminar flow over 50 to 60 percent of its wing chord.

In addition to the flight-test effort, computational fluid dynamics computer software codes and design methodologies were to be created, along with laminar flow control design criteria for use at supersonic speeds. The geometric asymmetry of the F-16XL-2 aircraft when fitted with the suction glove on the left wing required dedicated wind tunnel tests to determine the aerodynamic and stability and control characteristics of the modified aircraft before actual flight testing could begin. The first F-16XL-2 flight after the SLFC suction glove modification occurred on October 13, 1995. Evaluation of the active suction glove itself began on November 22, 1995, with the first supersonic flight test with the suction system operating occurring on January 24, 1996. The fight-test portion of the SLFC program with F-16XL-2 ended on November 26, 1996, after 45 research fights. During the 13-month flight research program, the NASA-industry SLFC team logged about 90 hours of flight time with F-16XL-2, much of it at speeds of Mach 2 at altitudes of 50,000 feet and above. The project demonstrated that laminar airflow could be achieved over a significant portion of a highly swept wing at supersonic speeds using an active suction system. A highly detailed synopsis of the SLFC flight research effort with F-16XL-2 is included in the closing section of this chapter.

SLFC Summary

Both F-16XL-1 and F-16XL-2 had configuration-specific shock and expansion waves, which influenced the laminar flow on the wings at supersonic conditions. Supersonic shock waves emanating from the canopies and engine inlets spread out over the wings and expansion waves coming from beneath the wing caused a highly three-dimensional flow field. These resulted in difficulties in obtaining laminar flow on the attachment-line region at the same test conditions. Despite these problems, which resulted from the decision to use the F-16XL as the SLFC research aircraft, NASA publicly stated that the supersonic laminar flow control flight experiments with the aircraft achieved about 70 to 80 percent of the initial research goals. Yet despite the somewhat promising results from the flight research program, there were other major difficulties with integration of active suction supersonic laminar flow control technologies into a commercial aircraft. Boeing strongly expressed their opinion that the manufacturing processes needed to produce a practical SLFC system for a commercial supersonic transport were so challenging that they were effectively a showstopper. Boeing had to try four times before they were able to fabricate a suction glove for F-16XL-2 that met the challenging smoothness and stiffness standards required to maintain supersonic laminar flow. Even then, some manufacturing discrepancies were simply tolerated in order to move the program forward. The surface contours of the wing glove had to be controlled to no more than a few thousandths of an inch. This had already proven very challenging to achieve on the F-16XL's small, stiff wing. It was well beyond Boeing's manufacturing capabilities to produce an active suction glove for a wing the size of that planned for the HSCT. Depending on the specific design approach, a wing of that size was estimated to require precision laser drilling of as many as a billion tiny holes in its laminar flow control suction panels.

In essence, Boeing felt that the SLFC-related manufacturing technology needed for a HSCT production line would be both very expensive and risky to develop. This was due to the precision required to produce active suction on a flexible airliner wing that was structurally an order of magnitude larger in size than that of the F-16XL wing. In addition to high manufacturing costs, other challenges with SLFC technology included costs associated with keeping the extremely small suction holes clear during routine day-to-day scheduled airline service. Commercial airline operations, by definition, would have involved routine flight in heavy rain with icing conditions often encountered. Additionally, airborne insects found in the vicinity of many commercial airfields would have resulted in insect accretion on the wing leading edges. These factors had a high potential to cause the boundary layer over the wing of an HSCT to prematurely transition from laminar to turbulent flow, increasing the drag due to skin friction and defeating the purpose of a suction-type SLFC system.[14]

By 1995, based on several industry design concepts, computer modeling, and wind tunnel tests, NASA had selected a Technology Concept Aircraft (TCA) as a common reference point for use with the HSR technology development and risk-reduction process. This single concept was intended to have improved aerodynamic performance and operational characteristics while also meeting environmental goals for engine emissions and noise pollution. An important rationale for the Technology Concept Aircraft was to serve as a basis to ensure that appropriate technology was available to meet both the needs of a practical and economically realistic design *and* its concurrent development schedule. The implications of this dual rationale had a major impact on the F-16XL SLFC program. In September 1996, the Airframe Management Team within the HSR program elected to terminate the F-16XL SLFC program.

This decision was based on a general agreement among both the Government and, especially, the aerospace industry members of the Airframe Management Team. The consensus within the team was that supersonic laminar flow control was not a near-term technology that could be available in time for integration into a High-Speed Civil Transport program on any realistic cost and development schedule.[15]

Endnotes

1. Cecil C. Rosen III began his professional career with Pratt & Whitney Aircraft in advanced jet engine design. He held a number of key positions at NASA, including manager of propulsion research and technology, director of aerospace research, and associate administrator of the Office of Aeronautics, where he managed the four NASA Research Centers (Ames, Langley, Lewis [later renamed Glenn], and Dryden).

2. Mark D. Bowles, *The "Apollo" of Aeronautics: NASA's Aircraft Energy Efficiency Program (1973–1987)* (Washington, DC: NASA SP-2009-574 2009).

3. Michael Fischer and Chandra S. Vemuru, "Application of Laminar Flow Control to the High Speed Civil Transport—The NASA Supersonic Laminar Flow Control Program," presented at the Aerospace Technology Conference and Exposition, Long Beach, CA, September 1991, SAE Paper 912115 (September 1, 1991).

4. As the subsequent SLFC test program with F-16XL-2 would reveal, achieving fully laminar flow over the entire surface of the HSCT wing would have been extremely difficult. Thus, the purported reductions in fuel consumption and HSCT gross weight that could be achieved by the use of SLFC were highly suspect. These facts, as well as the major manufacturing challenges in producing an active suction wing for the very large HSCT, were the primary reasons that the SLFC effort with the F-16XL was eventually cancelled.

5. Arthur G. Powell, "Supersonic LFC: Challenges and Opportunities," in *Proceedings of the NASA Langley Research Center First Annual High-Speed Research Workshop, Williamsburg, Virginia, May 14–16, 1991, Part 4* (April 1, 1992), pp. 1,823–1,840; Yorgo E. Saounatsos, "Technology Readiness and Development Risks of the New Supersonic Transport," *Journal of Aerospace Engineering* 11, no. 3 (July 1998): pp. 95–104.

6. Smolka would soon return to NASA Dryden as a NASA research pilot. Eric Hehs, "Marta Bohn-Myer: NASA Flight Researcher," *Code One Magazine* (April 1994).

7. Erik M. Conway, *High Speed Dreams: NASA and the Technopolitics of Supersonic Transportation, 1945–1999* (Baltimore, MD: Johns Hopkins University Press, 2005).

8. Jan R. Tulinius had conceived of the Active Aeroelastic Wing (AAW) concept in 1983. AAW was later evaluated on a modified F/A-18A under a jointly funded and managed Air Force Research

Laboratory–NASA Dryden Flight Research Center program. A total of 95 AAW research flights were completed between November 2002 and March 2005. Tulinius later was chief scientist for the North American Aviation Division of Rockwell International Corp before the company merged with Boeing.

9. The Hefner quote was provided in his comments on the manuscript of this book and is contained in correspondence between the author and Joseph Chambers, November 27, 2012.

10. Author unidentified, "F-16XL Aircraft Fly Out of Storage to Perform Flight Tests," *Aviation Week & Space Technology* 130, no. 13 (March 27, 1989): p. 27; author unidentified, "Arrow-wing F-16 Airborne Again," *Flight International* (March 25, 1989): p. 7.

11. Conway, *High Speed Dreams.*

12. Marta Bohn-Meyer had been at NASA Dryden since 1979. She served in positions that included director of flight operations, director of safety and mission assurance, deputy director of flight operations, and deputy director of aerospace projects. Bohn-Meyer became F-16XL Supersonic Laminar Flow Control project manager in 1990. In October 2001, she was selected as the NASA Dryden chief engineer. An accomplished aerobatic pilot and twice member of the U.S. Unlimited Aerobatic Team, Bohn-Meyer died when her Giles 300 aerobatic aircraft crashed near Yukon, OK, as a result of a catastrophic failure of the front canopy hinge. Alan Brown, "NASA Dryden Chief Engineer Marta Bohn-Meyer Dies in Airplane Crash," NASA DFRC Press Release 05-60, September 19, 2005.

13. In a 1994 interview with *Flight International*, Bohn-Meyer commented, "This [SLFC] is the kind of technology that will enable us to sharpen our pencils to design the HSCT." Quoted in Guy Norris, "Smooth and Supersonic," *Flight International* 145, no. 4421 (May 18, 1994): pp. 32–33. The same article quoted NASA sources as believing that SLFC applied to an HSCT design could reduce fuel consumption by 9 percent. That in turn, reportedly would have cut the aircraft TOGW by between 4 and 7 percent.

14. Boeing's Malcolm MacKinnon's perspective on SLFC manufacturing difficulties, as reported in Conway, *High Speed Dreams.* MacKinnon was the HSR deputy program manager.

15. Conway, *High Speed Dreams*; "NASA F-16XL Laminar-Flow Tests Will Aid HSCT Effort," *Flight International* (February 1, 1995).

F-16XL-1 with the active suction glove on the left wing that was used for research into super-sonic laminar flow control. The grey titanium active suction panel is visible on the inner region of the white wing glove. The passive outer leading edge of the wing glove is painted black in the region where a liquid-crystal sensor array was located. A video camera in the wingtip pod was used to record the liquid-crystal patterns. (NASA)

CHAPTER 9

Detailed Aspects of the F-16XL SLFC Research Effort

For NASA supersonic laminar flow research purposes, both F-16XL research aircraft were to be modified with the installation of titanium gloves smoothly faired into the wing with graphite and epoxy. The weight associated with these gloves had the potential to affect the flutter characteristics of the aircraft. For instance, the wing glove modification on F-16XL-1 weighed a total of 207 pounds. The wing gloves extended from the forward wing spar on the lower wing surface, around the leading edge, and aft to the 25- to 40-percent chord line on the upper wing surface of F-16XL-1. A glove fairing stretched further aft from the glove to the trailing-edge spar on the upper surface to ensure smooth airflow across the wing. The active suction wing glove installation later added to F-16XL-2 was even heavier and extended farther aft on the wing chord. Previous NASA experience with wing gloves had shown that changes in wing structural weight, stiffness, and airfoil shape resulted in shifts in wing torsion modes and vibrational frequencies. These had the potential of lowering the speed at which flutter could be encountered (flutter onset speed).

NASA F-16XL Flutter Testing

The effects of SLFC wing gloves on F-16XL aeroelastic and aeroservoelastic characteristics needed to be assessed to determine safe flutter flight envelopes. This required ground vibration and flight tests both before and after the glove modifications were installed on the aircraft. One ground vibration test (GVT) was performed with the basic F-16XL configuration to provide the baseline case. Another GVT was performed after the aircraft was modified with the glove. The GVTs showed that several structural modes involving the control surfaces were changed at higher excitation frequencies. Subsequent flight testing with the glove installed showed satisfactory structural damping levels and trends with the modified aircraft within the flight envelope approved for the SLFC research effort. The approved flight envelope for the F-16XL research aircraft as modified for the NASA SLFC research program had significant restrictions compared to the unmodified F-16XL aircraft. NASA Dryden research engineer David Voracek played a significant role managing and executing the F-16XL flutter test program.[1]

Flutter Test Objectives

During the original Air Force F-16XL flutter clearance program, two wing-tip configurations had been tested. One configuration consisted of AIM-9 launcher rails with missiles mounted on both wingtips. The other was the clean aircraft only without the missile launch rails mounted. Flutter clearances had been issued for these configurations out to a maximum dynamic pressure (max q) of 1,700 pounds per square feet. The clean-wingtip F-16XL configuration had been tested up to a maximum speed of Mach 1.6 at 30,000 feet. The NASA SLFC test program included an F-16XL configuration with wingtip-mounted missile launcher rails without AIM-9 missiles being carried. This configuration had not been evaluated during inflight flutter testing in the earlier program. Flutter analysis data provided by General Dynamics for the unmodified F-16XL-1 aircraft showed that the flutter frequencies for different fuel and wingtip store configurations ranged from 23.5 to 29.2 Hz. The wingtip-mounted missile launcher rail-only configuration (no missiles carried) was one of the configurations to be used during the SLFC flight research program. This configuration had flutter frequencies that ranged from 23.5 to 25.3 Hz. The addition of the wing glove was determined to affect aircraft control surface vibration modes above 20 Hz. The aircraft control surfaces were predicted to have the lowest flutter speeds based on analyses performed during the original F-16XL aircraft development effort. Potential changes in control surface vibration modes due to addition of the wing glove raised concerns about a high-frequency control surface vibration often referred to as buzz. Buzz normally occurs in the transonic flight region for most aircraft and can lead to structural failure.[2] Buzz is caused by the interaction of supersonic shock waves with the flexible structure of the control surface. The potential for control surface flutter coupled with the fact that the launcher rails-only configuration had never flight-tested for flutter were important factors in planning flutter test requirements for the modified F-16XL research aircraft.

There were two aspects of the F-16XL flutter test program: ground vibration testing and in-flight flutter tests. The two main objectives of flutter testing were first to assess the effect of the wing glove and its associated hardware on the structural characteristics of the modified aircraft that would be flown during the SLFC evaluation. The second test objective was to establish a safe flight envelope free of any flutter or aeroservoelastic instability. The desired flight envelope for the SLFC program with F-16XL-1 was defined as a dynamic pressure of 533 pounds per square foot up to an altitude of 32,000 feet. Mach number was then increased up to a max q of 1,008 pounds per square inch. This max q was maintained as altitude was increased up the wing glove structure's design temperature limit, which was 160 °F.[3] The flutter envelope for F-16XL-2 would later be further expanded to enable the SLFC research effort to encompass a flight envelope out to Mach 2.0 at altitudes well above 50,000 feet.

Ground Vibration Testing

Ground vibration tests used flight-ready F-16XL aircraft. Equipment that was not yet installed in the aircraft was simulated by ballast weights placed as close to the proper locations as possible. The aircraft was on its landing gear during vibration testing, and the landing gear struts were collapsed to eliminate potential nonlinearities that could affect vibration characteristics of the basic aircraft. The tires were deflated to one-half their normal pressure to provide a softer support. The fuel load included full fuselage tanks and empty wing tanks. The wing tanks were not fueled to ensure that the natural vibration modes of the wing structure and control surfaces were unaffected by the weight of the fuel in the internal wing tanks. All structural panels were fastened, and the canopy was closed and locked. The control surfaces were in the trimmed position for each test. Three electrodynamic shakers capable of generating a maximum force of 150 pounds were used to excite F-16XL-1's structure during GVT. One shaker was placed aft on the right wing launcher rail, a second shaker was placed forward on the left wing launcher rail, and a third shaker was suspended from an overhead crane and attached to the vertical stabilizer. A total of 180 piezoelectric accelerometers were attached on various locations to measure the structural response of the airframe during ground vibration testing.[4] A computerized workstation and data-acquisition and analysis system acquired, filtered, displayed, and recorded 183 channels of data. These provided comprehensive data on the 3 force inputs and the 180 accelerometer responses during GVTs on both the baseline and modified aircraft configurations.

Two GVTs were performed on the aircraft: one before the glove installation (used as the baseline GVT) and a second after the glove was installed on the aircraft (the modified GVT). The general procedure for each GVT was to install accelerometers at various locations on the aircraft. These were connected to a digital data-acquisition system. The aircraft was then excited by the three electrodynamic shakers using uncorrelated random signals with a frequency content of 1 to 50 Hz. Structural frequency response functions (FRFs) for the aircraft were estimated and subsequently used to determine the structural response frequencies and mode shapes below 30 Hz. The data were analyzed by estimating airframe modal parameters of frequency, damping, and mode shape and then comparing the GVT results from the baseline (unmodified) aircraft with GVT results from the modified aircraft to determine if there were significant modal changes caused by the wing glove installation.

Airframe structural vibration frequencies obtained during ground vibration testing using the baseline (unmodified) aircraft and the aircraft modified with the wing glove were compared. Small changes in structural response frequency existed between the two configurations. There were slight frequency shifts below 15 Hz because of the added mass of the wing glove with frequency shifts becoming greater at higher frequencies. Although most of the GVT data showed close agreement between the baseline and the modified aircraft, three differences in the control surface vibration modes were encountered. A previously identified 26.4-Hz symmetric control surface vibration mode with the unmodified aircraft was not apparent with the modified aircraft. The absence of this mode was believed to be the result of changes in wing mass and stiffness caused by the addition of the glove. The control surface vibration mode produces considerable deflection at the wing leading edge and the forward inboard wing. Since the glove covered this area of the wing, its mass and stiffness substantially reduced the modal response to the control surface deflections. An antisymmetric control surface vibration was also missing with the modified aircraft. As with the symmetric 26.4-Hz control surface mode, this mode had significant inboard wing motion on both the right and left wings. The wing glove was installed in an area where GVT of the unmodified aircraft showed significant deflections. The glove stiffened the wing, reducing its deflection and increasing the vibration frequency. The change in antisymmetric vibrational mode shape with the modified aircraft was restricted to the glove area, and vertical stabilizer and the fuselage motion remained unchanged. Another difference in modal data was observed in another antisymmetric control surface mode. The mode shape changed from antisymmetric to symmetric with the modified aircraft. One possible explanation given was that the 26.4-Hz symmetric mode was shifted up to 28 Hz because of the glove and coupled with the 28.8-Hz antisymmetric mode. There were no changes in structural vibration frequency of the airframe in the range where the structural notch filters were active in the flight control system. This led to the conclusion that there were no aeroservoelastic concerns for the modified aircraft.

In-Flight Flutter Testing

The F-16XL-1 was instrumented with seven accelerometers that sampled at a rate of 200 samples per second for in-flight flutter testing. Six of the accelerometers had a data-collection capability up to +10 g's. Since the g levels at the tip of the aircraft tailfin were much higher than those found at most other locations on the airframe, the accelerometer located there was designed to collect acceleration data up to a level of 75 g's. Other accelerometers were located on the forward and aft tips of both wings and on the left and right aileron beams. Accelerometer responses were telemetered from the test aircraft to the NASA Dryden Spectral Analysis Facility for near-real-time structural stability monitoring. Data from the accelerometers was routed to a spectrum

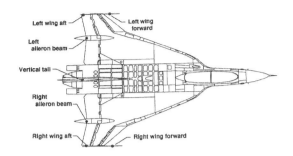

Accelerometer locations on the F-16XL airframe for use in flutter testing. (NASA)

analyzer that provided near-real-time frequency and structural-damping information while the planned flutter test points were actually in the process of being flown. Other relevant flight information such as Mach number, altitude, and airspeed were displayed on video monitors. This capability enabled flutter experts on the ground to provide important information to the pilot that was needed to safely and effectively progress through the flutter clearance envelope.

The F-16XL-1 obtained data at 14 flutter test points. These were flown in order of increasing dynamic pressure over a series of three test missions. In-flight data were collected during 60 seconds of stabilized flight at each test point with atmospheric turbulence providing the structural excitation. Lack of natural turbulence at some test points resulted in pilot-induced control surface pulses being used to supplement natural turbulence excitation. Accelerometer responses were monitored in real time to detect any imminent aircraft instabilities. These data were also used for determining in near-real-time the vibration-mode frequencies and damping characteristics of the airframe structure at each test point. In-flight results were thoroughly evaluated to estimate the structural frequency and damping responses before the aircraft was cleared to the next flutter test point. An in-depth analysis of flutter data was accomplished after each flight to provide higher confidence in the validity of estimated structural modal frequencies and damping values.

Aircraft flutter data were acquired at altitudes of 25,000 and 38,000 feet at Mach numbers ranging from 0.70 to 1.8. Trends for frequency and damping were only clear for six structural modes. The missing frequency and damping data could not be extracted from the structural response spectra because of lack of random atmospheric turbulence for excitation at these frequencies. Accelerometer data showed that some energy was imparted to the aircraft structure in the 20-Hz range. Original flutter analysis by GD had indicated that antisymmetric structural vibration modes above frequencies

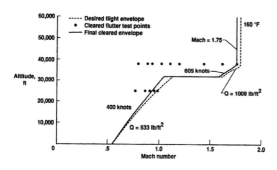

The F-16XL-1 flutter envelope approved for use during the SLFC research program. The vertical axis shows aircraft altitude in thousands of feet. (NASA)

of 20 Hz had the lowest flutter speeds. Results from ground vibration tests with the wing glove installed showed that significant changes occurred when structural vibration frequencies were above 20 Hz. However, real-time monitoring of these vibration modes during in-flight flutter testing did not indicate any structural instability. The flight envelope limits approved for the NASA F-16XL-1 SLFC experiment were defined as a maximum airspeed of 400 knots up to an altitude of 32,000 feet, then a maximum speed of no greater than 605 knots through 38,000 feet, and finally a maximum speed of 1.75 Mach above 38,000 feet. The final flutter envelope that was approved for the F-16XL-1 aircraft modified with the LFC wing glove is depicted in the accompanying photograph. The approved flutter envelope was somewhat reduced from the flight envelope originally desired for the SLFC research effort.[5]

F-16XL-1 Flutter Test Summary

Flutter-related tests studied the effects of the glove on the structural dynamics of the modified F-16XL aircraft. Ground vibration tests were performed before and after the installation of the wing glove. The effects of stiffness and mass changes on the vibration-mode characteristics of the aircraft were determined from the GVTs. The frequencies and shapes of the structural vibration modes did not significantly change below 20 Hz. Above frequencies of 20 Hz, several vibration modes involving the wing flight control surfaces were changed by the wing glove modification. However, in-flight flutter testing determined that the aircraft was free from any aeroelastic and aeroservoelastic instabilities within the very limited flight envelope that was approved for use during the SLFC program with the F-16XL. A safe and efficient flight flutter clearance program was possible because the stability of those structural modes for which frequency and damping could not be determined prior to the start of the flight-test effort was maintained through real-time monitoring of aircraft-mounted accelerometer responses.

F-16XL-1 with the active suction glove on the left wing that was used for research into supersonic laminar flow control. The grey titanium active suction panel is visible on the inner region of the white wing glove. The passive outer leading edge of the wing glove is painted black in the region where a liquid-crystal sensor array was located. A video camera in the wingtip pod was used to record the liquid-crystal patterns. (NASA)

F-16XL Supersonic Laminar Flow Control Research

Research with the F-16XL-1

The single-seat F-16XL-1 was fitted with an experimental suction-type wing glove mounted on the upper surface of the left wing. This perforated wing glove had both active suction and passive laminar flow sections. The design flight condition was Mach 1.6 at an angle of attack of 2 degrees and an altitude of 44,000 feet. The glove design was based on the use of a Navier-Stokes computational fluid dynamics computer code. The CFD code was coupled with a compressible linear stability theory that had been developed by NASA in the late 1980s for use in supersonic LFC design. A goal of the CFD methodology was to create a glove design that minimized suction requirements by defining suction pressures necessary to stabilize the boundary layer. The theory was to be validated by using the methodology to design the suction LFC glove for F-16XL-1 and then making a comparison with flight measured results from the aircraft.[6] At about the same time, a NASA-industry team used a thin-layer Reynolds-averaged Navier-Stokes CFD model to analyze the sensitivity of the boundary layer attachment line and crossflow velocity profiles to changes in aircraft angle of attack. As angle of attack increased, boundary-layer thickness and streamwise velocity profiles remained stable, the boundary-layer attachment line moved from the upper surface of the wing to the lower surface, and the crossflow velocity component on the upper surface of the wing decreased. This was important in determining the amount of suction needed to obtain laminar flow for any position on the wing.[7]

The wing gloves used on F-16XL-1 were designed and constructed by the North American Aviation (NAA) Division of Rockwell International in El Segundo, CA (North American Rockwell would later be absorbed by Boeing). Both the passive and active gloves, installed on the right and left wings, respectively, were designed with a modified NASA 65A003 airfoil. Foam and fiberglass fairings then blended the glove into the wing. The surface of the active suction glove on the left wing was manufactured from a thin titanium sheet whose porosity resulted from many tiny holes created using a high-energy laser. The porous laminar flow test area extended about 25 percent aft on the wing chord (or about 7 feet in the streamwise direction). The suction glove spanned 3.4 feet. The active glove had a uniform hole density of 2,500 holes per square inch across its porous titanium skin surface. Each hole was only 25 one-thousandths of an inch in diameter.

The suction system was designed to provide suction levels capable of producing laminar flow on the wing glove. Air from an array of 22 internal constant cross-section flutes that ran parallel to the glove's leading edge

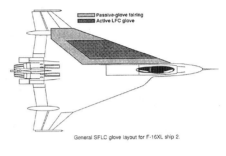

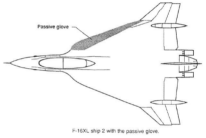

F-16XL passive and active glove configurations. (NASA)

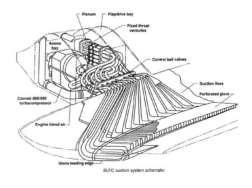

The SLFC active suction system used a turbocompressor adopted from the Convair 880 and 990 jetliners. It was tightly tailored to fit the confines of the F-16XL-1 aircraft. (NASA)

flowed inboard through suction tubes, ground adjustable ball valves, and venture tubes into a central plenum chamber connected to the turbocompressor that provided the suction to the panel. The turbocompressor was legacy technology, having been modified from an air-conditioning turbocompressor used in the Convair 880 and 990 jetliner family a quarter-century before, and was tailored for the SLFC experiment. During system operation, flow disturbances in the boundary layer were sucked through the porous panel and flowed through the internal suction system plumbing to the turbocompressor, as seen in the cutaway illustration of the system.

The F-16XL-1's Glove Instrumentation

The active suction wing glove installed on F-16XL-1 was initially instrumented with two rows of 41 flush static pressure orifices and three skin-temperature gauges. Thirty hot film sensors were installed on the glove in locations that were varied between flights. These hot film sensors were arranged in five rows on the active glove and one row on the passive glove. However, all rows of sensors were installed on the glove at the same time since sensors in one row could disrupt the airflow ahead of sensors in an adjacent row. For follow-on SLFC flight testing with F-16XL-1, higher density of hot film sensors were used to map the boundary-layer transition front. The higher sensor density was obtained by using a sheet with many sensors instead of the single-element sensors previously used. The use of liquid crystals as a technique to visualize boundary-layer transition on the passive glove was also investigated in this second phase of F-16XL-1 flight testing. A video camera mounted on the wingtip of the left wing was used to record liquid-crystal patterns on the passive region of the wing glove. For the liquid-crystal evaluation, a portion of the outboard active wing glove was painted black.

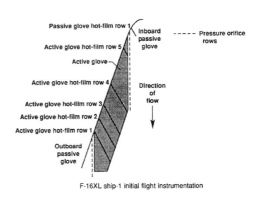

Test instrumentation used on the F-16XL-1 active suction wing glove. (NASA)

F-16XL-1 Supersonic Laminar Flow Control Research Summary

Thirty-one research flights were conducted with F-16XL-1 during the SLFC flight-test effort beginning in 1990. Pressure-distribution and transition data were obtained for the Mach number range from Mach 1.2 to Mach 1.7 and at an altitude range from 35,000 to 55,000 feet. During test missions flown in 1991 and 1992, limited supersonic laminar flow was achieved on the upper surface of the suction panel. However, laminar flow was achieved at a slightly lower Mach number and a slightly higher altitude than the suction glove design point. In fact, laminar flow at the glove design point of Mach 1.6 at an altitude of 44,000 feet was not achieved. The boundary layer transition and the pressure distribution data obtained from the SLFC flight tests were used to refine, correlate, and validate CFD computer codes. Calculated CFD pressure distributions were compared to the pressure distributions obtained at varying angles of attack during flight testing. In general, the CFD data at very low angles of attack agreed reasonably well with flight-test data. F-16XL-1 flight-test results demonstrated that SLFC using active suction on highly swept wings was feasible, but laminar flow prediction methodologies and CFD models were shown to require further refinement. Follow-on SLFC efforts with F-16XL-2 would result in more refined CFD methodologies and improved laminar flow prediction techniques. This aspect of the F-16XL SLFC test effort is discussed in the following section.

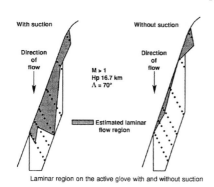

Laminar region on the active glove with and without suction

F-16XL-1 with an active suction glove installed on the left wing demonstrated limited laminar flow at supersonic conditions during flight testing conducted in 1991–1992. (NASA)

The F-16XL-2 Supersonic Laminar Flow Control Flight Research Program

The two-seat F-16XL was used for more extensive and comprehensive SLFC investigations that involved a more refined approach to the active suction wing glove design. As received from the Air Force, F-16XL-2 had incorporated the Large Normal Shock Inlet (LNSI) and a General Electric F110-GE-100 engine. NASA worked with GD and the Air Force to have the more powerful F110-GE-129 version of the engine fitted into the aircraft. The additional engine power gave the aircraft the capability to reach Mach 2.0 at an altitude of 55,000 feet when operating in full afterburner power. With the F110-GE-129 engine, F-16XL-2 was also able to demonstrate limited supercruise performance by maintaining Mach 1.1 at an altitude of 20,000 feet in full military power without resorting to the use of afterburner.[8]

The SLFC flight-test effort with F-16XL-2 was far more complex than the earlier tests with F-16XL-1, with regions of transition from laminar to turbulent flow over the wing glove explored at a wider range of supersonic Mach numbers. F-16XL-2 had been selected for this research effort because its cranked-arrow wing planform with the 70-degree in-board leading-edge sweep, its maximum speed (Mach 2.0), and its maximum altitude capabilities (55,000 feet) were similar to the wing planform, desired cruise speed (Mach 2.4), and cruise altitude (60,000 feet) of the proposed HSCT.[9] An additional advantage of using F-16XL-2 was that the second cockpit made it possible for a flight-test engineer to accompany the pilot on test missions. The flight-test engineer in the rear cockpit had the capability to monitor laminar flow conditions in real time. Most importantly, the flight-test engineer was able to vary the amount of suction pressure in the system during test missions, as were the ground controllers. The volume of boundary-layer airflow sucked through the holes into the glove was adjusted using a specially designed control panel. This allowed detailed investigations into the effects of variations in suction volume on the area distribution of the laminar flow region on the wing glove. As Jeffrey S. Lavell, NASA Langley project manager for the F-16XL SLFC test experiment, commented at the time: "We're not planning to just go up and get laminar flow at our test point and say we're done. We're going to vary a lot of parameters and get a lot of different data to increase the fidelity of our design codes. The purpose of this experiment, besides the demonstration, is to validate our CFD codes, which allow us to design these airfoils."[10]

NASA officials at the time noted that it might not be possible to achieve laminar flow over the entire supersonic transport wing using moderate suction levels for both practical and economic reasons. Although the goal of the research project was to demonstrate that laminar flow was feasible over 50 to 60 percent of the wing chord, NASA officials commented that a more realistic result might be in the 40- to 50-percent of wing chord region. Michael C. Fischer, principal SLFC project investigator at NASA Langley, was quoted as saying that industry was interested in a hybrid version of the laminar flow control system. This would limit active suction to the leading-edge region of a supersonic transport wing with the remainder of the wing shaped to provide the optimum pressure distribution needed to passively achieve laminar flow. This would do away with the cost, weight, and complexity of providing an active suction capability over the area of the entire wing. To this end, NASA planned to follow up the initial F-16XL-2 SLFC tests with follow-on investigations. These would involve covering the aft portion of the laminar flow test section with very thin tape to determine if the suction on the most critical section of the wing leading edge was adequate to maintain laminar flow over a significant portion of the wing farther aft on the chord. Also important was demonstrating that supersonic laminar flow was not easily disrupted by small changes in flight conditions. The latter could be caused by, for instance, small changes in angle of attack as the aircraft weight changed with fuel consumption during the course of long-range intercontinental flights.[11]

F-16XL-2 SLFC Test Planning and Management

The SLFC research program with F-16XL-2 involved a combination of in-house and contractor efforts. These included wind tunnel testing, piloted simulations, computational aerodynamics, hardware design, tooling and fabrication, software development and validation, test aircraft modification, and flight testing. A NASA-industry team consisting of representatives from the Langley Research Center, the Dryden Flight Research Center, the Boeing Commercial Airplane Group, McDonnell-Douglas Corporation, and Rockwell International provided technical support. NASA Langley provided overall technical management and wind tunnel test data. Industry contributions included the design and fabrication of the SLFC test hardware. Dryden Flight Research Center was responsible for the installation and operation of all flight hardware and the conduct of flight testing. The NASA-industry team arrangement was designed to facilitate the rapid development of SLFC technology and the direct transfer of the technology to industry.[12] Specific objectives of the NASA SLFC flight-test program with F-16XL-2 were to

- Achieve 50- to 60-percent wing chord laminar flow on a highly swept wing at supersonic speeds,
- Validate CFD codes and design methodology for supersonic laminar flow wings, and
- Establish initial LFC suction system design criteria to enable industry to more accurately determine the benefits and integrate the SLFC concept into the HSCT.

Design, development, and installation of the wing glove, the suction system, the shock wave diverter fences, a turbulence diverter, and preflight and postflight monitoring of excrescences were critical elements of the SLFC flight research effort, and these aspects are discussed in detail in the following sections.

The F-16XL-2 SLFC experiment was to be conducted in two test phases. The first phase, using a passive wing glove on the right wing of the aircraft, studied the effects of wing leading-edge radius and very high Reynolds number (Re) on the location of the boundary-layer attachment line.[13] A primary goal of the passive glove experiment was to obtain detailed surface pressure distribution data in the highly swept inner-wing leading-edge region. These data were obtained for a Mach number range of 1.4 to 2.0 and over an altitude range from 45,000 to 50,000 feet. These aerodynamic data were then used in the design of the active suction laminar flow wing glove that was installed over a portion of the left wing in the second phase of the SLFC project. Unlike the active suction glove used on F-16XL-1, which had uniform hole spacing, the glove on F-16XL-2 was optimized for supersonic laminar flow with variable spacing of its suction holes.

Team members from the NASA Dryden Flight Research Center, NASA Langley Research Center, Boeing Commercial Airplane Group, McDonnell-Douglas Corporation, and Rockwell International supported this phase of the project.[14] NASA staff members with senior responsibilities for the F-16XL-2 SLFC flight-test experiment included Jeffrey S. Lavell, NASA Langley program manager; Marta R. Bohn-Meyer and Carol A. Reukauf, Dryden program managers; Lisa J. Bjarke, Dryden principal engineer; Mark Collard, Dryden operations engineer; and Dana D. Purifoy, Dryden's primary project pilot. Scott G. Anders and Michael C. Fischer, both from the LaRC, produced an excellent in-depth technical report that thoroughly documented the SLFC flight-test experiment with F-16XL-2. Their report provided extensive documentation of the research objectives, test design, aircraft modifications, and results, including the achievements and limitations of this most ambitious SLFC flight-test effort. The discussion of the F-16XL-2 SLFC experiment in the following sections is heavily based on their published work. It goes into relatively significant depth in order to provide insight into the major challenges that existed in accomplishing the ambitious goals of the SLFC project.[15]

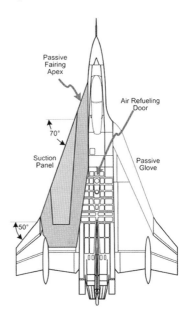

The F-16XL-2 was fitted with a General Electric F110-GE-129 engine. The passive wing glove on the right wing and active suction glove on the left wing give it a distinctive asymmetric planform. (Lockheed Martin via Robert Wetherall)

Supporting Research: Wind Tunnel and Flight Tests

The SLFC program included experiments in low-disturbance-level supersonic tunnels, tests with a 1/15-scale wind tunnel model with the modified wing configuration, and precursor flight tests with the actual F-16XL-2 aircraft. These efforts, described in more detail in the following sections, were designed to reduce technical risk, enhance the design of the final experiment, and satisfy safety of flight concerns that resulted from the asymmetric test configuration.[16]

Passive Wing Glove Tests

A passive laminar flow glove was installed on the leading edge of the F-16XL-2's right wing. It was used to provide information on airflow over a wing with a leading-edge radius and shape that was similar to that planned for the active

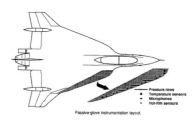

Passive-glove instrumentation layout.

The passive wing glove was instrumented to collect information on supersonic flow over the wing leading edge. (NASA)

suction glove. The passive glove was constructed from foam and fiberglass and it extended the leading edge of the right wing forward by a few inches. Five rows of flush pressure orifices located in the passive glove measured pressure profiles across the leading edge. Hot films mounted on the surface of the wing glove were used to determine the location where the boundary layer transitioned from laminar to turbulent flow.

Aerodynamic Flow Fixes

The basic design of the F-16XL aircraft created several areas of concern that required the development and installation of "aerodynamic fixes" to help ensure that the airflow over the active suction wing glove would not excessively disrupt formation of smooth laminar flow. Data were also collected to address several concerns related to the final active suction wing glove design. These included determining the canopy-closure shock wave location on the upper wing surface, evaluating the effectiveness of the preliminary shock wave blocker-fence design, and an evaluation of leading-edge turbulence-diverter concepts. Two rows of pressure belts were installed on XL-2's upper wing surface in the vicinity of where the canopy-closure shock wave was predicted from CFD assessments. The actual canopy-closure shock wave location turned out to be somewhat forward of the CFD-predicted location, but it was still where it would be blocked effectively by a wing-mounted shock fence. To assess the effectiveness of a shock wave fence in blocking the inlet shock wave system, a 10-inch-tall aluminum fence with a 60-degree swept leading edge was mounted on XL-2's right wing at butt line (BL) 45. The aluminum shock fence was 90 inches long in the chordwise direction and was 3/8-of-an-inch thick. It was mounted at the missile attachment point originally intended for an AIM-120 AMRAAM missile. The inlet diverter is the wedge-shaped structure centrally located between the undersurface of the fuselage and the engine inlet on the standard F-16, as well as on the F-16XL. The inlet diverter was a significant feature of the F-16 design and prevented the turbulent boundary layer on the lower fuselage from entering the engine inlet. Ingestion of this turbulent airflow would have disrupted engine performance, especially at higher angles of attack.

Shock Wave Fence Design Options

Five rows of flush static pressure orifices were installed on the passive glove on both the upper and lower surfaces of the leading edge. Pressure measurements from these sensors were used to evaluate the effectiveness of an underwing shock fence in blocking pressure disturbances on the wing leading edge. The pressure belts on the lower surface were primarily used to determine the effec-

tiveness of the shock fence. The 10-inch high shock fence that was initially tested was found to reduce the strength of the pressure disturbances caused by the inlet shock wave system. However, it did not entirely eliminate their influence on airflow on the wing glove. CFD calculations using a detailed grid model of the F-16XL-2 fitted with the 10-inch-tall shock fence were compared to flight-test results with the fence. The flight-test data and the CFD results with the shock wave blocker fence both on and off the aircraft compared favor-ably. Based on this success, CFD was then used to assess

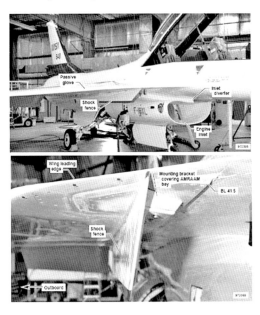

Initially, the F-16XL-2 had a 10-inch-tall shock wave fence under its starboard wing, as seen above. (NASA)

several possible shock wave fence configurations. This assessment resulted in the decision to develop two different 20-inch-tall shock wave blocker fences for the next phase of the project—the active suction SLFC flight-test effort. The two shock wave fences used in the research effort are described in detail in a following section.

Transonic and Supersonic Wind Tunnel Tests

Concerns that the asymmetric wing planform of the modified F-16XL-2 might create excessive pitchup tendencies along with diminished directional control led to a decision by NASA to structure a special wind tunnel test program. The goals and objectives of the wind tunnel test effort with the modified aircraft model were intended to

- Determine the stability and control characteristics of the F-16XL-2 aircraft with the asymmetric wing planform,

The F-16XL-2 in flight showing its Langley-tested shock wave fence under the port wing. (NASA)

- Obtain force and moment coefficients needed to upgrade the existing F-16XL simulator model,
- Verify CFD design software codes with actual measured surface pressures, and
- Determine the effectiveness of proposed supersonic shock wave diverter fences in minimizing the effects of the inlet/diverter shock wave on the leading edge of the wing glove.

A ¹⁄₁₅-scale model of the modified F-16XL aircraft was used to obtain required force and moment data. Transonic testing was done in the Langley 8-Foot Transonic Pressure Tunnel, and supersonic wind tunnel tests were conducted in the Langley Unitary Plan Wind Tunnel. The model was tested with both the gloved wing and the baseline wing to compare the stability and control characteristics of the two configurations. Different shock fence designs were also tested using this model. A dedicated NASA Langley team that included Gaudy Bezos-O'Connor, Stan J. Miley, Paul M. Vijgen, and Jeffrey K. Viken coordinated and conducted the wind tunnel test effort. Approximately 2,800 hours of wind tunnel test time were accumulated in preparation for the SLFC flight-test program.

Flight Simulator Upgrade

Aerodynamic data derived from NASA transonic and supersonic wind tunnel testing was used to predict aircraft performance and handling qualities with the XL-2's asymmetric wing configuration. Using these wind tunnel data, NASA engineers at Dryden reprogrammed the computer software in the F-16XL simulator model to ensure that the characteristics of the modified aircraft were accurately represented. NASA Dryden research pilots Dana D. Purifoy and Mark P. Stucky evaluated the handling qualities, safety, and performance of the new aerodynamic configuration in the upgraded flight simulator prior to the start of in-flight testing with the modified aircraft. Their evaluation showed no significant adverse effects on aircraft handling qualities with the asymmetric configuration up to the 3-g maneuver limitation that NASA established for the SLFC experiment. In-flight characteristics of the modified F-16XL-2 aircraft were later found to compare well with those of the upgraded simulator.

The Active Suction Wing Glove

The active suction wing glove was designed by a combined NASA and contractor team that included engineers from the Langley Research Center, the Dryden Flight Research Center, Rockwell International, Boeing, and McDonnell-Douglas. Modifications to the F-16XL-2 included the installation of the active suction test panel and related suction system components on the left wing and in portions of the fuselage. The glove design included an extension of the wing leading edge that continued the 70-degree in-board wing leading-edge sweep into the forward fuselage, similar to the configuration of the HSCT wing. Other modifications included new instrumentation, power supplies, signal conditioning units, cables, wiring, suction ducting, a plenum chamber, suction control valves and flow meters, a suction turbocompressor, and passive foam-fiberglass contour fairings. The turbocompressor was installed in the bay that previously held the 20-mm ammunition magazine. A titanium suction panel and a foam-fiberglass passive fairing covered about 75 percent of the upper wing surface of the left inner segment of the cranked-arrow wing. Its outer metal surface was perforated with 12 million extremely small, laser-cut holes. A suction system drew a very small portion of the boundary layer through the porous surface of the wing glove and was intended to expand the region of laminar flow to reduce aerodynamic drag. The glove was instrumented to measure laminar flow and other variables that affected laminar flow at various flight conditions. These included surface imperfections on the wing surface and surface pressure variations caused by the acoustic environment or produced by supersonic shock waves impinging on the wing glove's surface.

The perforated wing glove for F-16XL-2 and its aerodynamic fairing were designed by Boeing using a constrained direct iterative surface curvature (CDISC) design methodology. Originally developed by NASA Langley, CDISC was coupled with a three-dimensional, thin-layer Navier-Stokes flow solver computer program to create the final wing glove design.[17] Boeing fabricated the wing glove, constructed of sheets of titanium 0.040 inches thick. The active portion of the glove was perforated with more than *12 million* laser-drilled holes. These holes nominally were 0.0025 inches in diameter and were spaced at distances that ranged from 0.010 to 0.055 inches, depending on the required suction porosity. The inverse conical shape of the individual holes provided the perforated surface through which suction was applied to remove instabilities in the boundary layer. The exit diameter of each hole was double the entrance diameter. This taper was intended to ensure that small particles ingested into the holes passed through and did not obstruct airflow through the hole. The titanium suction panel extended 17 feet outward along the leading edge of the wing and back to 60 percent of the wing chord. This was much larger than the active suction wing glove used during earlier SLFC tests with F-16XL-1, whose suction panel only extended aft to 30 percent of the wing chord.

The active suction panel was physically bounded by the apex—an aluminum substructure with a carbon-fiber cover and a carbon-fiber passive fairing that blended the suction panel with the existing wing contour. Inner support structures in the apex region of the wing continued the 70-degree swept wing directly into the forward fuselage. The maximum thickness of the suction panel, measured above the existing left wing, was about 5.5 inches. This increased to 7 inches in the region where the fairing around the suction panel joined the fuselage. The test panel and related suction system components were installed on the left wing and in portions of the fuselage. This installation included instrumentation, power supplies, signal conditioning units, cables, wiring, suction ducting and plenum, suction control valves and flow meters, a turbocompressor, an apex extension, and passive fairings. The perforated titanium suction panel was positioned near the center of the inner segment of the highly swept left wing.[18]

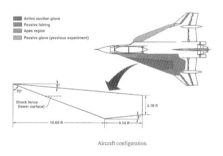

The physical dimensions of the F-16XL-2 SLFC active suction wing glove and the location of the shock fence on the underside of the left wing are shown in this NASA drawing. (NASA)

Design Flight Conditions

The design point for the SLFC experiment of Mach 1.9 and 50,000 feet was selected based on the performance capabilities of the modified F-16XL-2 with the F110-GE-129 turbofan engine. The foam-fiberglass passive glove area surrounding the suction panel was designed to blend the test panel smoothly into the basic wing and was an integral element of the aerodynamic design. Boeing designed the SLFC suction panel and fairing geometry using an inverse wing design methodology originally developed by NASA Langley coupled with a three-dimensional thin-layer Navier Stokes CFD flow solver.[19] Design flight conditions for the SLFC research experiment were based on the results from CFD analyses and previous laminar flow flight experiments with F-16XL-2. A passive laminar flow wing glove had been installed on the right-side leading edge of the aircraft. It was flight tested before the active suction glove was ever installed on the left wing to verify the aerodynamic design approach used in the leading-edge region. The SLFC design point, Mach 1.9 at an altitude of 50,000 feet, was within the achievable F-16XL-2 flight envelope with the modified aircraft. Depending on drag and engine performance, XL-2 could achieve Mach numbers and altitudes that were higher than the supersonic laminar flow design point. The calculated Reynolds number at the SLFC design condition was 22.5 million. The actual Reynolds number during any test run was dependent on the local dynamic viscosity of the air. Since the viscosity of the air depends on the local air temperature at the test altitude, it varied somewhat for each test flight. Thus, the actual Reynolds number at specific test conditions also varied somewhat between each flight.

Design Pressure Distribution

The pressure distribution over the gloved F-16XL-2 wing was designed to minimize development of airflow disturbances that could cause the boundary layer to transition from laminar to turbulent conditions. The steep leading-edge curvature of the wing's upper surface resulted in the airflow being rapidly accelerated through the region of aerodynamic crossflow. This acceleration was followed by the development of a gradual, favorable pressure gradient that acted to stabilize Tollmien-Schlichting wave disturbances.[20] The lack of spanwise gradients in the design pressure distribution allowed for nearly unswept isobars or streamlines across the upper surface of the wing at the design angle of attack.[21] Although the design pressure distribution over the wing was very important in obtaining laminar flow, active suction was essential to obtain extensive laminar flow region over the highly swept inner region of the F-16XL's cranked-arrow wing. To obtain this suction, extensive modifications to the aircraft were required.

Suction System

The suction panel had 20 individually controlled independent suction regions. Seven were located on the upper surface of the glove and 13 were in the leading-edge region. The suction system consisted of 20 individual collector ducts (one for each independent region), 20 individual mass flow sensors and control valves, a common plenum chamber, a master control valve, and a turbocompressor. The turbocompressor turbine was driven by engine bleed air; this allowed the compressor to provide the low-pressure source for the suction system. Exhaust

The engine bleed air–powered turbocompressor used with the active SLFC suction system was installed in F-16XL-2's ammunition bay, formerly used to house the 20-mm rounds used by its M61 Vulcan cannon. The overboard flow vent that exited on the upper right side of the aircraft is in the foreground. (NASA)

from the compressor and turbine was dumped overboard on the right side of the aircraft, behind the rear cockpit (the side of the aircraft opposite from the suction panel on the left wing). The design suction pressure distribution on the wing glove had been derived by Boeing using linear, boundary-layer stability theory calculations. The Boeing analysis was correlated with wind tunnel and flight-test data and was used to establish the design criteria for the maximum and minimum suction levels. The suction control system was designed to achieve the design suction pressure distribution as closely as possible by varying the suction applied to the panel surface at different locations. Suction was provided by a modified Boeing 707 cabin air–pressurization turbocompressor that was fed by bleed air ducted from the aircraft's GE F110 engine. The turbocompressor was installed in the large bay just aft of the cockpit normally used to house the F-16's 20-mm ammunition drum. All air exiting the turbocompressor was vented overboard through an exit duct on the right side of the aircraft. Originally designed as an auxiliary power unit for the Boeing 707 jet airliner, the turbocompressor had been modified by the Allied Signal Corporation under contract to NASA Dryden to meet airflow requirements of the SLFC experiment. This modification included an upgrade to enable the turbocompressor to safely run at higher speed (allowable rpm) to provide greater suction pressure.

The turbo compressor installation in the F-16XL presented interesting issues related to reliability and operational safety. Turbines are, by their nature, highly energetic and highly loaded, and thus subject to potentially dangerous failures. The turbo compressor had failed catastrophically during development testing of the suction system design. The existing ammunition bay in which the turbo compressor was installed was located aft of the cockpit and in relatively close proximity to the aircraft's hydrazine-powered emergency power unit (EPU)

The turbocompressor exhaust duct exited the F-16XL-2 in the center-of-black region behind the rear cockpit. Note the special fairing mounted over the canopy frame to minimize shock wave formation. (NASA)

and the fuselage fuel cells.[22] Concerns with the integrity of the design in the event of an in-flight failure prompted the decision to add additional protection around the turbocompressor bay. General Dynamics technician Steve Slaughter was assigned to come up with an internal structural reinforcement approach within the existing F-16 fuselage ammunition bay. Slaughter graphically described this task in his own words: "I had to develop an armor system for NASA because they were blowing up the cabin pressurization turbo pump they used for boundary layer control. Had to 'invent' and install the panels in 7 days to meet the flight test schedule. That gun breech where the pump is located is kinda bad if the pump grenades: Hydrazine APU, Fuel—bummer when it lets go."[23]

The suction flow rate through the surface in each region of the suction panel was determined by the perforation hole spacing and was controlled by varying the pressure in the internal suction regions. The rate of air drawn through the holes was measured by mass flow sensors and controlled by butterfly flow control valves (FCVs). The air passed into a common plenum chamber then through a large duct, where the master FCV was located. When insufficient quantities of air were drawn through the master FCV, a surge valve opened, providing supplemental air to the turbocompressor. As noted earlier, the suction panel was divided into 20 regions, 13 of which were located in the leading edge.

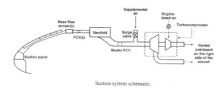

Suction system schematic.

Schematic of the F-16XL-2 active wing glove suction system. (NASA)

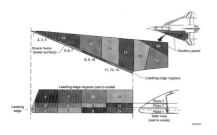

There were 20 separate suction regions on the F-16XL-2 wing glove, and different suction levels could be applied to each region. (NASA)

Three so-called flutes provided suction to the regions located in the leading edge. Each suction region had its own mass flow sensor and flow control valve. A suction control system in the rear cockpit was used by the flight-test engineer to control the master FCV and the 20 individual control valves through a special onboard computer. The onboard computer interfaced in real time with uplinked command signals sent to the aircraft from the mission control room at Dryden. These uplinked signals controlled the individual control valves, setting the individual suction levels for each region on the panel. In this way, a variety of suction distributions could be evaluated on each flight to determine their effects on laminar flow.

Design and Fabrication of the F-16 XL-2's Suction Panel and System Hardware

Existing NASA design databases for surface waviness, steps, gaps, and roughness, developed and used in previous subsonic laminar flow experiments, were used in designing the F-16XL-2 wing glove. To ensure that the desired design surface pressures were achieved on the surface of the wing glove, the contour and shape of the suction panel had to be manufactured to extremely precise tolerances. Allowable manufacturing deviation was no more than 20 one-thousandths of an inch in the leading-edge region of the wing. As the distance progressed aft on the wing glove, allowable manufacturing tolerances were relaxed to fifty one-thousandths of an inch. These manufacturing tolerances had been derived from computer calculations in which the wing panel was evaluated with different levels of manufacturing tolerance in a simulated supersonic flow field. Maximum allowable surface wavelengths and heights, steps and gaps, and three-dimensional roughness values were based on flight-test and wind tunnel databases. Surface waviness, in particular, was an area of concern. The presence of steps and gaps in the wing surface was another area of concern. The design criteria for aft-facing steps were more restrictive than for forward-facing steps. Any airflow along a gap was to be avoided whenever possible. Accepted limits for steps and gaps during fabrication and assembly of the wing glove were set at a maximum height of three one-thousandths of an inch for forward-facing steps.

The aft-facing step-height manufacturing limit was set at only one-thousandth of an inch. The gap-width limit in areas where airflow moved over the gap was set at two and one half one-thousandths of an inch.

An attempt was made to minimize any three-dimensional roughness caused by steps and gaps in the panel design effort. The perforated titanium skin was formed in two continuous sheets joined at one seam in an attempt to eliminate the need for rivets and sources of roughness. Finally, porosity of the suction surface depended on both individual diameter of the suction holes and relative hole spacing. The nominal diameter of the laser-drilled holes was 25 one-thousandths of an inch for the entire panel. Porosity was varied by changing the spacing between the holes on different regions of the panel. The 20 suction regions contained 123 patches, or individual panel areas that had a specific, constant hole spacing. Despite major efforts at maintaining high quality control standards, the processes used in manufacturing, installing, and maintaining the wing panel and glove were determined to contribute to unanticipated variations in panel porosity.

On left: The laminar flow wing glove during the positioning process on F-16XL-2's left wing, February 1995. On right: The F-16XL-2 after the laminar flow wing glove was mounted on the wing and the forward wing fairing was installed. Note how far forward on the fuselage the left wing extended. (Both images NASA)

Structural and Suction System Design

The entire suction panel and its associated substructure were designed to be mounted over the existing left inner wing of F-16XL-2. The panel extended about 12 inches upstream of the original left-wing leading edge, giving the aircraft its unique asymmetric appearance. Aluminum structural ribs that provided panel stiffness and a means for securely attaching the structure to the existing wing were bonded to the lower surface of the suction panel. An apex region in-board of the suction panel provided structural support and continued the cantilevered structure inward to the F-16XL-2 forward fuselage while maintaining a constant 70-degree leading-edge wing-sweep angle. The wing glove, suction system, associated instrumentation, and a shock fence that was added to the underside of the left wing added about 1,700 pounds to the aircraft weight. The panel and suction system had been developed by a contractor team headed by Rockwell under a contract to NASA Langley. Detailed aerodynamic and structural design and fabrication of the suction panel was done by Boeing with McDonnell-Douglas responsible for design of the complete suction system up to the point where it joined the turbocompressor. Both companies were under contract to Rockwell, who was the prime contractor to Langley for the SLFC program with F-16XL-2. The laminar flow wing glove was installed on the aircraft in NASA Dryden aircraft maintenance facilities in February 1995.

F-16XL-2 Unique Flow-Field Features

Certain features unique to the basic F-16XL-2 aircraft produced flow field disturbances at supersonic speed. These in turn altered the pressure distribution on the surface of the suction panel, affecting the ability to achieve laminar

A faired gun trough fairing was added to F-16XL-2 to minimize shock wave influences on the laminar flow wing glove. (NASA)

flow. Significant shock waves that were produced by the canopy and the engine inlet were areas of primary concern. A secondary issue was the lower strength shock wave produced by the 20-mm cannon trough. The shock wave from the canopy windshield intersected the wing leading edge in the area of butt line 30 to 35, depending on Mach number. However, since the suction glove was located further outboard on the wing, beyond BL 41.5, shock waves emanating from the windshield could not interact with the suction panel and adversely affect laminar flow. The shock wave created by the cannon trough was mainly resolved by mounting an aluminum fairing over the trough.[24]

Shock Wave/Wing Glove Flow-Field Interaction

If not taken into account, shock waves unique to the F-16XL-2 configuration would have interacted with the flow field over the active suction wing glove, resulting in a highly three-dimensional flow field. This phenomenon would have made laminar flow difficult to achieve over the entire wing glove. Two distinct supersonic shock waves were produced by the F-16XL engine inlet. One of these came from the inlet diverter and the other from the inlet face itself. Additionally, a shock wave emanating from the canopy joint created unfavorable pressure gradients and caused undesirable boundary-layer transition on the upper surface of the laminar flow glove. To minimize these problems, several shock wave blockers were designed, installed, and tested on XL-2 during the SLFC program.

Inlet Shock System

Inlet shock waves propagated outward across the lower surface of the wing and crossed the leading edge near midspan. This would have adversely affected the extent of laminar flow on the upper surface of the wing. Boeing, who was responsible for the aerodynamic design of the suction panel and fairings, recommended the installation of a shock fence on the lower surface of the wing to block the inlet shock waves. Numerous design iterations using CFD and results from supporting flight and wind tunnel tests were used during development of the wing shock fences used in the SLFC flight-test program.

Canopy-Closure Shock

Due to the three-dimensional geometry of F-16XL-2's canopy, the airflow over the canopy expanded as the physical canopy profile extended into the fuselage contour. At the location where this expansion ended, a so-called "closure" shock wave was produced. This shock wave moved outward across the wings, as shown in the accompanying drawing, where the effects of Mach number variation on shock wave location are indicated. The canopy-closure shock wave was a factor in the design of the suction panel because the pressure produced by the shock wave was likely to cause loss of laminar flow on the glove. The suction panel was designed so that only the rearmost portion was intersected by the canopy-closure shock wave at Mach 2.0. In addition, suction pressures in the rearmost area of the glove surface could be tailored to compensate for the presence of the canopy-closure shock wave pressure disturbance. A separate suction region provided higher suction pressures to deal with the boundary layer disturbance caused by the closure shock wave.[25]

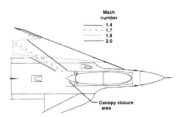

The canopy-closure shock wave impingement locations on the upper surface of F-16XL-2 are illustrated for several representative cruise Mach numbers. (NASA)

Shock Wave Diverter Fences

As noted earlier, the engine inlet configuration of the F-16XL raised concerns that shock waves generated by the engine inlet and diverter would impact on a critical region of the leading edge of the laminar flow suction glove, reducing the possibility of obtaining supersonic laminar flow. During previous SLFC flight testing, a 10-inch-tall shock fence with a 60-degree leading edge had been used to reduce the effects of the inlet diverter shock wave on the wing leading edge. The 10-inch-tall shock fence was only partially effective. Two different 20-inch-tall shock fences were designed for the second phase of the

SLFC test program with F-16XL-2. They were known by the sweep angle of the leading edge of each shock fence. The first fence that was flown was known as the 60-degree shock fence. This fence was based on the 10-inch-tall fence used during the previous phase of the F-16XL-2 laminar flow project. The 60-degree shock fence was installed on the test aircraft during 19 of the 45 research flights flown in the second phase of the SLFC program with F-16XL-2. However, this fence was unable to block the shock wave coming from the engine inlet face. This shock wave had not been identified in earlier

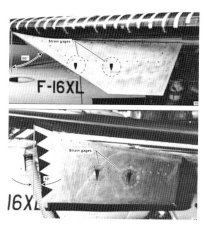

Different underwing shock wave fences were used to block the shock waves produced by the engine inlet from affecting the airflow on the leading edge of the wing glove. (NASA)

The F-16XL-2 seen with the 60-degree shock fence installed under the left inner wing in this November 1996 NASA Dryden photo. The fence was designed to block the shock waves that emanated from the engine inlet system. (NASA)

flight testing because the leading edge of the wing without the SLFC glove had been located farther in-board and aft. A shock fence designed to more effectively block both inlet shock waves was then constructed that featured a 10-degree leading-edge sweep angle. However, the leading edge of this 10-degree fence was submerged in supersonic flow and produced a shock wave of its own that spread out over the wing glove. Unfortunately, this was exactly what the shock fence was designed to prevent. The 10-degree shock fence was installed on the aircraft for 24 SLFC research flights. The aluminum shock fences were mounted onto an existing AIM-120 missile attachment station. Both shock fences were fitted with strain gages to ensure that their design structural load limits were not exceeded during the flight-test program.

Two test flights were flown without the 10-degree or the 60-degree shock fences installed to obtain baseline data on shock wave effects produced by the basic aircraft. As expected, supersonic laminar flow was not achieved on these flights due to shock wave impingement on the boundary layer. In-flight measurements of the pressure distributions on the in-board segment of the F-16XL-2 wing over the Mach number range from 1.4 to 2.0 provided a baseline to determine the location of shock waves on the panel. This was very important to ensure that these shock waves did not invalidate or compromise follow-on testing to determine the effectiveness of the SLFC experiment. Results from these tests were analyzed and reported by Lisa J. Bjarke of NASA Dryden and Stephen F. Landers and John A. Saltzman, research engineers with PRC, Inc., the NASA Dryden systems engineering test-support contractor.[26]

Turbulence Diverter

A boundary-layer turbulence diverter that consisted of a narrow longitudinal slot was installed on the extended leading edge of the left wing, in-board of the active suction panel. This slot allowed the turbulent boundary layer that normally would have flowed outboard from the leading edge where it attached to the fuselage to be swept aft by the airflow. This allowed a new laminar flow boundary-layer attachment line to be formed on the inboard leading edge of the suction panel. The turbulence diverter design was based on experience gained with three different diverter configurations test flown on F-16XL-2 during the previous phase of the SLFC project.[27]

Unique features of the modified F-16XL-2 aircraft included the active suction laminar flow wing glove, the extended left-wing apex, the turbulence diverter (the darker strip along the intersection of the left wing with the forward fuselage), and the shock wave fence under the left wing. (NASA)

Test Instrumentation

The F-16XL-2 was highly instrumented for the SLFC research effort. A flight-test nose boom was used to determine airspeed and airflow angles. In addition to the aerodynamic vanes used to measure angles of attack and sideslip, the nose boom also provided measurements of total and static pressure. The aircraft was also instrumented to measure total temperature, Euler angles, accelerations, and flight control surface positions.[28] The wing glove was extensively instrumented. There were over 450 pressure taps, 151 thermocouples, 40 microphones, mass flow sensors, and up to 50 hot-film anemometers. An array of pressure taps installed on the left wing was used to obtain both surface and internal pressure measurements. Of the 454 surface pressure taps, 200 were located on the active suction panel with 113 of these positioned in the leading-edge region. The remaining 254 surface pressure taps were located on passive regions of the glove fairing surrounding the suction panel, including the apex portion of the inner wing. Seventy-two internal pressure taps monitored the pressure within the suction flutes. Twenty mass flow sensors were inserted in the ducts between the surface of the suction panel and the flow control valves. They measured the suction flow rate in each region of the system.[29]

Hot-film sensors with temperature-compensated anemometer systems were used on or around the suction panel on both the upper and lower surfaces. The sensors were mounted such that their active elements were nearly perpendicular to the airflow, with the temperature elements adjacent and slightly aft of the hot-film sensors to avoid possible flow disturbance over the active elements of the hot-film sensors. Twenty-four hot-film sensors were mounted directly to the titanium surface on the edge of the active suction region on the wing upper surface. The number of hot films on the active suction surface varied from 0 for the first eight flights to 31 for the final flights. The location of these hot films was varied between flights as different areas of the suction panel were investigated. Although the number of usable lower-surface hot films was limited to 15, the location and number of these sensors also varied throughout the flight phase. Initially, 14 lower-surface hot films were used, the first of which was mounted to the carbon-fiber panel just forward of the turbulence diverter. The other 13 were mounted directly to the titanium surface on the edge of the suction-panel regions.[30]

Data Recording and Interpretation

All instrumentation data were telemetered to the control room in real time during SLFC research flights. Air data and aircraft parameters were measured at a rate of 50 samples per second. Wing glove pressure data were obtained at 12.5 samples per second. Mass flow data were obtained at 60 samples per second. Telemetered hot-film data were acquired at 100 samples per second. Data from the hot-film sensors were used to determine the boundary-layer state. The dynamic portion of the hot-film signal was "quieter" for laminar flow than for turbulent flow because the temperature-compensated hot-film sensors required less voltage input to keep the temperature constant for laminar flow. During laminar flow conditions, the hot-film sensors required less voltage because there was less mixing in the boundary layer, thus there was less convective heat transfer away from the sensor than in turbulent flow. Consequently, the laminar flow signal had lower voltage amplitude. Conversely, for turbulent flow, the heat transfer rates increased and the data showed rapid fluctuations. Extensive flow mixing within the boundary layer led to data signals with higher amplitudes. High-amplitude voltage spikes in the hot-film data were an indication of transitional flow. Spikes in the direction of positive voltage indicated a mostly laminar signal with turbulent bursts. Spikes in the direction of negative voltage indicated a mostly turbulent signal with laminar bursts. Boundary-layer transition from laminar to turbulent flow was indicated by a maximum occurrence of high-amplitude (positive voltage) spikes.[31]

Surface Imperfections (Excrescences)

Excrescences, or imperfections on the suction panel surface such as rough spots, dimples, and surface contamination caused by dirt or insect impacts, were long known to prevent the development of laminar flow on an airfoil. Such surface imperfections cause disturbances in the boundary layer and "trip" the airflow from laminar to turbulent flow.[32] NASA Dryden personnel performed extensive inspections of the wing glove before and after each flight and kept detailed records about the locations of any surface imperfections. By such means, odd behavior or a lack of repeatability in laminar flow data was sometimes linked to insect impacts on the wing glove. Impacts encountered during or shortly after takeoff were particularly difficult to correlate with unusual laminar flow occurrences noted during flight. Often the remnants from these insect impacts had eroded away and were no longer obvious during postlanding inspection. In an attempt to minimize the dirt and insect impact problem, the suction panel was thoroughly cleaned before each flight-test mission.[33]

Research pilot Dana Purifoy flew the highly modified F-16XL-2 on its first flight with the asymmetrical wing configuration on October 13, 1995. Wingtip-mounted flutter excitation vanes are fitted on both wingtip missile launchers. (NASA)

The F-16XL-2 SLFC Flight-Test Effort

Forty-five SLFC research flights were flown with F-16XL-2 between October 13, 1995, and November 26, 1996. NASA research pilot Dana D. Purifoy flew the highly modified asymmetric aircraft on its first flight on October 13, 1995. Flight-test engineer Mark Collard occupied the rear seat on the 64-minute flight during which the aircraft reached an altitude of 30,000 feet and a Mach number of 0.78. The NASA Dryden project manager for the Phase 2 SLFC effort, Marta Bohn-Meyer, was the ground controller for this 1.1-hour mission, which essentially consisted of a functional check flight (FCF) of the aircraft and its systems. The active suction system was not operated on the first flight.

During the first Phase 2 SLFC research flight, an excessive pressure differential involving the laminar flow test section on the left wing was observed. Under certain flight conditions, the difference in pressure between the upper surface of the wing and a narrow cavity where the test section was attached to the original wing exceeded the acceptable limit of 0.75 psi. Concerns were expressed that continued exposure to the higher pressure differential could damage the attachment mechanism that held the active suction laminar flow test section to the basic wing structure. It was believed that the higher-than-expected pressure differential occurred during flight at higher angles of attack that were not typical of cruise conditions, perhaps even during takeoff and landing approach. A flight restriction that limited the aircraft to no more than 2 g's during subsonic flight at lower altitudes was chosen to mitigate the issue. This, plus some other improvised modifications to better seal the wing glove, kept the pressure differential to within acceptable limits. The modified F-16XL-2 aircraft had been originally been cleared for flight to an angle of attack of 15 degrees and a 3-g limit.[34]

The second F-16XL-2 research flight on November 25, 1995, involved structural loads and flutter clearance tests, evaluation of the handling qualities with the asymmetrical configuration, and engine and air refueling systems checks. The flight-test effort very quickly expanded to include investigations of turbocompressor and suction system performance and the collection of supersonic laminar flow data at the design Mach number and altitude. Dana Purifoy flew the first 12 missions from the front seat with Mark Collard flying as test engineer in the rear cockpit. On February 28, 1996, NASA research pilot Mark P. Stucky flew in the rear cockpit on his initial checkout flight in the aircraft with Dana Purifoy instructing from the front seat. On the next flight, Mark Stucky was in the front seat but the mission was terminated after 0.5 hours due to an in-flight emergency caused by a right main landing gear door failure. Stucky completed his F-16XL flight checkout on March 6.

F-16XL crewmembers were required to wear the NASA Combined High Altitude and Gravity System (CHAGS) during research flights conducted above an altitude of 50,000 feet. NASA's CHAGS ensemble was based upon the British "Jerkin" system, which had been in use for nearly 20 years. The oxygen regulator associated with the CHAGS system was designed to provide aircrew protection up to 9 g's, as well as protection from decompression at high altitudes. Dana Purifoy eventually flew 38 of the 45 research missions conducted during the Phase 2 SLFC effort. Sixteen of these were flown at altitudes above 50,000 feet. Air refueling tanker support was used on many research flights to extend the time that laminar flow data could be collected at high supersonic speeds. Dana Purifoy, who had flown the first flight with F-16XL-2 in the asymmetric configuration, also flew F-16XL-2 on the 45th and last flight of the Phase 2 SLFC program, on November 26, 1996.[35]

During the Phase 2 SLFC program with F-16XL-2, a number of in-flight anomalies were encountered. Nine in-flight emergencies (IFEs) were declared, resulting in termination of the test mission and an early return to base (RTB). Two of these were due to problems with landing gear doors. The remaining in-flight emergencies were related to issues with the F-16XL's flight control system that required SLFC test missions to be aborted early. Laminar flow data was collected on 34 flights. The special laminar flow test instrumentation on the aircraft and the turbocompressor and active laminar flow suction system generally functioned well. In one case, the turbocompressor experienced an rpm overspeed, but it automatically shut itself down as it was designed to do. Detailed mission logs containing flight objectives, test point accomplishment, and postflight commentary for each Phase 2 SLFC flight-test mission with F-16XL-2 are contained in Appendix H.[36]

F-16XL-2 SLFC Flight-Test Results

The Supersonic Laminar Flow Control Phase 2 research program with F-16XL-2 was intended to achieve laminar flow over 50 to 60 percent of the highly swept inner wing chord at supersonic speeds. In addition, flight-test data was to be used to validate computational fluid dynamics computer codes and glove suction design methodologies. Laminar flow test data was obtained at a wide variety of flight conditions throughout nearly each SLFC research flight. However, the primary focus of flight testing was at conditions associated with supersonic flight at Mach 2. Primary data collection altitudes ranged from 50,000 feet to 55,000 feet. Angles of attack during laminar flow test collection ranged from +2 degrees to +4 degrees, and angles of sideslip were either zero or 1.5 degrees nose-right. The flight-test program was primarily conducted at these flight conditions instead of at the wing glove design conditions, which were Mach 1.9 at an altitude of 50,000 feet with a 3.3-degree angle of attack and zero angle of sideslip. Those wing glove design conditions had been determined from previous SLFC flight-test results and from analysis of CFD simulation results. However, flight testing at those design conditions did not result in supersonic laminar flow on the glove. The angles of attack and sideslip angles used during flight testing were based on those that would be seen at cruise conditions by the planned High-Speed Civil Transport. These were an angle of attack of 3.5 degrees with zero sideslip. Maneuvers that were typically performed during the SLFC flight-test effort involved steady-state pushovers to a predesignated angle of attack, which was then maintained while laminar flow data were collected. These smooth pushovers were performed with and without sideslip, and data-collection runs typically lasted about 10 seconds. Achieving and maintaining laminar flow was found to be very sensitive to changes in aircraft angles of attack and sideslip.[37]

Wing Pressure Distributions

During flight-test missions, the pressure distribution over the suction glove had been measured at constant intervals on the surface of the wing from BL 50 to BL 110 both with and without active suction applied to the glove. Several variables had influenced the glove pressure distribution including pressure disturbances caused by the engine inlet shock wave and the canopy-joint shock wave. The maximum level of laminar flow that was achieved on the wing glove occurred at an altitude of 53,000 feet with a 3.7-degree angle of attack and −1.5 degrees of sideslip. At these flight conditions, the Reynolds number was 22.7 million and laminar flow extended aft over the wing to 46 percent of the wing chord. With the 60-degree shock fence installed, laminar flow was observed as far aft as 42 percent of the wing chord. This occurred at an altitude of 53,000 feet, at an angle of attack of 3.4 degrees with an angle of sideslip of −1.5 degrees. This represented the maximum amount of laminar flow observed with the 60-degree shock fence installed.

Boundary-Layer Attachment Line

Obtaining and maintaining a laminar, leading-edge boundary-layer attachment line on a highly swept wing at supersonic speeds is a primary concern if laminar flow is to be achieved over a significant portion of the wing glove. Lower surface hot films placed near the leading edge were used to identify the spanwise extent of laminar flow at the attachment line. Many variables affected the attachment-line and boundary-layer state; foremost were the flight conditions, the shock fences, and the turbulence diverter. Their respective influences are discussed in the following subsections.

Flight Condition and Shock Fence Effects

Key parameters in laminar flow experiments are Reynolds number, angle of attack, and angle of sideslip. Test data were acquired over the Mach number range from 1.9 to 2.0 and at altitudes ranging from 50,000 to 55,000 feet. A completely laminar attachment line was not attainable without a shock fence installed because of the inlet shock effects on the airflow over the wing glove.

Turbulence Diverter Effects

CFD investigations conducted prior to the SLFC flight-test program had been used to predict the local flow field over the aircraft. These had showed that any turbulence created by the in-board row of hot films would not contaminate the hot films located farther downstream. However, CFD results had also indicated that the in-board region of the suction panel's upper surface would experience a turbulent boundary layer. This turbulent boundary layer was formed because the turbulence diverter was not removing all of the oncoming turbulent flow. This prevented a laminar boundary layer from being formed on the in-board region of the suction panel. In addition, the turbulence diverter may also have been generating a vortex that would cause turbulent flow along the in-board edge of the glove. To verify this theory, the gap in the turbulence diverter was filled with low-density foam and room-temperature vulcanizing silicon, and it was coated with epoxy. When filled, the turbulence diverter was no longer able to remove the turbulent boundary layer to allow a laminar flow attachment line to form. Instead, the boundary-layer attachment line was now completely turbulent, regardless of panel suction levels or flight conditions. Both the turbulence diverter and the canopy-joint shock were identified as the cause of the turbulent in-board upper-surface region. The forward portion of the turbulent in-board region was thought to most likely be caused by a vortex generated by the turbulence diverter. The aft portion of the turbulent in-board region on the wing was caused by the shock wave disturbance generated by the canopy joint.

Suction Effects on Transition

Obtaining the optimum suction pressure distribution on the panel proved to be highly challenging. The suction system design had been optimized for flight conditions at Mach 1.9 at an altitude of 50,000 feet. Successful laminar flow results were consistently obtained at Mach 2.0 and an altitude of 55,000 feet. The suction system was usually not turned on until the aircraft was approaching flight-test conditions, thus there was time to observe the behavior of the hot films with the suction system off. The lower surface hot films often showed laminar flow without active suction at altitudes and Mach numbers ranging from 1.7 to 1.93 and at 45,000 to 50,000 feet. These same sensors often indicated a transition from laminar to turbulent flow when design suction pressure level was applied. This was caused by too much suction being present in the regions where the boundary layer transitioned from laminar to turbulent flow. The design suction levels that were believed necessary to overcome the leading-edge pressure disturbance from the engine inlet shock wave had been analytically determined using CFD prior to the start of the flight-test program. The need for a lower-than-design suction pressure level was found to occur only on the boundary-level attachment line. Hot films in other regions on the glove often showed laminar flow with design suction levels.

F-16XL-2 SLFC Program Summary

The maximum region of laminar flow achieved over the wing glove during the entire SLFC program with F-16XL-2 is illustrated in the accompanying diagram.

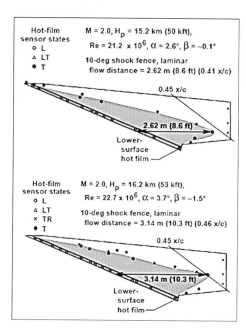

The maximum extent of supersonic laminar flow on the F-16XL-2 active suction wing glove was achieved at Mach 2.0 at an altitude of 53,000 feet. (NASA)

Both laminar flow cases shown were obtained with the 10-degree sweep shock wave fence on the left wing. Hot films on the lower surface of the wing were used to indicate the presence of laminar flow. In the first case shown, a laminar flow region that extended 8.6 feet along the surface of the wing glove was attained at Mach 2.0 at 50,000 feet. During this test, the aircraft was at an angle of attack of 2.6 degrees, somewhat lower than the desired angle of attack for the High-Speed Civil Transport at its supersonic cruise condition. The second case shows laminar flow at Mach 2.0 at 53,000 feet at an angle of attack of 3.7 degrees. These flight conditions were closer to the desired HSCT cruise angle of attack and altitude. Laminar flow extended as far aft as 46 percent of the wing chord equivalent to a distance of 10.3 feet from the wing leading edge. The best supersonic laminar flow was produced at Mach 2.0 and an altitude of 53,000 feet. On the last flight of the SLFC program, on November 26, 1996, laminar flow was measured over the wing as far aft as 42 percent of the chord.

Conclusion and Possible Follow-On Efforts

During NASA's research efforts with both F-16XLs, data on various aspects of supersonic laminar flow control was obtained, and it indicated that "significant progress toward accomplishing the goal was achieved."[38] However, laminar flow was not achieved at the wing glove design point of Mach 1.9 at an altitude of 50,000 feet. Boundary-layer transition data were obtained on the suction glove at Mach 2.0 and altitudes of 53,000 to 55,000 feet. The best laminar flow results were obtained at Mach 2.0 at an altitude of 53,000 feet. At an angle of attack of 3.7 degrees, which was near the desired cruise angle of attack for the High-Speed Civil Transport, laminar flow was obtained over the wing glove to a streamwise location of 46 percent of the wing chord. The Reynolds number during this test run was 22.7 million. Laminar flow was consistently obtained to a minimum of 42 percent of the wing chord at Mach 2.0 at 50,000 feet using the suction levels determined to be optimum from flight testing. The Reynolds number at these conditions was 21.2 million.

The conceptual HSCT would have experienced a much higher Reynolds number than was seen during the SLFC experiment with F-16XL-2. At the HSCT's cruise conditions of Mach 2.4 at 60,000 feet, the Reynolds number would have been about 200 million versus the 22.7 million seen during laminar flow test missions with the F-16XL. This led NASA to investigate the use of the much larger Russian Tupolev Tu-144 supersonic transport as a more representative test bed for follow-on SLFC research. The large, slender delta-winged Russian supersonic airliner would have had the additional advantage of avoiding the laminar flow contamination issues that had been caused by shock wave impingement on the F-16XL's wing glove. In late 1992, Dennis M. Bushnell, NASA Langley chief scientist, held preliminary discussions on the possibility of using the Tu-144 with Tupolev officials who were supportive of the concept. In March 1993, Joseph R. Chambers, then head of the NASA Langley Flight Applications Division, and Kenneth J. Szalai, the director of the NASA Dryden Flight Research Center, formally proposed the concept of using one of the retired Tu-144s for SLFC experimentation at Dryden. Louis J. Williams, the HSR Phase 1 program manager, had already been considering the possibility of a NASA Tu-144 research project. To this end, the HSR Program Office had issued a contract through the Air Force to the North American Aviation Division of the Rockwell Corporation. The North American contract was for a feasibility assessment of restoring a Tu-144 for NASA use as a SLFC test bed.

By mid-1993, direct discussions were in progress between NASA and Tupolev. Wesley L. Harris, NASA associate administrator for aeronautics, was a strong advocate of the joint U.S.-Russian

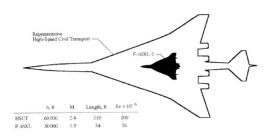

	h, ft	M	Length, ft	Rc × 10⁻⁶
HSCT	60 000	2.4	310	200
F-16XL	50 000	1.9	54	56

Comparison of the F-16XL with the proposed HSCT. (NASA)

research effort. Preliminary estimates were that it would cost at least $40 million to return the Russian aircraft to flightworthy status. Extensive airframe modifications were needed to incorporate active suction laminar flow gloves and a purpose-designed suction system into the Tu-144; these were estimated to cost at least another $50 million. However, North American's engineering assessment indicated that the existing wing on the Tu-144 routinely rippled during supersonic flight at Mach 2 due to the effects caused by heating on the structure. These ripples were considered to be large enough to totally disrupt any possibility of successfully achieving supersonic laminar flow with an active suction system. The North American study recommended the development and integration of a new purpose-designed wing with an original Tu-144 fuselage to create a new SLFC flight demonstrator for use in NASA SLFC research (an approach that was curiously similar to what GD had done in creating the SCAMP/F-16XL). However, this approach would have cost far more than the relatively small NASA HSR program could afford. The NASA research effort with the Tu-144 was limited to a restricted budget of only $15 million. The Tu-144 effort went forward with a joint U.S.-Russian 10-flight-test program that investigated various areas of interest to the HSR program, but these did not include SLFC research.[39]

Endnotes

1. David F. Voracek, "Ground Vibration and Flight Flutter Tests of the Single-Seat F-16XL Aircraft with a Modified Wing," NASA TM-104264 (June 1993).

2. Control surface buzz was first encountered in the United States in the early 1920s, but it became a serious problem two decades later, as aircraft approached the speed of sound during high-speed dives. The aileron buzz phenomenon was demonstrated to pilots (including the author) during their initial check-out flight in the two-seat version of the F-80, the T-33. Michael W. Kehoe, "A Historic Overview of Flight Flutter Testing," NASA TM 4720 (October 1995); N.C. Lambourne, "Control Surface Buzz," (London: Aeronautical Research Council, Ministry of Aviation, R&M No. 3364, 1964).

3. Dynamic pressure (commonly referred to as "q") is the difference between the stagnation pressure and the static pressure on an object in a fluid flow. The stresses on an aircraft are directly proportional to the dynamic pressure. The maximum allowable aerodynamic load on the airframe is reached at "maximum q," which is a critical parameter in aircraft design and flight test. Dynamic pressure q is defined by the equation $q = \frac{1}{2}\rho v^2$ where ρ is air density and v is the velocity.

4. A piezoelectric sensor uses the piezoelectric effect to measure parameters such as pressure, acceleration, strain, or force. Piezoelectricity is the electrical charge that accumulates in certain solid materials (notably crystals, certain ceramics, and biological matter such as bone, DNA, and various proteins) in response to applied mechanical stresses. The word "piezoelectricity" means electricity resulting from pressure. Discovered in the 19th century by the French Curie brothers, the first practical application of a piezoelectric device was in a hydrophone system, designed to detect submerged submarines, developed in France during the First World War.

5. Lura Vernon, "In-Flight Investigation of a Rotating Cylinder-Based Structural Excitation System for Flutter Testing," NASA TN 4512 (June 1993).

6. C.J. Woan, P.B. Gingrich, and M.W. George, "Validation of a Supersonic Laminar Flow Concept," presented at the 29th AIAA Aerospace Sciences Meeting, Reno, NV, January 1991, AIAA paper 1991-0188 (1991).

7. J. Flores, E. Tu, B. Anderson, and S. Landers, "A Parametric Study of the Leading Edge Attachment Line for the F-16XL," presented

at the 22nd AIAA Fluid Dynamics, Plasma Dynamics and Lasers Conference, Honolulu, HI, June 24–26, 1991, AIAA paper 91-1621 (June 1991).

8. Hehs, "Marta Bohn-Meyer."

9. Michael Fischer and Chandra S. Vemuru, "Application of Laminar Flow Control to the High Speed Civil Transport—The NASA Supersonic Laminar Flow Control Program," presented at the Aerospace Technology Conference and Exposition, Long Beach, CA, September 1991, SAE paper 912115 (September 1, 1991).

10. Laurie A. Marshall, "Summary of Transition Results from the F-16XL-2 Supersonic Laminar Flow Control Experiment," presented at the AIAA Applied Aerodynamics Conference, Denver, CO, August 14–17, 2000, AIAA paper 2000-4418 (August 2000); Bruce A. Smith, "F-16XL Flights Could Aid in HSCT Design," *Aviation Week & Space Technology* (October 23, 1995).

11. Ibid.

12. Michael C. Fischer, "F-16XL Supersonic Laminar Flow Control Program Overview," *NASA Langley Research Center First Annual High-Speed Research Workshop, Part 4*, NASA (April 1, 1992), pp. 1,811–1,820.

13. Reynolds number (R_e) is used to determine the dynamic similarity between different experimental cases in fluid dynamics, e.g., comparing results obtained with the F-16XL to those from the very much larger High-Speed Civil Transport. Named after the English physicist Osborne Reynolds (1842–1912), R_e is also used to characterize differences in flow states, such as laminar or turbulent flow. A dimensionless number, R_e provides a measure of the ratio of inertial forces (which determine how a fluid resists changes in motion) to viscous forces. The calculation of R_e includes fluid density and viscosity, its velocity, and a characteristic surface dimension. For aircraft, the mean aerodynamic chord (mac) of the wing is often used for this purpose. R_e is defined as follows:
$R_e = (\rho vL)/\mu = (vL)/v$
where:
v is the mean velocity of the object relative to the fluid
L is a characteristic linear dimension such as the mac
μ is the dynamic viscosity of the fluid
v is the kinematic viscosity, where $v = \mu/\rho$
ρ is the density of the fluid

14. Marshall, "Summary of Transition Results."

15. Scott G. Anders and Michael C. Fischer, "F-16XL-2 Supersonic Laminar Flow Control Flight Test Experiment," NASA Technical Publication (TP) 1999-209683 (1999).

16. Ibid.

17. Navier-Stokes equations describe how the velocity, pressure, temperature, and density of a moving fluid are related and include the effects of viscosity on the flow. The highly complex equations were derived independently by G.G. Stokes, in England, and M. Navier, in France, in the early 1800s. Navier-Stokes equations are too difficult to solve analytically. In the past, approximations and simplifications were used to form a group of solvable equations. Today, high-speed computers solve approximations of the Navier-Stokes equations using a variety of analytic techniques. This technical area is known as computational fluid dynamics, or CFD. John D. Anderson, "NASA and the Evolution of Computational Fluid Dynamics," Case 7 in Hallion, *NASA's Contributions to Aeronautics*, Vol. 1.

18. Smith, "F-16XL Flights Could Aid in HSCT Design."

19. The constrained direct iterative surface curvature (CDISC) design tool that was used by Boeing in designing the wing glove for F-16XL-2 had been developed at the NASA Langley Research Center. The CDISC methodology consisted of a set of linear aerodynamic relations between the flow properties of velocity and pressure related to the local surface curvature. These relations allowed for rapid surface modifications to drive toward a specified distribution of pressures and velocities. Other constraints based upon geometry, desirable pressure features, total integrated forces, and more were incorporated into the CDISC methodology, which was used for aerodynamic design in subsonic, transonic, and supersonic airflows for both simple two-dimensional cases and complex three-dimensional geometries.

20. A Tollmien–Schlichting (T-S) wave is a streamwise instability that occurs within the airflow moving through the boundary layer. It is one of the ways in which the airflow within the boundary layer transitions from laminar to turbulent flow. T-S waves are initiated when some external pressure disturbance (generated from, for example, a supersonic shock wave) interacts with the airflow. T-S waves slowly amplify as they move downstream, eventually growing large enough that the flow transitions from laminar to turbulent condition. T-S waves were discovered in Germany in the early 20th century by

Ludwig Prandtl. They are named for two of his students, Walter Tollmien and Hermann Schlichting.

21. An isobar connects regions of equal pressure in a flow field.

22. The emergency power unit (EPU) on the F-16 is powered with hydrazine from a tank located inside the right wing strake. Hydrazine is a highly toxic and dangerously unstable compound. It was first used by the Germans as a rocket fuel during World War II. The Messerschmitt Me 163B rocket fighter plane, described as being more dangerous to its pilots than to the enemy, was hydrazine-powered. It experienced a number of catastrophic explosions attributed to the unstable nature of its fuel. Hydrazine is commonly used as a monopropellant for maneuvering thrusters on spacecraft. It powered the Space Shuttle Auxiliary Power Units (APUs). The Curiosity rover that landed on Mars in August 2012 employed hydrazine-powered thrusters during its descent to the surface.

23. Wetherall, "F-16XL First Flight 25th Anniversary Celebration.".

24. Stephen F. Landers, John A. Saltzman, and Lisa J. Bjarke, "F-16XL Wing Pressure Distributions and Shock Fence Results from Mach 1.4 to Mach 2.0," NASA TM 97-206219 (1997).

25. Ibid.

26. Ibid.

27. Ibid.

28. In analyzing moving the motion of a rigid body, the *xyz* system is referred to as the space coordinates with the body coordinates known as the *XYZ* system. Space coordinates are treated as unmoving while the body coordinates are rigidly embedded in the moving body (in this case, the aircraft). Aerospace engineers use the terms yaw, pitch, and roll to refer to rotations about the *x*-, *y*-, and *z*-axes, respectively, often calling these the Euler angles. NASA Glenn Research Center.

29. The individual sensors that were used to correlate valve position with mass flow in each of the 20 suction regions on the wing glove were laboratory-calibrated at NASA Langley prior to the F-16XL-2 SLFC flight-test missions. Anders and Fischer, "F-16XL-2 Supersonic Laminar Flow Control Flight Test Experiment."

30. Ibid.

31. Ibid.

32. An excrescence is an imperfection, accumulation, or growth on a surface. In the case of an aircraft wing, excrescences produced by manufacturing variations and accumulated insect impacts are very common. Developed by NACA beginning in the late 1930s, natural

laminar flow airfoils had their maximum thickness located further aft on the wing chord than conventional airfoils. The WWII North American Aviation (NAA) P-51 Mustang was the first production aircraft to be fitted with a laminar flow airfoil that had been collaboratively designed by NAA and NACA. But while it could be attained by a carefully cleaned and polished P-51 aircraft in a full-size wind tunnel, laminar flow rarely if ever existed in practice due to manufacturing imperfections and dirt and insect impact accumulations on the wing leading edges.

33. Laurie A. Marshall, "Boundary-Layer Transition Results From the F-16XL-2 Supersonic Laminar Flow Control Experiment," NASA TM 1999-209013 (December 1999); Saltzman and Bjarke, "F-16XL Wing Pressure Distributions."

34. Bruce A. Smith, "Dryden Analyses Test Section Problem," *Aviation Week & Space Technology* 9 (November 6, 1995): p. 76.

35. A former Air Force test pilot, Dana D. Purifoy joined NASA as a research test pilot in August 1994. A distinguished graduate of EPNER, the French Test Pilot School (which he attended as a U.S. Air Force exchange pilot), Purifoy later served as project manager for NASA's Aeronautics Test Program at the DFRC. He accumulated over 5,000 flying hours in more than 100 different aircraft. NASA, *NASA People: Dana D. Purifoy*, September 2010, *http://www.nasa.gov/centers/dryden/news/Biographies/Pilots/bd-dfrc-p013.html*, accessed August 9, 2011.

36. The F-16XL-2 SLFC Mission Test Logs, Document 6 in Albert L. Braslow, *A History of Suction-Type Laminar Flow Control with Emphasis on Flight Research* (Washington, DC: NASA Monograph in Aerospace History Number 13, 1999).

37. Ibid.

38. Ronald D. Joslin, "Overview of Laminar Flow Control," NASA TP 1998-208705 (1998).

39. Robert A. Rivers, "NASA's Flight Test of the Russian Tu-144 SST," Case 15 in Hallion, *NASA's Contributions to Aeronautics*, Vol. 2; Conway, *High Speed Dreams*.

F-16XL-1 was used in its basic unmodified aerodynamic configuration for the CAWAP flight-test effort. (NASA)

CHAPTER 10

Other NASA F-16XL Flight Research Efforts

Although the main thrust of NASA flight testing with the F-16XL was focused on research into supersonic laminar flow control, as discussed in the previous chapter, the two aircraft were also used for flight research into other areas that were important to risk reduction and technology transfer for the proposed High-Speed Civil Transport. These included research oriented toward understanding issues associated with noise in the vicinity of airfields, sonic boom signature measurement and prediction, measurement of vortical flow over highly swept wing planforms, and the cooperative development of computational fluid dynamics tools and design methodologies. A comprehensive program of analytical and wind tunnel testing was closely associated with these research efforts. Flutter envelope flight clearances were defined via ground and flight testing for both F-16XL aircraft as they were modified to support NASA SLFC research efforts. Separately, the F-16XL tested a new flutter excitation system concept that was evaluated and qualified over the flight envelope from subsonic through transonic to high-speed supersonic flight conditions. This flutter excitation system has since been widely adopted in the international flight-test community. Each of these research efforts with the F-16XL is discussed in further detail in the following sections.

Vortex Flap Flight-Test Planning

The Flight Applications Division at NASA Langley, led by Joseph R. Chambers, was responsible for high-lift aspects of the High-Speed Research program. Takeoff noise had been identified as a major problem of the High-Speed Civil Transport with its highly swept cranked-arrow wing. Very high takeoff thrust levels are required to compensate for the low-lift and high-drag characteristics of such highly swept low aspect ratio wings. Since supersonic transports were optimized for good long-range supersonic cruise performance, they had poor cruise performance at subsonic conditions and especially in their landing configuration. This was the consequence of the high induced drag that resulted from their low aspect ratio wings. NASA Langley research efforts were focused on improving the subsonic lift and drag characteristics of supersonic transports with highly swept low aspect ratio wings. Wind tunnel and computer-based aerodynamic studies were used to assess various wing leading-edge high-lift design approaches that could be used to improve HSCT performance. These included fixed camber configurations, deflectable cambered flaps, and vortex flaps.

By 1993, a flight-test program designed to obtain detailed information on leading-edge vortex flaps at high-lift subsonic conditions was approved using F-16XL-1 as the test bed aircraft. As previously discussed, NASA Langley researchers had conducted low-speed and transonic vortex flap wind tunnel tests during the early 1980s in conjunction with the original F-16XL development effort. By the 1990s, interest in low-speed, high-lift devices had increased within the High-Speed Research program, driven by the need to improve takeoff and landing performance and reduce HSCT noise. Langley had obtained an F-16 on loan from the Air Force to conduct ground crew and pilot training in preparation for receiving F-16XL-1 for the planned high-lift/noise program. The aircraft arrived at Langley on April 15, 1993. On October 5, it was painted in a striking black-and-gold color scheme to enhance the use of flow visualization techniques for the planned flights, which would encounter strong vortical flows. However, the decision was made to transfer the aircraft back to Dryden, and it departed Langley on October 22, 1993. While F-16XL-1 was at Langley, it had been used for simulation-to-flight flying qualities work. During this effort, NASA pilots flew on back-to-back flights in Langley's fixed-base Differential Maneuvering Simulator (DMS) and the F-16XL-1 to evaluate tasks and perceived handling qualities with the fixed-base simulator. This test effort lasted about 1 month, during which time two pilots, including James W. Smolka, flew the aircraft. This work was monitored by engineers from the Air Force Research Laboratory (AFRL).[1]

Langley researcher David E. Hahne conducted wind tunnel tests that used an F-16XL model with several different leading-edge flap configurations. Testing focused on selection of a vortex flap concept that was intended to be built and tested on the inner segment of the F-16XL wing with its 70-degree sweep. The proposed vortex flap flight research program with the F-16XL would also investigate unconventional thrust-management concepts. Using these approaches, power would be reduced at certain takeoff conditions to reduce noise in the vicinity of airfields. Noise intensity in the airport vicinity would be measured while the F-16XL used different thrust-management approaches in combination with extended leading-edge vortex flaps. NASA Langley engineers designed and implemented a piloted simulation of the modified F-16XL in the DMS at Langley in preparation for the actual vortex flap flight-test effort that was to use a modified F-16XL-1. By 1996, all the wing tooling needed to install the vortex flaps had been delivered to NASA Dryden in anticipation of an eventual F-16XL flight-test effort. When the flight research effort with the aircraft modified with vortex flaps was eliminated from further consideration that same year, the vortex flap tooling was placed in storage at Dryden. All tooling related to the vortex flight research effort with F-16XL was later destroyed after the entire NASA High-Speed Research program was cancelled in 1999.[2]

Acoustic Research

Airport noise was one of the major issues that needed to be addressed in determining the environmental and public acceptability of a civil supersonic transport. These heavy aircraft would have been powered by large, high-thrust engines operating at high nozzle pressure ratios (NPRs) and high exhaust-jet velocities. Concerns existed not only for the noise produced in the vicinity of the airport during takeoff and landing but also for the noise footprint produced along the flightpath during climb out to cruise altitude. This noise footprint extended outward for a distance of up to 50 miles from the takeoff runway. To determine the engine noise for these supersonic transport designs, NASA Langley had developed computer-based acoustic prediction software programs such as the Aircraft Noise Prediction Program (ANOPP). However, these programs had been developed and validated using data acquired from earlier turbofan engine designs whose nozzle bypass ratios and flight speeds were lower than those planned for future supersonic transports. Doppler amplification of the noise forward of the aircraft flightpath was also a concern for these higher speed aircraft. For these reasons, NASA Langley and NASA Dryden jointly planned and conducted flight tests to acquire in-flight acoustic data for high nozzle bypass ratio engines.

Flyover and static tests of the F-16XL-2 powered by the General Electric GE F110-GE-129 engine were used to study the acoustics of high-NPR engines, like those planned for use in an HSCT. Flight-test objectives were to assess noise during the subsonic climb-to-cruise (CTC) phase of operations using an aircraft equipped with high–nozzle bypass ratio engines and to obtain an improved noise database to validate aircraft noise predictive software codes. Engine exhaust flow properties (mass flow, temperature, pressure, velocity, and Mach number) were key factors in determining acoustic characteristics. An engine cycle computer program was used to calculate parameters for comparison with parameters measured during in-flight tests. The engine computer program and follow-on calculations were also used to calculate engine exhaust

The two-seat F-16XL-2 powered by the F110-GE-129 engine seen on a test flight from NASA Dryden in October 1991. (NASA)

properties where in-flight measurements were not possible. These tests were performed in conjunction with NASA Langley as part of a study to investigate the acoustic characteristics of jet engines operating at high nozzle pressure conditions. Dryden was responsible for the planning and conduct of the flyover tests, recording and analyzing flight data, determining the aircraft space position, determining engine exhaust gas flow properties, and conducting a ground static acoustic survey. NASA Langley responsibilities included the design and setup of the microphone array, recording the noise measurements, merging the acoustic and space position data, analyzing and evaluating the acoustic data, and correlating these data with Dryden-determined engine exhaust properties.

The F-16XL acoustic research effort included F-16XL flights over a microphone array at varying speeds and altitudes. Noise levels were determined during subsonic climb-to-cruise conditions, and acoustic data collection was used to enable predictive computer software codes to be refined and validated. In the subsonic climb-to-cruise portion of the study, flyovers of the acoustic array were conducted at altitudes from 3,800 feet to 12,300 feet and from Mach 0.3 to Mach 0.95 at intermediate (non-afterburning) power settings. During acoustic data collection for the evaluation of aircraft noise prediction computer software codes, tests were flown at an altitude of 3,800 feet and at speeds from Mach 0.3 to Mach 0.95. Ground-level engine testing was conducted at power settings ranging from idle to intermediate to establish baseline exhaust noise levels at ground static conditions. The final test report summarizing the acoustic flight-test program was prepared by NASA Dryden research engineers Jon K. Holzman, Lannie D. Webb, and Frank W. Burcham, Jr.[3] Separately, NASA Langley research staff members Jeffrey J. Kelly, Mark R. Wilson, John Rawls, Jr., Thomas D. Norum, and Robert A. Golub correlated the acoustic test results with predictions obtained from the NASA-developed ANOPP computer program. They produced and published a detailed acoustic flight-test database based on the results from the F-16XL flight-test effort.[4]

Acoustic Test Instrumentation

F-16XL-2 was instrumented to measure both aircraft and engine parameters. In addition, measurements of acoustic, meteorological, and aircraft space-positioning were collected from sensors on the ground. Mach number and altitude were obtained from the Pitot static probe on the F-16XL-2 noseboom. Pressures from the Pitot probe were fed to the aircraft central air data computer, where Mach number and altitude were calculated. The aircraft also had an inertial navigation system (INS) for accurate velocity and position determination. Angle of attack and angle of sideslip were measured by vanes on the F-16XL-2 flight-test noseboom. These data were recorded at a rate of 10 samples per second by an onboard system on a 10-bit pulse code modulation (PCM) data system, and the data was also transmitted to the ground. The F-16XL-2 was also equipped with a C-band radar beacon to aid in precise spatial positioning.

The General Electric F110-GE-129 turbofan was equipped with a digital electronic engine control (DEEC) unit. The F110 engine was extensively instrumented for the acoustic test effort in support of the High-Speed Research effort. Engine parameters were used as inputs into the F110-GE-129 engine computer program and acoustic analyses. Results from the F110 engine computer program were used for comparison with flight-test results. They included throttle position, engine face total temperature, fan discharge total pressure,

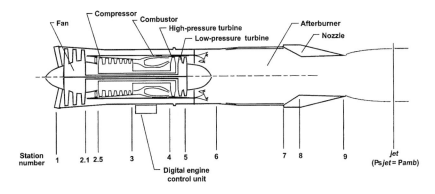

A cutaway view of the General Electric F110-GE-129 turbofan engine shows the engine station number locations. (NASA)

compressor discharge static pressure, core engine fuel flow, fan rotor speed, core rotor speed, engine exhaust gas temperature (EGT), and exhaust nozzle throat area.

Acoustic Measurements

Noise propagation in the vicinity of airfields was a major concern with the supersonic transport. Public perceptions of noise were known to be significantly affected by weather conditions. For this reason, meteorological conditions were significant inputs into the aircraft noise prediction program, and weather conditions during the flight-test missions needed to be measured. They were determined from four main sources: F-16XL-2 onboard measurements, weather balloons, a ground weather station at the acoustics van, and a tethered balloon located near the flyover array.

Onboard measurements obtained from the F-16XL-2 primarily consisted of winds-aloft data determined from the aircraft inertial system and total temperature measured at the F110 engine face. A tethered balloon was located near the array of microphones at the flyover location on Rogers Dry Lake. It was raised and lowered on a 1,500-foot-long line to support meteorological data collection during the acoustic test missions.

During flyover tests, acoustic data were measured with an analog and digital microphone array. The array was positioned along a defined flyby line on Rogers Dry Lake. This location provided a good proximity to the tracking radar; was an adequate distance from the Edwards, CA, main runway; and had a large, flat area suitable for acoustics measurements. The analog microphone setup was similar to the setup used by NASA Dryden during static ground run engine acoustic testing. The NASA Dryden FPS-16 radar was used to track the C-band radar beacon on the aircraft during the acoustic flyovers. Ground test controllers in the mission control room assisted the F-16XL pilot in lining up for each test, establishing the time for beginning and completing data runs, and determining track validity for each flyover. These data were also used by NASA Langley in their postflight analyses to determine the spatial position of the aircraft. This was important for correlation with the acoustic data collected by the microphone arrays.

For static signature measurements, an array consisting of 24 microphones was located on a large, flat taxiway area at NASA Dryden. The microphones were placed every 7.5 degrees on an arc that was located 99 feet from the engine exhaust centerline. The microphones were mounted upside down inside protective windscreens. The microphone diaphragms were located 0.5 inches above a thin aluminum plate taped to the surface of the concrete or asphalt. This test arrangement enabled acoustic exhaust noise from the F-16XL to be recorded without interference by ground reflections. The NASA Dryden acoustics research van was used to record the 24 channels of microphone data. Two 14-track tape recorders were installed in the mobile trailer. Twelve channels of acoustic data were recorded on each of the two recorders. The remaining tape channels were used to record the time and the pilot's event marker. Each of the 24 microphone stations was battery-powered and consisted of a condenser microphone, a preamplifier, and a line driver amplifier. The trailer also contained a weather station for recording local temperatures, wind velocity, and wind direction in the area of the microphone array. The trailer also had UHF radios for communication with the test aircraft.

Test Procedures

To satisfy test objectives, acoustic levels were measured during the F-16XL's subsonic climb-to-cruise altitude and data necessary to validate the aircraft noise predictive software computer code was collected. In both cases, collection of acoustic data was desired when the aircraft was located more than 10 to 15 degrees above the horizon as measured from the center of the acoustic microphone array. Data collection start- and end-point distances from the acoustic array depended on the flight altitude of the F-16XL-2 aircraft during each flyover pass. At the lowest test altitude, which was 1,500 feet above ground level (AGL), this start- and end-point distance was approximately 1 nautical mile from the acoustic data-collection microphone array. The F-16XL pilot flew the planned flyovers across the acoustic test array using visual navigation cues, inputs from his onboard inertial navigation system, and radio directions from the test controller in the mission control room.

Climb-To-Cruise Tests

The flight matrix for the climb-to-cruise runs consisted of level flight accelerations over the acoustic array at various Mach numbers and altitudes. During these runs, the engine power setting was held constant at the intermediate level in order to obtain maximum engine nozzle pressure ratio. Test altitudes varied from 3,800 feet to 32,300 feet, and Mach numbers ranged from 0.30 to over Mach 0.90. To establish the desired climb-to-cruise condition, the pilot initially stabilized the aircraft at the desired altitude just below the desired Mach number. As the airplane approached the start point for acoustic data collection, the throttle was advanced to the intermediate power setting based on a radio call from the mission control room. The engine was allowed to stabilize for approximately 5 seconds before the start of the test run. The aircraft accelerated through the desired test conditions in level flight depending on the degree of excess thrust available. Some acoustic runs were initiated directly over the center of the array with the run terminating when the elevation angle was again 15 degrees above the horizon. At some flight-test conditions, the aircraft speed brakes were deployed to reduce aircraft acceleration during acoustic data acquisition. The climb-to-cruise tests resulted in a significant change in Mach number during test runs caused by the excess engine thrust available with the F-16XL-2. Mach numbers during test runs ranged from Mach 0.30 to Mach 0.95.

Aircraft Noise Prediction Program Code Evaluation Tests

The aircraft noise prediction program software code evaluation tests were flown at constant Mach numbers and at an aircraft altitude of 3,800 feet above sea level (1,500 feet above the local ground level). The throttle was set at the power required for level flight at constant speed. For these runs, the pilot coordinated his overflight of the microphone array with the mission control room. Once the engine power was set, it was not changed during the data-collection run and small changes in Mach number were allowed to occur. Speed brakes were not used during ANOPP data-collection test runs.

Static Ground Tests

For F-16XL-2 ground static tests, the aircraft was secured to tiedown points and engine power setting was varied to achieve various engine pressure ratio increments between idle power and intermediate power and then back to idle. The engine was stabilized for 1 minute at each test point, then acoustic data was acquired for 30 seconds. All static testing was conducted with the wind speed below 5 knots to minimize wind effects on noise measurements. Atmospheric data during ground acoustic testing were obtained from the NASA Dryden acoustics van and from observations taken at other locations around the Air Force Flight Test Center.

Analytical Techniques

Jet-mixing and shock cell noise are the two primary sources of noise for engines with high NPRs during takeoff and subsonic climb. Engines of this type were to be used on the proposed HSCT. Engine noise is primarily affected by aircraft velocity and Mach number, exhaust velocity at the engine exhaust exit, and the engine nozzle bypass ratio. For purposes of acoustic analysis, engine exhaust characteristics were defined at the nozzle exit and also at a location somewhat behind the nozzle exit where the engine exhaust was assumed to be fully expanded. Jet-mixing noise primarily results from the difference between the fully expanded nozzle jet velocity and the free-stream air velocity. Shock cell noise is related to the difference between the Mach number of the fully expanded jet and the Mach number at the engine nozzle exit and is based on the nozzle expansion ratio.

F110-GE-129 Digital Engine Model

Flight-test and ground-test data collected from the instrumented engine could not measure values of pressure, temperature, velocity, and mass flow directly at the engine nozzle exit. Measurements from the instrumented engine did not directly provide the data needed for the evaluation of climb-to-cruise and validation of the aircraft noise acoustic predictive software codes. For these reasons, a General Electric F110 digital engine performance computer model was used to calculate some of the parameters needed for the acoustic evaluation. Other engine performance parameters were computed separately using follow-on calculations. The F110-GE-129 engine performance model (also referred to as the "engine deck") was a digital computer-based FORTRAN software language–based computer program. It predicted engine parameters and performance consistent with that of a nominal F110-GE-129 engine. This aerothermodynamic model was used to calculate various F110 engine operating parameters that would otherwise be difficult or impossible to measure because of excessively high temperatures and/or inaccessibility of certain areas internal to the engine to installation of test instrumentation. Input parameters used for the analysis consisted of altitude, Mach number, engine-face total temperature, and throttle setting.

The engine computer program modeled engine performance based on the measured airplane flight parameters previously inputted into the program. Some parameters needed for the acoustic analysis could not be measured in flight, and these were computed by the engine model. These nonmeasurable parameters included gross thrust, nozzle pressure ratio, the ratio of the exhaust nozzle effective exit-plane area to its effective throat area, the ratio of exhaust nozzle flow exit-plane static pressure to ambient static pressure, the exhaust nozzle mixed-jet total temperature at the throat, the mass flow rate at the exhaust nozzle throat, and other useful exhaust nozzle exit-stream parameters, such as throat total pressure, the exhaust nozzle total throat pressure, and the specific heat ratio of the exhaust gas at the nozzle entrance. The engine deck also calculated many other parameters that could be compared to actual in-flight data obtained from engine measurements.

Selected flight-test parameters were compared with the times associated with pilot call outs for the selected inbound distance to the acoustic test array, the overhead point, and the selected outbound distance. Results determined that Mach number, altitude, exhaust nozzle throat area, and throttle setting were the main controllable parameters that determined test data quality. Constant throttle setting and exhaust nozzle throat area along with a constant or slowly accelerating Mach number and a relatively constant altitude yielded the most consistent test results.

Acoustic Research Test Summary

F110-GE-129 engine parameters were measured during test flights with F-16XL-2 at NASA Dryden and compared with parameters calculated using the General Electric F110-GE-129 engine computer program. Erroneous results could have occurred if the flight-test engine installed in F-16XL-2 was significantly different from the nominal engine modeled in the engine computer program. For this reason, engine parameters were measured during flights with the F-16XL. These measurements, along with altitude and Mach number, were compared with F110 parameters calculated using the engine computer program. A comparison of results showed very good agreement, confirming that the computer model of the General Electric F110-GE-129 engine was a good representation of the actual engine flown in F-16XL-2. Ground static testing, climb-to-cruise data, and flyover data showed good to excellent agreement between measured and estimated noise signatures that were produced using the NASA Langley Aircraft Noise Prediction Program.

F-16XL Cranked-Arrow Wing Aerodynamics Project

The F-16XL aircraft provided a unique opportunity for computer model correlation and CFD code validation with in-flight and wind tunnel data. This would provide a valuable contribution to the design of an HSCT with its similar highly swept cranked-arrow wing configuration. A series of vortex flow studies based on the aerodynamics of the F-16XL were led by NASA Langley's John E. Lamar. This project was known as the Cranked-Arrow Wing Aerodynamics Project (CAWAP). Lamar's team of researchers included Langley's Clifford J. Obara, Susan J. Rickard, and Bruce D. Fisher, as well as Dryden's David F. Fisher. The CAWAP research approach was planned to take advantage of the detailed measurements and analyses of F-16XL vortex flow characteristics that had been created in conjunction with NASA wind tunnel and flight-test research efforts. Data obtained from these efforts included static and dynamic pressures on the surface of the F-16XL cranked-arrow wing, detailed boundary-layer measurements, and airflow visualization on the upper surface of the cranked-arrow wing. The flow visualization studies used cameras installed at various locations on F-16XL-1 to image large numbers of tufts located on the upper wing surface. Flight-test results were correlated with data derived from CFD studies. As the effort evolved, CAWAP became the basis for a series of follow-on multinational studies and analyses of vortex flow when the effort was expanded, becoming known as the Cranked-Arrow Wing Aerodynamics Program International (CAWAPI).[5]

As originally planned, CAWAP was intended to be divided into three phases of flight testing. These were based on the modifications to the F-16XL wing configuration to support anticipated HSCT technology and risk-reduction needs. Phase 1 was structured to use the basic F-16XL-1 with no modifications. Data from this phase was to serve as the technical baseline for the follow-on phases. Phase 2 modifications would have extended the cranked-arrow wing farther forward into the

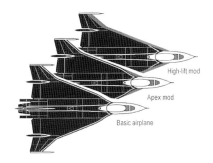

The CAWAP flight-test program was originally intended to be conducted in three phases, with the F-16XL-1 wing planform progressively modified for each phase as depicted above. (NASA)

fuselage, removing the distinctive S-curve at the wing apex. The S-curve had been incorporated into the F-16XL wing design as a result of earlier NASA Langley wind tunnel testing. It was intended to minimize the pitchup problems that would be encountered with an air superiority fighter during aggressive maneuvering at very high angles of attack. However, the S-curve at the apex of the wing was not needed for a civil transport aircraft. The Phase 2 configuration, with its continuous 70-degree swept wing leading edge, was more representative of the cranked-arrow wing that was planned to be used on the future supersonic transport.

NASA Langley had previously conducted wind tunnel tests of a large (18-percent) scale F-16XL model fitted with a wing similar to that which was to be installed on F-16XL-1 for the CAWAP Phase 2 test effort. To compensate for the pitch instability caused by the extended wing leading edges at higher angles of attack, the test model was equipped with a thrust-vectoring capability. Phase 3, the final CAWAP flight-test phase, would have incorporated a high-lift (vortex flap) device along the entire leading edge of the F-16XL-1 wing. The exact configuration of this final high-lift device would have been determined from wind tunnel experiments, CFD predictions, and the results of flight testing with the F-16XL aircraft in the Phase 2 configuration. However, the CAWAP Phase 3 configuration, with

A free-flight model of the F-16XL with the wing apex modification seen during high-AoA free-flight testing in the Langley 30- by 60-foot wind tunnel. (NASA)

its NASA-developed high-lift vortex flaps, was planned to be fully representative of the HSCT conceptual design in its takeoff or landing configuration.[6]

A significant objective of the flight-test effort associated with the CAWAP was to verify the performance of proposed high-lift concepts for the HSCT while ensuring acceptable compliance with community noise standards. The first step in this process would establish a ground-to-flight noise correlation for the aircraft with the cranked-arrow wing planform. The original intent of the program was that all three F-16XL-1 wing planform configurations would be flown, with the resulting data used to calibrate design and analysis tools as well as noise prediction codes. In addition, advanced operating procedures for possible use with the HSCT during takeoff and landing would have been evaluated during flight testing. The final CAWAP objective would have assessed the integration and operation of high-lift devices on a highly swept cranked-arrow wing in realistic operational scenarios that were representative of actual airline service.

Program Rescope

In the spring of 1994, during preparations for Phase 1 of the planned CAWAP effort, the remainder of the three-phase flight-test effort was cancelled by NASA. Sufficient funding was provided to complete the Phase 1 effort using F-16XL-1 in its baseline configuration. Test objectives were revised to focus on documenting flow physics at both high-lift and transonic conditions and to characterize the stability and control of the aircraft. The approach was still on a combined wind tunnel, CFD, and flight-test-correlation approach. However, only the baseline (unmodified) F-16XL wing configuration would be used for the remainder of the CAWAP effort. The first CAWAP flight occurred at Dryden on November 21, 1995. The CAWAP flight-test program ended in April 1996, never having progressed beyond the Phase 1 effort. This decision effectively ended the entire NASA F-16XL flight-test effort within the HSR program, although F-16XL-1 would be upgraded with a digital

F-16XL-1 was used in its basic unmodified aerodynamic configuration for the CAWAP flight-test effort. (NASA)

flight control system for potential use as a pneumatic vortex control (PVC) test bed prior to finishing its test flying days at Dryden. This aspect of the flight-test program is discussed separately.

CAWAP Data Collection

The CAWAP flight-test program was designed to maximize the quality, quantity, and availability of data that could be collected with F-16XL-1. Pressure-based data were to be collected using surface static pressure ports, boundary-layer rakes, and modified Preston tubes. Video recordings would be used to image tufts, surface oil patterns, and surface liquid crystals mounted on the upper surface of the wings. To ensure the validity of test data, precise geometric data on the upper surface of the F-16XL-1 was determined using photogrammetry and compared with the original numerical surface description of the aircraft. Data from surface-mounted hot films would also be collected and analyzed. The pressure and surface flow data were intended to be used to establish the effects of variations in Mach number on local airflow on the wing. Hot-film data would determine the conditions under which the boundary layer transitioned from laminar to turbulent flow. Details of the complex set of instrumentation that were installed on the aircraft for the CAWAP effort are described in more detail below.

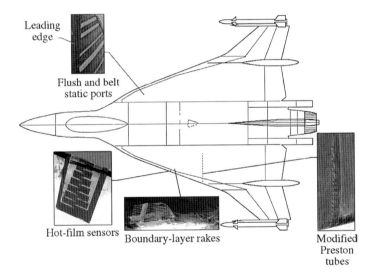

A wide variety of specialized sensors and tailored test instrumentation was installed on F-16XL-1 to collect accurate airflow data for the CAWAP flight-test effort. (NASA)

F-16XL-1 was fitted with a highly sophisticated pressure instrumentation system. The layout of this system on the aircraft included a large number static pressure ports distributed on the wing surface as well as boundary-layer rakes and modified Preston tubes.[7] The static pressure ports were either belt- or flush-mounted on the surface of the wing. The static ports were connected to

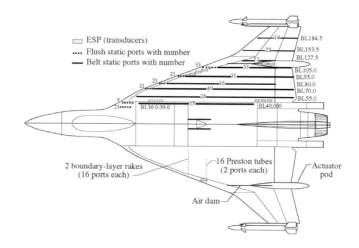

An extensive suite of pressure instrumentation systems was installed on F-16XL-1 during the CAWAP test effort. (NASA)

electronically scanning pressure (ESP) modules inside the wing through tubes. Individual pressure tubes inside each pressure belt measured two separate values of pressure. This was done by sealing each tube about halfway along its length with separate pressures collected from one forward and one aft pressure port.

Static pressures on the wing surface were measured using 337 static ports. These included flush static pressure ports installed in the leading-edge region of the right wing and in the streamwise belts. Eleven ESP transducers were distributed at various locations on the wing. During the flight-test effort, only 326 of the 337 static pressure ports provided reliable data. Of these, 280 were on the upper wing surface and 46 on the lower surface. The static ports were distributed so that there were sufficient numbers at any given butt line or fuselage station location to enable the surface pressures on the wing to be correlated with aerodynamic cross flow. Another consideration that drove the pressure collection layout on the aircraft was coverage of other regions of special interest, especially the apex of the wing and the areas forward and aft of the trailing-edge control surface hinge lines.

Boundary-layer pressure measurements were obtained using two 2-inch-high pressure rakes at a time. The pressure rakes were mounted at four different positions on the left wing. The most in-board of the rakes was used as a control. Each rake had 16 active tubes with 15 used to measure total pressures and 1 to measure static pressure. The two rakes were connected to a 32-port ESP module located inside the wing. Each rake was mounted on the upper surface of the wing and was oriented into the local flow at an average angle based on the results from CFD predictions. The local flow at and slightly above the wing surface was used to establish the rake orientation angles for specific aircraft flight conditions. Finally, 16 modified Preston tubes were aligned with the local flow on the wing near fuselage station FS 330. They were used to determine the local skin friction across the left wing. Through a process of calibration, the pressure change between the total pressure and the static tubes was related to the local skin friction.

Video data was recorded with six external cameras. Two cameras were mounted at the top of the vertical tail, one was on either side of the fuselage behind the canopy, and one was located in the nose of each wingtip-mounted dummy AIM-9 missile shape. Video recordings were used to image tufts, surface oil patterns, and surface liquid crystals mounted on the upper surface of the wings.

The F-16XL-1 was heavily instrumented for the CAWAP research program. The aircraft is seen during a data-collection run at an angle of attack of 21 degrees at an altitude of 17,500 feet. The surface tufts, pressure belts, and visual reference markings are readily discernible. (NASA)

Wind Tunnel Testing

Wind tunnel testing for comparison purposes with the results from computational fluid dynamics analyses and flight-test data was mainly accomplished using three subscale F-16XL models. The first of these was a 0.11-scale F-16XL model, which was tested in the NASA Ames 11-Foot Tunnel. This model was used to estimate loads on the aircraft from Mach 0.60 to Mach 2.0 prior to the start of NASA Dryden flight testing with F-16XL-1. A total of 190 pressure ports, located in streamwise rows, were distributed on the left upper wing surface and the right lower wing surface. During the tests, angle of attack was varied from –2 degrees to nearly 29 degrees. Separately, a 0.18-scale F-16XL model was tested in the NASA Langley 30- by 60-Foot Full-Scale Tunnel. For these tests, Mach number was kept below 0.08 and angle of attack was varied from –5 degrees to 30 degrees. Angle of sideslip was varied between –20 degrees and 20 degrees. This 18-percent-scale wind tunnel test model had 30 right-wing-mounted, flush upper static pressure surface ports positioned in both streamwise and spanwise rows. These pressure port locations were duplicated on the actual F-16XL-1 aircraft in order to ensure the most valid comparison between the wind tunnel test results and in-flight data. Force, moment, and pressure data on the aircraft were obtained from these wind tunnel test efforts.

A 0.18-scale instrumented F-16XL model was tested in the NASA Langley 30- by 60-foot Full-Scale Tunnel to obtain precise vortical data for comparison with airflow results predicted from CFD modeling. (NASA)

The final wind tunnel test for comparison purposes used an instrumented 0.04-scale wind tunnel model of the F-16XL. It was tested in the NASA Langley Basic Aerodynamic Research Tunnel, colloquially known as the BART. Test conditions included Mach numbers up to 0.165 with angle of attack varying from 5 to 20 degrees. This model was fitted with 82 pressure ports divided between the right upper wing surface and the left lower wing surface. The pressure port locations correlated with those on the 0.18-scale wind tunnel model, and they were duplicated on the actual F-16XL-1 aircraft. Flow visualization tests were conducted with this $1/25$-scale F-16XL-1 wind tunnel model during 1992. During these tests, the airflow over the top of the model was illuminated by three laser sheets. A fine mist of smoke was then introduced upstream from the model into the wind tunnel. The laser

A $1/25$-scale F-16XL-1 model was tested in the Basic Aerodynamics Research Tunnel at NASA Langley Research Center in 1992. Laser light sheets illuminate the vortex flow field around the model. (NASA)

sheets captured the vortex created by air flowing over the F-16XL leading-edge extension at a moderately high angle of attack. The vortex core was visualized as it flowed downstream over the model from the left to the right.[8]

CFD Modeling

The last major source of data in the CAWAP effort was generated by computational fluid dynamics modeling. A Navier-Stokes CFD computer program, modified to incorporate a turbulent boundary layer, was used to determine airflow characteristics across the F-16XL-1 model using a multiblock, patched grid that was superimposed on the aircraft geometry. In its original version, this grid used 750,000 tiny triangles superimposed over the surface geometry of F-16XL-1. To improve the fidelity of the results from the computational fluid dynamics analyses, the final version of this particular patchwork grid was greatly increased in size to encompass 1,460,000 triangles. During the course of the CAWAP effort, CFD analyses were conducted over a variety of simulated flight conditions to enable results from computer modeling to be correlated with data derived from wind tunnel models and F-16XL-1 flight testing.

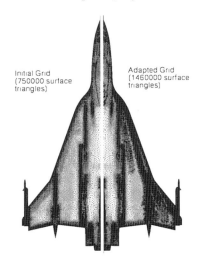

The geometric grids used for precisely modeling F-16XL geometry were very intricate in order to produce high-fidelity CFD results. (NASA)

CAWAP International

Based on the success of CAWAP in fostering the use of CFD to analyze high-AoA airflow over complex aircraft like the F-16XL, NASA moved on to sponsor a similar multinational initiative. This would result in CAWAP being expanded to encompass a broader community of nations and academic institutions in both Europe and the United States. The U.S. delegation to the NATO Research and Technology Organization (RTO) Air Vehicle Technology (AVT) Symposium, held in Germany in the spring of 2000, had proposed a set of independent CFD-based aerodynamic studies that would be conducted by cooperating nations. National organizations (either government research facilities or academic institutions) would use their CFD techniques to predict the vortical flow aerodynamics around the F-16XL aircraft. The results from these independent CFD analyses could then be compared with actual flight-test results. This would enable an evaluation of multinational capabilities to accurately predict the aerodynamics around a complex aircraft like the F-16XL. This would be followed by refinements to existing CFD techniques within these multinational organizations. The goal of the CAWAPI effort was to increase the Technology Readiness Level (TRL) of computational fluid dynamics tools and techniques for use in the development of advanced military aircraft (in particular, high-performance fighters) by allied nations. The TRL approach was a NASA innovation conceived by Stan Sadin at NASA Headquarters in 1974. With some variation, it has since been widely adapted by organizations and agencies around the world, including the U.S. Department of Defense.[9] (Appendix G furnishes a list of the nine TRLs as defined by NASA.)

NASA agreed to provide highly detailed geometrical data and grids on the F-16XL to appropriately authorized nations to enable the various participating national organizations to accomplish these independent CAWAPI research efforts. Overall sponsorship of the effort would come under the NATO RTO. Direct management was assigned to the Performance, Stability & Control, and Fluid Physics Technical Committees operating under the RTO AVT working group. During a meeting in Norway in the spring of 2001, a variety of vortex flow topics were discussed with two topics selected for further study. These were the international expansion of the NASA CAWAP (F-16XL flight-test and CFD) effort and a separate Vortex Flow Experiment.[10] Since both topics involved vortex flows around slender wings, they were merged into a single proposal in the fall of 2002. The proposal was submitted to the NATO RTO for approval. In the spring of 2003, the RTO approved the project as AVT-113, "Understanding and Modeling Vortical Flows to Improve the Technology Readiness Level for Military Aircraft." The expanded CAWAP activity was then designated CAWAPI to denote the multinational involvement. CAWAPI would eventually involve the creation of a Virtual Laboratory at NASA Langley for facilitating secure data storage and transmission among participating member nations.[11]

The objectives of the CAWAP International effort were contained in the "Terms of Reference," a document prepared by the Air Vehicle Technology working group. This document called for participating nations to cooperate in the following ways:[12]

> Assess various CFD codes against F-16XL-1 flight and wind tunnel data sets in order to increase the Technology Readiness Level (TRL) of CFD computer software codes to a value of 5, where a TRL of 5 was defined by NATO (using the NASA definition) as "Component and/or breadboard verification in a relevant environment";

Develop best practices for each CFD code based on the data sets; and

Incorporate appropriate or upgraded turbulence models into the respective codes to provide for improved agreement between wind tunnel, flight-test, and CFD results.

These objectives were to be accomplished by assigning responsibility for certain aspects of the effort to each of the participating groups. In particular, NASA agreed to do the following.[13]

Supply export-controlled geometry in various formats of the F-16XL-1 aircraft to participating partners once formal Memorandum-of-Agreements are in place.

Make available F-16XL-1 flight pressures, images, skin friction, and boundary layer measurements to the team.

Supply data formats and coordinate necessary database services.

The completion date for these actions was originally set for December 2005 but was later extended to December 2007. The U.S. International Traffic in Arms Regulations (ITAR) restricted unlimited open-level dissemination of the highly detailed F-16XL aircraft geometry. This created some complications for NASA in meeting its CAWAPI agreements. An acceptable solution that was adopted consisted of the creation of the CAWAPI Virtual Laboratory, housed in an electronically secure facility located at the NASA Langley Research Center. This electronically secure virtual laboratory was subsequently used to securely transfer F-16XL aircraft geometry and highly detailed CFD grids among the authorized CAWAPI participants.[14]

Participating CAWAPI organizations eventually included four airframe companies: EADS, in Germany; Turkish Aircraft Industries; Boeing Phantom Works, in St. Louis, MO; and Lockheed Martin Aeronautics Company, in Fort Worth, TX. Two government research laboratories also played major roles. These were the National Aerospace Laboratory (NLR) in the Netherlands and the NASA Langley Research Center in the United States. In addition, there were six independent university-led research efforts, three in Europe and three in the United States. The European academic research efforts were led by the Royal Institute of Technology/Swedish Defense Research Agency, the University of Glasgow/ University of Liverpool in the United Kingdom, and Vrije Universiteit Brussel/ Numeca (the Free University of Brussels) in Belgium. Participating American universities were the University of Tennessee-Chattanooga SimCenter, the United States Air Force Academy, and the University of Wyoming.[15]

CAWAPI Summary

The NASA-developed Technology Readiness Level approach coupled with the NATO-sponsored CAWAPI effort improved the technical capabilities of U.S. and allied aeronautical organizations to use state-of-the-art CFD techniques. The CAWAPI research effort was accomplished under the auspices of the NATO RTO. A dedicated working group (designated AVT-113) composed of independent researchers from various nations and research establishments was able to independently evaluate the airflow on and around a highly precise computer-based geometric model of the F-16XL aircraft. The F-16XL model had been provided using approved secure technology transfer procedures that were specially developed for the CAWAPI effort. The latest CFD methodologies were used to prepare predictions of the airflow over the F-16XL using the geometric model and a detailed F-16XL flight-test dataset provided via NASA Langley under the CAWAPI effort. Results from actual F-16XL flight test was compared to CFD predictions produced by participating U.S. and allied research organizations. With appropriate refinements to CFD models, the results produced by these organizations were shown to agree very closely with NASA in-flight measurements. Representative illustrations of predicted vortical airflow over the F-16XL under various flight conditions, prepared by teams from the United Kingdom, the Netherlands, NASA, the U.S. Air Force Academy, and Lockheed Martin, are shown below.[16]

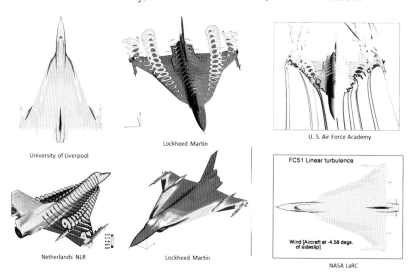

Some examples of vortical airflow over the F-16XL as graphically predicted using the CFD modeling capabilities of various national organizations. (NATO)

Dynamic Ground Effects on a Cranked-Arrow Wing

The High-Speed Civil Transport program motivated renewed research into dynamic ground effect based on the known sensitivity of low aspect ratio slender wings to this phenomenon. The primary objective of the cranked-arrow wing dynamic ground effect test program was to obtain ground effect data containing sufficient detail and accuracy to enable analysis of the dynamic nature of the problem. A second objective of the research effort was to develop an engineering model of dynamic ground effect and evaluate an algorithm based on this model using flight-test data. The F-16XL, with its low aspect ratio cranked-arrow wing, had a wing configuration that was similar to that planned for the HSCT. Thus, it was selected as the research aircraft for the dynamic ground effect test effort. The test approach and data analysis methods were similar to those used on previous ground effect flight-test programs. The one significant difference was the differential global positioning system (DGPS) that provided highly accurate spatial position information as the F-16XL closed with the runway. NASA Dryden researcher Robert E. Curry analyzed the flight-test results and prepared the formal test report covering the dynamic ground effects research effort.[17]

Ground effect had originally been studied as a steady-state situation in which incremental changes to aerodynamic forces and moments on an aircraft due to its proximity to the ground were determined as a function of the aircraft's height above the ground. Conventional wind tunnels were used to predict steady-state ground effects, and results were successfully correlated with steady-state analytical methods. During a series of flight tests of low aspect ratio aircraft beginning in the late 1960s, distinct differences were observed between the data obtained from steady-state wind tunnel testing (holding height above the ground constant) and dynamic flight data (descending to the ground). This was verified through subsequent wind tunnel experiments in which the dynamic conditions of descending flight were simulated. Flight testing confirmed the distinction between steady-state and dynamic data and identified trends that depended on the aircraft's rate of descent close to the ground. Earlier test data either were limited to constant rates of descent (or sink rate) for a given run or the data were limited to a constant glide-path angle. During typical landing approaches, both the sink rate and the glide-path angle vary continuously during the portion of flight influenced by ground effect. Although flight testing can obtain data in more realistic dynamic scenarios, aircraft must be operated within a small range of vertical and horizontal velocities to ensure flight safety. As the aircraft approaches the ground, its flightpath flattens out as the rate of descent is reduced immediately prior to touchdown—a phenomenon referred to in aviation jargon as "flare." Many other parameters (angle of attack, dynamic pressure, control surface positions) also tend to vary during the final stages of a landing approach, complicating the determination of aerodynamic ground effects.[18]

Flight-Test Techniques

Twenty-four dynamic landing approaches into ground effect were accomplished on seven different research flights with F-16XL-1 at NASA Dryden. The flight-test technique that was used was for the pilot to lower the landing gear and begin the landing approach descent at a predetermined glide slope and angle of attack. After stabilizing on the final approach, the pilot held the power constant and made minimal control surface inputs. As the aircraft descended close to the runway and reacted to ground effect, the pilot held the throttle constant and maintained a constant angle of attack using sidestick inputs to the flight control system. The approach into ground effect maneuver was considered complete when the aircraft touched down or the pilot adjusted the throttle. This maneuver was termed a "constant alpha approach." The use of a constant throttle setting and nearly constant angle of attack eliminated the source of many potential errors and greatly simplified subsequent data analysis.

During the ground effect evaluation, constant alpha approach maneuvers at a range of glide-slope angles were flown. The pilot used the instrument landing system (ILS) glide-slope indicator as an aid in setting up the initial condition. The flightpath angle for a typical constant AoA landing approach was nearly constant during the descent down to a height of about one wingspan above the ground. Then the flightpath began to round out naturally as the F-16XL responded to the increase in lift as it entered the ground effect region near the runway. On some occasions during these constant alpha maneuvers, the aircraft automatically flared to level flight before touching down. Of course, the flightpath angles that could be practically used during the ground effect evaluation were limited by aircraft/landing gear structural and tire restrictions on allowable vertical and horizontal touchdown speeds. Flightpath angles to the horizontal that were observed during the ground effect flight-test evaluation ranged from -1 to -3 degrees at altitudes above ground effect height (generally one wingspan). However, this flightpath envelope decreased to a range between 0 and -1.9 degrees by a height above the ground of one-half of the aircraft wingspan.

During a more typical F-16XL landing, unlike the controlled test maneuvers used during the ground effect evaluation, the flightpath angle tended to vary continuously during final approach. However, the range of flightpath angles that were encountered during typical landings was still within the envelope of the landing approach maneuvers used in the ground effect study. The initial angle of attack for all F-16XL landing approaches ranged from 11 to 13 degrees.

F-16XL-1 is seen during landing rollout with its drag chute deployed and the speed brakes on either side of the engine nozzle in the open position. (NASA)

Results and Discussion

The F-16XL was used to determine force and moment coefficient changes due to ground effects. Incremental changes in lift coefficient, normalized to the out-of-ground effect (OGE) lift coefficient, were compared for a variety of aircraft configurations with different wing aspect ratios. All aircraft configurations indicated the same general trend: dynamic ground effect lift data was less affected by the influence of the ground than had been indicated from steady-state wind tunnel–derived test data. In the case of the F-16XL, the normalized lift coefficient increased by over 20 percent at an aircraft height of 0.3 wingspans from the ground. This distance represented a height of about 11 feet above the ground, or just as the aircraft neared touchdown with its landing gear extended. The normalized drag coefficient increment as the aircraft approached ground level was also positive but was comparatively much smaller. Both flight test and wind tunnel data consistently indicated a moderate nose-down pitching moment increment when in the influence of ground effect. Wind tunnel data for the variation in lift increment in ground effect was evaluated with the dynamic ground effect data obtained from actual flight testing.

Flight-test results, obtained under dynamic conditions, showed significantly lower changes in the lift coefficient in ground effect than had been indicated from wind tunnel data obtained under steady-state conditions. This fundamental difference between wind tunnel and dynamic test results was consistent with the data obtained from other aircraft configurations for which steady-state and dynamic lift data were available. Both the steady-state and the dynamic

F-16XL ground effect data followed similar trends to those observed in ground effect with other aircraft, both in wind tunnel and actual flight testing. For comparative purposes, the incremental change in lift coefficient in ground effect normalized to the lift coefficient out-of-ground effect for the F-16XL was compared with various other aircraft configurations. These other aircraft included delta wings with differing leading-edge sweep angles, the F-104 with its low aspect ratio straight wing, the F-15 with a conventional horizontal tail, and the X-29 with its forward-swept wing and canard configuration. The F-16XL flight-test effort enabled NASA to develop a more accurate engineering model of dynamic ground effect. This dynamic ground effect model was validated with highly precise data obtained during the F-16XL flight-test effort and dynamic wind tunnel testing.

Sonic Boom Probing Experiment

NASA required sonic boom propagation data to validate and refine computer prediction software codes. These sonic boom propagation prediction codes would be used by the Sonic Boom Integrated Technology Development Team within the NASA High-Speed Research program to assess the environmental impact of High-Speed Civil Transport designs. The Lockheed SR-71 was selected as the sonic boom–generating aircraft for the test because of its large size and supersonic endurance. It was flown at speeds from Mach 1.25 to Mach 1.6 at altitudes of 31,000 and 48,000 feet in steady, level flight. These Mach numbers were far slower than the proposed cruise speed of the HSCT (Mach 2.4), but they were selected to ensure that an existing NASA fighter-type aircraft could be used for the sonic boom probing experiment. A probing aircraft that could match the speed of the SR-71 was important. Small differences in closure speed maximized the amount of data that could be collected during each probing pass and increased the resolution of the shock waves. Also, an increased number of probing passes were possible when the probing aircraft was able to maneuver in close proximity to the SR-71. The F-16XL was selected for the probing experiment since it had good supersonic performance and endurance. Equipped with special pressure instrumentation in and behind its flight-test nose boom to collect sonic boom pressure signatures, the F-16XL was used as the near-field sonic boom probing aircraft because of its ability to fly in formation with the SR-71 up to speeds of about Mach 1.5. In addition, the F-16XL had greater supersonic endurance than the majority of supersonic fighter-type aircraft available at NASA Dryden. However, the SR-71 had much greater supersonic endurance than the F-16XL, and aerial refueling was routinely used to maximize data collection on each flight.

F-16XL-1 was used for sonic boom probing tests with the NASA SR-71. The F-16XL's speed brakes are extended in this photo taken at subsonic speed; however, the F-16XL had a difficult time maintaining formation with the SR-71 above Mach 1.5. (NASA)

F-16XL Sonic Boom Overpressure Instrumentation

The overpressures produced by the shock waves from the SR-71 were measured using four independent systems in the F-16XL. The first system measured the pressure differences between two flush pressure ports located ±37.5 degrees from the top of the noseboom. The second system used flush ports offset ±90 degrees. The transducers that measured the overpressure differentials between the pressure ports sampled at a rate of 200 samples per second. These transducers were accurate to within ±1 psi. The third system used an absolute digital pressure transducer to record the indicated static pressure close to the nose boom. The fourth and last system measured indicated total pressure using a transducer that was plumbed into the aircraft total pressure line close to the nose boom.

There was some concern that the orientation of the flush ports with the incident shock wave from the SR-71 would affect the overpressure readings. Probing data taken from below the SR-71 showed that the ±37.5-degree ports gave the same overpressure readings as the ±90-degree ports when the F-16XL aircraft was steady in pitch and yaw. The two sets of ports also gave the same overpressures when probing data were gathered to the side of the SR-71 aircraft. Thus, for steady level flight, the orientation of the ports to the incident shock wave had no effect on the overpressure data. However, pressure port readings were affected by changes in both pitch and yaw angle. To determine these effects, angular sweeps in pitch and yaw were conducted while the F-16XL was flying at high supersonic speeds but was not actively involved in probing the SR-71 shock waves. The ±90-degree ports showed pressure variations with changes in aircraft pitch attitude. Since slight pitch changes occurred when the F-16XL was conducting probing maneuvers below the SR-71, the resultant overpressure data from the ±90-degree ports were slightly affected. The data from the pressure ports at the ±37.5-degree locations were steady during pitch changes but were affected by yaw changes. Because yaw generally remained steady while probing below the SR-71, the pressure ports located at the ±37.5-degree locations on the noseboom were determined to provide more valid overpressure data than did those located at the ±90-degree locations.

Another test to determine the accuracy of the overpressure instrumentation installed in the F-16XL was conducted using sonic booms generated by a NASA Dryden McDonnell-Douglas F/A-18 aircraft. During this test, the F-16XL was stationary on the ground with its overpressure instrumentation system operational. Several portable automatic triggering system (PATS) sonic boom recorders were placed with their pressure sensors at the same height and a few feet to the side of the F-16XL's noseboom. The F/A-18 was flown at a speed of Mach 1.20 at an altitude of 30,000 feet over the F-16XL aircraft and the PATS recorders, both of which measured the differential pressures produced by the sonic boom. The data measured by the differential pressure transducers on the stationary F-16XL compared favorably to the overpressures measured by the adjacent ground-based PATS units.

An extensively instrumented Lockheed YO-3A aircraft (69-18010, itself a remarkable research aircraft, originally the last of 10 special quiet observation aircraft produced for service during the Vietnam War) was also used to measure SR-71 sonic boom signatures. Virtually silent in flight, it flew at relatively low altitudes that ranged from 21,000 to 38,000 feet below the SR-71 flight altitude. The YO-3 recorded data from 17 SR-71 passes. Sonic boom signatures at ground level as well as atmospheric data were recorded for each test mission. Results showed that shock wave patterns varied with SR-71 gross weight, Mach number, and cruise altitude. For example, noncoalesced shock wave signatures were measured by the YO-3A while flying at a distance that was 21,000 feet below the SR-71's acoustic test cruise altitude of 31,000 feet. At the time, the SR-71 was at a low gross weight and was cruising at Mach 1.25.[19]

Computer predictions had shown that some planned SR-71 flight conditions could result in severely distorted sonic boom signatures reaching ground sensors due to possible turbulence in the atmosphere nearest the ground. Because this turbulent atmospheric layer could extend several thousand feet above ground level, researchers decided to use an airborne platform to record the sonic booms above this layer to provide undistorted signature data. The YO-3A aircraft was flown along the predetermined SR-71 flight track at a

A NASA Lockheed YO-3A was used to measure the sonic boom signatures emanating from a Lockheed SR-71 flying at supersonic speed at much higher altitudes. (NASA)

cruise altitude of 10,000 feet. It maintained an indicated airspeed of about 65 knots while it recorded sonic boom signatures above the turbulent atmospheric layer. During data-collection flights, the YO-3A stayed at a distance that was up range from the array of sonic boom recorders on the ground to avoid producing any interference with their data. Sonic boom signatures were recorded by the YO-3A as the SR-71 passed overhead. The F-16XL aircraft could not probe at this relatively low altitude at supersonic speeds because of aircraft and airspace limitations.[20]

F-16XL Probing Maneuvers

Probing maneuvers began with the F-16XL behind the SR-71's tail shock wave. The F-16XL then moved forward through the SR-71 shock wave pattern ending ahead of the bow shock wave. Then, the F-16XL aircraft slowed down and repeated the probe moving from the bow shock wave backward past the tail shock. Because the shock waves sweep behind the SR-71, longitudinal separation existed between the tail of the SR-71 aircraft and the nose of the F-16XL aircraft. During probing maneuvers, the F-16XL attempted to maintain level flight with no lateral offset from the SR-71. While some probing maneuvers were quite level with very little lateral offset, most had some variability in altitude and lateral offset. The F-16XL pilot had several indications of crossing the shock wave pattern when he probed within a distance of about 1,000 feet from the supersonic SR-71. These indications included the pilot feeling the pressure changes within the cockpit, his being slightly jostled by the shock waves, and his being able to hear the roar of the SR-71's engines when positioned aft of the tail shock. When probing maneuvers were conducted at vertical separations that were greater than about 1,000 feet, the pilot was unaware when he had penetrated the shock wave pattern. Pressure and temperature data from both the SR-71 and F-16XL were recorded on the aircraft and transmitted to the control room in real time. Pressure data collected from the F-16XL was displayed in real time in the control room. The ground controller advised the F-16XL pilot when he was ahead of or behind the SR-71 shock wave system to enhance his sonic boom data-collection opportunities.

Probing Maneuver Test Summary

Three NASA aircraft were used during the SR-71 Sonic Boom Experiment. The SR-71 was the primary sonic boom generator; the F-16XL was the supersonic probing aircraft; and the YO-3A was the far-field, slow-speed microphone platform. Test aircraft were equipped with instrumentation systems that included specialized pressure sensors on the F-16XL and differential carrier phase Global Positioning System (GPS) on the SR-71 and F-16XL. Prior to the start of the flight-test effort, the accuracy of these instruments was validated during ground and airborne calibration tests. During the sonic boom evaluation, the SR-71 was flown at three flight conditions to assess the effects of Mach number and altitude on boom propagation. Gross weight of the SR-71 during the supersonic test runs ranged from 73,000 to 118,000 pounds. The SR-71 generated sonic booms over the speed range from Mach 1.25 to Mach 1.6 at constant altitudes of 31,000 to 48,000 feet. The F-16XL probed the sonic boom signatures at nearly the same speed as the SR-71 while the YO-3A operated at much lower altitudes and was overflown by the SR-71.

The F-16XL measured the SR-71's near-field shock wave pattern from distances that varied from very close proximity to the aircraft to more than 8,000 feet below. The YO-3A collected sonic boom signatures from distances ranging from 21,000 to 38,000 feet below the SR-71. The F-16XL gathered sonic boom data during 105 probing maneuvers on seven flights; the SR-71 made 17 passes over the YO-3A's acoustic sensors. In addition, an array of several types of ground-based sonic boom recorders were used to complete the sonic boom propagation dataset with a total of 172 signatures recorded. Atmospheric data were gathered for flight data analysis and for use with sonic boom propagation prediction codes. The results from the SR-71 sonic boom probing tests were analyzed and published by NASA Dryden researchers Edward A. Haering, Jr., L.J. Ehernberger, and Stephen A. Whitmore. The detailed acoustic overpressure data obtained from the F-16XL, YO-3A, and ground-based sensors were used by researchers at NASA Langley to validate sonic boom propagation prediction computer software codes.[21]

F-16XL Flutter Excitation System Test

The F-16XL was also used to evaluate an airframe excitation system for use in subsonic, transonic, and supersonic aircraft flutter testing. The excitation system had been conceived and patented by former NASA Langley employee Wilmer Reed, who had retired in the early 1980s after a 34-year career with NASA. During his long career, Reed had gained international recognition for innovative research and his patented ideas relating to aircraft flutter and aero-elasticity.[22] The airframe-mounted structural excitation system developed by Reed consisted of a wingtip-mounted vane with a rotating slotted cylinder at the trailing edge. As the cylinder rotated during flight, the flow was alternately deflected upward and downward through the slot, resulting in a periodic lift force at twice the cylinder's rotational frequency. Primary objectives of the excitation research effort with the F-16XL were to determine the system's ability to generate adequate force levels necessary to excite the aircraft's structure and to evaluate the frequency range over which the system could excite aircraft structural modes. Excitation parameters such as sweep duration, sweep type, and energy levels were assessed, and results from the flutter exciter vane were compared with results from atmospheric turbulence excitation alone at the same flight conditions. The comparison indicated that the vane with a rotating slotted cylinder provided data of higher quality with less variation than results obtained from atmospheric turbulence. The flight-test evaluation of the flutter excitation system used F-16XL-2 as the test bed. Detailed test results were reported on by NASA Dryden research engineer Lura Vernon.[23]

Background: Structural Excitation Systems

NASA Dryden had extensive experience and a long history of in-flight flutter testing using a variety of structural excitation systems. Natural atmospheric turbulence had often been used as the structural excitation mechanism during flutter testing. However, natural atmospheric turbulence is difficult to find and usually does not excite all aircraft structural vibration modes. Pilot-induced control surface pulses were frequently used in conjunction with atmospheric turbulence to excite the aircraft structure. However, these pilot-initiated control surface impulses typically did not excite structural vibration modes above a frequency of about 5 Hz. Other means of structural excitation included sinusoidal control surface excitation, rotary inertia exciters, pyrotechnic thrusters (known in the flight-test community as "bonkers"), and oscillating aerodynamic vanes. Each of these had been used previously and successfully in flutter test projects. However, each of these techniques, briefly discussed in the following paragraphs, had disadvantages that prevented them from being used consistently for aircraft flutter testing.[24]

Rotary Inertial Exciter

A rotary inertia exciter consists of a rotating unbalanced weight attached to a shaft. As the unbalanced weight rotates, a sinusoidal varying force is applied to the surface to which it is attached.[25] The excitation force produced is proportional to the rotational acceleration. At high rotational frequencies, the excitation force levels are high; however, at lower rotational frequencies, the force levels produced are low and may be insufficient to excite the aircraft structure. Adding mass to the exciter increases the amount of excitation force that is produced. Unfortunately, that could also affect the flutter characteristics of the aircraft.

Pyrotechnic Thrusters ("Bonkers")

Pyrotechnic bonkers are small, single-shot solid propellant rockets with very rapid burn times. Attached to various locations on the airframe, they provide a short-duration impulse to the aircraft structure, exciting a number of aircraft structural modes. They have maximum thrust levels that range from 400 to 4,000 pounds. Disadvantages include low reliability under vibration and at the extreme cold conditions encountered in high-altitude flight testing, as well as difficulties in synchronizing ignition. The number of possible impulses per flight-test mission is also limited.[26]

Sinusoidal Control Surface Excitation

In sinusoidal control surface excitation, the aircraft control surfaces are preprogrammed through the flight control system to oscillate through a predetermined frequency range. The effective excitation frequency range was limited by the frequency response capability of the control surface actuator. This method also required modifications to the aircraft control system software, a process that was costly and time consuming.

Externally Mounted Aerodynamic Vanes

Earlier flutter research determined that externally mounted oscillating aerodynamic vanes were effective in producing vibrational forces on the aircraft structure. These devices were designed to oscillate either symmetrically or asymmetrically at the desired excitation frequencies. However, they were clumsy, produced large loads on the exciter system, and required relatively large amounts of external power. Typically, aircraft systems were used as power sources, and installation was costly and time-consuming.[27]

The DEI Flutter Exciter System

Disadvantages of earlier flutter excitation methods led to the need to develop a more effective structural excitation system for use in flight test programs. A structural excitation system that adequately excites all modes of interest was required to verify the absence of flutter within the aircraft flight envelope. With NASA Langley encouragement and support, Dynamic Engineering, Inc., (DEI) of Hampton, VA, designed, developed, and tested a relatively low-cost flutter excitation system that was capable of generating the required in-flight forces on aircraft structures. The DEI flutter exciter system was tested on the two-seat F-16XL aircraft at NASA Dryden to determine its effectiveness as a structural excitation system. The DEI exciter concept incorporated a wingtip-mounted vane with a rotating slotted cylinder attached behind the trailing edge. This system was designed to be a lightweight, self-contained structural excitation device that could be rapidly installed on a variety of aircraft with minimal interface with normal aircraft systems.

Test Objectives

The F-16XL flutter exciter flight-test effort was designed to determine the ability of the vane exciter system to develop the force levels necessary to excite the aircraft structure. The frequency range over which various aircraft structural vibration modes were excited would be measured. Various parameters such as exciter sweep duration, sweep type, and energy levels were also to be determined. The exciter vane was installed on F-16XL-2's left wingtip, and the aircraft was instrumented with nine accelerometers to collect structural vibration data. The accelerometers were located on the wingtips, in the aileron actuator housing, in the fuselage, and on the vertical tail. Since a conventional flutter clearance had been conducted during the development of the basic aircraft, the NASA flutter test effort was initially focused on evaluating the vane exciter system.[28]

DEI Flutter Exciter System Description

The DEI flutter excitation system consisted of three main components. These were a cockpit control panel, an electronics box, and the fixed-vane exciter that was designed for installation on the exterior of the airframe. Installation of the system on the F-16XL required mounting the control box in the cockpit, mounting the electronics box in the instrumentation bay, and routing the necessary electrical wiring through the F-16XL's leading-edge flap to the fixed-vane exciter at the wingtip. A cockpit control panel located in the aft cockpit controlled the excitation system. Eighty work hours were required to install the flutter exciter system on the F-16XL's left wingtip.[29]

Operating Modes

The exciter system incorporated several operating modes. These were constant frequency, linear or logarithmic sine sweeps, sweep frequency range and duration, a quick-stop feature for free-decay response measurements, and high- or low-force amplitude options. The exciter system was capable of excitation at frequencies up to 50 Hz with the force level measured by a bending-moment strain gauge that was mounted near the root of the exciter vane. The fixed-vane exciter consisted of a diamond-shaped symmetric airfoil section and a rotating slotted cylinder at the trailing edge. The vane was attached to the wingtip of the F-16XL using an adapter plate that was specially designed to slide into the wingtip-mounted AIM-9 missile launcher. The vane had a span of 1.0 foot, an area of 0.85 square feet, and it weighed 10 pounds. A ground vibration test showed that the weight of the vane did not change the vibration characteristics of the F-16XL wing structure.

Exciter Operation

During flutter testing, the two slots in the cylinder attached to the exciter vane generated periodic forces that excited the aircraft structure. As the cylinder rotated during flight, the flow was alternately deflected upward and downward through the slots, resulting in a periodic lift force at twice the cylinder's rotational frequency. The cylinder was rotated through 180 degrees for each full sinusoidal forcing period. The amplitude of the excitation force depended upon the dynamic pressure and the amount that the slot was open. The amount that the slot was open was controlled by the direction of rotation of the slotted cylinder. Reversing the rotational direction of the cylinder drive motor caused half of the spanwise slot opening to be blocked by an inner cylinder in the in-board slot. Closing the in-board slot attenuated the excitation force by half in flight. The lift force produced by the vane rotating cylinder concept was analogous to that of an oscillating vane. The rotating cylinder's main advantage was that it required a small amount of power to overcome the aerodynamic and frictional forces opposing its rotation. A low-wattage electric servomotor requiring only 28 volts ran the exciter system. It operated from the normal aircraft power supply. The design condition for the exciter vane was Mach 1.2 at 10,000 feet (a dynamic pressure of 1,467 pounds per square foot) at an angle of attack of 4 degrees. The vane stalled at an angle of attack of about 12 degrees.

Exciter Test Procedures

The flutter excitation system was tested in subsonic, transonic, and supersonic flight conditions. Exciter force sweeps covered the primary structural vibration modes of interest on the F-16XL. Data on structural excitation via random atmospheric turbulence were also acquired at each test point to compare with the forced excitation data. Linear sweeps were used to assess the effects of exciter vane test duration on structural excitation characteristics. Logarithmic sweeps were compared with linear exciter force sweeps of the same duration. Structural response data were acquired for frequencies corresponding to the

F-16XL's symmetric and antisymmetric wing bending modes. The accelerometer response data and strain-gauge load data were telemetered to a ground station for real-time data collection and monitoring to observe structural response levels. Data were sampled at a rate of 200 samples per second.[30]

Exciter Sweep Compared With Random Atmospheric Turbulence Excitation
At each stabilized test point, 60 seconds of aircraft random response data generated by natural atmospheric turbulence excitation was collected before the exciter sweep response data were collected. Frequency and damping estimates were obtained at each flight condition for each type of excitation. A comparison was made of the left wing's response to excitation caused by random atmospheric turbulence and forced excitation produced from the exciter vane. At Mach 0.9 at 30,000 feet, the pilot reported encountering light to moderate atmospheric turbulence. From atmospheric turbulence excitation, only the 8-Hz mode was well excited. Natural atmospheric turbulence did not excite any of the structural modes above 14 Hz. In comparison, all expected structural modes were excited by the exciter vane. Excitation provided by the exciter vane was superior to natural atmospheric turbulence for use in flutter test programs.

The most critical flutter frequencies for this F-16XL configuration were predicted to be in the range of 20 to 30 Hz. It was important that these modes were excited to ensure detection of any impending aeroelastic instabilities. The exciter vane provided excitation at these frequencies while atmospheric turbulence did not. For every flight condition, the forced excitation data yielded higher structural damping values than those obtained from atmospheric turbulence data. Structural damping estimates for the forced excitation data were often as much as twice the value of the data for the atmospheric turbulence. This is attributed to the fact that the amplitudes for the vibration modes that were excited by atmospheric turbulence had a very low signal-to-noise ratio. The modes were not well excited and were contaminated by noise; therefore, the damping levels were difficult to calculate accurately.

Static Forces
The exciter vane was mounted at a 0-degree angle with respect to the launcher rail. No attempt was made to determine a mounting angle that would minimize static loads at planned flight conditions. The static loads generated at different Mach numbers were measured. At Mach 0.8, when the aircraft was at an angle of attack of 6.5 degrees, the vane generated 160 pounds of upward force. The magnitude of the static loads on the wing decreased until the aircraft reached Mach 1.7. At that speed and with an aircraft angle of attack of 2 degrees, 30 pounds of downward force was measured.

Dynamic Forces

The dynamic forces generated by the exciter vane at each Mach number were given in pounds, peak to peak, and were all for the high-force setting (cylinder slot 75 percent open). Overall, the average dynamic force increased with increasing Mach number, which was expected because dynamic pressure was also increasing. The dynamic forces ranged from about 50 pounds at Mach 0.8 to almost 90 pounds at Mach 1.7 (all at a 30,000-foot altitude). These loads were less than expected. For the design condition of Mach 1.2 at 10,000 feet (equivalent to a dynamic pressure of 1,467 pounds per square foot), wind tunnel and flight-test data had estimated a pound peak-to-peak force range produced by the exciter of 409 pounds. The force level produced by the exciter at a flight condition of Mach 1.7 at an altitude of 30,000 feet (where the dynamic pressure was 1,271 pounds per square foot) was expected to be close to the this wind tunnel prediction. However, the exciter used on the F-16XL-1 had been modified by the addition of an internal plug that reduced the exciter slot opening by 25 percent. This, as well as the local airflow conditions over the F-16XL launcher rail, affected the excitation forces that were produced. While lower force levels had been predicted, these dynamic force levels were more than sufficient to excite F-16XL structural modes of interest.

Force Roll-Off

The exciter vane generated adequate force across the entire flutter frequency range of interest (5 to 35 Hz). The dynamic force peaked at two frequencies that corresponded to antisymmetric structural modes. The increase in force at these frequencies was most likely caused by an inertial reaction of the exciter as these structural modes are excited. An increase in amplitude was also seen at the sweep cutoff frequency at 35 Hz. This was a result of the excitation frequency approaching the exciter vanes first bending mode, which is at 43 Hz.

Logarithmic and Linear Sweeps Compared At Mach 0.9, the effects of logarithmic and linear force exciter sweeps were nearly identical. As Mach number increased, the logarithmic sweep did not excite the control surface modes in the important frequency range from 20 to 30 Hz as well as the linear sweep did. This trend was even more pronounced for longer sweep durations. Overall, the linear sweep was more consistent in exciting aircraft structural modes over the range of Mach numbers tested with F-16XL-2. To determine the effect of different sweep durations on structural airframe response, linear sweeps from 5 to 35 Hz were performed for time periods of 60, 30, 15, and 7 seconds. Overall, the 30- and 60-second sweeps produced about the same level of structural response, regardless of Mach number, and these levels were considered adequate for aircraft flutter testing.

Excitation Energy Distribution

During the evaluation flights, the vane assembly was mounted on the left wingtip of the aircraft. Accelerometers were mounted both on the left and right wingtips. The response from the accelerometer was used to measure the energy transferred from the left wing to the right wing during exciter operation. Symmetrical and antisymmetric wing bending modes were excited well on both wingtips; however, one of the launcher pitch modes was not excited on the right wing. The exciter, as well as the aft accelerometer, was placed near the node line for this mode. There was sufficient energy to excite this mode on the left side of the aircraft. However, there was insufficient energy to excite this mode on the right side. In addition, the higher frequency control surface modes were not excited as well on the right wing when compared to the left wing. Overall, vibration modes above 20 Hz were not excited well on the side of the aircraft opposite where the exciter was installed. This flight-test deficiency was overcome by adding a vane exciter to the right wingtip missile launcher. Vane exciters were mounted on both wingtip missile launchers during the subsequent flutter clearance effort with F-16XL-2 after it had been modified for a later phase of the supersonic laminar flow control effort resulting in an asymmetric wing configuration.

F-16XL-2 was fitted with wingtip-mounted DEI excitation vanes for flutter testing with the asymmetrical wing configuration that was used for NASA supersonic laminar flow research. (NASA)

Flutter Excitation System Results

The objectives for the flight-test effort were to determine the capability of the DEI vane excitation system, to develop adequate force levels needed to excite the aircraft structure, and to determine the frequency range over which the system could excite aircraft structural modes. The system was found to adequately excite most F-16XL structural modes during flight tests in the subsonic and transonic flight regimes. The structural response data quality obtained with the exciter was superior to that obtained with random atmospheric turbulence. Responses from the forward and aft accelerometers on the left wing indicated that all modes that had been previously identified during ground vibration tests were excited, with the exception of a vertical fin mode and a symmetric wingtip missile launcher pitch vibration mode. All expected structural vibration modes in a frequency bandwidth of 5 to 35 Hz were excited, while atmospheric turbulence alone only excited the wing's first bending mode. The vertical fin mode was not excited because the excitation energy was not transmitted to the vertical fin from the wingtip exciter vane. Since the exciter vane was mounted on the vibrational node line for the symmetric launcher pitch mode, this mode was not expected to be excited.[31]

Best results were obtained with 30- and 60-second linear frequency sweeps. Shorter-duration sweeps and logarithmic sweeps did not always sufficiently excite aircraft structural modes above 20 Hz. Because the exciter system was mounted on the left wingtip of the aircraft, energy distribution to the right side of the aircraft was of concern. The symmetric and antisymmetric wing bending modes were excited well on both wingtips; however the missile launcher pitch mode on the right-wing launcher pitch mode was not excited. In addition, vibration modes above 20 Hz were not excited well on the side opposite the single flutter exciter. This deficiency was overcome by adding a second exciter vane to F-16XL-2's right wingtip for use in subsequent flutter testing after the aircraft was modified with an asymmetric wing glove configuration. The relatively simple installation, precise excitation control, low-power requirements, and effectiveness over a large frequency range showed the vane exciter system to be a viable solution for aircraft flutter testing. Today, the vane-type flutter excitation system is now nearly universally used in flutter testing of new or modified aircraft designs around the world.

F-16XL Digital Flight Control System Upgrade

F-16XL-1 was modified with a digital FBW flight control system that replaced the original analog FBW flight control system in 1997. Gerald D. "Gerry" Budd was the NASA Dryden manager for the F-16XL Digital Flight Control System Upgrade Envelope Expansion Flight Test Project, during which 10 flights were flown over a 12-week period. Designed by the Lockheed Martin Tactical Systems Division in Fort Worth, TX, the new digital flight control system used revised software and new hardware that had been developed for the Air Force F-16C/D digital upgrade program (integrated into Block 40 production aircraft). The new software was specifically tailored to the F-16XL's aerodynamics, flight control system characteristics, and operational flight envelope. The original F-16XL flight control laws were rewritten in digital format using a flight parameter sampling time of 64 cycles per second. Other changes to the digital flight control system included both new and modified gains and filters. Existing electronic and flight control system hardware components were retained, but control over leading-edge-flap scheduling, air data management, and AoA-related functions was moved to the digital flight control computer.

The rationale for upgrading the F-16XL to a digital flight control system had been to support a possible joint Air Force–NASA flight research effort intended to investigate the use of Pneumatic Vortex Control across the full aircraft flight envelope. Under this approach, F-16XL-1 would have been specially modified as a flying test bed for PVC research with appropriate provisions made to its entire flight control system. Jay M. Brandon was the lead NASA Langley researcher for the effort doing all the simulations of the upgraded aircraft. Patrick C. Stoliker was the primary research contact at NASA Dryden with Ken A. Norlin of Dryden's Simulation Laboratory providing simulation support and expertise. Dr. Lawrence A. Walchli in the Advanced Development Branch at the Air Force Research Laboratory at Wright-Patterson AFB, OH, was responsible for managing the proposed PVC program; however, available funding ran out and the effort was cancelled before the aircraft was ever modified.[32]

Restricted Flight Envelope

The F-16XL was originally designed to operate out to Mach 2.0, up to an altitude as high as 60,000 feet, with a maneuvering load capability as high as 9.0 g's. However, restrictions were placed on F-16XL-1's allowable flight envelope with the DFCS as a result of issues identified during pilot-in-the-loop simulator testing. The piloted simulator had predicted that the aircraft with the digital flight control system would experience an increase in roll rate of about 25 percent over that available with the original analog system. The aircraft instrumentation was not adequate to monitor the increased structural loads that could be encountered at such high roll rates. As a result, the aircraft was restricted to operations with the Cockpit Stores Configuration Switch in the CAT III mode only.[33] When the CAT III mode was engaged, the maximum possible commanded roll rate was automatically reduced by 75 degrees per second. The piloted simulation had also identified a deficiency in the digital flight control system that would have allowed the aircraft to exceed the 9.0-g limiter during aggressive maneuvering. This resulted in another restriction that required that

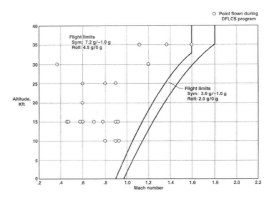

Flight envelope restrictions and maneuver limits were imposed on F-16XL-1 during the DFCS evaluation. (NASA)

the aircraft be operated with the g-limiter set no higher than 7.2 g's. This was intended to eliminate the potential to exceed the 9.0-g structural operating limit during flight testing with the DFCS. For the handling qualities evaluation, allowable test points were restricted to a flight envelope that was defined by a maximum Mach number of 1.6, a maximum angle of attack of 18 degrees, and a maximum flight altitude of 35,000 feet.

Flown by NASA research pilot Dana Purifoy, F-16XL-1 takes off on the initial flight in the Digital Flight Control System evaluation project on December 16, 1997. (NASA)

Handling Qualities Tasks

The DFCS flight-test evaluation began in December 1997 and ended in March 1998. The flight envelope clearance program consisted of 10 flights to collect maneuvering performance and handling qualities data. The first flight in the DFCS evaluation occurred on December 16, 1997. NASA research pilot Dana D. Purifoy performed systems functional checks and handling qualities maneuvers out to a speed of Mach 0.6 and 300 knots during the 1 hour 25 minute flight.[34] During DFCS evaluation flights, doublets were performed in all three axes. Other maneuvers included windup turns, −1.0 negative-g pushovers, steady heading sideslips, and 360-degree rolls at most flight conditions.[35] Flight data was analyzed using standard handling qualities analysis techniques, and where possible, results were compared with qualitative pilot handling qualities assessments. Pilot comments and Cooper-Harper ratings (CHR) were obtained for close trail formation flight and air-to-air tracking maneuvers and during powered landing approaches with the landing gear and flaps extended.[36] Additional maneuvers that were flown during the evaluation included 180-degree over-the-top rolls; pitch, roll, and normal acceleration captures; rolls with higher g loadings; and g-loaded roll reversals. Handling qualities evaluation tasks included normal acceleration captures, pitch attitude captures, bank angle captures, air-to-air tracking, and close trail formation flight. Detailed descriptions of the handling qualities tasks and criteria used to assess F-16XL performance during the DFCS evaluation are contained in Appendix I. The Cooper-Harper Rating Scale, used by the NASA research pilots to assess aircraft handling qualities, is also included in Appendix I.

Test Results

Pilot comments on aircraft performance in the lateral (roll) axis during handling qualities maneuvers flown with the DFCS were generally positive. F-16XL roll characteristics with the DFCS were considered to be "very similar to the analog aircraft."[37] Performance during lateral handling qualities tasks was rated as good. Performance during steady-state formation flying tasks was rated as adequate and given primarily level 2 CHRs (good, with negligible deficiencies). However, the NASA research pilots noted that adequate performance was not possible while executing rapid roll reversals during maneuvering flight tasks in routine or trail formation, and they typically gave level 3 CHRs (fair, with some mildly unpleasant tendencies) to these tasks. During air-to-air tracking tasks, the aircraft received CHR level 2 ratings for gross acquisition and level 2 to level 3 ratings for fine tracking. Pilots frequently reported encountering a "pitch bobble" while attempting to track targets. The pitch bobble had the greatest negative effect during fine tracking. Pitch bobble was the biggest reason for the "less than adequate" performance (level 3) pilot ratings given at some flight conditions.

During the evaluation of the digital flight control system, pitch and roll data were obtained at both subsonic and supersonic flight conditions. Conventional flight control analysis techniques were applied to the longitudinal (pitch axis) flight-test data. These pitch control analyses had predicted level 2 to level 3 CHR handling qualities, depending on flight conditions, with improvement in handling qualities predicted as aircraft speed increased. However, this trend was not seen in the actual pilot ratings and comments. Pilots rated the aircraft at near the CHR level 2 to level 3 handling qualities border regardless of flight conditions. This was largely attributed to the high estimated time delay inherent in the digital flight control system as it was implemented in F-16XL-1. Pilot comments on F-16XL-1 performance during the DFCS handling qualities task evaluation along with their Cooper-Harper ratings are contained in Appendix I.

DFCS Test Summary

During the F-16XL-1 DFCS Upgrade project, nine flights had been flown over a 12-week period. Pilot comments and Cooper-Harper ratings were obtained for air-to-air tracking and close trail formation flight tasks at a number of subsonic flight conditions. Pilot comments during lateral handling qualities tasks were generally favorable. However, the two NASA research pilots were critical of a pitch bobble that degraded performance during fine tracking tasks typical of air-to-air gunnery. This pitch bobble led to level 3 CHR ratings (fair with some mildly unpleasant deficiencies) at some flight conditions. Pilots also commented that adequate aircraft performance could not be obtained during roll reversals during close trail formation flight. This also resulted in CHR level 3 ratings (mildly unpleasant) for roll reversal tasks at some flight conditions. At the conclusion of the project, Gerry Budd, who served as the NASA Dryden project manager for the F-16XL digital flight control system evaluation, was quoted in a 1998 NASA Dryden news release as stating, "The aircraft and the new control system work very smoothly together and have proven to be a good combination."[38] However, the aircraft had some flight control limitations related to higher maneuverability tasks involving, for instance, high-g maneuvering and air-to-air tracking tasks. The NASA observations were consistent with earlier Air Force and GD findings that the F-16XL flight control system needed additional development effort. If the aircraft had been extensively modified for a PVC research effort, as originally envisioned, the flight control system would likely have been upgraded to address such concerns.

Endnotes

1. The discussion of the F-16XL-1's use at NASA LaRC is based on comments from Jay Brandon via Joe Chambers and technical details reported in: Jay M. Brandon, Louis J. Glaab, Phillip W. Brown, and Michael R. Phillips, "Ground-to-Flight Handling Qualities Comparisons for a High Performance Airplane," NASA TM 111925, presented at the Atmospheric Flight Mechanics Conference held in Baltimore, MD, August 7–9, 1995, published as AIAA Paper 95-3457 (August 1995).

2. Wetherall, "F-16XL First Flight 25th Anniversary Celebration."

3. Jon K. Holzman, Lannie D. Webb, and Frank W. Burcham, Jr., "Flight and Static Exhaust Flow Properties of an F110-GE-129 Engine in an F-16XL Airplane During Acoustic Tests," NASA TM 104326 (November 1996).

4. Jeffrey J. Kelly, Mark R. Wilson, John Rawls, Jr., Thomas D. Norum, and Robert A. Golub, "F-16XL and F-18 High Speed Acoustic Flight Test Data Base," NASA CD TM-100006 (1996).

5. J.E. Lamar and C.J. Obara, "Review of Cranked-Arrow Wing Aerodynamics Project: Its International Aeronautical Community Role," AIAA Paper 2007-0487 (January 2007).

6. Ibid.

7. A Preston tube consists of a circular Pitot tube placed directly on the surface of an object in a fluid flow. It is named for British engineer J.H. Preston, who showed in 1953 that the stagnation pressure measured from a Pitot tube located on a surface can be related to the surface shear stress (skin friction) by the Prandtl-Karman "law of the wall" for turbulent flow. The law states that fluid properties near the wall are related to the surface shear stress. J.H. Preston, "The Determination of Turbulent Skin Friction by Means of Pitot Tubes," *Journal of the Royal Aeronautical Society* 58, no. 109 (1954).

8. A laser was used as the illumination source because of the fineness of its beam and the monochromatic nature of laser light. These characteristics enabled more precise evaluation of the flow field around the model.

9. Technology Readiness Levels is a NASA-developed systematic metric/measurement system that supports assessments of the maturity of a particular technology. The first NASA TRL scale had seven levels; a revised scale with nine levels gained widespread acceptance and remains in use today. The TRL approach is incorporated in the NASA Management Instruction addressing integrated technology planning for all programs at NASA. It has been adopted by

the DoD, the European Space Agency, NATO, and many other organizations and agencies around the world. John C. Mankins, "Technology Readiness Levels: A White Paper," Office of Space Access and Technology, NASA Headquarters (April 6, 1995).

10. James M. Luckring, "An Overview of the RTO Symposium on Vortex Flow and High Angle of Attack Aerodynamics," in *Proceedings of the 2002 International Council of the Aeronautical Sciences (ICAS) Congress* (2002).

11. John E. Lamar and James M. Luckring, "The Cranked-Arrow Wing Aerodynamics Project and its Extension to the International Community as CAWAPI: Objectives and Overview," chapter 3 in *Summary Report of Task Group AVT-113*, RTO-TR-AVT-113 AC/323 (AVT-113) TP/246 (October 2009).

12. Ibid.

13. Ibid.

14. John E. Lamar, Catherine K. Cronin, and Laura E. Scott, "Virtual Laboratory Enabling Collaborative Research in Applied Vehicle Technologies," in *Proceedings of the NATO RTO AVT-113 Symposium on Flow Induced Unsteady Loads and the Impact on Military Application*, a conference held in Budapest, Hungary, April 25–29, 2005, NATO RTO-TR-AVT-113 (October 2009).

15. Lamar and Luckring, "The Cranked-Arrow Wing Aerodynamics Project." The participation of the Swedish defense research establishment in this NATO-sponsored project was one of the interesting aspects of the CAWAPI effort.

16. J.E. Lamar and K.S. Abdol-Hamid, "USM3D Unstructured Grid Solutions for CAWAPI at NASA LaRC," AIAA Paper 2007-0682 (2007); Kenneth Badcock, Oklo Boelens, Adam Jirasek, and Arthur Rizzi, "What Was Learned from Numerical Simulations of F-16XL (CAWAPI) at Flight Conditions," AIAA Paper 2007-0683 (2007).

17. Robert E. Curry, "Dynamic Ground Effect for a Cranked Arrow Wing Airplane," NASA TM 4799 (August 1997).

18. Ibid.

19. Edward A. Haering, Jr., L.J. Ehrenberger, and Stephen A. Whitmore, "Preliminary Airborne Measurements for the SR-71 Sonic Boom Propagation Experiment," presented at the 1995 High Speed Research Program Sonic Boom Workshop, NASA Langley Research Center, Hampton, VA, September 12–13, 1995, NASA TM-104307 (1995).

20. The YO-3A was based on a Schweizer sailplane design, and it was fitted with a highly modified engine and a special quiet propeller

design to minimize its acoustic signature. Dryden's had been based at the NASA Ames Research Center in Mountain View, CA, to measure the in-flight acoustic signatures of helicopters. Its quiet signature and excellent slow-speed flight characteristics made it an excellent airborne complement to the F-16XL for recording sonic boom signatures. Haering et al., "Preliminary Airborne Measurements for the SR-71 Sonic Boom Propagation Experiment," Ibid.; "Lockheed YO-3A Quiet Star," Western Museum of Flight, Torrence, CA, *http://www.wmof.com/yo-3a.htm*, accessed September 26, 2012.

21. Edward A. Haering, Jr., "SR-71 Experiment on Propagation of Sonic Booms," *NASA Tech Briefs* 20, no. 1 (January 1996): pp. 68–69.

22. Dynamic Engineering, Inc. (DEI), had been established in 1972 in Newport News, VA, near the NASA Langley Research Center. The company began by building wind tunnel models for Langley Research Center test programs. At DEI, Reed recognized the need to increase the safety and minimize the cost and hazards associated with aircraft flight flutter testing. He conceived and patented the DEI Flutter Exciter, now used worldwide in flight flutter testing of new or modified aircraft designs. NASA, "Aircraft Flutter Testing," *Spinoff*, NASA (1997), p. 62; Reed provided his reflections on his career in aeroelastic research and flutter testing at Langley in "Aeroelasticity Matters."

23. Lura Vernon, "In-Flight Investigation of a Rotating Cylinder-Based Structural Excitation System for Flutter Testing," NASA TM-4512 (January 1993). Vernon would later become NASA Dryden's chief technologist.

24. Ibid.

25. This technique was first used in Germany during in-flight flutter test efforts with larger multiengine aircraft in 1935. Michael W. Kehoe, "A Historic Overview of Flight Flutter Testing," NASA TM 4720 (October 1995); see also Ernst Heinrich Hirschel, Horst Prem, and Gero Madelung (eds.), *Aeronautical Research in Germany from Lilienthal until Today* (Berlin: Springer-Verlag, 2004).

26. The term "bonkers" is post-WWII British slang meaning crazy or mad. It is often associated with impressive fireworks displays on Guy Fawkes Day in England, which may account for the origin of the term in the context of pyrotechnic thrusters. Officially, the British referred to these structural excitation devices as lateral thrust units. Wingtip and vertical-fin-mounted bonkers were used in the 1960s during flutter testing of the delta-wing Fairey FD. 2 supersonic

research aircraft. The FD. 2 was extensively modified for the British SST program, becoming the BAC 221 when fitted with a highly swept ogee-shaped wing mounted on its extended fuselage (a modification very much in the fashion of the later F-16XL). This ogee wing planform was subsequently adopted for the Anglo-French Concorde SST design. Wingtip and fin-mounted bonkers were also used in the Concorde flutter test program. "BAC. 221: Slender-delta Research Aircraft," *Flight International* (July 23, 1964); Jon Lake, "Fairey Deltas: FD.1, FD.2, & BAC 221," *Wings of Fame*, vol. 11 (London: Aerospace Publishing Company, 1998); Robert Rosenbaum, "Survey of Aircraft Subcritical Flight Flutter Testing Methods," NASA CR-132479 (August 1974).

27. This flutter technique was pioneered at the German Aviation Research Institute (*Deutsche Versuchsanstalt für Luftfahrt* [DVL]) during the 1930s; Hirschel et al., *Aeronautical Research in Germany*.

28. Vernon; Ibid. Later, after F-16XL-2 was modified with the active-suction wing glove and the extended left wing leading edge, DEI flutter excitation vanes were installed on both wingtips. The two-vane flutter exciter configuration was used during flutter investigation of F-16XL-2 in the asymmetric configuration. These flutter tests were conducted in conjunction with the NASA SLFC research effort.

29. Vernon, "In-Flight Investigation."

30. Ibid.

31. Ibid.

32. Information on planned use of F-16XL-1 for PVC research came from Jay Brandon and is contained in correspondence between the author and Joseph Chambers, November 27, 2012. The feasibility of F-16XL as a full-scale flying test bed with PVC as the primary control effector across the full aircraft flight envelope was the subject of a joint NASA–Air Force Research Laboratory investigation. Under this effort, a highly detailed F-16XL simulation provided by NASA DFRC was installed at Wright Laboratory. The F-16XL simulation was modified to assess multiaxis (wing, forebody, and vertical tail–mounted) PVC devices and determine required lateral/directional closed-loop performance and PVC mass flow levels for a potential follow-on full-scale flight-research program. See: John Valasek and Lawrence A. Walchli, "High Speed, Low Angle-of-Attack Pneumatic Vortex Control," AIAA Papers 98-4449 and A98-37266 (1998); Ken A. Norlin, "Flight Simulation Software at NASA Dryden Flight Research Center," NASA TM-104315 (October 1995).

33. The CAT III position on the F-16 Cockpit Stores Configuration Switch limits the attainable roll rate by approximately 40 percent to provide departure resistance. The CAT III position is normally used when the F-16 is carrying heavy air-to-ground weapons payloads. USAF, F-16C/D Blocks 25, 30, and 32 Flight Manual, USAF T.O. 1F-16C-1 (May 14, 1990).

34. Marty Curry, "NASA F-16XL Makes First Flight with Digital Flight Control System," NASA Dryden Research Center News Release 97-50 (December 17, 1997).

35. A doublet is a standard flight-test maneuver in which the pilot applies full control surface defection in one direction. As aircraft motion reaches its maximum point, the controls are then deflected fully in the opposite direction.

36. NASA Ames research pilot George Cooper developed a handling qualities rating system based on the need to quantify pilot judgment. Cooper's approach established specific definitions of pilot tasks and related performance standards. It accounted for demands placed on the pilot by the aircraft in accomplishing a given control task to some level of precision. The Cooper Pilot Opinion Rating Scale was initially published in 1957. The rating system was modified in collaboration with Robert "Bob" Harper of the Cornell Aeronautical Laboratory in 1969. As the Cooper-Harper Handling Qualities Rating Scale, it remains the standard for measuring flying qualities. Paul F. Borchers, James A. Franklin, and Jay W. Fletcher, *Flight Research at Ames: Fifty-Seven Years of Development and Validation of Aeronautical Technology* (Washington, DC: NASA, 1998).

37. Susan J. Stachowiak and John T. Bosworth, "Flight Test Results for the F-16XL with a Digital Flight Control System," NASA TP-2004-212046 (March 2004).

38. NASA, "NASA F-16XL Completes Digital Flight Control System Verification," NASA DFRC News Release 98-21 (April 14, 1998).

The F-16XL-1 is seen during ground taxi tests at the Dryden Flight Research Center on June 28, 2007. Neither of the two F-16XLs moved under its own power after this date. (NASA)

CHAPTER 11

Final Research Options and Retirement

In 2005, Boeing had identified potential low–sonic boom flight demonstrator configurations under a Sonic Boom Mitigation Project study contract with NASA. The Boeing assessment produced a matrix that contained 22 flight demonstrator configurations. These included modified F-5s, F-15s, F-16s, F-18s, Russian Sukhoi Su-27s, and even entirely new X-planes designed from scratch. However, the Boeing study identified a modification of the F-16XL as the most cost-effective option for a low-boom flight demonstrator. They proposed a low–sonic boom research aircraft that was based on an extensively modified F-16XL-1. The Boeing low–sonic boom flight demonstrator would have incorporated a new lengthened nose and a sweptback V-type windscreen similar to those that had been used on the earlier Convair F-102 and F-106 fighters and the Lockheed SR-71. These modifications were intended to reshape and reduce the strength of the shock wave produced at the forward end of the aircraft by tailoring the area distribution and certain features of the basic aircraft. Other modifications to the aircraft included a canopy closeout fairing, a reshaping of the forebody chine and wing leading edge, raked wingtips, drooped ailerons, a rear-fuselage stinger-type extension above the nozzle carrying a small horizontal tail, and the fitting of an overexpanded engine nozzle. These modifications were intended to reduce the strength of the shock wave coming from the aft end of the aircraft. Boeing also noted that this combination of modifications to the F-16XL-1 would preclude achieving the low-drag supersonic characteristics that also would have been desirable in a high-speed research aircraft.[1]

In 2007, F-16XL-1 was again being considered for future research projects involving sonic boom investigations, presumably to include the low–sonic shock flight demonstrator effort. The feasibility of upgrading the aircraft systems and returning the aircraft to full flight-ready status was considered in an F-16XL Return to Flight and Supportability Study. Equipping F-16XL-1 with the more powerful General Electric F110-GE-129 engine in place of its Pratt & Whitney F100-PW-200 engine was an option, as were systems upgrades

The F-16XL-1 is seen during ground taxi tests at the Dryden Flight Research Center on June 28, 2007. Neither of the two F-16XLs moved under its own power after this date. (NASA)

intended to improve the digital flight control and avionics systems. However, funding was not provided to proceed with these upgrades, which would have brought the aircraft systems closer to the standard of new production F-16s. A NASA Dryden spokesman stated at the time, "F-16XL-1 is now being looked at for possible research efforts that are as yet undefined. It is being thoroughly inspected to assess its health and the feasibility of bringing it back to flyable status."[2] In conjunction with this evaluation, the aircraft systems were brought back to basic flightworthy status. NASA research pilot Jim Smolka, who had been project pilot on the earlier supersonic laminar flow control experiments, successfully taxi-tested F-16XL-1 at Dryden in late June of 2007. This would be the final time that either F-16XL moved under its on power.

In 2009, NASA Langley researcher Peter Coen, principal investigator for the supersonics project in NASA's fundamental aeronautics program, stated in an interview with *Aviation Week & Space Technology* that proceeding with a low–sonic shock flight demonstrator was a "fairly high priority." He went on to note that the NASA aeronautics budget was not large enough to support such a program without help from other agencies and industry partners. "We can't do it without significantly modifying an existing aircraft or building something new. The F-16XL is an aircraft we have." Boeing had continued work on their F-16XL low–sonic shock flight demonstrator concept under NASA contract. Coen stated that the Boeing work "looks promising" and "initial design studies have been encouraging with respect to shock mitigation of the forebody, canopy, inlet, wing leading edge and aft lift/volume distribution features." He went on to comment that the Boeing team was moving from initial concept validation to optimizing the detailed design configuration and "the modified F-16XL appeared to be fairly low in cost." Coen added a realistic qualifier noting: "We will not necessarily get everything we want. We will not be able to explore low boom and low drag at the same time. But it (the low sonic shock flight demonstrator) will give us a shaped front and aft signature and we can use the resulting aircraft in studies related to sonic boom acceptability."[3]

In any case, NASA did not proceed with the F-16XL low–sonic shock flight demonstrator project after the contract with Boeing ended later in 2009. This resulted in a NASA decision to permanently retire both F-16XLs. The single seat F-16XL-1 is now exhibited at the Dryden Flight Research Center at Edwards, CA. As of December 2012, the two-seat F-16XL-2 was still at Dryden pending a decision on future restoration and possible exhibition at the National Museum of the United States Air Force at Wright-Patterson AFB, OH.

Endnotes

1. Graham Warwick, "Boeing Studies F-16XL Low-Sonic-Boom Demonstrator," *Aviation Week & Space Technology* (March 23, 2009); Lawrence R. Benson, "Softening the Sonic Boom: 50 Years of NASA Research," Case 4 in Hallion, *NASA's Contributions to Aeronautics.*
2. NASA Dryden Flight Research Center, "Return to Flight and Supportability Study," Solicitation Number NND07204397Q-DAC, DFRC Code A (Research and Development) (June 20, 2007); John Croft, "NASA Could Put F-16XL Back in the Air," *Flight International* (October 7, 2007); Wetherall, "F-16XL First Flight Anniversary Celebration: The NASA Years."
3. Warwick, "Boeing Studies F-16XL Low-Sonic-Boom Demonstrator."

F-16XL-1 over Texas on first flight L-M. (Lockhead Martin)

CHAPTER 12

Summary and Observations

Summary

The F-16XL program began as a private venture by the General Dynamics Corporation in the mid-1970s, not long after the F-16 had entered service with the Air Force. GD had observed that the F-16, whose highly innovative design concept was highly focused on the lightweight air combat fighter mission, was being increasingly used on ground attack missions. In that role, the range and performance of the small F-16 were limited by the weight and drag of large loads of external stores when compared to larger strike aircraft. Initially known by the acronym SCAMP (Supersonic Cruise and Maneuver Prototype), the initiative also was oriented to address emerging Air Force interest in supersonic combat capability. GD proposed to develop an inexpensive experimental prototype derived from the F-16 to validate improved transonic/supersonic cruise and maneuverability along with expanded air-to-ground capabilities. A key aspect of the GD F-16XL business development approach and marketing strategy involved interesting the Air Force in supporting the development and eventual production of a new aircraft that would share much in common with the existing F-16's airframe, engine, avionics, and subsystems. The F-16XL was seen by GD as providing the Air Force with a more affordable procurement option to replace the much larger F-111 in the demanding deep-strike mission, one that could lead to follow-on production contracts.

NASA support had been extremely productive during both the YF-16 Lightweight Fighter technology demonstration and the follow-on F-16 Full-Scale Development program, and it proved quite effective in resolving difficult technical issues such as airframe flutter when carrying certain external stores. This encouraged GD to develop a collaborative arrangement with NASA for SCAMP research that would effectively exploit ongoing NASA supersonic transport and fighter research efforts based on the use of aerodynamically efficient cranked-arrow-wing planforms. The final F-16XL prototype configuration, featuring a stretched F-16 fuselage along with a cranked-arrow wing, was in many significant ways the direct result of this collaborative effort with

NASA. The Air Force supported the GD F-16XL prototyping initiative, providing equipment (including two F-16A fuselages), test facilities, and partial funding for a flight demonstration. However, as the requirement for an F-111 replacement evolved, the Air Force concept changed to include close-in and beyond-visual-range air-to-air capabilities along with advanced all-weather ground attack. The aircraft that would meet this requirement was now referred to by the Air Force as the Dual-Role Fighter. In its marketing, General Dynamics strove to convince both Congress and the Air Force that the F-16XL could meet the DRF requirement and complement, rather than compete with the larger F-15E for the deep-strike mission. However, Congress directed that only one aircraft would be funded for production, with the decision to be based on a comparative evaluation of the F-16XL and the F-15E.

The F-16XL flew for the first time on July 3, 1982, at Carswell AFB, TX, adjacent to the Fort Worth Division of General Dynamics, where the two experimental prototypes had been built. The subsequent Air Force flight-test evaluation of the F-16XL was conducted at the Flight Test Center at Edwards Air Force Base from 1982 to 1983 using the Combined Test Force (CTF) approach that had been successfully used during the Lightweight Fighter Program. The CTF included both military and contractor participation in nearly all aspects of the flight-test effort, which unfolded very rapidly with 369 flights accomplished by May 15, 1983. During the evaluation, the F-16XL demonstrated many outstanding capabilities. Its range, payload, and supersonic performance were far superior to those of the standard F-16, and its spin resistance and out-of-control recovery characteristics were outstanding. Demonstrated takeoff and landing distances were longer than desired, and the aircraft was unable to cruise supersonically without the use of afterburner. The aircraft's relatively low thrust-to-weight ratio combined with the high induced drag produced by its low aspect ratio wing resulted in rapid loss of airspeed during sustained subsonic high-g maneuvering. These issues were important considerations in the Air Force DRF decision, which was based on results from F-15E and F-16XL flight testing as well as other sources of information, including the outcomes of computerized war games. Faced with challenging budgetary choices, the Air Force elected to fund the F-15E as its DRF, along with the high-stealth F-117 and Advanced Tactical Fighter (ATF). Limited F-16XL flight testing continued until October 1985, by which time the two prototypes had accumulated a total of nearly 800 sorties before being placed in storage.

During the 1990s, NASA was pursuing a complex program of High-Speed Research (HSR) that included investigations into many aspects related to commercial supersonic flight. The potential application of supersonic laminar flow control (SLFC) capability to a highly swept cranked-arrow wing was an area of high interest to the HSR program. A flight demonstration to reduce the perceived high level of SLFC technology risk would support development and production of a future High-Speed Civil Transport (HSCT). Since the F-16XL cranked-arrow-wing planform closely resembled conceptual HSCT designs, their ready availability presented a unique opportunity for an SLFC technology flight-test effort. NASA arranged for the two F-16XL prototypes to be transferred to the Dryden Flight Research Center, where they were used for a series of HSR-related test projects during the 1990s, with tests involving SLFC research being the most challenging. Highly modified and specially instrumented, the F-16XL experimental prototypes evaluated the technical feasibility of the active suction SLFC concept as well as contributed to other areas important to HSCT development and risk reduction. Experiments with the F-16XLs had produced a very large volume of technical data by the time NASA decided to end the research program in late 1996. NASA research with the F-16XL furthered the state of the art in aerodynamics, acoustic, and sonic boom phenomenology, and it was a major contributor to improved understanding of vortex flow over highly swept delta wings. In addition, it made major contributions to development and validation of computational fluid dynamics (CFD) capabilities and design tools and methodologies across the aerospace community.

Observations and Lessons Learned

NASA provided extensive technical support during F-16XL engineering development and design refinement. Notable aspects of NASA support included innovative wing design methodology and analytical procedures developed at LaRC, wind tunnel model testing, the use of performance predictions based on wind tunnel test results, and important inputs into the design of the F-16XL's specially tailored digital flight control system. The latter was based in part on successful pilot-in-the-loop testing in the Differential Maneuvering Simulator at NASA Langley. Thousands of hours of wind tunnel testing were accomplished by the first flight of the F-16XL, in July 1982. An unusually large number of configuration variables were evaluated during the cooperative wind tunnel test effort with NASA. These included a wide variety of wing planforms, vertical tails, leading-edge flaps, vortex fences, wingtips, spoilers, different fuselage stretches, forebody strake designs, airfoils and camber variations, and even potential canard arrangements. In addition, geometrically and dynamically scaled models of different weapons, external stores, and guided missiles were tested on the final F-16XL configuration prior to eventual flight testing. By the time the Air Force F-16XL program ended in late 1985, over 4,000 wind tunnel test hours had been completed, most of that in NASA wind tunnels.

Computer-aided design (CAD) and computer-aided manufacturing (CAM) systems were extensively used in the F-16XL development in an early demonstration of the power of these technologies to enhance aeronautical design and system engineering effectiveness. Computer-based structural analysis, design, and manufacturing systems had greatly benefited from a major NASA initiative known as NASTRAN (NASA Structural Analysis System), which was managed under Langley Research Center leadership. NASTRAN led to the development and widespread use of many commercially developed CAD/CAM systems. In designing the F-16XL, GD employed a Lockheed-developed CAD/CAM system called CADAM; it played a major role in the successful design, manufacture, and smooth integration of the complex cranked-arrow wing into the prototype flight demonstration aircraft.

In another early demonstration of advanced technologies, the F-16XL's wing skins were constructed of aeroelastically tailored composite laminates. These were more adaptable to being formed into the compound curvature surfaces of the cranked-arrow wing with its complex combination of wing camber and twist. Designed to deform favorably under heavy loads while meeting the strength requirements of a minimum-weight, damage-tolerant structure, the F-16XL's aeroelastically-tailored composite wing skins resulted in significant weight savings. An additional benefit was reduced manufacturing cost since the composite wing skins did not require machine milling or chemical etching like metallic skins. Other important structural benefits were increased stiffness and better rigidity along with improved durability. Widespread use of advanced composite structures in the aerospace industry was heavily influenced by NASA- and Air Force–sponsored research efforts with many aerospace companies, including General Dynamics.

Extensive wind tunnel, spin tunnel, and drop model test efforts conducted at NASA facilities were critically important to F-16XL flight control system functionality and effectiveness. Design of the leading-edge flaps and programming of the software used in the F-16XL's computerized fly-by-wire flight control system capitalized on Langley research efforts on deep stall recovery and automatic spin prevention. An automatic pitch override capability provided pitch-rocking commands to the flight control system in the event of a stabilized deep stall, and manual pitch override allowed the angle-of-attack limiter to be bypassed, providing full-pitch-command authority to enable the pilot to break a deep stall. These features, developed in close cooperation with NASA experts, provided a significant contribution to the F-16XL's very high resistance to inadvertent loss of control or spin development; this was convincingly demonstrated during extensive flight testing that involved aggressive maneuvering to extreme pitch attitudes and angles of attack.

The F-16XL's refined low-drag aerodynamic design, along with its ability to carry a much larger quantity of internal fuel in its large cranked-arrow wing and stretched fuselage, provided significantly increased range and combat radius compared to the standard F-16C. With twice the ordnance payload, combat radius was nearly 50 percent greater than that of the F-16C. Its instantaneous turn rate was exceptional, but there was a significant loss of sustained turn capability due to the high induced drag produced by the low aspect ratio wing and the relatively low thrust-to-weight ratio of the aircraft. The F-16XL's exceptional rolling ability partially offset the loss of sustained maneuver capability; however, high energy loss experienced during aggressive combat maneuvering was a major concern to the Air Force.

The F-16XL had a very high approach speed under heavyweight conditions, with touchdown speeds well above 170 knots. It was reportedly smooth, responsive, and stable during landing approach, but its approach angle of attack was limited by restricted over-the-nose visibility and also to ensure adequate aft-fuselage clearance with the runway. The aircraft was more stable than the standard F-16 during aerodynamic braking after touchdown, with pitch control reported as being more positive. The F-16XL did not achieve the goal of decreased landing distance relative to the standard F-16. Its much longer landing distance was primarily due to its very high approach and touchdown speeds. Several approaches to increase the effective lift coefficient of the aircraft were being investigated by GD in cooperation with NASA Langley in an attempt to reduce final approach and touchdown speeds. These included fitting vortex flaps to the inner wing leading edge, modifications to the wing trailing edge and the elevons, and changes to the digital flight control system intended to optimize landing approach characteristics.

An interesting phenomenon involving a longitudinal oscillation in the pitch axis, commonly referred to by the test pilots as "pitch gallop," affected the F-16XL's ability to effectively track maneuvering aerial targets. To determine the cause of the anomaly, an in-flight-excitation test procedure was devised and used to obtain aircraft frequency responses at any condition within the flight envelope. Flight testing using this methodology revealed a disagreement between the analytical model of the aircraft flight control system and the actual flight control system in the aircraft. The pitch gain turned out to be slightly out of phase in the frequency range where the longitudinal oscillation existed and was not detected during preflight pilot-in-the-loop simulations of the flight control system.

NASA F-16XL Flight Research

The main thrust for NASA use of the F-16XL was supersonic laminar flow research in support of technology risk reduction efforts oriented to a future HSCT. In this regard, laminar flow technology potentially offered significant reductions in fuel consumption, but practical application of the technology to a production aircraft had proven fruitless despite a long series of attempts over the years that had included many flight-test programs. Laminar flow technology, especially as it related to the supersonic flight regime, had significant risks that involved airframe design, system integration, production engineering, and manufacturing feasibility. Operations and maintenance of an HSCT fitted with SLFC in routine airline service also faced many uncertainties. A program of SLFC flight research was needed if these risks were to be mitigated in time for integration into any HSCT. This was the primary motivation for NASA's selection of the two idle F-16XLs for modification into SLFC test beds. In addition, the modified airframes would also be used for NASA research into a number of other issues associated with reducing technical risk and operational feasibility for a viable commercial supersonic transport.

F-16XL-1 arrived at NASA Dryden in March 1989 where it was modified for laminar flow research. Its first flight with a highly instrumented laminar flow wing glove occurred in May 1990. A perforated titanium active suction wing glove with a turbocompressor was installed in the aircraft in 1992 for initial SLFC investigations. In 1995, after being returned to its original aerodynamic configuration and fitted with acoustic pressure sensors, F-16XL-1 was used with a NASA Lockheed SR-71 and a Lockheed YO-3 in a research project intended to further quantify sonic boom phenomenology. In 1997, it was modified and tested with a digital fly-by-wire (FBW) flight control system (DFCS) that replaced the original analog FBW flight control system for potential use in a NASA program that would have tested nonconventional pneumatic control effectors on the aircraft. However, a proposed flight-test program of this technology using F-16XL-1 was not pursued.

A more ambitious program of supersonic laminar flow control testing used the two-seat F-16XL-2, which had been assigned to Dryden in February 1991. The SLFC flight research effort with F-16XL-2 was intended to achieve laminar flow over 50 to 60 percent of its wing chord. In addition to the flight-test effort, CFD computer software codes and design methodologies were to be created along with laminar flow control design criteria for use at supersonic speeds. Prior to its delivery, NASA had arranged for the more powerful General Electric F110-GE-129 turbofan engine to be installed in F-16XL-2 for SLFC testing, replacing the F110-GE-100 engine used during the earlier Air Force flight-test program. Initial F-16XL-2 testing was accomplished during 1991–1992 using a passive wing glove designed by McDonnell-Douglas Corporation and built at the NASA Dryden Flight Research Center. Data from initial flight testing was used to calibrate computer software design codes, particularly in the leading-edge boundary-layer region. Preventing the turbulent boundary layer on the fuselage from contaminating the boundary layer attachment-line region on the wing leading edge was a major technical issue that was also addressed in early flight testing with F-16XL-2. The data obtained was subsequently used to design the active suction glove that would be installed for the next phase of SLFC testing.

Work began on the active suction glove in 1992 in a collaborative effort between Boeing, McDonnell-Douglas, Rockwell, and NASA. Designed to fit on the inner left wing, the glove's leading edge extended forward into the fuselage to better replicate the HSCT wing. This resulted in a pronounced asymmetric configuration when the glove was installed on F-16XL-2 at NASA Dryden. Constructed of inner and outer titanium skins and aluminum stringers, the glove covered about 75 percent of the upper-wing surface and 60 percent of the leading edge. A turbocompressor mounted in the fuselage provided suction to draw air through nearly 12 million laser-drilled holes via a highly complex manifold system that employed 20 independently moving computer-controlled valves. The geometric asymmetry of the F-16XL-2 with the active suction glove required dedicated wind tunnel tests to determine the aerodynamic and stability and control characteristics of the modified aircraft before actual flight testing could begin. A wind tunnel model of F-16XL-2 fitted with the active suction glove was subjected to about 2,800 hours of testing to validate its aerodynamic characteristics. In addition to wind tunnel testing, a computer simulation of the aircraft with the glove modification was evaluated in a flight simulator at Dryden to ensure that aircraft handling qualities were not adversely affected by the asymmetrical aerodynamic configuration. Since the objectives of the SLFC project were oriented to application of the technology to a transport aircraft, high-g, high-AoA maneuvering was not required in the test program, and the SLFC glove was designed for 3-g flight conditions.

Evaluation of the active suction glove began in November 1995, and the first supersonic flight test with the suction system operating occurred in January 1996. The fight-test portion of the SLFC project with F-16XL-2 ended in November 1996 after 45 research fights during which about 90 hours of flight time were logged, much of it at speeds of Mach 2 at altitudes of 50,000 feet and above. The project demonstrated that laminar airflow could be achieved over a significant portion of a highly swept wing at supersonic speeds using an active suction system. However, the F-16XL had configuration-specific shock and expansion waves, which affected laminar flow over the wings at supersonic conditions. Supersonic shock waves emanating from the canopies and engine inlets spread out over the wings, and expansion waves coming from beneath the wing caused a highly three-dimensional flow field. These resulted in difficulties in obtaining consistent laminar flow at the same test conditions. Despite these problems, the SLFC experiments with the F-16XL achieved about 70 to 80 percent of the initial goals.

HSCT Integration Issues

Despite the promising results from the flight research program, there were other major difficulties with integration of active suction supersonic laminar flow control technologies into a commercial transport aircraft. Industry experts strongly expressed their opinion that the manufacturing processes needed to produce a practical SLFC system on a commercial supersonic transport were so challenging that they were effectively a showstopper. Boeing had to try four times before they were able to fabricate a suction glove for F-16XL-2 that met the challenging smoothness and stiffness standards required to maintain supersonic laminar flow. Even then, some manufacturing discrepancies were simply tolerated in order to move forward. Surface contours on the wing glove had to be controlled to no more than a few thousandths of an inch. This had already proven very challenging to achieve on the relatively small, stiff F-16XL wing and was assessed to be well beyond the manufacturing capabilities needed to produce an active suction glove for the much larger wing planned for the HSCT. Depending on the specific design approach, a wing of that size was estimated to require precision laser drilling of as many as a billion tiny holes in its laminar flow control suction panels. The manufacturing technology needed for an HSCT production line was considered both very expensive and risky to develop due to the precision required to produce active suction on a flexible airliner wing that was an order of magnitude larger in size than the F-16XL. In addition to high manufacturing costs, other challenges with SLFC technology included costs associated with keeping the extremely small suction holes clear during routine day-to-day scheduled airline service. Commercial airline operations, by definition, would have involved routine flight in heavy rain with icing conditions often encountered. Additionally, airborne insects found in the vicinity of many commercial airfields would have resulted in insect accretion on the wing leading edges. These factors had a high potential to cause the boundary layer over the wing of an HSCT to prematurely transition from laminar to turbulent flow, increasing the drag due to skin friction and defeating the purpose of a suction-type SLFC system.

Program Conclusion

In 1995, based on industry design concepts, computer modeling, and wind tunnel tests, NASA selected a Technology Concept Aircraft (TCA) as a common reference point for use in subsequent high-speed research technology development and risk reduction. This single concept was intended to have both improved aerodynamic performance and operational characteristics while also meeting environmental goals for engine emissions and noise pollution. An important rationale for the Technology Concept Aircraft was to serve as a basis to ensure that appropriate technology was available to meet both the needs of a practical and economically realistic design *and* its concurrent development schedule. The implications of this dual rationale had a major impact on the F-16XL SLFC project. In September 1996, the Airframe Management Team within the NASA HSR program elected to terminate the F-16XL SLFC project. This decision was based on a general agreement among both the Government and, especially, the aerospace industry members of the Airframe Management Team. The consensus within the team was that supersonic laminar flow control was not a near-term technology that could be available in time for integration into an HSCT program on any realistic cost and development schedule.

A Retrospective Assessment

In retrospect, the F-16XL was a remarkably productive research effort, whose impact and benefits extended far beyond its original purpose. Begun as a long-range strike variant of the basic F-16A air combat fighter, the F-16XL made its greatest contribution as a test bed for a series of technological approaches to enable efficient supersonic cruising flight. NASA (and the NACA before it) had made use of military prototypes for basic and applied research purposes many times before, but rarely with such productive results. The complex double-delta cranked-arrow wing planform, studied extensively in wind tunnels and by predictive analytical methodologies, received an important in-flight validation and exploration going well beyond earlier experience with similar (if not so sophisticated) planforms, such as that employed on the path-breaking Swedish Saab J 35 Draken of the 1950s. The benefits of that research will influence civil and military design choices and design trades for decades to come.

While the F-16XL did not enter service with the United States Air Force, it possessed a design configuration suitable for subsequent long-range inhabited and remotely piloted reconnaissance and strike systems, and thus military interest in the test program went beyond the immediate interest in the F-16XL-F-15E Strike Eagle "competition." In the civil sense, the configuration selected by the General Dynamics design team for what became the F-16XL reflected NASA's long-standing interest in deriving and refining highly efficient aerodynamic planforms for supersonic flight, applicable to supersonic commercial aircraft. While the anticipated market for supersonic airliners did not emerge so that the double-delta arrow wing could have been applied to a "second generation" follow-on to the Anglo-French Concorde and the Soviet-era Tupolev Tu-144, market interest in smaller commercial supersonic aircraft remains high, and, therefore, it is quite possible that the planform will be adopted by designers seeking to build super-cruising commercial business jets capable of spanning the oceans. If so, the flight-test and developmental lessons learned from the F-16XL program will continue to benefit the progression of aeronautical science.

Finally, the story of the F-16XL explains much about the organization of American aerospace science and technology, the adaptation of that technology for military and civil purposes, and the workings of aerospace professionals, industry, and the test and evaluation communities of both the military and NASA.

NASA, through its years of refined study at Langley Research Center (and building on earlier legacy work from the days of the NACA at what were then the Langley and Ames aeronautical laboratories), had matured a concept to the point that it could be applied to both civil and military aircraft; all that was required was a justification to do so. That justification came about through the recognition that the F-16 aircraft family would be primarily dedicated to air-to-surface attack, with a secondary air-to-air mission. Thus, the arrow wing, with its promise of enhanced long-range efficiencies, excellent high-speed properties, and ability to carry greater ordnance loads, was immediately attractive to the General Dynamics team.

The General Dynamics design team had the insight, inventiveness, and innovative spirit to recognize that, in the era of fly-by-wire flight control technology, they could take the basic configuration of the F-16A and, with a straightforward modification, transform it into an aircraft with quite different properties and qualities. This is not an innocuous point; since the time of the Wright brothers themselves, many design teams have been better at invention than at innovation. In the case of General Dynamics, the F-16 team possessed a rare willingness to "play" with their basic configuration to fulfill new purposes and generate new capabilities—a commendable corporate spirit of innovation. The seeming simplicity of their resulting design belied the complex analysis and subtle "under the skin" changes necessitated if one were to move successfully from the deceptively conventional planform of the original F-16A to the elegance of the arrow-wing F-16XL. While constrained by such issues as landing gear location and properties, the resulting aircraft was, in its own fashion, a remarkable accomplishment. Had it not faced the F-15E Strike

Eagle, it is altogether possible that it might have served as the basis for a larger, more powerful, and more capable production variant, the F-16XL functioning in much the same fashion for that ultimate production machine as the earlier YF-16 had for the original F-16A.

The Air Force and NASA test teams on the aircraft performed with the characteristic excellence that has come to distinguish flight testing and flight research in the skies over what was then the Air Force Flight Test Center (now the Air Force Test Center) and the NASA Dryden Flight Research Center. As noted earlier, Air Force flight testing quickly confirmed that while the F-16XL had outstanding range, payload, and supersonic performance when compared to the F-16A from whence it sprang, it had other deficiencies in takeoff and landing distance, turn performance, and thrust-to-weight ratio that, taken together with changes in Air Force operational requirements, mitigated against its being placed in production. Accordingly, the service selected a different design for derivative development, the McDonnell-Douglas (now Boeing) F-15E Strike Eagle.

It was at this juncture in its brief history that the F-16XL, seemingly destined for the scrapheap or museum, received a reprieve: its opportunity to function as a technology demonstrator and configuration research aircraft to validate not only the cranked-arrow planform but also a range of other concepts and technologies (most notably supersonic laminar flow control) applicable to sustained, efficient, supersonic cruising flight, supporting NASA's long-standing interest in High-Speed Research leading to possible High-Speed Civil Transports. Under NASA auspices, the F-16XL flew for over another decade, expanding knowledge not merely of the properties and characteristics of the cranked-arrow wing, but on related subjects such as sonic boom propagation and validation of CFD tools and analytical methodologies.

In sum, the F-16XL was an important research tool in the furtherance of understanding of supersonic cruising vehicle design. Though not used for the combat purposes for which it was originally conceived, it nevertheless proved an important weapon in the continuing struggle of humanity to master movement through the third dimension.

The F-16XL-2 during radar signature testing conducted by General Dynamics. (Lockheed Martin)

F-16XL First Flight Certificate

3 July 1982

Fighting Falcon

To: F-16XL Team Members
From: D. R. Kent

2 July 1982 - F-16XL Rollout
3 July 1982 - F-16XL First Flight

These are dates I'm sure we will all long remember. They represent the culmination of an extraordinary achievement by all of you who participated in the birth of this beautiful aircraft.

When we started the project in November 1980, we knew that to fly 19 months later represented a most ambitious and difficult undertaking. But because of your dedication and personal sacrifices and those of your family, the challenge was met - indeed, we beat the schedule! I am sure you shared with me the thrill and sense of pride when F-16XL-1 took to the air on Saturday morning, 3 July.

As a result of your skill and efforts, we can now offer our country an important new defense weapon - the F-16XL Fighting Falcon.

Please accept my thanks for your outstanding performance.

Vice President &
Program Director
F-16XL

GD F-16XL First Flight Certificate

F-16XL Weapon Separation Log

Flt	Date	A/C	Load-Out and/or Configuration	Weapons Released	Mission Notes
37	8/24/82	1	Twelve Mk-82 bombs	Twelve Mk-82	.75 M/ 13 K/ 1 g
45	1/24/83	2	Twelve Mk-82	Two Mk-82	—
46	1/25/83	2	Twelve Mk-82	Twelve Mk-82	.75 M/ 5 K
47	1/26/83	2	Six CBU-58 bombs, two 370 gal. tanks	Six CBU-58	.75 M/ 5 K
60	10/13/82	1	Six Mk-82	One Mk-82	500 kt/ 1,500 ft
61	10/14/82	1	Six Mk-82	One Mk-82	480 kt/ 500 ft/ 25-deg bank
64	10/18/82	1	Six Mk-82	One Mk-82	500 kt/ 500 ft/ 2 g's
67	10/19/82	1	Six Mk-82	One Mk-82	500 kt/ 500 ft/ 4 g's
69	10/20/82	1	Six Mk-82	One Mk-82	540 kt/ 500 ft/ 2 g's

Flt	Date	A/C	Load-Out and/or Configuration	Weapons Released	Mission Notes
71	10/21/82	1	Six Mk-82	One Mk-82	540 kt/ 500 ft/ 4 g's
72	10/22/82	1	Six Mk-82	One Mk-82	540 kt/ 500 ft/ 4 g's
85	3/9/83	2	Twelve Mk-82	Twelve Mk-82	.90 M/ 5 K
86	3/9/83	2	Two Mk-82	One Mk-82	.90 M/ 10 K/ 30-deg dive
87	3/10/83	2	Six Mk-82, twelve pylons	One Mk-82	.90 M/ 10 K/ 2 g's
88	3/10/83	2	Two Mk-82, twelve pylons	One Mk-82	90 M/ 10 K/ 47-deg dive
89	3/11/83	2	Six Mk-82, twelve pylons	One Mk-82	.88 M/ 9.6 K/ 4.3 g's
91	3/11/83	2	Two Mk-82, twelve pylons	One Mk-82	.90 M/ 9 K/ 3.8 g's
177	4/14/83	1	Twelve Mk-82	One Mk-82	Bomb impact survey
246	1/27/84	2	Twelve Mk-82	Eight Mk-82	.75 M/ 5 K
247	1/31/84	2	Twelve Mk-82	Eight Mk-82	.90 M/ 5 K
248	2/2/84	2	Two Mk-84 bombs	Two Mk-84	.75 M/ 5 K

Flt	Date	A/C	Load-Out and/or Configuration	Weapons Released	Mission Notes
249	2/21/84	2	Two Mk-84	Two Mk-84	.75 M/ 5 K
250	2/28/84	2	Two Mk-84	Two Mk-84	.80 M/ 5 K
251	3/5/84	2	Two Mk-84	Two Mk-84	.90 M/ 10 K
257	4/12/84	2	Two Mk-84	Two Mk-84	.90 M/ 5 K
265	5/9/84	2	Four Mk-84	Four Mk-84	.75 M/ 5 K
266	5/17/84	2	Four Mk-84 (Tandem Carriage)	Four Mk-84	.75 M/ 15 K
375	3/29/85	1	One AGM-65 Maverick missile	One AGM-65	.75 M/ 10 K/ 10-deg dive

F-16XL Flight-Test Activity Through October 1, 1985

Milestone Data			
Item	**F-16XL-1**	**F-16XL-2**	**Total**
1st Flight-Last Flight	7/3/82–8/14/85	10/29/82–10/1/85	—
1st Supersonic Flight	Flt 2 (7/9/82)	Flt 1 (10/29/82)	—
Maximum "G" Flight	9.0 g's (Flt 20, 7/28/82)	—	—
Maximum Mach Number	1.95M (Flt 19, 7/28/82)	1.6M (Flt 25, 12/7/82)	—
Maximum Altitude	50K ft (Flt 11, 7/24/82)	50K ft (Flt 212, 9/13/83)	—
Longest Range Demo	1,985 nm (Flt 224, 9/23/83)	—	—
1st Flt w/ GE 110 Slimline Engine	—	Flt 274 (7/19/84)	—
1st Flt w/ Large Normal Shock Inlet	—	Flt 311 (6/26/85)	—

Flight Data			
Item	**F-16XL-1**	**F-16XL-2**	**Total**
Total Number of Flights	437	361	798
Total Air-to-Air Flights	318 (72.8 percent)	230 (63.7 percent)	548 (68.7 percent)
Total Air-to-Ground Flights	119 (27.2 percent)	131 (36.3 percent)	250 (31.3 percent)

Flight Hour Data			
Item	**F-16XL-1**	**F-16XL-2**	**Total**
Total Number of Flight Hours	532.6	407.1	939.7
Total Air-to-Air Flight Hours	400 (75.1 percent)	283.1 (69.5 percent)	683.1 (72.7 percent)
Total Air-to-Ground Flight Hours	132.6 (24.9 percent)	124 (30.5 percent)	256.6 (27.3 percent)
Average Hours Per Flight	1.22	1.13	1.18

Aerial Refueling			
Item	**F-16XL-1**	**F-16XL-2**	**Total**
1st Aerial Refueling Flight	Flt 26 (8/12/82)	Flt 30 (1/7/83)	—
Number of Refueling Flights	71	56	127
Number of "Wet" Refuelings	100	75	175
Longest Flight with Refueling	4.5 hrs (Flt 89, 12/15/82) two aerial refuelings	4.0 hrs (Flt 33, 1/11/83), two aerial refuelings	—
Longest Flight without Refueling	4.0 hrs (Flt 224, 9/23/83) with two 600 gal tanks	2.5 hrs (Flt 5, 11/8/82) 2.5 hrs (Flt 68, 2/22/83)	—

Gunfire Data			
Item	**F-16XL-1**	**F-16XL-2**	**Total**
1st Gun-Firing Flight	Flt 163 (4/1/83)	Flt 32 (1/10/83)	—
Number of Gun-Firing Flights	8	7	15
Number of 20-mm Rounds Fired	4,763	2,600	7,363

Weapon Data			
Item	**F-16XL-1**	**F-16XL-2**	**Total**
Number of Bomb Drop Flights	14	31	45
Mk-82 bombs dropped/flights	89/14	129/23	218/37
CBU-58 bombs dropped/flights	0	6/1	6/1
Mk-84 bombs dropped/flights	0	18/7	18/7
Flights Carrying Mk-82	71	80	151
Flights Carrying CBU-58	7	1	8
Flights Carrying Mk-84	1	20	21
Flights Carrying BDU-38	7	15	22
Flights Carrying SUU-65	20	11	31
AGM-65 Carriage Flights	5	0	5
AGM-65 Launches/ Flights	1/1	0	1/1

F-16XL Flight-Test Objectives Accomplished

Purpose/Flight-Test Objectives	Number of Flights	
	F-16XL-1	F-16XL-2
Performance	75	65
Stability and Control (S&C)	38	16
Flutter Expansion Envelope	10	8
Stability and Control (High Angle of Attack)	43	—
Stability and Control (Structural Loads)	—	26
Stability and Control (Speed Break Loads)	8	—
Stability and Control (Pitch Gallop Investigation)	11	—
Stability and Control (Landing Handling Qualities)	5	—
Stability and Control (Aft Center-of-Gravity Envelope Expansion	22	—
Stability and Control (Inflight Excitation [Random/Sinusoid])	37	—
Stability and Control (G-Overshoot Investigation)	6	—
Performance/Stability & Control (Combined)	13	9
Performance/Stability & Control w/ Locked LEF	24	—

Purpose/Flight-Test Objectives	Number of Flights	
	F-16XL-1	F-16XL-2
Flutter/Stability & Control (Combined)	7	2
Flutter/Performance (Combined)	6	—
Propulsion—F110 Slimline Engine Envelope Expansion	—	32
Propulsion/S&C/ Performance—F110 Engine w/ LNSI Using JP-4 Fuel	—	30
Propulsion—F110 Engine w/ LNSI Using JP-8 Fuel	—	13
Propulsion—High-Speed Envelope Expansion	—	9
Hinge Moment Evaluation w/ Modified LEF	—	5
Helmet Mounted Display Evaluation	—	3
Weapon Separation/Gun Firing/Air Combat Maneuvering Instrumentation (ACMI) Pod Range	14	28
Vibration Test Maneuvers	8	—
Elevon Loads Survey	—	5
ECS/Drag Chute Deployment	2	—
Air Data Calibration	4	3
Aerial Refueling	2	3
Operational Utility Evaluation (OUE) Testing	42	29
Special Test Objectives	9	6
Reliability & Maintainability Evaluation	7	2
Ferry Flights (General Dynamics Forth Worth to/ from Edwards AFB)	10	8

Purpose/Flight-Test Objectives	Number of Flights	
	F-16XL-1	F-16XL-2
Functional Check Flights (Engine/FCC/etc.)	9	15
VIP Demonstration/Practice	—	35
Used as Target and/or Chase Aircraft	7	—
Pilot Training/Checkout/Familiarization	18	9
TOTAL FLIGHTS BY EACH AIRCRAFT	437	361

F-16XL Flight-Test Logs

Appendix E-1: F-16XL-1 FLIGHT LOG						

F-16XL-1 Pilots

BR	Burnett	D	Dryden	N	Newman	T	Thomas
BS	Bushnell	F	Fergione	O	Oestricher	W	Wolfe
C	Cary	K	Knight	P	Payne		
CG	Caughlin	M	McKinney	S	Svendsen		

Flt.	Date	Hrs	Pilot	Mission	Configuration	Notes
1	7/3/82	1.0	M	FCF	A/A	—
2	7/9/82	2.1	M	Performance/ S&C	A/A	First Supersonic
3	7/17/82	1.9	M	Performance/ S&C	A/A	—
4	7/18/82	1.3	M	Performance	A/A	—
5	7/18/82	2.3	M	Ferry to EAFB	A/A	—
6	7/20/82	.9	BS	Pilot Fam./ AS Calibration	A/A	—
7	7/22/82	.8	W	Performance	A/A	—
8	7/22/82	1.5	M	Flutter	A/A	—
9	7/23/82	.9	BS	Performance	A/A	—
10	7/23/82	1.5	W	Flutter	A/A	—

Flt.	Date	Hrs	Pilot	Mission	Configuration	Notes
11	7/24/82	1.2	BS	Performance/ S&C	A/A	—
12	7/24/82	.9	W	Performance	A/A	—
13	7/24/82	.8	W	Performance/ S&C	12 Mk-82	—
14	7/26/82	.6	M	Flutter	12 Mk-82	—
15	7/27/82	.7	W	Performance	12 Mk-82	—
16	7/27/82	.5	M	Performance	12 Mk-82	—
17	7/27/82	.8	W	Performance	12 Mk-82	—
18	7/27/82	.8	D	Pilot Familiarization	12 Pylons	—
19	7/27/82	1.2	BS	Performance	A/A	—
20	7/28/82	1.1	M	Performance/ S&C	A/A	9 g
21	7/29/82	1.1	BR	Pilot Familiarization	A/A	—
22	8/3/82	.5	T	Pilot Familiarization	A/A	Lost System A Hyd.
23	8/6/82	.9	K	Pilot Familiarization	A/A	—
24	8/9/82	.8	W	Flutter/S&C	A/A	—
25	8/12/82	1.8	W	Data Calibration	A/A	—
26	8/12/82	1.8	BS	Air Refueling (A/R)	A/A	—
27	8/13/82	1.4	T	Pilot Familiarization	A/A	—
28	8/13/82	1.1	M	Flutter	A/A	—

Flt.	Date	Hrs	Pilot	Mission	Configuration	Notes
29	8/16/82	1.4	M	S&C	A/A	—
30	8/17/82	1.1	BS	AoA Cal.	A/A	—
31	8/17/82	.7	T	Performance	12 Mk-82	—
32	8/17/82	.5	M	Flutter	12 Mk-82	—
33	8/18/82	.5	D	Performance	12 Mk-82	—
34	8/18/82	1.8	BR	Performance	12 Mk-82	—
35	8/23/82	1.0	W	S&C	A/A	—
36	8/23/82	1.4	BS	S&C	A/A	—
37	8/24/82	.7	W	Weapon Separation	12 Mk-82	—
38	8/25/82	.4	W	Flutter	12 Mk-82	—
39	8/25/82	.9	T	S&C	A/A	—
40	8/26/82	1.7	BS	—	A/A	—
41	8/26/82	1.7	D	—	A/A	—
42	8/28/82	.7	W	S&C	A/A	—
43	9/22/82	2.4	W	Ferry to GDFW	A/A	—
44	9/22/82	.7	M	FCF	—	—
45	9/22/82	2.4	BR	Ferry to EAFB	A/A	—
46	9/23/82	.8	W	Loads	A/A	—

Flt.	Date	Hrs	Pilot	Mission	Configuration	Notes
47	9/27/82	1.6	BS	—	12 Mk-82	—
48	9/28/82	.9	T	—	12 Mk-82	—
49	9/28/82	2.4	BR	Performance	12 Mk-82	—
50	9/30/82	1.8	D	—	12 Mk-82	—
51	10/1/82	1.8	T	S&C	A/A	—
52	10/1/82	2.7	BS	Performance	A/A	—
53	10/4/82	.9	M	Loads	A/A, 2 fore. AMRAAMs	—
54	10/4/82	1.8	T	Performance	A/A	—
55	10/11/82	.5	M	Flutter	A/A	—
56	10/11/82	1.3	W	S&C	A/A	—
57	10/11/82	1.0	M	S&C	A/A	—
58	10/12/82	.8	W	S&C	A/A	—
59	10/13/82	.9	BS	S&C	6 Mk-82	—
60	10/13/82	.8	W	Weapon Separation	6 Mk-82	—
61	10/14/82	.7	T	Weapon Separation	6 Mk-82	—
62	10/14/82	.9	W	S&C	6 Mk-82	—
63	10/15/82	1.0	BS	Performance	6 Mk-82	—
64	10/18/82	.9	T	Weapon Separation	6 Mk-82	—

Flt.	Date	Hrs	Pilot	Mission	Configuration	Notes
65	10/18/82	1.0	BS	S&C	A/A	—
66	10/19/82	.9	T	Performance	6 Mk-82	—
67	10/19/82	.7	W	Weapon Separation	6 Mk-82	—
68	10/19/82	.8	C	Pilot familiarization	A/A	—
69	10/20/82	.7	T	Weapon Separation	6 Mk-82	—
70	10/20/82	.7	BR	Separation Practice	6 Mk-82	—
71	10/21/82	.6	W	Weapon Separation	6 Mk-82	—
72	10/22/82	.6	BR	Weapon Separation	A/A	—
73	10/25/82	.8	BS	Performance	A/A	—
74	10/25/82	1,4	M	Performance	A/A	—
75	10/26/82	.9	BS	S&C	A/A	—
76	10/27/82	2.1	D	Ferry to GDFW	A/A	—
77	11/8/82	1.6	M	FCF	A/A	—
78	11/8/82	2.5	BR	Ferry to EAFB	A/A	—
79	11/9/82	1.0	M	S&C	A/A	—
80	12/3/82	.8	BS	Performance	A/A	—
81	12/7/82	.9	BS	S&C/ Performance	2 BDU-38, 2 370-gal. tanks	—
82	12/7/82	.7	T	Flutter	2 BDU-38, 2 370-gal. tanks	—

Flt.	Date	Hrs	Pilot	Mission	Configuration	Notes
83	12/10/82	.7	D	Performance	12 Mk-82	—
84	12/13/82	.7	T	Flutter/S&C	6 CBU-58, 2 370-gal. tanks	—
85	12/13/82	.5	M	Flutter	6 CBU-58, 2 370-gal. tanks	—
86	12/14/82	.5	T	Performance	6 CBU-58, 2 370-gal. tanks	—
87	12/15/82	.7	BS	Performance	6 CBU-58, 2 370-gal. tanks	—
88	12/16/82	.9	T	Performance	6 BDU-38, 2 370-gal. tanks	—
89	12/15/82	4.5	D	—	A/A	—
90	12/16/82	.4	T	Performance	6 CBU-58, 2 370-gal. tanks	—
91	12/17/82	1.7	C	Performance	6 CBU-58, 2 370-gal. tanks	—
92	12/17/82	1.1	BS	Performance	6 BDU-38, 2 370-gal. tanks	—
93	12/20/82	1.5	BR	Performance	A/A	—
94	12/20/82	1.0	T	Performance	A/A	—
95	12/21/82	1.3	C	Performance	A/A	—
96	12/21/82	1.1	T	Performance	12 Mk-82	—
97	1/11/83	1.0	T	S&C	A/A	—
98	1/12/83	.6	W	S&C	A/A	—
99	1/12/83	2.5	C	Performance	12 Mk-82	—
100	1/13/83	.8	T	Performance	12 Mk-82	—

Flt.	Date	Hrs	Pilot	Mission	Configuration	Notes
101	1/14/83	3.3	T	Performance	6 SUU-65, 2 370-gal. tanks	—
102	1/24/83	.7	M	S&C	A/A (with spin chute)	—
103	1/28/83	.8	M	High AoA	A/A (with spin chute)	—
104	1/28/83	1.0	BS	SFO practice	A/A (with spin chute)	—
105	1/31/83	1.9	W	High AoA	A/A (with spin chute)	—
106	2/1/83	.8	BS	High AoA	A/A (with spin chute)	—
107	2/4/83	1.5	M	High AoA	A/A (with spin chute)	—
108	2/7/83	1.7	M	High AoA	A/A (with spin chute)	—
109	2/8/83	2.6	BS	High AoA	A/A (with spin chute)	—
110	2/9/83	2.3	M	High AoA	A/A (with spin chute)	Weather abort (WX)
111	2/9/83	2.6	W	High AoA	A/A (with spin chute)	—
112	2/11/83	1.5	M	High AoA	A/A (with spin chute)	—
113	2/14/83	2.5	M	High AoA	A/A (with spin chute)	—
114	2/15/83	.6	BS	High AoA	A/A (with spin chute)	—
115	2/16/83	1.1	BS	High AoA	A/A (with spin chute)	—
116	2/16/83	1.1	BS	High AoA	A/A (with spin chute)	—
117	2/16/83	1.1	W	High AoA	A/A (with spin chute)	—
118	2/18/83	.7	W	High AoA	12 Mk-82 (with spin chute)	48K wheels tires brakes

Flt.	Date	Hrs	Pilot	Mission	Configuration	Notes
119	2/18/83	2.7	BS	High AoA	12 Mk-82 (with spin chute)	—
120	2/22/83	.5	BS	High AoA	12 Mk-82 (with spin chute)	—
121	2/22/83	.5	BS	High AoA	12 Mk-82 (with spin chute)	—
122	2/22/83	.5	BS	High AoA	12 Mk-82 (with spin chute)	—
123	2/24/83	.7	M	High AoA	12 Mk-82 (with spin chute)	—
124	2/24/83	.9	M	High AoA	12 Mk-82 (with spin chute)	—
125	2/25/83	1.3	M	High AoA	A/A (with spin chute)	—
126	3/3/83	.7	BS	High AoA	12 Mk-82 (with spin chute)	—
127	3/3/83	.7	BS	High AoA	12 Mk-82 (with spin chute)	—
128	3/3/83	.5	M	High AoA	12 Mk-82 (with spin chute)	—
129	3/4/83	1.1	D	High AoA	A/A (with spin chute)	—
130	3/4/83	.9	C	High AoA	A/A (with spin chute)	—
131	3/4/83	.7	BR	High AoA	A/A (with spin chute)	—
132	3/8/83	2.4	C	OUE	A/A plus 2 ACMI pods	—
133	3/8/83	1.0	D	Ferry	A/A plus 2 ACMI pods	—
134	3/9/83	2.4	BR	OUE	A/A plus 2 ACMI pods	—
135	3/9/83	.9	C	Ferry	A/A plus 2 ACMI pods	—
136	3/10/83	1.3	D	OUE	A/A plus 2 ACMI pods	—

Flt.	Date	Hrs	Pilot	Mission	Configuration	Notes
137	3/10/83	1.1	D	OUE	A/A plus 2 ACMI pods	—
138	3/10/83	.9	BR	Ferry	A/A plus 2 ACMI pods	—
139	3/11/83	2.5	C	OUE	A/A plus 2 ACMI pods	—
140	3/11/83	1.2	D	Ferry	A/A plus 2 ACMI pods	—
141	3/14/83	2.4	BR	OUE	A/A plus 2 ACMI pods	—
142	3/14/83	.7	BR	Ferry	A/A plus 2 ACMI pods	—
143	3/15/83	1.2	T	Propulsion	A/A plus 2 ACMI pods	—
144	3/15/83	2.4	C	OUE	A/A plus 2 ACMI pods	—
145	3/15/83	.5	C	Ferry	A/A plus 2 ACMI pods	—
146	3/16/83	2.0	BR	OUE	A/A plus 2 ACMI pods	—
147	3/16/83	.6	BR	Ferry	A/A plus 2 ACMI pods	—
148	3/22/83	2.7	D	OUE	A/A plus 2 ACMI pods	—
149	3/23/83	.7	D	Ferry	A/A plus 2 ACMI pods	—
150	3/23/83	.8	M	Flutter	A/A with clean wingtips	—
151	3/24/83	.8	T	Flutter	A/A with clean wingtips	—
152	3/24/83	.5	T	S&C	A/A with clean wingtips	—
153	3/25/83	.8	D	S&C	A/A	—
154	3/25/83	1.9	BS	OUE	A/A	—

Flt.	Date	Hrs	Pilot	Mission	Configuration	Notes
155	3/28/83	.6	BR	OUE	12 Mk-82	—
156	3/29/83	.9	D	OUE	12 Mk-82	—
157	3/29/83	1.8	C	OUE	12 Mk-82	—
158	3/29/83	.7	C	Ferry	12 Mk-82	—
159	3/30/83	.8	C	OUE	12 Mk-82	—
160	3/31/83	.8	C	OUE	A/A	—
161	3/31/83	.6	M	Flutter	A/A	—
162	4/1/83	1.3	BR	OUE	12 Mk-82	—
163	4/1/83	1.0	C	OUE	12 Mk-82	—
164	4/4/83	1.2	C	OUE	12 Mk-82	—
165	4/4/83	1.2	BR	OUE	12 Mk-82	—
166	4/5/83	2.0	C	OUE	A/A plus 2 ACMI pods	—
167	4/5/83	.6	C	Ferry	A/A plus 2 ACMI pods	—
168	4/8/83	.9	BS	S&C	12 Mk-82	—
169	4/6/83	1.7	D	OUE	6 Mk-82	—
170	4/7/83	.6	BS	S&C	12 Mk-82	—
171	4/7/83	1.1	C	OUE	6 Mk-82	—
172	4/8/83	1.3	BR	OUE	12 pylons	—

Flt.	Date	Hrs	Pilot	Mission	Configuration	Notes
173	4/11/83	1.5	D	OUE	12 Pylons	—
174	4/11/83	1.9	D	OUE	12 Mk-82	—
175	4/11/83	.9	D	Ferry	12 Mk-82	—
176	4/13/83	1.1	C	OUE	12 Mk-82	—
177	4/14/83	1.5	D	Impact Survey	12 Mk-82, 2 AMRAAMs	—
178	4/15/83	1.4	BR	OUE	2 BDU-38, 2 370-gal. tanks	—
179	4/18/83	1.4	M	Flutter	12 Mk-82, 2 AMRAAM	—
180	4/18/83	1.6	C	OUE	12 Mk-82, 2 AMRAAM	—
181	4/19/83	.7	M	Flutter	12 Mk-82, 2 AMRAAM	—
182	4/19/83	1.6	D	OUE	12 Mk-82, 2 AMRAAM	—
183	4/21/83	2.2	D	OUE	A/A, 2 AMRAAM	—
184	4/22/83	1.7	BS	Air Data Calibration	A/A, 2 AMRAAM	—
185	4/29/83	1.2	D	Performance	A/A	—
186	5/2/83	1.3	BR	Performance	A/A	—
187	5/2/83	.8	T	Performance	A/A	—
188	5/3/83	.6	C	Performance	12 Mk-82	—
189	5/3/83	1.0	D	Performance	12 Mk-82	—
190	5/4/83	1.2	C	Performance	12 Mk-82	—

Flt.	Date	Hrs	Pilot	Mission	Configuration	Notes
191	5/4/83	1.8	T	Performance	12 Mk-82	—
192	5/5/83	1.0	T	Performance	2 BDU-38, 2 370-gal. tanks	—
193	5/5/83	2.3	C	Performance	2 BDU-38, 2 370-gal. tanks	—
194	5/6/83	1.2	BS	Performance	A/A	—
195	5/6/83	2.1	D	Performance	A/A	—
196	5/9/83	1.3	T	Performance	6 SUU-65, 2 370-gal. tanks	—
197	5/10/83	1.2	BS	Performance	A/A	—
198	5/11/83	1.4	T	OUE	6 SUU-65, 2 370-gal. tanks	—
199	5/12/83	1.4	BR	—	A/A	—
200	5/13/83	1.6	BS	Performance	6 Mk-82	—
201	5/17/83	1.1	M	Performance	6 SUU-65, 2 370-gal. tanks	—
202	6/3/83	.9	BS	Performance	6 SUU-65, 2 370-gal. tanks	—
203	6/3/83	.9	T	Flutter	A/A, 2 370-gal. tanks	—
204	6/7/83	.6	M	Flutter	A/A, 2 370-gal. tanks	—
205	6/14/83	.9	D	FCS	A/A	—
206	6/28/83	1.1	BR	FCS	A/A	—
207	7/7/83	.7	W	FCS	A/A	—
208	7/15/83	1.9	BS	Flutter	6 AGM-65	—

Flt.	Date	Hrs	Pilot	Mission	Configuration	Notes
209	7/19/83	.8	M	Performance	6 SUU-65	—
210	7/20/83	1.5	BS	Performance	6 SUU-65	—
211	7/25/83	2.1	D	Ferry	A/A	—
212	8/15/83	2.0	C	Ferry	A/A	—
213	9/2/83	2.2	BS	Performance	6 Pylons	—
214	9/6/83	2.1	BS	Performance	6 SUU-65	—
215	9/7/83	2.6	T	Performance	6 SUU-65	—
216	9/8/83	2.4	T	Performance	6 SUU-65	—
217	9/14/83	1.5	BS	Performance	6 SUU-65	—
218	9/15/83	2.0	T	Flutter	A/A, 2 600-gal. tanks	—
219	9/16/83	.9	W	Performance	A/A, 2 600-gal. tanks	—
220	9/19/83	1.7	T	Performance	A/A, 2 600-gal. tanks	—
221	9/19/83	.9	T	Flutter	A/A, 2 600-gal. tanks	—
222	9/21/83	.9	BS	Performance	6 SUU-65	—
223	9/22/83	.5	D	FCF	Tandem Pylons	—
224	9/23/83	4.0	D	Extended Cruise	A/A, 2 600-gal. tanks	—
225	9/26/83	.7	BS	Performance	6 SUU-65, 2 370-gal. tanks	—
226	9/27/83	1.0	BS	Performance	6 SUU-65, 2 370-gal. tanks	—

Flt.	Date	Hrs	Pilot	Mission	Configuration	Notes
227	9/28/83	3.8	C	Extended Cruise	A/A, 2 600-gal. tanks	—
228	10/7/83	.8	BS	FCS	A/A	—
229	10/11/83	1.3	T	FCS	A/A	—
230	10/13/83	1.1	F	Loads	A/A, 2 AMRAAMs	—
231	10/18/83	1.2	W	S&C	A/A	—
232	10/20/83	1.3	BS	S&C	A/A	—
233	10/21/83	1.1	BS	FCS	A/A	—
234	10/25/83	1.6	D	FCS	A/A	—
235	10/28/83	1.0	T	FCF	A/A	—
236	10/28/83	.2	D	FCF	A/A	—
237	10/28/83	.2	T	Performance	6 SUU-65, 2 370-gal. tanks	—
238	10/28/83	.3	T	Performance	6 SUU-65, 2 370-gal. tanks	—
239	10/28/83	.4	T	Performance	6 SUU-65, 2 370-gal. tanks	—
240	11/2/83	.5	T	Performance	6 SUU-65, 2 370-gal. tanks	—
241	11/3/83	.5	T	Performance	6 SUU-65, 2 370-gal. tanks	—
242	11/3/83	.8	T	Performance	6 SUU-65, 2 370-gal. tanks	—
243	11/9/83	1.2	T	FCS	A/A	—
244	11/17/83	1.1	T	FCS	A/A	—

Flt.	Date	Hrs	Pilot	Mission	Configuration	Notes
245	11/21/83	1.1	T	FCS	A/A	—
246	12/7/83	1.5	F	FCS	A/A	—
247	12/9/83	1.4	F	Performance	A/A, 2 370-gal. tanks	—
248	12/9/83	3.3	F	Ferry to GDFW	A/A, 2 370-gal. tanks	—
249	12/22/83	2.5	F	Ferry to EAFB	A/A, 2 370-gal. tanks	—
250	1/9/84	1.0	W	Landings	A/A	—
251	1/16/84	1.5	T	FCS	A/A	—
252	1/25/84	1.4	T	Aerial Refueling	6 SUU-65, 2 370-gal tanks	—
253	2/1/84	1.3	P	Pilot Familiarization	A/A, 2 370-gal tanks	—
254	2/13/84	1.3	T	FCS	A/A	—
255	2/15/84	1.3	P	Flutter	A/A, 2 370-gal. tanks	—
256	2/23/83	1.5	T	Performance	A/A, 2 370-gal. tanks	—
257	2/28/63	1.9	F	Proficiency	A/A, 2 370-gal. tanks	—
258	3/7/83	.9	W	Proficiency	A/A	—
259	3/12/83	1.4	W	Handling Qualities	A/A	—
260	3/14/83	.8	T	Handling Qualities	A/A	—
261	3/22/84	1.8	F	Handling Qualities	A/A	—
262	3/27/84	1.1	P	Proficiency	A/A	—

Flt.	Date	Hrs	Pilot	Mission	Configuration	Notes
263	3/28/84	1.3	T	Handling Qualities	A/A	—
264	4/26/84	.9	T	Vibration	A/A	—
265	4/27/84	.8	T	Vibration	A/A	—
266	5/1/84	2.5	W	Ferry to GDFW	A/A, 12 pylons	—
267	5/7/84	2.7	W	Ferry to EAFB	A/A, 12 pylons	—
268	5/7/84	.8	W	Vibration	12 Mk-82	—
269	5/11/84	.6	P	Vibration	12 Mk-82	—
270	6/6/84	1.4	P	FCP	A/A, 12 pylons	—
271	6/7/84	.9	P	Vibration	12 Mk-82	—
272	6/8/84	.9	T	Gun Firing	A/A, 12 pylons	—
273	6/11/84	1.2	W	S&C	A/A	—
274	6/13/84	.9	W	S&C	A/A	—
275	6/15/84	.8	T	S&C	A/A	—
276	6/18/84	1.5	F	ARI	A/A	—
277	6/22/84	.7	F	FCF	A/A	For ECS
278	6/22/84	.8	F	Propulsion	A/A, 6 pylons	—
279	6/29/84	.9	T	FCF	A/A, spin chute straps	For instrumentation
280	7/6/84	1.0	P	S&C	A/A, spin chute straps	—

Flt.	Date	Hrs	Pilot	Mission	Configuration	Notes
281	7/10/84	1.0	F	Locked LEF	A/A, spin chute straps	—
282	7/11/84	.9	T	Locked LEF	A/A, spin chute straps	—
283	7/13/84	.8	T	Locked LEF	A/A, spin chute straps	—
284	7/24/84	1.0	T	Locked LEF	A/A, spin chute straps	—
285	7/25/84	1.0	W	Locked LEF	A/A, spin chute straps	—
286	7/26/84	.9	W	Locked LEF	A/A, spin chute straps	—
287	7/27/84	.6	W	Locked LEF	A/A, spin chute straps	—
288	8/7/84	1.2	T	High AoA	A/A, spin chute	—
289	8/8/84	1.0	W	High AoA	A/A, spin chute	—
290	8/9/84	2.0	W	High AoA	A/A, spin chute	—
291	8/11/84	1.1	T	High AoA	A/A, spin chute	—
292	8/16/84	1.2	F	High AoA	A/A, spin chute	—
293	8/16/84	.8	F	High AoA	A/A, spin chute	—
294	8/17/84	1.3	P	High AoA	A/A, spin chute	—
295	8/20/84	.8	T	High AoA	A/A, spin chute	—
296	8/21/84	1.1	W	High AoA	A/A, spin chute	—
297	8/22/84	.8	F	High AoA	A/A, spin chute	—
298	8/22/84	.7	F	High AoA	A/A, spin chute	—

Flt.	Date	Hrs	Pilot	Mission	Configuration	Notes
299	8/23/84	1.8	W	High AoA	A/A, spin chute	—
300	8/24/84	.9	W	High AoA	A/A, spin chute	—
301	8/24/87	.9	W	High AoA	A/A, spin chute	—
302	8/27/84	2.2	T	High AoA	A/A, spin chute	—
303	8/28/84	2.2	T	High AoA	A/A, spin chute	—
304	8/29/84	1.1	T	High AoA	A/A, spin chute	—
305	8/29/84	.6	T	High AoA	A/A, spin chute	—
306	8/30/84	1.0	W	High AoA	A/A, spin chute	—
307	8/31/84	1.0	T	High AoA	A/A, spin chute	—
308	8/31/84	1.2	T	High AoA	A/A, spin chute	—
309	9/6/84	1.0	W	High AoA	A/A, spin chute	—
310	9/7/84	1.0	T	High AoA	A/A, spin chute	—
311	9/7/84	,6	T	High AoA	A/A, spin chute	—
312	9/10/84	2.4	W	High AoA	A/A, spin chute	—
313	9/12/84	2.1	T	High AoA	A/A, spin chute	—
314	9/14/84	.7	W	High AoA	A/A, spin chute	—
315	9/17/84	1.3	W	High AoA	A/A, spin chute	Changed ECA
316	9/18/84	2.5	W	High AoA	A/A, spin chute	—

Flt.	Date	Hrs	Pilot	Mission	Configuration	Notes
317	9/19/84	1.0	T	High AoA	A/A, spin chute	—
318	9/20/84	2.3	W	High AoA	A/A, spin chute	—
319	9/21/84	1.4	T	High AoA	A/A, spin chute	Added Ballast
320	9/24/84	1.7	W	High AoA	A/A, spin chute	Remv. Ballast Chute
321	9/25/84	1.0	T	High AoA	A/A, spin chute	—
322	9/26/84	2.7	W	High AoA	A/A, spin chute	—
323	10/2/84	2.3	T	High AoA	A/A, spin chute	—
324	10/3/84	1.5	F	High AoA	A/A, spin chute	ECA #3
325	10/4/84	1.0	F	High AoA	A/A, spin chute	—
326	10/11/84	1.0	T	Locked LEF	A/A, spin chute straps	—
327	10/16/84	1.0	P	Locked LEF	A/A, spin chute straps	—
328	10/18/84	.8	T	Locked LEF	A/A, spin chute straps	—
329	10/23/84	.9	T	FCS	A/A	FCC #3, ECA #2
330	10/30/84	.7	W	Locked LEF	A/A	ECA #4
331	11/1/84	.7	W	Locked LEF	A/A	—
332	11/27/84	1.1	P	Locked LEF	A/A	—
333	11/29/84	.7	T	Locked LEF	A/A	—
334	12/7/84	.8	P	VIP Practice	A/A	FCC #4, ECA #2

Flt.	Date	Hrs	Pilot	Mission	Configuration	Notes
335	12/11/84	.8	T	S&C	A/A	—
336	12/14/84	.9	P	Locked LEF	A/A	—
337	12/17/84	1.0	T	Locked LEF	A/A, spin chute	ECA #4
338	1/3/85	.9	P	Locked LEF	A/A	—
339	1/4/85	.7	F	Locked LEF	A/A	—
340	1/15/85	1.5	F	Locked LEF	A/A	—
341	1/30/85	1.1	T	R&M	A/A	—
342	1/31/85	1.4	P	R&M	A/A	ECA #2
343	2/4/85	1.9	P	R&M	A/A	—
344	2/5/85	1.0	T	R&M	A/A	—
345	2/4/85	1.9	P	S&C	6 AGM-65	—
346	2/5/85	1.0	T	S&C	6 AGM-65	—
347	2/6/85	1.1	F	S&C	6 AGM-65	—
348	2/7/85	1.4	F	R&M	A/A	—
349	2/11/85	1.1	T	R&M	A/A	—
350	2/14/85	.6	P	Gun Firing	A/A	510 20mm rounds
351	2/15/85	1.1	T	R&M	A/A	—
352	2/21/85	.8	F	Env. Vibration	A/A	—

Flt.	Date	Hrs	Pilot	Mission	Configuration	Notes
353	2/25/85	1.0	T	S&C	A/A	—
354	2/25/85	.8	P	S&C	A/A	—
355	2/26/85	.9	T	S&C	A/A	—
356	2/26/85	.9	P	S&C	A/A	—
357	2/27/85	.9	T	S&C	A/A	—
358	2/27/85	1.3	P	S&C	A/A	—
359	3/1/85	.6	T	Flutter	2 Mk-84, 2 370-gal. tanks	—
360	3/5/85	1.4	T	In-Flight Excitation	A/A	FCC #2, ECA #3
361	3/7/85	1.1	F	In-Flight Excitation	A/A	—
362	3/8/85	1.0	P	In-Flight Excitation	A/A	—
363	3/8/85	1.1	F	In-Flight Excitation	A/A	—
364	3/11/85	2.4	P	In-Flight Excitation	A/A	—
365	3/11/85	1.5	T	In-Flight Excitation	A/A	—
366	3/12/85	1.4	F	In-Flight Excitation	A/A	—
367	3/12/85	1.7	P	In-Flight Excitation	A/A	—
368	3/14/85	1.3	F	In-Flight Excitation	A/A	—
369	3/15/85	1.2	P	Gunfire Vibration	A/A	—
370	3/19/85	1.6	T	In-Flight Excitation	A/A	—

Elegance in Flight

Flt.	Date	Hrs	Pilot	Mission	Configuration	Notes
371	3/20/85	1.0	P	In-Flight Excitation	A/A	—
372	3/20/85	1.1	T	In-Flight Excitation	A/A	—
373	3/22/85	1.1	P	SFO Practice	A/A, 6 pylons	—
374	3/26/85	1.0	P	AGM-65 Rehearsal	6 AGM-65	—
375	3/29/85	.7	P	AGM-65 Launch	6 AGM-65	1 AGM-65 Fired
376	4/4/85	1.2	P	In-Flight Excitation	A/A	—
377	4/5/85	.9	T	G-Overshoot	A/A	—
378	4/8/85	.8	F	Performance	A/A	—
379	4/9/85	1.1	T	Performance	A/A	—
380	4/10/85	.8	T	In-Flight Excitation	A/A	—
381	4/11/85	1.5	F	In-Flight Excitation	A/A	—
382	4/11/85	.8	F	In-Flight Excitation	A/A	—
383	4/12/85	1.7	T	S/B Loads	A/A, 2 aft AMRAAMs	—
384	4/15/85	.7	F	In-Flight Excitation	A/A	—
385	4/17/85	1.0	F	S/B Loads	A/A, 2 AMRAAMs	—
386	4/17/85	1.2	D	S/B Loads	A/A, 2 AMRAAMs	—
387	4/18/85	.6	F	S/B Loads	A/A, 2 AMRAAMs	—
388	4/18/85	1.4	D	Performance	A/A	—

Flt.	Date	Hrs	Pilot	Mission	Configuration	Notes
389	4/22/85	1.0	T	In-Flight Excitation	A/A	—
390	4/22/85	.7	P	In-Flight Excitation	A/A	—
391	4/24/85	.8	T	In-Flight Excitation	A/A	—
392	4/24/85	.9	P	In-Flight Excitation	A/A	—
393	4/26/85	1.1	T	In-Flight Excitation	A/A	—
394	4/26/85	.8	T	In-Flight Excitation	A/A	—
395	5/8/85	1.0	T	In-Flight Excitation	A/A	—
396	5/8/85	.9	D	In-Flight Excitation	A/A	—
397	5/13/85	.9	P	In-Flight Excitation	A/A	—
398	5/15/85	.7	P	In-Flight Excitation	A/A	—
399	5/16/85	1.2	P	In-Flight Excitation	A/A	—
400	5/21/85	.9	T	In-Flight Excitation	A/A	—
401	5/22/85	1.1	F	In-Flight Excitation	A/A	—
402	5/23/85	1.4	P	In-Flight Excitation	A/A	—
403	5/28/85	1.5	P	Demo Practice	A/A	—
404	5/29/85	1.2	T	Proficiency	A/A	—
405	5/30/85	.9	P	In-Flight Excitation	A/A	—
406	5/30/85	.8	T	R&M Excitation	A/A	—

Flt.	Date	Hrs	Pilot	Mission	Configuration	Notes
407	5/31/85	1.3	T	In-Flight Excitation	A/A	—
408	6/11/85	1.7	F	Proficiency	A/A	—
409	6/12/85	1.3	F	Proficiency	A/A	—
410	6/13/85	1.0	T	In-Flight Excitation	A/A	—
411	6/14/85	.8	P	In-Flight Excitation	A/A, 2 370-gal. tanks	—
412	6/17/85	1.0	T	Performance	6 Mk-82, 2 370-gal. tanks	—
413	6/18/85	1.3	P	Target	A/A, 6 pylons	—
414	6/19/85	1.1	T	Proficiency	A/A, 6 pylons	—
415	6/19/85	1.4	P	Proficiency	A/A, 6 pylons	—
416	6/20/85	1.2	P	Performance	A/A, 6 pylons	—
417	6/24/85	1.3	F	Proficiency	A/A, 6 pylons	—
418	6/28/85	1.0	T	Performance	A/A, 6 pylons, 2 370-gal. tanks	—
419	7/1/85	1.4	T	Performance	A/A, 6 pylons, 2 370-gal. tanks	—
420	7/2/85	1.9	D	Target	A/A, 6 pylons.	—
421	7/3/85	.8	F	Performance	A/A, 6 pylons, 2 370-gal. tanks	—
422	7/3/85	1.2	CG	TR-1	A/A, 6 pylons	—
423	7/9/85	1.4	D	In-Flight Excitation	A/A	—
424	7/11/85	3.0	CG	TR-2	A/A	—

Flt.	Date	Hrs	Pilot	Mission	Configuration	Notes
425	7/16/85	1.5	CG	Proficiency	A/A	—
426	7/17/85	1.1	P	In-Flight Excitation	A/A	—
427	7/18/85	.8	D	Chase	A/A	—
428	7/18/85	1.0	CG	G-Overshoot	A/A	
429	7/18/85	.8	D	Chase	A/A	
430	7/23/85	.7	CG	G-Overshoot	A/A	
431	7/25/85	1.3	P	Proficiency	A/A	
432	7/30/85	1.3	CG	G-Overshoot	A/A	
433	7/30/85	.6	F	G-Overshoot	A/A	
434	7/30/85	1.8	P	Target	A/A	
435	8/1/85	1.4	CG	In-Flight Excitation	A/A	
436	8/13/85	1.0	CG	FCF	A/A	FCC #4, ECA #2
437	8/14/85	2.5	D	Ferry to GDFW	A/A	

Appendix E-2: F-16XL-2 FLIGHT LOG						
F-16XL-2 Pilots						

BR	Burnett	D	Dryden	N	Newman	T	Thomas
BS	Bushnell	F	Fergione	O	Oestricher	W	Wolfe
C	Cary	K	Knight	P	Payne		
CG	Caughlin	M	McKinney	S	Svendsen		

Test Observers/Aircraft Familiarization/VIPs

AL	Aldrich	AN	Anderson	BA	Barter	BE	Berry
BK	Beckel	BO	Bond	BU	Buck	BY	Byron
CA	Cathey	CH	Chain	CR	Craig	DA	Dana
DR	Darner	DU	Dunn	DW	Dwyer	ET	Ettinger
FI	Fischer	GA	Garland	GE	Gentry	GL	Gilcrist
GO	Goodall	GT	Gorton	GU	Gutierrez	HA	Hall
HF	Haeffner	HG	Hoag	HM	Hoffman	HO	Horton
HP	Heimple	HT	Hartinger	HU	Huete	HY	Hayashi
JO	Johnson	JY	Joyce	KE	Kerby	KI	Kirk
LA	Lapidot	LR	Larson	LU	Leuthauser	MA	Manley
MD	Meade	ME	Meschko	MH	Mathes	MI	McInerney
ML	McMullen	MM	McMonagle	MO	Monahan	MU	Mauley
OD	Odgers	OL	Oliver	PA	Palmer	PH	Phillips
RB	Robinson	RE	Reed	RO	Ropelewski	RU	Russ
RY	Rhynard	SC	Schofield	SK	Skantze	SM	Smith
SP	Sprague	ST	Stott	SW	Swalm	TA	Talty
TH	Thayer	TI	Tierney	WE	Welch	YT	Yates

Flt.	Date	Hrs	Pilot	Mission	Configuration	Notes
1	10/29/82	1.0	W/M	FCF	A/A	—
2	11/1/82	1.3	M/W	S&C	A/A	—
3	11/1/82	1.1	W/D	Performance	A/A	—
4	11/8/82	1.4	O/W	Pilot Familiarization	A/A	—
5	11/8/82	2.5	D/W	Ferry to EAFB	A/A	—
6	11/16/82	1.0	BS/D	Loads/ Propulsion	A/A	—

Flt.	Date	Hrs	Pilot	Mission	Configuration	Notes
7	11/17/82	.8	M/C	Loads/ Propulsion	A/A	Abort auto transfer to alternative
8	11/17/82	.8	T/D	Loads	A/A	—
9	11/18/82	.7	T/BR	Performance	A/A	—
10	11/18/82	1.0	BS/C	Performance	A/A	—
11	11/19/82	1.3	T/C	Loads	A/A	—
12	11/22/82	1.2	T/D	Loads	A/A	—
13	11/23/82	1.1	M/D	Loads	A/A	—
14	11/23/82	1.0	C/D	Performance	A/A	—
15	11/24/82	.9	T/C	Performance	A/A	—
16	11/24/82	.9	BS/T	Performance	A/A	—
17	12/1/82	1.0	BS/D	FCF	A/A	New aft control
18	12/1/82	1.0	W/BR	Propulsion	A/A	—
19	12/1/82	1.7	T/C	Air Data Calibration	A/A	—

Flt.	Date	Hrs	Pilot	Mission	Configuration	Notes
20	12/2/82	1.3	BS/W	Performance	A/A	—
21	12/3/82	1.3	W/C	Loads	A/A	—
22	12/03/82	1.7	C/N	OCU	A/A	—
23	12/6/82	1.2	D/C	Air Data Calibration	A/A	—
24	12/6/82	1.0	W/D	S&C	A/A	—
25	12/7/82	1.0	W/C	Flutter	A/A; no tip missiles	—
26	12/7/82	1.3	W/D	Performance	A/A; no tip missiles	—
27	12/7/82	1.1	BR/T	Performance	Clean aircraft	—
28	1/6/83	.4	W/D	FCS and S&C	A/A	48K landing gear
29	1/7/83	.8	W/T	Performance	A/A	—
30	1/7/83	.7	BS/D	—	A/A	—
31	1/10/83	1.3	T/BR	S&C	A/A	—
32	1/10/83	1.3	W/D	Gun Firing	A/A	—

Flt.	Date	Hrs	Pilot	Mission	Configuration	Notes
33	1/12/83	4.0	BS/D	—	A/A	—
34	1/13/83	.7	W/C	S&C	A/A	—
35	1/13/83	2.1	D/BR	Performance	A/A	—
36	1/14/83	1.2	W/BS	Loads	A/A	—
37	1/14/83	3.7	BS/D	—	A/A	—
38	1/17/93	.9	D/BS	Loads	A/A	—
39	1/17/83	.9	T/D	Performance	A/A	—
40	1/18/83	1.1	T/D	Loads	A/A	—
41	1/18/83	.8	BS/ OD	Demo	A/A	—
42	1/20/83	.8	BS/ SK	Demo	A/A	—
43	1/20/83	.4	M/D	Hinge Moments	A/A	—
44	1/21/83	1.7	BS/S	Hinge Moments	A/A	—
45	1/24/83	.3	BS/ BR	Weapon Separation	12 Mk-82	Short "pickle" button

Flt.	Date	Hrs	Pilot	Mission	Configuration	Notes
46	1/25/83	.4	BS/C	Weapon Separation	12 Mk-82	—
47	1/26/83	.3	M/BR	Weapon Separation	6 CBU-58, 2 370-gal. tanks	—
48	1/27/83	.5	BR/N	Performance	12 Mk-82	—
49	1/27/83	.5	BR/N	Performance	12 Mk-82	—
50	2/2/83	.8	BS/D	S&C	12 Mk-82	—
51	2/4/83	.8	W/C	S&C	A/A	—
52	2/4/83	3.3	BS/N	—	12 Mk-82	—
53	2/7/83	.8	T/BR	Loads/S&C	A/A	—
54	2/7/83	.9	T/C	Loads/S&C	A/A	—
55	2/8/83	1.4	T/C	Loads/S&C	12 Mk-82	—
56	2/8/83	3.1	D/BS	—	12 Mk-82	—
57	2/9/83	.5	T/D	Loads/S&C	A/A	—
58	2/11/83	.6	T/BR	Loads/S&C	A/A	—
59	2/14/83	.7	T/S	Loads/S&C	A/A	—
60	2/14/83	.9	T/S	Loads/S&C	A/A	—
61	2/15/83	1.1	BR/N	Ferry	A/A; no tip missiles	—
62	2/15/83	1.0	BR/N	ACMI Check	A/A; ACMI pods	—
63	2/15/83	1.1	BR/N	Ferry to EAFB	A/A; no tip missiles	—

Flt.	Date	Hrs	Pilot	Mission	Configuration	Notes
64	2/16/83	1.1	M/S	S&C/ Propulsion	A/A	High AoA FCS
65	2/17/83	.9	T/AL	Loads	A/A	—
66	2/17/83	.8	W/GA	Loads	A/A	—
67	2/17/83	2.2	C/D	Ferry to GDFW	A/A	—
68	2/22/83	2.5	M/–	Ferry to EAFB	A/A	New paint scheme
69	2/22/83	.9	T/BR	S&C/Loads	A/A	—
70	2/23/83	.9	T/N	Loads	A/A	48K wheels
71	2/23/83	.7	D/BR	Pilot Proficiency	A/A	—
72	2/24/83	.7	C/BR	Pilot Proficiency	A/A	—
73	2/24/83	.8	BR/C	Pilot Proficiency	A/A	—
74	2/25/83	.4	T/HA	Loads	12 Mk-82	—
75	2/25/83	.5	T/N	Loads	12 Mk-82	—
76	2/28/83	1.1	T/S	S&C	12 Mk-82	—
77	2/28/83	1.0	M/BR	High AoA	A/A	—
78	3/3/83	.8	T/ME	Loads	A/A	—
79	3/3/83	1.2	C/N	OUE	4 AMRAAM, 2 ACMI	—

Flt.	Date	Hrs	Pilot	Mission	Configuration	Notes
80	3/4/83	1.2	AN/M	Demo	4 AMRAAM, 2 ACMI	—
81	3/4/83	.8	C/-	Ferry	4 AMRAAM, 2 ACMI	—
82	3/4/83	.7	C/BR	Ferry to EAFB	4 AMRAAM, 2 ACMI	—
83	3/7/83	1.1	C/N	OUE	4 AMRAAM, 2 ACMI	—
84	3/7/83	1.1	BS/T	Performance	A/A	—
85	3/9/83	.4	T/D	Weapons Separation	12 Mk-82	—
86	3/9/83	.6	BS/N	Weapons Separation	2 Mk-82, 12 pylons	—
87	3/10/83	.7	T/N	Weapons Separation	6 Mk-82, 12 pylons	—
88	3/10/83	.8	BS/N	Weapons Separation	2 Mk-82, 12 pylons	—
89	3/11/83	.7	BS/N	Weapons Separation	6 Mk-82, 12 pylons	—
90	3/11/83	.6	BS/BR	Weapons Separation	2 Mk-82, 12 pylons	—
91	3/11/83	.6	BS/N	Weapons Separation	2 Mk-82, 12 pylons	—
92	3/14/83	.5	BS/T	Flutter	2 BDU-38, 2 370-gal. tanks	—

Flt.	Date	Hrs	Pilot	Mission	Configuration	Notes
93	3/15/83	.8	BS/S	Flutter	2 BDU-38, 2 370-gal. tanks	—
94	3/15/83	1.5	T/DU	Flutter	2 BDU-38, 2 370-gal. tanks	—
95	3/16/83	.7	BS/DU	S&C	2 BDU-38, 2 370-gal. tanks	—
96	3/16/83	.8	T/RY	S&C	2 BDU-38, 2 370-gal. tanks	—
97	3/17/83	.7	D/MD	Performance	2 BDU-38, 2 370-gal. tanks	—
98	3/17/83	1.9	C/BR	OUE	4 AMRAAM, 2 ACMI	—
99	3/17/83	.5	C/BR	Ferry	4 AMRAAM, 2 ACMI	—
100	3/17/83	2.5	T/D	KC-10 Refueling	4 AMRAAM, 2 ACMI	—
101	3/18/83	.6	M/S	Loads	2 BDU-38, 2 370-gal. tanks	—
102	3/18/83	2.2	T/HY	KC-10 Refueling	2 BDU-38, 2 370-gal. tanks	—
103	3/18/83	1.0	M/GU	Performance	2 BDU-38, 2 370 gal. tanks	—
104	3/21/83	1.9	D/N	OUE	4 AMRAAM, 2 ACMI	—
105	3/21/83	.7	BS/HO	Turn Study	12 Mk-82	—

Flt.	Date	Hrs	Pilot	Mission	Configuration	Notes
106	3/21/83	.8	BR/C	OUE	12 Mk-82	—
107	3/22/83	.8	T/HU	Performance	12 Mk-82	—
108	3/22/83	.7	C/N	OUE	12 Mk-82	—
109	3/23/83	.6	D/S	OUE	12 Mk-82	—
110	3/23/83	.8	BR/C	OUE	12 Mk-82	—
111	3/24/83	1.1	BR/D	OUE	12 Mk-82	—
112	3/24/83	.7	BS/BA	Performance	12 Mk-82	—
113	3/24/83	.7	D/N	OUE	12 Mk-82	—
114	3/25/83	.9	BR/N	OUE	12 Mk-82	—
115	3/25/83	1.9	BS/HO	Performance	12 Mk-82	—
116	3/25/83	1.0	C/BR	OUE	12 Mk-82	—
117	3/28/83	1.2	T/GU	Performance	A/A	—
118	3/29/83	.9	M/T	Performance	A/A	—
119	3/29/83	1.9	D/N	OUE	A/A	—
120	3/29/83	1.0	D/N	Ferry	A/A	—
121	3/31/83	.9	D/M	OUE	12 Mk-82	—
122	3/31/83	.9	T/BS	VIP Practice	12 Mk-82	—

Flt.	Date	Hrs	Pilot	Mission	Configuration	Notes
123	4/1/83	.7	M/HU	Propulsion	A/A	—
124	4/1/83	.7	BS/S	Performance	A/A	—
125	4/4/83	1.1	D/N	OUE	4 AMRAAM, 2 ACMI	—
126	4/4/83	1.1	D/N	Ferry	4 AMRAAM, 2 ACMI	—
127	4/4/83	.7	C/S	Performance	A/A	—
128	4/5/83	.7	T/LU	Performance	A/A	—
129	4/6/83	.6	D/DU	Performance	2 BDU-38, 2 370-gal. tanks	—
130	4/6/83	1.9	C/S	Performance	2 BDU-38, 2 370-gal. tanks	—
131	4/7/83	.6	D/S	Performance	2 BDU-38, 2 370-gal. tanks	—
132	4/7/83	1.1	T/F	Performance	A/A, 2 370-gal. tanks	—
133	4/8/83	1.3	BS/G	Performance	A/A	—
134	4/11/83	2.0	BR/C	OUE	A/A	—
135	4/11/83	1.2	BR/C	Ferry	A/A	—
136	4/12/83	.7	BO/BS	Demo	12 Mk-82	—
137	4/13/83	.7	D/N	Performance	12 Mk-82	—
138	4/13/83	1.1	BR/C	OUE	A/A	—

Flt.	Date	Hrs	Pilot	Mission	Configuration	Notes
139	4/14/83	.6	M/S	S&C	A/A	—
140	4/15/83	1.2	T/N	Performance	A/A	—
141	4/15/83	1.4	C/N	OUE	A/A	—
142	4/18/82	1.6	BR/D	OUE	A/A	—
143	4/19/83	.8	BS/D	Propulsion	A/A	—
144	4/19/83	1.6	C/BS	OUE	A/A	—
145	4/20/83	.7	BS/D	Gun Firing	A/A	—
146	4/21/83	.8	BS/N	Performance	6 SUU-65, 2 370-gal. tanks	—
147	4/21/83	.9	T/S	Performance	6 SUU-65, 2 370-gal. tanks	—
148	4/22/83	2.0	T/D	Performance	6 SUU-65, 2 370-gal. tanks	—
149	4/22/83	.9	C/BR	OUE	6 SUU-65, 2 370-gal. tanks	—
150	4/25/83	2.1	T/D	Performance	12 Mk-82	—
151	4/26/83	1.2	BS/ HM	OUE	A/A	—
152	4/27/83	1.0	T/S	Performance	12 Mk-82	—
153	4/27/83	1.7	C/D	Performance	12 pylons	—
154	4/28/83	1.1	D/W	Performance	6 Mk-82	—

Flt.	Date	Hrs	Pilot	Mission	Configuration	Notes
155	4/28/83	1.3	BS/ SC	Performance	6 Mk-82	—
156	4/29/83	.9	T/S	Loads	6 SUU-65, 2 370-gal. tanks	—
157	4/29/83	.8	T/-	S&C	6 SUU-65, 2 370-gal. tanks	—
158	5/2/83	1.1	T/W	S&C/ Performance	6 SUU-65, 2 370-gal. tanks	—
159	5/2/83	1.2	BS/N	Performance	6 SUU-65, 2 370-gal. tanks	—
160	5/3/83	.7	BS/N	Loads	2 BDU-38, 2 370-gal. tanks	—
161	5/3/83	.7	T/HG	Loads	2 BDU-38, 2 370-gal. tanks	—
162	5/4/83	.7	BS/S	Gun Comp.	A/A	—
163	5/4/83	1.0	BS/D	Gun Firing	A/A	—
164	5/5/83	.7	BS/D	Gun Firing	A/A	—
165	5/5/83	.7	BS/D	Performance	A/A	—
166	5/6/83	.7	T/S	Loads	12 Mk-82	—
167	5/6/83	1.2	BR/ OL	Ride Quality Evaluation	12 Mk-82	—
168	5/10/83	1.0	C/BR	FCF	A/A	—
169	5/11/83	2.3	C/D	OUE	A/A	—
170	5/16/83	.7	BS/ BU	Demo	12 Mk-82	—

Flt.	Date	Hrs	Pilot	Mission	Configuration	Notes
171	5/16/83	.9	D/KE	Demo	12 Mk-82	
172	5/19/83	1.0	T/MO	Demo	12 Mk-82	—
173	5/26/83	.5	BS/W	H-S Envelope Expansion	A/A	—
174	6/3/83	.6	BS/HP	H-S Envelope Expansion	A/A	—
175	6/7/83	.5	T/D	H-S Envelope Expansion	A/A	—
176	6/8/83	.6	T/CR	Demo	A/A	—
177	6/9/83	1.0	RE/D	Demo	A/A	—
178	6/9/83	.7	M/BR	H-S Envelope Expansion	A/A	—
179	6/10/83	.6	BS/C	H-S Envelope Expansion	A/A	—
180	6/10/83	.5	T/GA	H-S Envelope Expansion	A/A	—
181	6/10/83	.5	BS/N	H-S Envelope Expansion	A/A	—
182	6/13/83	1.4	T/S	H-S Envelope Expansion	A/A	—
183	6/17/83	.7	BS/HT	Demo	A/A	FCC #1
184	6/21/83	.5	BS/S	H-S Envelope Expansion	A/A	—
185	6/23/83	.7	BS/YT	Demo	12 Mk-82	—
186	6/27/83	1.0	T/SM	S&C	A/A	—
187	6/29/83	1.3	BR/PH	Demo	12 Mk-82	—
188	7/7/83	.8	T/S	Flutter	2 Mk-84	—

Flt.	Date	Hrs	Pilot	Mission	Configuration	Notes
189	7/8/83	.5	W/T	Flutter	2 Mk-84	—
190	7/12/83	.7	W/D	Flutter	4 Mk-84	—
191	7/13/84	1.9	T/S	Performance	4 Mk-84	—
192	7/14/83	.7	W/GU	Flutter	12 Mk-82, 2 370-gal. tanks	—
193	7/14/83	1.8	T/SP	Performance	12 Mk-82, 2 370-gal. tanks	—
194	7/21/83	1.0	M/BS	Engine FCF	A/A	Installed engine 7
195	7/22/83	3.9	D/N	—	A/A	—
196	7/25/83	1.0	T/S	Engine FCF	A/A	Installed engine 6
197	7/26/83	.9	GO/T	Demo	12 Mk-82	—
198	7/27/83	.9	T/S	Photo Flight	12 Mk-82	—
199	7/28/83	2.7	T/PA	Photo Flight	12 Mk-82	—
200	8/1/83	1.6	BS/W	Hinge Moments	A/A	9.4° LEF, FTR 57
201	8/2/83	2.0	W/M	Hinge Moments	A/A	0° LEF, FTR 24
202	8/10/83	1.2	T/N	Hinge Moments	A/A	9.4° LEF, FTR 57
203	8/12/83	1.1	DA/D	Demo	A/A	—
204	8/17/83	.9	BS/TH	Demo	12 Mk-82	—
205	8/23/83	.9	T/CH	Demo	12 Mk-82	—

Flt.	Date	Hrs	Pilot	Mission	Configuration	Notes
206	8/26/83	.9	SW/B	Demo	12 Mk-82	—
207	8/31/83	.9	B/S	Engine FCF	12 pylons	Installed engine 7
208	8/31/83	.9	M/BE	Demo	12 Mk-82	—
209	9/2/83	1.0	M/RO	Demo	12 Mk-82	—
210	9/6/83	1.0	W/SC	Performance	A/A, 1 300-gal. tank	—
211	9/7/83	1.1	D/MM	Performance	A/A, 1 300-gal. tank	—
212	9/8/83	.7	BR/C	Performance	6 SUU-65, 1 300 gal. tank	—
213	9/9/83	.9	C/BR	Performance	6 SUU-65, 1 300-gal. tank	—
214	9/9/83	1.0	C/BR	Performance	6 SUU-65, 1 300-gal. tank	—
215	9/14/83	.9	W/S	Flutter	4 Mk-84	—
216	9/14/83	.8	W/S	Flutter	4 Mk-84	—
217	9/15/83	1.0	W/N	S&C	4 Mk-84	—
218	9/15/83	.8	W/N	S&C	4 Mk-84	—
219	9/16/83	1.7	BS/ MA	Flutter	4 Mk-84	—
220	9/16/83	.8	C/D	Flutter	4 Mk-84	—
221	9/19/83	.7	BS/KI	Demo	12 Mk-82	—
222	9/22/83	.9	T/CA	Demo	12 Mk-82	—

Flt.	Date	Hrs	Pilot	Mission	Configuration	Notes
223	9/23/83	.9	BR/N	OUE	4 Mk-84	—
224	10/3/83	1.3	F/T	Pilot Checkout	12 pylons	—
225	10/4/83	.9	T/ML	Demo	12 Mk-82	—
226	10/4/83	.9	F/BS	Pilot Checkout	12 Mk-82	—
227	10/12/83	.8	BS/D	Loads	A/A	—
228	10/14/83	1.2	F/BR	S&C	4 Mk-84	—
229	10/17/83	.9	T/LR	Demo	12 Mk-82	—
230	11/2/83	1.0	F/BR	Engine FCF	A/A	Installed engine 6
231	11/4/83	.6	T/MI	Demo	12 Mk-82	—
232	12/1/83	1.2	T/P	Engine FCF	12 pylons	Installed engine 7
233	12/5/83	1.3	BS/T	Demo Practice	12 Mk-82	—
234	12/6/83	1.3	F/T	Demo Practice	12 Mk-82	—
235	12/6/83	1.4	T/MU	Demo Practice	12 Mk-82	—
236	12/8/83	.8	LA/T	Demo	12 Mk-82	—
237	12/8/83	.6	LA/T	Demo	12 pylons	—
238	12/14/83	1.5	BS/DW	HMD Evaluation	A/A, FLIR pod	—
239	12/15/83	.9	T/HF	Demo	12 Mk-82	—
240	12/16/83	.5	BS/DW	HMD Evaluation	A/A, FLIR pod	—

Flt.	Date	Hrs	Pilot	Mission	Configuration	Notes
241	12/16/83	1.5	BS/ DW	HMD Evaluation	A/A, FLIR pod	—
242	1/3/84	1.4	P/T	Pilot Checkout	12 pylons	—
243	1/4/84	.8	P/BR	Pilot Checkout	12 Mk-82	—
244	1/12/83	.2	T/BY	Demo	12 Mk-82	Engine surging
245	1/18/84	.6	P/T	Engine FCF	12 pylons	—
246	1/27/84	.5	F/T	Weapon Separation	12 Mk-82	8 separated
247	1/31/84	.5	T/F	Weapon Separation	12 Mk-82	8 separated
248	2/2/84	.5	F/T	Weapon Separation	2 Mk-84	2 separated
249	2/21/84	.5	P/T	Weapon Separation	2 Mk-84	2 separated
250	2/28/84	.5	P/F	Weapon Separation	2 Mk-84	2 separated
251	3/5/84	.6	T/P	Weapon Separation	2 Mk-84	2 separated
252	3/16/84	.8	F/P	Proficiency	2 pylons	—
253	3/19/84	1.1	GT/T	Demo	12 Mk-82	—
254	3/21/84	.9	T/GL	Demo	12 Mk-82	
255	3/27/84	.9	T/AD	Demo	12 Mk-82	
256	4/5/84	.6	F/P	Weapon Separation	2 Mk-84	2 separated
257	4/12/83	.5	P/F	Weapon Separation	2 Mk-84	2 separated

Flt.	Date	Hrs	Pilot	Mission	Configuration	Notes
258	4/16/84	1.1	ET/T	Demo	12 Mk-82	—
259	4/17/84	.7	P/T	S&C	12 pylons	—
260	4/18/84	.9	P/T	S&C	12 pylons	—
261	4/19/84	1.0	WE/T	Demo	2 Mk-84	—
262	4/25/84	.5	T/C	Propulsion	2 Mk-84	—
263	4/26/84	.9	T/FI	Demo	2 Mk-84	—
264	5/1/84	.7	P/MH	Engine FCF	A/A	Changed aft control
265	5/9/84	1.0	F/P	Weapon Separation	4 Mk-84	—
266	5/17/84	.9	T/F	Weapon Separation	4 Mk-84	—
267	5/18/84	1.3	F/P	R&M	A/A, 12 pylons	—
268	5/21/84	.8	T/BK	Demo	12 Mk-82	—
269	5/29/84	1.1	P/ST	R&M	12 pylons	—
270	5/31/84	.9	T/RU	Demo	12 Mk-82	—
271	5/31/84	.9	T/GE	Demo	A/A	—
272	6/4/84	2.4	W/P	Ferry to GDFW	A/A, no tip missiles	—
273	7/18/84	.8	F/W	Engine FCF	A/A	Installed F110 Slimline
274	7/19/84	1.0	W/T	Engine FCF	A/A	—
275	7/20/84	2.2	T/W	Ferry to EAFB	A/A, no tip missiles	—

Flt.	Date	Hrs	Pilot	Mission	Configuration	Notes
276	7/30/84	1.5	T/P	Propulsion	A/A	—
277	8/7/84	1.2	F/P	Propulsion	A/A	—
278	8/8/84	1.7	P/T	Propulsion	A/A	—
279	8/9/84	1.4	T/P	Propulsion	A/A	—
280	8/10/84	1.0	P/F	Propulsion	A/A	—
281	8/13/84	2.8	F/P	Propulsion	A/A	—
282	8/17/84	.5	F/T	Propulsion	A/A	Abort, lakebed landing
283	8/20/84	1.2	T/F	Propulsion	A/A	—
284	8/21/84	2.0	F/P	Propulsion	A/A	Abort, low P/P
285	10/9/84	1.4	F/T	Engine FCF	A/A	Flex-Line PS14 Man.
286	10/10/84	2.1	T/F	Propulsion	A/A	—
287	10/22/84	1.5	P/T	Performance	A/A	—
288	10/23/84	1.3	P/W	Performance	A/A	—
289	10/24/84	1.0	T/W	Propulsion	A/A	—
290	10/25/84	.7	W/P	Propulsion	A/A	—
291	10/29/84	1.1	P/W	Propulsion	A/A	New aft control.
292	10/30/84	1.2	W/P	Propulsion	A/A	—
293	10/31/84	.8	W/P	Propulsion	A/A	—
294	10/31/84	.8	W/P	Performance	A/A	—

Flt.	Date	Hrs	Pilot	Mission	Configuration	Notes
295	11/1/84	2.6	P/W	Propulsion	A/A	—
296	11/2/84	1.7	P/F	Performance	A/A	—
297	11/2/84	2.3	F/T	Propulsion	A/A	—
298	11/6/84	1.5	T/P	Propulsion	A/A	—
299	11/7/84	.7	P/F	Propulsion	A/A	No A/B light
300	11/8/84	.5	F/T	Propulsion	A/A	New A/B igniter
301	11/9/84	2.1	T/P	Propulsion	A/A	—
302	11/13/84	2.1	T/P	Propulsion	A/A	—
303	11/15/84	2.0	W/T	Propulsion	A/A	—
304	11/16/84	2.3	T/W	Propulsion	A/A	—
305	11/19/84	1.7	P/F	Propulsion	A/A	—
306	11/20/84	1.9	F/P	Propulsion	A/A	A/B nozzle damage
307	1/11/85	.8	T/F	FCF, Spray Bar Evaluation	A/A	—
308	1/23/85	.7	P/T	Spray Bar Evaluation	A/A	—
309	1/25/85	.9	F/T	Propulsion	A/A	—
310	1/28/85	2.0	F/–	Ferry to GDFW	A/A	—
311	6/26/85	1.1	D/P	FCF	A/A	LNSI, spray bar, mixer
312	6/28/85	1.3	P/D	FCF	A/A	—

Flt.	Date	Hrs	Pilot	Mission	Configuration	Notes
313	6/28/85	2.3	P/D	Ferry to EAFB	A/A	—
314	7/10/85	1.4	F/D	Spray Bar Evaluation	A/A	—
315	7/12/85	1.5	D/F	S&C, Performance	A/A	—
316	7/15/85	.6	D/P	S&C, Performance	A/A	—
317	7/16/85	.9	D/ME	S&C, Performance	A/A	—
318	7/17/85	.7	P/CG	S&C, Performance	A/A	—
319	7/18/85	1.0	P/CG	S&C, Performance	A/A	—
320	7/25/85	.8	F/P	S&C	A/A	—
321	7/26/85	.8	F/CG	S&C	A/A	—
322	7/26/85	1.0	F/CG	S&C	A/A	—
323	7/29/85	1.5	CG/F	S&C, Performance	A/A	—
324	8/1/85	1.1	F/CG	Spray Bar Evaluation	A/A	Phi ratio set
325	8/2/85	1.5	P/F	Propulsion, Performance	A/A	—
326	8/5/85	1.5	P/D	Propulsion, Performance	A/A	—

Flt.	Date	Hrs	Pilot	Mission	Configuration	Notes
327	8/6/85	1.4	P/TA	Locked LEF	A/A	—
328	8/7/85	.9	D/P	Locked LEF	A/A	—
329	8/7/85	1.2	P/D	Propulsion, Performance	A/A	—
330	8/9/85	.8	D/P	Performance	A/A	—
331	8/9/85	.9	P/D	Performance	A/A	—
332	8/14/85	2.0	CG/P	S&C	A/A	—
333	8/14/85	1.3	P/CG	S&C	A/A	—
334	8/16/85	1.8	CG/P	S&C	A/A	—
335	8/22/85	1.5	F/CG	Propulsion	A/A	—
336	8/23/85	1.5	CG/F	S&C	A/A	—
337	8/23/85	.7	P/F	Propulsion	A/A	—
338	8/26/85	1.1	F/CG	Propulsion	A/A	—
339	8/26/85	1.2	P/F	S&C	A/A	—

Flt.	Date	Hrs	Pilot	Mission	Configuration	Notes
340	8/27/85	2.3	CG/F	S&C	A/A	—
341	8/27/85	2.3	F/P	S&C	A/A	—
342	8/29/85	1.4	CG/P	Propulsion	A/A	First JP-8 flight
343	8/30/85	1.1	P/RB	Propulsion	A/A	—
344	9/3/85	1.5	CG/D	Propulsion	A/A	—
345	9/4/85	1.5	D/CG	Propulsion	A/A	—
346	9/5/85	1.3	CG/JY	Propulsion	A/A	—
347	9/6/85	1.4	D/CG	Propulsion	A/A	—
348	9/6/85	.9	CG/DR	Propulsion	A/A	—
349	9/13/85	.7	P/F	Propulsion	A/A	—
350	9/13/85	1.3	F/CG	Propulsion	A/A	—
351	9/16/85	1.0	CG/P	Propulsion	A/A	—
352	9/16/85	1.0	P/D	S&C	A/A	FCC #4
353	9/17/85	1.4	D/CG	S&C/ Propulsion	A/A	—
354	9/17/85	1.2	P/JO	Propulsion	A/A	—
355	9/18/85	1.5	CG/D	Propulsion	A/A	—
356	9/19/85	2.1	D/TI	S&C	A/A	FCC #1

Flt.	Date	Hrs	Pilot	Mission	Configuration	Notes
357	9/24/85	1.2	F/CG	FCC Checkout	A/A	FCC #3
358	9/25/85	2.2	P/CG	Performance	A/A	FCC #1
359	9/27/85	.6	P/CG	Engine FCF	A/A	Installed engine 6
360	9/30/85	1.0	P/ET	Engine FCF	A/A	Abort, data system
361	10/1/85	2.2	CG/P	Ferry to GDFW	A/A, no tip missiles	—

F-16XL VIP Flights

Flt	Date	Hrs	Pilot	VIP and Position
1983				
41	1/18/83	0.8	Bushnell	Maj. Gen. Peter W. Odgers, USAF, Commander, Air Force Flight Test Center, Edwards AFB, CA
42	1/20/83	0.8	Bushnell	Gen. Lawrence A. Skantze, USAF, Commander, Air Force Systems Command, Andrews AFB, MD
102	3/18/83	2.2	Thomas	Col. Melvin Hayashi, USAF, Commander, Air Force Test Pilot School, Edwards AFB, CA [for KC-10 refueling]
136	4/12/83	0.7	Bushnell	Lt. Gen. Robert M. Bond, USAF, Vice Commander, Air Force Systems Command, Andrews AFB, MD
170	5/16/83	0.7	Bushnell	Maj. Gen. John T. Buck, USAF, Vice Commander, Aeronautical Systems Division, W-PAFB, OH
171	5/16/83	0.9	Dryden	Col. Michael C. Kerby, UAAF, Commander, 57th Fighter Weapons Wing, Nellis AFB, NV
172	5/19/83	1.0	Thomas	Brig. Gen. George L. Monahan, USAF, Director, F-16 SPO, Aeronautical Systems Division, W-PAFB, OH
176	6/7/83	0.6	Thomas	Maj. Gen. Thomas L. Craig, DCS for Requirements, HQ Tactical Air Command, Langley AFB, VA
177	6/8/83	1.0	Dryden	Maj. Gen. Robert H. Reed, USAF, DCS for Operations, HQ Tactical Air Command, Langley AFB, VA

Flt	Date	Hrs	Pilot	VIP and Position
1983				
183	6/17/83	0.7	Bushnell	Gen. James V. Hartinger, USAF, Commander, USAF Space Command, Peterson AFB, CO
185	6/23/83	0.7	Bushnell	Brig. Gen. Ronald W. Yates, USAF, Director, Tactical Systems, Aeronautical Systems Division, W-PAFB, OH
187	6/29/83	1.3	Burnett	Maj. Gen. Richard W. Phillips, Jr., Commander, AF Operational Test and Evaluation Center, Kirtland AFB, NM
197	7/26/83	0.9	Thomas	Maj. Gen. Harry A. Goodall, USAF, Commander, 17th AF, U.S. Air Forces in Europe, Ramstein AB, Germany
203	8/12/83	1.1	Dryden	William Dana, NASA Research Pilot, NASA Dryden Flight Research Center, Edwards, CA
204	8/17/83	0.9	Bushnell	Hon. Paul Thayer, Deputy Secretary of Defense
205	8/23/83	0.9	Thomas	Maj. Gen. John T. Chain, USAF, DCS Plans and Operations, HQ USAF
206	8/26/83	0.9	Bushnell	Maj. Gen. Thomas S. Swalm, USAF, Commander, Tactical Air Warfare Center, Eglin AFB, FL
208	8/31/83	0.9	McKinney	F. Clifton Berry, *Air Force Magazine* staff reporter
209	9/2/83	1.0	McKinney	Robert Ropelewski, *Aviation Week & Space Technology* senior editor
221	9/19/83	0.7	Bushnell	Maj. Gen. William Kirk, DCS for Operations, U.S. Air Forces in Europe, Ramstein AB, Germany
222	9/22/83	0.9	Thomas	Lt. Gen. Carl H. Cathey, USAF, Vice Commander, U.S. Air Forces in Europe, Ramstein AB, Germany

Flt	Date	Hrs	Pilot	VIP and Position
1983				
225	10/4/83	0.9	Thomas	Lt. Gen. Thomas McMullen, USAF, Commander, Aeronautical Systems Division, Wright-Patterson AFB, OH
229	10/17/83	0.9	Thomas	Maj. Gen. Gerald D. Larson, USAF, Commander, Air Force Inspection and Safety Center, Norton AFB, CA
231	11/4/83	0.6	Thomas	Maj. Gen. Thomas McInerney, USAF, DCS for Operations and Intelligence, Pacific Air Forces, Hickam AFB, HI
237	12/8/83	0.6	Thomas	General Amos Lapidot, Chief of Staff, Israeli Air Force
239	12/15/83	0.9	Thomas	Maj. Gen. Fred A. Haeffner, USAF, Vice Commander, Pacific Air Forces
1984				
253	3/19/84	1.1	Thomas	Maj. Gen. William Gorton, USAF, Director of Operational Requirements, Office of the DCS for RD&A, HQ USAF
254	3/21/84	0.9	Thomas	RADM Paul Gilcrist, USN, Assistant CNO, Pentagon
255	3/27/84	0.9	Thomas	Brig. Gen. Jimmie Adams, USAF, Special Assistant for Tactical Modernization, RD&A, HQ USAF
258	4/16/84	1.1	Thomas	Col. Robert Ettinger, USAF, Deputy F-16 Program Director, ASD, Wright-Patterson AFB, OH
261	4/19/84	1.0	Thomas	Lt. Gen. Larry Welch, USAF, DCS for Programs and Resources, HQ USAF
263	4/26/84	0.9	Thomas	Maj. Gen. Eugene Fischer, USAF, Commander, Tactical Fighter Weapons Center, Nellis AFB, NV
268	5/21/84	0.8	Thomas	Maj. Gen. Robert Beckel, USAF, Director of Operations, Office of the DCS, Plans and Operations, Headquarters USAF

Flt	Date	Hrs	Pilot	VIP and Position
1984				
270	5/31/84	0.9	Thomas	Maj. Gen. Robert Russ, USAF, DCS for RD&A, HQ USAF
271	5/31/84	0.9	Thomas	Col. Jerauld Gentry, USAF, Office of the DCS for RD&A, HQ USAF
1985				
360	9/30/85	1.0	Payne	Col. Robert Ettinger, USAF, Vice Commander, Air Force Flight Test Center, Edwards AFB, CA

NASA Technology
Readiness Levels

TECHNOLOGY READINESS LEVELS

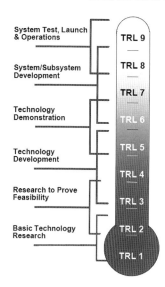

System Test, Launch & Operations — **TRL 9** — Actual system "flight proven" through successful mission operations

System/Subsystem Development — **TRL 8** — Actual system completed and "flight qualified" through test and demonstration (Ground or Flight)

TRL 7 — System prototype demonstration in a space environment

Technology Demonstration — **TRL 6** — System/subsystem model or prototype demonstration in a relevant environment (Ground or Space)

Technology Development — **TRL 5** — Component and/or breadboard validation in relevant environment

TRL 4 — Component and/or breadboard validation in laboratory environment

Research to Prove Feasibility — **TRL 3** — Analytical and experimental critical function and/or characteristic proof-of-concept

Basic Technology Research — **TRL 2** — Technology concept and/or application formulated

TRL 1 — Basic principles observed and reported

NASA Technology Readiness Levels Thermometer. (NASA)

NASA Technology Readiness Levels

TRL 1 Basic principles observed and reported: Transition from scientific research to applied research. Essential characteristics and behaviors of systems and architectures. Descriptive tools are mathematical formulations or algorithms.

TRL 2 Technology concept and/or application formulated: Applied research. Theory and scientific principles are focused on specific application area to define the concept. Characteristics of the application are described. Analytical tools are developed for simulation or analysis of the application.

TRL 3 Analytical and experimental critical function and/or characteristics proof-of-concept: Proof of concept validation. Active Research and Development (R&D) is initiated with analytical and laboratory studies. Demonstration of technical feasibility using breadboard or brassboard implementations that are exercised with representative data.

TRL 4 Component/subsystem validation in laboratory environment: Standalone prototyping implementation and test. Integration of technology elements. Experiments with full-scale problems or data sets.

TRL 5 System/subsystem/component validation in relevant environment: Thorough testing of prototyping in representative environment. Basic technology elements integrated with reasonably realistic supporting elements. Prototyping implementations conform to target environment and interfaces.

TRL 6 System/subsystem model or prototyping demonstration in a relevant end-to-end environment (ground or space): Prototyping implementations in full-scale realistic problems. Partially integrated with existing systems. Limited documentation available. Engineering feasibility fully demonstrated in actual system application.

TRL 7 System prototyping demonstration in an operational environment (ground or space): System prototyping demonstration in operational environment. System is at or near scale of the operational system, with most functions available for demonstration and test. Well integrated with collateral and ancillary systems. Limited documentation available.

TRL 8 Actual system completed and "mission qualified" through test and demonstration in operational environment (ground or space): End of system development. Fully integrated with operational hardware and software systems. Most user documentation, training documentation, and maintenance documentation completed. All functionality tested in simulated and operational scenarios. Verification and Validation (V&V) completed.

TRL 9 Actual system "mission proven" through successful mission operations (ground or space): Fully integrated with operational hardware/software systems. Actual system has been thoroughly demonstrated and tested in its operational environment. All documentation completed. Successful operational experience. Sustaining engineering support in place.

F-16XL Flight Research: NASA SLFC Program and Overall

	Appendix H-1: F-16XL-2 SUPERSONIC LAMINAR FLOW CONTROL RESEARCH FLIGHTS								
SLFC Flt	Date	Hrs	Test Points	Pilot	Back-Seater	Test Controller	Max Alt	Objectives	Comments
1995									
1	10/13/95	1.1	5	Purifoy	Collard	Bohn-Meyer	30K	Functional check (FC) flight	
2	10/25/95	0.9	4	Purifoy	Collard	Bohn-Meyer	50K	Loads clearance, load/handling qualities (HQ) evaluation, air refueling checks, engine checks, flutter clearance, pressure differential (P/D), performance	
3	11/5/95	1.35	15	Purifoy	Collard	Bohn-Meyer	40K	Loads clearance, flutter clearance, load/HQ evaluation, engine checks, in-flight refueling checks	
4	11/22/95	3.7	38	Purifoy	Collard	Bohn-Meyer	50K	Loads expansion, supersonic laminar flow control (SLFC) data	

Elegance in Flight

SLFC Flt	Date	Hrs	Test Points	Pilot	Back-Seater	Test Controller	Max Alt	Objectives	Comments
1996									
5	1/24/96	2.6	7	Purifoy	Collard	Bohn-Meyer	50K	Turbocompressor (T/C) functional checks, suction system evaluation, SLFC data	
6	1/26/96	1.8	26	Purifoy	Collard	Bohn-Meyer	50K	Loads clearance, T/C performance and oil bypass, serve-on-mass-flow mode checks	
7	2/1/96	0.4	0	Purifoy	Collard	Bohn-Meyer		SLFC data at design Mach and altitude, T/C startup procedure evaluation, servo-on-mass flow mode evaluation	In-flight emergency (IFE); left main landing gear door non-retract forced return to base (RTB)
8	2/2/96	2.5	20	Purifoy	Collard	Bohn-Meyer	50K	SLFC data at design Mach and altitude, T/C startup procedure evaluation, servo-on-mass flow mode evaluation	
9	2/9/96	2.6	19	Purifoy	Meyer	Bohn-Meyer	50K	SLFC data on leading edge (LE). Evaluate River Run for flight operations	
10	2/15/96	1.2	0	Purifoy	Collard	Bohn-Meyer		Servo-on-mass-flow mode evaluation, use of hot films (HFs) to determine existence of laminar flow, turbocompressor would not start	

366

SLFC Flt	Date	Hrs	Test Points	Pilot	Back-Seater	Test Controller	Max Alt	Objectives	Comments
11	2/22/96	1.6	4	Purifoy	Collard	Bohn-Meyer	50K	FC of T/C after shutoff valve (SOV) replacement, SLFC with hot films, communication problem between Onboard Suction System Computer-Communications (OSSC-C) and downlink—no suction	
12	2/28/96	3.2	11	Purifoy	Stucky	Yamanaka	50K	SLFC off, begin checkout of second pilot, recurrency training for backup controller. Validate OSSC system, validate air traffic control (ATC) communications	
13	3/1/96	0.5	0	Stucky	Purifoy	Collard	50K	SLFC with suction system on and off	IFE, due to right main gear door remaining down
14	3/6/96	2.1	19	Stucky	Purifoy	Collard	50K	Complete flight qualification of second pilot, SLFC data with suction on/off, red phone training for backup structures engineer	
15	3/8/96	2.3	14	Stucky	Meyer	Collard	50K	SLFC data with suction on	

SLFC Flt	Date	Hrs	Test Points	Pilot	Back-Seater	Test Controller	Max Alt	Objectives	Comments
16	3/15/96	2.4	34	Purifoy	Collard	Yamanaka	50K	SLFC data to determine minimum suction requirements on rooftop regions 14 & 15 and LE	
17	3/21/96	1.0	7	Stucky	Collard	Yamanaka	50K	SLFC data to document baseline shock fence configuration	T/C experienced revolutions per minute (RPM) overspeed with auto shutdown
18	4/17/96	3.1	50	Purifoy	Collard	Yamanaka	50K	Update loads envelope, SLFC data for no shock fence configuration. Determined minimum g-limit for suction during pushover maneuvers	
19	4/23/96	1.4	16	Purifoy	Collard	Bohn-Meyer	50K	Determine effectiveness of new larger shock fence	
20	4/26/96	3.1	49	Purifoy	Meyer	Bohn-Meyer	50K	Complete evaluation of shock fence configuration	Flight control system (FCS) caution light—but cleared
21	5/1/96	1.1	14	Purifoy	Bohn-Meyer	Collard	50K	Define suction distribution with new shock fence	FCS caution— declared IFE

SLFC Flt	Date	Hrs	Test Points	Pilot	Back-Seater	Test Controller	Max Alt	Objectives	Comments
22	5/1/96	0.8	0	Purifoy	Collard	Yamanaka			FCS caution— declared IFE. First Combined High Altitude and Gravity System (CHAGS) flight. Had replaced electronic component assembly (ECA)
23	5/8/96	0.8	14	Purifoy	Bohn-Meyer	Yamanaka			FCS caution— declared IFE. Had replaced channel D power inverter
24	5/16/96	1.0	1	Purifoy	Collard	Yamanaka	55K	FCS checkout, loads clearance at 55K, SLFC research data	
25	5/17/96	1.0	0	Purifoy	Collard	Yamanaka			FCS caution— declared IFE, airborne interface control subsystem (AICS) box was functional
26	5/26/96	0.9	16	Purifoy	Collard	Yamanaka	55K	FCS checkout, loads clearance at 45K, 42K, and 40K; SLFC data	
27	5/31/96	1.25	13	Purifoy	Meyer	Yamanaka	50K		SLFC data, FCS caution— declared IFE

SLFC Flt	Date	Hrs	Test Points	Pilot	Back-Seater	Test Controller	Max Alt	Objectives	Comments
28	6/7/96	3.1	31	Stucky	Collard	Yamanaka	50K	SLFC data to obtain increased laminar flow	
29	6/12/96	2.0	15	Purifoy	Collard	Yamanaka	55K	SLFC data with lower surface masking (unsuccessful). Tufts and video	
30	6/14/96	0.9	8	Stucky	Collard	Yamanaka	50K	SLFC data masking lower surface perforations (unsuccessful). Tufts, takeoff (T/O) delayed due to pyro inspection	
31	6/26/96	3.0	21	Purifoy	Meyer	Bohn-Meyer	50K	SLFC suction level verification of extent of laminar flow	
32	6/28/96	2.0	31	Purifoy	Meyer	Bohn-Meyer	50K	SLFC data with filled turbulence diverter (unsuccessful)	
33	7/8/96	2.0	24	Purifoy	Bohn-Meyer	Yamanaka	53K	SLFC data with gap filled beneath shock fence, varying alphas	
34	7/12/96	1.8	15	Purifoy	Collard	Yamanaka	53K	Investigate best suction levels at Mach 2.0 with top region 11 masked & det. turbulence wedge angle from HF on inboard suction panel	
35	7/13/96	2.0	18	Purifoy	Collard	Yamanaka-Wilcox	53K	Investigate best suction levels at Mach 2.0 with top of region 11 masked	

SLFC Flt	Date	Hrs	Test Points	Pilot	Back-Seater	Test Controller	Max Alt	Objectives	Comments
36	7/15/96	3.0	31	Purifoy	Collard	Yamanaka-Wilcox	53K	Investigate best suction levels at Mach 2.0 with no masking, varying alpha and beta	
37	7/26/96	3.0	34	Purifoy	Collard	Yamanaka-Wilcox	53K	Code calibration data	
38	8/16/96	3	41	Purifoy	Bohn-Meyer	Collard-Wilcox	53K	Code calibration data and baseline data for shock fence toe-in	
39	8/28/96	2.7	27	Purifoy	Collard	Yamanaka-Wilcox	53K	Evaluate results of shock fence toe-in, checkout canopy ring mod technique	
40	9/13/96	3.2	13	Stucky	Collard	Yamanaka-Wilcox	54K	Determine effectiveness of canopy fairing, get more info on turbulence wedge angle	
41	9/20/96	3.1	43	Purifoy	Collard	Yamanaka-Wilcox	55K	Determine effectiveness of canopy fairing, get more info on turbulence wedge angle, rooftop suction reduction	
42	10/4/96	2.9	48	Purifoy	Collard	Wilcox	55K	Determine effectiveness of canopy fairing, obtain SLFC data for rooftop, LE, and uniform suction reduction	
43	10/24/96	3.2	48	Purifoy	Bohn-Meyer	Collard	52K	Using the 60° shock fence, obtain data on the optimum flight conditions. Also, obtain Anderson Current Loop data.	

SLFC Flt	Date	Hrs	Test Points	Pilot	Back-Seater	Test Controller	Max Alt	Objectives	Comments
44	11/13/96	1.3	0	Purifoy	Collard	Wilcox	51K		FCS caution light for LE flap (LEF). RTB declaring IFE
45	11/26/96	2.7	43	Purifoy	Collard	Wilcox	53K	Using the 60° shock fence obtain data for code calibration and the inboard turbulent region. Also, obtain Anderson Current Loop data and Optical Sensor data.	
Total Hrs and Test Points		**90.6**	**796**						

APPENDIX H-2: IN CONTEXT—OVERALL F-16XL TEST OBJECTIVES AND FLIGHT SUMMARY		
Objectives	**Number of Flights**	
	F-16XL-1	**F-16XL-2**
Performance	75	65
Stability and Control (S&C)	38	16
Flutter Expansion Envelope	10	8
S&C (High Angle of Attack)	43	—
S&C (Structural Loads)	—	26
S&C (Speed Break Loads)	8	—
S&C (Pitch Gallop Investigation)	11	—
S&C (Landing Handling Qualities)	5	—
S&C (Aft Center-of-Gravity Envelope Expansion)	22	—
S&C (Inflight Excitation [Random/Sinusoid])	37	—
S&C (G-Overshoot Investigation)	6	—
Performance/S&C (Combined)	13	9
Performance/S&C w/ Locked LEF	24	—
Flutter/S&C (Combined)	7	2
Flutter/Performance (Combined)	6	—
Propulsion—F110 Slimline Engine Envelope Expansion	—	32
Propulsion/S&C/Performance—F110 Engine w/ Large Normal Shock Inlet (LNSI) Using JP-4 Fuel	—	30
Propulsion—F110 Engine w/ LNSI Using JP-8 Fuel	—	13
Propulsion—High-Speed Envelope Expansion	—	9
Hinge Moment Evaluation w/ Modified LEF	—	5
Helmet Mounted Display Evaluation	—	3
Weapon Separation/Gun Firing/Air Combat Maneuvering Instrumentation (ACMI) Pod Range	14	28
Vibration Test Maneuvers	8	—
Elevon Loads Survey	—	5
Environmental control system (ECS)/Drag Chute Deployment	2	—
Air Data Calibration	4	3
Aerial Refueling	2	3
Operational Utility Evaluation (OUE) Testing	42	29
Special Test Objectives	9	6
Reliability & Maintainability Evaluation	7	2
Ferry Flights (General Dynamics Forth Worth to/from Edwards AFB)	10	8

Elegance in Flight

Objectives	Number of Flights	
	F-16XL-1	F-16XL-2
Functional Check Flights (Engine/Flight Control Computer/etc.)	9	15
VIP Demonstration/Practice	—	35
Used as Target and/or Chase Aircraft	7	—
Pilot Training/Checkout/Familiarization	18	9
TOTAL FLIGHTS BY EACH AIRCRAFT	**437**	**361**

Pilot Rating of F-16XL-1 DFCS Handling Qualities

This appendix presents the handling qualities tasks and related task descriptions used by the two NASA research pilots in their evaluation of F-16XL-1 aircraft handling qualities with the digital flight control system (DFCS). The comments, ratings, and Cooper-Harper scores are reproduced verbatim from the original NASA Dryden F-16XL-1 DFCS report without attribution to specific pilots. The Cooper-Harper Handling Qualities Rating Scale (commonly referred to as the CHR scale) is reproduced for convenience in cross-referencing the NASA pilot ratings assigned to the F-16XL DFCS later in this appendix.[1]

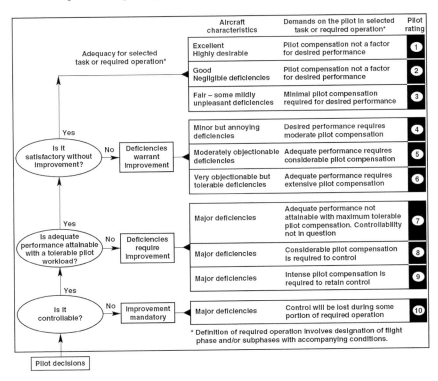

Cooper-Harper Rating Scale (NASA)

Handling Qualities Tasks, Task Descriptions, and Ratings

Normal Acceleration Captures Task Description:

From 1.0 *g* trim conditions, the pilot performed an abrupt symmetric pull up to capture 2.0 *g*. Pilots also performed 3.0 *g* captures starting from 2.0 *g* windup turns. Pilots commented on the initial and final aircraft response, pitch and roll attitude performances, and stick forces using abrupt inputs.

Flight Condition: Mach 0.6, 25K:

2.0 *g* capture from wings level: "Full abrupt stick input. Easy to capture. Bobbled to 1.7 *g*. Predictable."

3.0 *g* capture from 2.0 *g* windup turn: "Got right to 3 *g* with full aft stick. Easy to capture. Starting to bleed off—really can't get much more than that."

Flight Condition: Mach 0.9, 25K:

2.0 *g* capture from wings level: "Expected faster initial acceleration at higher speed. Was still relatively easy to capture. I did spike it down to about 1.6 *g*, then recaptured the 2 *g* pretty well."

3.0 *g* capture from 2.0 *g* windup turn: "Spiked to 3.5 *g*. Eased off to capture 3 *g*. Good, predictable response."

Pitch Attitude Captures Task Description:

From 1.0 *g* trim conditions, pilots captured 5° changes in pitch attitude using abrupt stick inputs. Pitch attitude captures were also performed using 2.0 *g* windup turns as the starting point. Pilots commented on the initial and final aircraft response and stick forces using abrupt inputs.

Flight Condition: Mach 0.6, 25K:

5° pitch attitude capture from wings level: "Trying to use abrupt inputs to really capture it. Three degree overshoot and a little bit of bobble as I settled in on it."

5° pitch attitude capture from constant altitude 2.0 *g* windup turn: "Moved right to 5° with full aft stick. Very easy to capture. Got about all you're going to get."

Flight Condition: Mach 0.9, 25K:

5° pitch attitude capture from wings level: "Negligible overshoot. Three quick half-degree bobbles. Predictable and good."

5° pitch attitude capture from constant altitude 2.0 g windup turn: "Using gyro in cockpit. Can't use HUD. Response seems a bit quicker—maybe due to differences in gauges. Predictable."

Bank Angle Captures Task Description:

From 1.0 g trim conditions, the pilot captured target bank angles using full stick force. Target bank angles of ± 30° and ± 90° were captured starting from a 1.0 g trim reference point. Target bank angles of ± 90° were also captured using 90° opposite bank as the starting point of the maneuver. Pilots commented on the initial and final aircraft response, roll attitude performances, and stick forces using abrupt inputs.

Flight Condition: Mach 0.6, 15K:

30° bank angle captures from wings level: "Nice response. Ten degree overshoot. Very easy."

90° bank angle captures from wings level: "Moderate roll mode time constant. Builds up gradually."

Flight Condition: Mach 0.9, 15K:

30° bank angle captures from wings level: "Much more abrupt roll response. On left capture, went to 40°, came back with another overshoot to 35°, then captured it nicely. Better on right—did not overshoot. Crisp roll response."

90° bank angle captures from wings level: "A little bit of bobble. Two small amplitude bobbles. Seems like a nice smooth response. Easy to capture."

Flight Condition: Mach 0.6, 25K:

30° bank angle captures from wings level: "One overshoot of about three degrees on left capture. Pretty easy to capture. Nice crisp, quick movement—easier than the simulator. Bigger overshoot on left capture—probably 10 to 12°, but came back with no overshoot to capture. A good crisp acceleration."

90° bank angle captures from wings level: "Nice acceleration. Easy to check with negligible overshoot. Kind of a smooth roll rate. Easy to capture."

Flight Condition: Mach 0.8, 25K:

90° bank angle captures from wings level: "Moderate roll rate. Easy to anticipate. Easy to lead. Minimum compensation."

90° bank angle captures from 90° opposite bank: "Fifteen degree overshoot on right capture. Performance right on limit of desired. Increased workload."

Flight Condition: Mach 0.9, 25K:

30° bank angle captures from wings level: "Nice acceleration. Spiked to just under 45° on left capture, then came back to 30° with no problems. Nice forces. Ten degree overshoot on right capture. Came back with a one to two degree overshoot then captured. Nice crisp response."

90° bank angle captures from wings level: "Slight ratcheting. Not quite as fast as expected. Starts off well, but steady state is slower than expected. Stuck around 70° then captured."

Flight Condition: 18° alpha, 30K:

90° bank angle captures from wings level: "Right—coupled with pitch. Adequate. A couple of oscillations. Slow roll rate. Left—smooth and predictable—captured real well."

90° bank angle captures from 90° opposite bank: "Desired performance. No problems with pitch. Easy to anticipate."

Air-to-Air Tracking Task Description:

In this maneuver, the F-16XL attempted to track a target aircraft from ranges of 1,000 to 1,500 feet. Once the F-16XL was in a position behind the target, the target aircraft performed a 3.0 *g* turn. When the target was 30° off the nose, the F-16XL pilot maneuvered to acquire the target in his gunsight pipper. When the target was acquired, the F-16XL pilot fine-tracked for 2 to 3 seconds and then called for the target aircraft to reverse his turn followed by a repeat in the opposite direction. This task was then repeated with random maneuvering of the target up to 3.0 *g* with unannounced reversals. To achieve desired performance in gross acquisition, the pilot had to be able to track the target within a 50 mm diameter on the pipper, with one overshoot and no PIO allowed. Adequate performance required that the target be kept within 75 mm with two overshoots and no PIO tendencies. In fine tracking, desired performance kept the target within a ±10 mil diameter on the pipper for 2 seconds without PIO. Adequate performance was achieved when the target was tracked within an accuracy region of ± 20 mils without PIO encountered. Pilots commented on any undesirable motions, predictability, aggressiveness effects and compensation techniques.[2]

Flight Condition: Mach 0.8, 10K:

"Desired performance on gross acquisition—nice response. Fine tracking not quite adequate. Pitch bobble - 8 mils."
CHR: gross acquisition - 4; fine tracking - 7.

Flight Condition: Mach 0.9, 10K:

"Could get desired on gross acquisition—nice handling qualities. Couldn't get adequate in finetracking."
CHR: gross acquisition - 3; fine tracking - 7.

Flight Condition: Mach 0.6, 15K:

"No PIO tendency. Twenty mils edge twice during gross acquisition. Adequate performance not possible for fine tracking. Slight pitch bobble. No major deficiencies."
CHR: gross acquisition - 6; fine tracking - 7.

Flight Condition: Mach 0.9, 15K:

"Nice crisp performance on gross acquisition. Able to get it there without any overshoots. Desired. Right at ten mils or so. Real nice handling qualities for gross acquisition. Not quite adequate performance on fine tracking."
CHR: gross acquisition - 4; fine tracking - 7.

Flight Condition: Mach 0.6, 25K:

"Three *g* tracking task not doable at this flight condition. With full afterburner and full aft stick, it is just lagging. Can't match target's pitch rate. At 45° and full aft stick, can't match target's turn rate. Just continues to bleed. Have to go off the plane and cut across, and still can't get the nose back to him."

"Two *g* tracking—two overshoots on gross acquisition. Once to edge, once a couple of mils past. Not able to get adequate performance during fine tracking. Transitory, two to four mils off target. Cycles around target. No real PIO tendency."
CHR: gross acquisition - none given; fine tracking - 6 or 7.

Flight Condition: Mach 0.9, 25K:

"Crisper response. Able to get desired performance on gross acquisition. Could not keep adequate in fine tracking. Would be stable on exhaust and bobble to wingtip. In a period of ten seconds, a bobble put it out to almost twice the adequate performance level allowance."
CHR: gross acquisition - 3; fine tracking - no rating.

Flight Condition: Mach 0.9, 25K:

> "Desired performance on gross acquisition. Crisper response. Could not keep within desired for fine tracking. A bobble would put out to adequate performance."
> CHR: gross acquisition - 3; fine tracking - 4.

Flight Condition: 250 KCAS, 15K:

> "Easy to get desired for gross acquisition—within 15 mils. Real smooth, some pitch bobble in fine tracking."
> CHR: gross acquisition - 3; fine tracking - 4.

Flight Condition: 280 KCAS, 15K:

> "PIO tendency in pitch axis. Similar to analog airplane - maybe better. Pitch bobble (four mils). Nice and stable."
> CHR: none given.

Flight Condition: 350 KCAS, 15K:

> "Easy, nice handling qualities, no overshoot in gross acquisition. Preferred speed range for fine tracking."
> CHR: gross acquisition - 2; fine tracking - 3.

Flight Condition: 400 KCAS, 15K:

> "Easy gross acquisition. Within 30 mils without overshoot. Most pitch bobble during fine tracking at this speed range. Seemed to decrease at other speeds."
> CHR: gross acquisition - 3; fine tracking - 4.

Flight Condition: 11° alpha, 15K, Powered Approach

> "Easy to get desired for gross acquisition. Some pitch bobble seen in fine tracking; no roll bobble. More pitch bobble with increased aggressiveness."
> CHR: gross acquisition - 2; fine tracking - 3.
> "Two overshoots in gross acquisition. Sensitive. Pitch heavier than roll. Energy low. Tendency to couple in roll - impacts predictability."
> CHR: gross acquisition - 5; fine tracking - 3.
> Nose seems to bobble. Pitch bobble - 5 mils.
> CHR: gross acquisition - 3; fine tracking - 3.

Close Trail Formation Flight Task Description:

In this maneuver, the F-16XL followed the tail of the lead airplane with increasing aggressiveness though s-turn maneuvers. For the initial evaluation, the lead airplane maneuvered up to 3.0 *g*. The desired performance goal was that both the lateral and vertical displacement of the tracking pipper be kept within ±1 tailpipe diameter from the tailpipe of the lead aircraft without a PIO being encountered. Adequate tracking performance was achieved when the lateral and vertical pipper displacement was within ±2 tailpipe diameters without PIO. Pilots evaluated aircraft handling responses during steady tracking and reversals by the lead aircraft. Cooper-Harper ratings were given for both gross acquisition and fine tracking based on the desired and adequate performance margins.

Flight Condition: Mach 0.8, 10K:

"Desired performance in steady state. Very nice handling qualities. Need to lag for quicker reverse. For slower reverse, can get adequate performance, but not desired."
CHR: steady state - 4; reversals - 6.

Flight Condition: Mach 0.9, 10K:

No comments.
CHR: steady state - 4; reversals - 7.

Flight Condition: Mach 0.6, 15K:

"Able to maintain adequate performance steady state. Adequate performance not possible for reversals."
CHR: steady state - 5; reversals - 7.

Flight Condition: Mach 0.9, 15K:

"Able to maintain desired performance for the majority of the time in steady state. For a number of seconds after a reversal, unable to maintain adequate. Probably five or more diameters away."
CHR: steady state - 4; reversals - 7.

Flight Condition: Mach 0.6, 25K:

"Can get desired performance in steady state for both longitudinal and lateral–directional. Any movement puts me to adequate, or not even adequate, even if he is calling the reversals. We can't match the *Ps*, so we start drifting back. Difficult to evaluate at greater ranges."
CHR: steady state - 4; reversals - 5 or 6.

Flight Condition: Mach 0.9, 25K:

"Noticed a couple of PIO bobbles that were outside of adequate then got settled out. Not the most predictable thing. Could have mainly desired for an extended period of time, then have adequate, or not even adequate performance for straight and level flight. Relatively predictable and able to meet adequate the majority of the time in turns."

CHR: none given.

Flight Condition: 280 KCAS, 15K:

"Control harmony good. Can see difference between pitch and roll. Adequate. Very similar to analog aircraft. No tendency roll–ratchet. Six to seven mil cycling in pitch."

CHR: none given.

Endnotes

1. Susan J. Stachowiak and John T. Bosworth, "Flight Test Results for the F-16XL with a Digital Flight Control System," NASA TP-2004-212046 (March 2004).
2. A mil is a unit of angular measurement. It is equal to the angle subtended by an arc equal to one one-thousandth of the distance to the object or target being tracked.

Acronyms, Abbreviations, Nomenclature, and Symbols

A	Area
A/B	Afterburner
A/R	Aerial Refueling
A-A, A/A	Air-to-Air
AB, A/B	Afterburner
AC, ac	Aerodynamic Center
ACEE	Aircraft Energy Efficiency
ACF	Air Combat Fighter
ACMI	Air Combat Maneuvering Instrumentation
ACMR	Air Combat Maneuvering Range
AEDC	Arnold Air Engineering Center
AF	Air Force
AFB	Air Force Base
AFCD	Advanced Fighter Capability Demonstrator
AFE	Alternate Fighter Engine
AFFTC	Air Force Flight Test Center
AFFTC	Air Force Test and Evaluation Center
AFHQ	Air Force Headquarters
AFOTEC	Air Force Operational Test and Evaluation Center
AFRL	Air Force Research Laboratory
AFSC	Air Force Systems Command
A-G	Air-to-Ground
AGARD	Advisory Group for Aeronautical Research and Development
AGL	Above Ground Level
AGM	Air-to-Ground Missile
AHS	American Helicopter Society
AIAA	American Institute of Aeronautics and Astronautics
AICS	Airborne Interface Control Subsystem
AIM	Air Intercept Missile

Alpha	Angle of Attack
Alt	Altitude, Alternative
AMRAAM	Advanced Medium Range Air-to-Air Missile
AMT	Airframe Management Team
ANOPP	Aircraft Noise Operations Prediction Program
AoA, AOA	Angle of Attack
APU	Auxiliary Power Unit
AR	Aspect Ratio
ARC	Ames Research Center
ARI	Aileron Rudder Interconnect
AS	Airspeed
ASD	Aeronautical Systems Division
ATC	Air Traffic Control
ATF	Advanced Tactical Fighter
ATIS	Airborne Test Instrumentation System
AVT	Air Vehicle Technology
AW&ST	Aviation Week and Space Technology
b	Wingspan
BART	Basic Aerodynamics Research Tunnel
BDU	Bomb Dummy Unit
Beta	Sideslip Angle
BFM	Basic Fighter Maneuvers
BL	Butt Line (or Buttock Line)
BVR	Beyond Visual Range
C, c	Chord
CAD	Computer-Aided Design
CADAM	Computer-Aided Design and Manufacturing
cal	Calibration
CAM	Computer-Aided Manufacturing
CAP	Combat Aircraft Prototype
CAS	Calibrated Airspeed
CASI	Canadian Aeronautics and Space Institute
CAT	Category
CAWAP	Cranked Arrow Wing Aerodynamics Program
CAWAPI	Cranked Arrow Wing Aerodynamics Program International
CBO	Congressional Budget Office
CBU	Cluster Bomb Unit
Cd	Drag Coefficient
CDC	Control Data Corporation
CDISC	Constrained Direct Iterative Surface Curvature

CFD	Computational Fluid Dynamics
CG, cg	Center of Gravity
CHAGS	Combined High Altitude and Gravity System
CHR	Cooper-Harper Rating
CIC	Close-in-Combat
CINC	Commander in Chief
C_L	Lift Coefficient
Cmd	Command
CNI	Communications, Navigation, Identification
Cp	Coefficient of Pressure
CP	Complete
CTF	Combined Test Force
Ctr	Center
DARPA	Defense Advanced Research Programs Agency
DCS	Deputy Chief of Staff
DD	Department of Defense
DEC	Digital Equipment Corporation
DEEC	Digital Electronic Engine Control
Deg	Degrees
DEI	Dynamics Engineering Incorporated
Demo	Demonstration
det	Determine
DFCS	Digital Flight Control System
DFE	Derivative Fighter Engine
DFRC	Dryden Flight Research Center
DFSG	Dual Role Fighter Steering Group
DGLR	German Society for Aeronautics and Astronautics
DGPS	Differential Global Positioning System
DMS	Differential Maneuvering Simulator
DO	Director of Operations
DoD	Department of Defense
DoDD	Department of Defense Directive
DOR	Director of Operational Requirements
DOT&E	Director of Operational Test and Evaluation
DRF	Dual Role Fighter
DT&E	Development Test and Evaluation
DVL	Deutsche Versuchsanstalt für Luftfahrt (Aviation Research Institute)
EADS	European Aeronautic Defense and Space Company
EAFB	Edwards Air Force Base
ECA	Electronic Component Assembly

ECS	Environmental Control System
EGT	Exhaust Gas Temperature
ENGR	Engineering
ENG	Engineering
Env	Environmental
EPU	Emergency Power Unit
ESP	Electronically Scanning Pressure sensor
ETF	Enhanced Tactical Fighter
Eval	Evaluation
EWC	Equal Weight Composite
Ext	Extended
f	Feet
Fam	Familiarization
FARs	Federal Acquisition Regulations
FAST	Fuel and Sensor Tactical
FBW	Fly-by-Wire
FC	Functional Check
FCC	Flight Control Computer
FCF	Functional Check Flight
FCS	Flight Control System
FCV	Flow Control Valve
FLCS	Flight Control System
FLIR	Forward Looking Infrared
FLT	Flight
FM	Frequency Modulation
FO	Flight Operations
FORTRAN	**For**mula **Tran**slating System
FRC	Flight Research Center
FRF	Frequency Response Function
FS	Fuselage Station
FSD	Full Scale Development
FSED	Full Scale Engineering Development
FSW	Forward Swept Wing
ft	feet
FTR	Flight Test Request
FTW	Fort Worth
FW	Fort Worth
FWC	Fighter Weapons Center
FWD	Forward
G, g	Normal Acceleration
Gal	Gallon

GAO	General Accounting Office
GD	General Dynamics
GDFW	General Dynamics Forth Worth
GE	General Electric
GFE	Government Furnished Equipment
Gnd	Ground
GPS	Global Positioning System
GVT	Ground Vibration Test
HF	Hot Film
Hi	High
HLFC	Hybrid Laminar Flow Control
HMD	Helmet Mounted Display
Hp	Pressure Height
HQ	Handling Qualities, Headquarters
Hrs	Hours
H-S	High-Speed
HSCT	High-Speed Civil Transport
HSR	High-Speed Research
HUD	Head-Up Display
Hyd	Hydraulic
Hz	Hertz
ICAS	International Council of the Aeronautical Sciences
IDA	Institute for Defense Analyses
IEEE	Institute of Electrical and Electronic Engineers
IES	Institute for Environmental Studies
IFE	In-flight Emergency
IFF	Identification, Friend or Foe
IFFCS	Integrated Fire and Flight Control System
IGE	In-Ground Effect
IIR	Imaging Infrared
ILS	Instrument Landing System, Integrated Logistic Support
ILSP	Integrated Logistics Support Plan
in	Inches
inbrd	Inboard
INS	Inertial Navigation System
insp	Inspection
instl	Install/Installation
IPE	Improved Performance Engine
IPT	Integrated Product Team
IR&D	Independent Research and Development

ISA	Instruction Set Architecture
ISA	International Society for Automation
ITAR	International Traffic in Arms Regulations
ITD	Integrated Technology Development
ITEA	International Test and Evaluation Association
JAST	Joint Advanced Strike Technology
JFS	Jet Fuel Starter
JP	Jet Propulsion
JTT	Joint Test Team
K, k	Thousand
KCAS	Knots Calibrated Airspeed
kft	Thousands of feet
KW	Kilowatts
L	Laminar Flow
L	Length
L/D	Lift-to-Drag Ratio
LANTIRN	Low Altitude Navigation Targeting Infra-Red Night
LaRC	Langley Research Center
Lb, lb	pound
LE	Leading Edge
LEF	Leading Edge Flap
LEFT	Leading Edge Flap Test
LFC	Laminar Flow Control
LFCPO	Laminar Flow Control Program Office
LNSI	Large Normal Shock Inlet
LODE	Low Aerodynamic Drag Ejector
LT	Laminar Flow with Turbulent Bursts
LTV	Ling Temco Vought
LWF	Light Weight Fighter
M	Mach number
m	meters
MAC, mac	Mean Aerodynamic Chord
Max	Maximum
MDC	McDonnell-Douglas Corporation
MER	Multiple Ejector Rack
MFD	Multi-Function Display
MIL	Military
MIL-STD	Military Standard
MK	Mark
mm	millimeter
mph	miles per hour

MPO	Manual Pitch Override
MSIP	Multi Stage Improvement Program
MTBM	Mean Time Between Maintenance
MTOGW	Maximum Takeoff Gross Weight
NACA	National Advisory Committee for Aeronautics
NASTRAN	NASA Structural Analysis System
NATO	North Atlantic Treaty Organization
NLF	Natural Laminar Flow
NM, nm	Nautical Miles
NPR	Nozzle Pressure Ratio
NTPS	National Test Pilot School
NTSB	National Transportation Safety Board
OCU	Operational Conversion Unit
OGE	Out of Ground Effect
ops	Operations
OSD	Office of the Secretary of Defense
OSSC	Onboard Suction System Computer
OSSC-C	Onboard Suction System Computer-Communications
OT&E	Operational Test and Evaluation
OUE	Operational Utility Evaluation
P&W	Pratt and Whitney
P/D	Pressure Differential
PA	Pitch Axis
PACAF	Pacific Air Forces
Pamb	Ambient Pressure
PATS	Portable Automatic Triggering System
PCM	Pulse Code Modulation
PIO	Pilot Induced Oscillation
PMT	Propulsion Management Team
POM	Program Objective Memorandum
prov	Provisions
PS	Pressure Sensor
PSI, psi	Pounds per Square Inch
Ps_{jet}	Static Pressure in the Jet Exhaust
PVC	Pneumatic Vortex Control
PWT	Propulsion Wind Tunnel
Q, q	Dynamic Pressure
q max	Maximum Dynamic Pressure
R&D	Research and Development
R&M	Reliability and Maintainability

RAM	Radar Absorbing Materials
RCS	Radar Cross Section
RD&A	Research, Development, and Acquisition
R_e	Reynolds Number
Req	Requirements
RFP	Request for Proposals
RPM	Revolutions per Minute
RTB	Return to Base
RTO	Research and Technology Organization
S	Wing Area
S&C	Stability and Control
S/B	Speed Brake
SAC	Strategic Air Command
SAE	Society of Automotive Engineers
SAM	Surface to Air Missile
SAR	Selected Acquisition Report
SAR	Synthetic Aperture Radar
SBIR	Small Business Independent Research
SC	Spin Chute
SCAMP	Supersonic Cruise and Maneuver Prototype
SCAR	Supersonic Cruise Aircraft Research
SCAT	Supersonic Commercial Air Transport
SCIF	Supersonic Cruise Integrated Fighter
SCR	Supersonic Cruise Research
SEC	Secondary
Sep	Separation
SETP	Society of Experimental Test Pilots
SFO	Simulated Flame Out
SFTE	Society of Flight Test Engineers
SLFC	Supersonic Laminar Flow Control
SLST	Sea Level Static Thrust
SMS	Stores Management System
SOC	Statement of Operational Capability
SOF	Safety of Flight
SON	Statement of Operational Need
SOV	Shut Off Valve
Spec	Specification
SPO	System Program Office
SS, ss	Supersonic
SST	Supersonic Transport
ST	Start

SUU	Suspended Underwing Unit
sym	Symmetric
Sys	Systems
T	Turbulent Flow
T/C, TC	Turbocompressor
T/O	Takeoff
T/W	Thrust to Weight Ratio
TAC	Tactical Air Command
Tact	Tactical
TACT	Transonic Aircraft Technology
TC	Turbocompressor
TCA	Technology Concept Aircraft
TE	Trailing Edge
TER	Triple Ejector Rack
TFX	Tactical Fighter Experimental
TL	Turbulent Flow with Laminar Bursts
TMD	Tactical Munitions Dispenser
TMT	Technology Management Team
TOGW	Takeoff Gross Weight
TPS	Test Pilot School
TR	Transition
TRL	Technology Risk Level
T-S	Tollmien-Schlichting (Wave)
Turb	Turbulence
UAE	United Arab Emirates
UHF	Ultra High Frequency
Ult	Utility
USAF	United States Air Force
USAFE	United States Air Forces in Europe
USDR&E	Under Secretary of Defense for Research and Engineering
UT	University of Tennessee
v	Velocity
V&V	Verification and Validation
VAX	Virtual Address eXtension
VGI	Variable Geometry Inlet
VHS	Very High Frequency
vib	Vibration
VLM-SA	Vortex Lattice Method coupled with Suction Analogy
VIP	Very Important Person
w	With

WBS	Work Breakdown Structure
WL	Water Line
W-PAFB	Wright-Patterson Air Force Base
WSO	Weapons System Officer
WT	Wingtip
WVR	Within Visual Range
WX, Wx	Weather
x	Chord-wise Distance from the Leading Edge
x/c	Chord Location (Non Dimensional)

Greek Symbols

μ	Dynamic Viscosity
α	Angle of Attack
β	Sideslip Angle
η	Wing Crank Location Measured from Aircraft Centerline
Λ	Wing Sweep Angle
ν	Kinematic Viscosity
ρ	Air Density
σ	Radar Cross Section

Acknowledgments

I would like to acknowledge the outstanding support and contributions provided to me by a number of individuals during research and preparation of this book on the elegant and graceful General Dynamics (GD) (later Lockheed-Martin) F-16XL.

First and foremost, Dr. Richard P. Hallion—senior consultant, Science & Technology Policy Institute (STPI) of the Institute for Defense Analyses (IDA), chronicler of the history of the National Aeronautics and Space Administration (NASA) Dryden Flight Research Center (DFRC), and later the Air Force Flight Test Center (AFFTC) chief historian at Edwards Air Force Base, CA— graciously discussed his recollections of the F-16XL flight-test effort and provided access to official AFFTC histories from the time. Those contributions provided invaluable insights into the flight-test program and were indispensable assets in describing details of the U.S. Air Force (USAF) evaluation of the aircraft.

Two employees of Lockheed-Martin, the successor company to General Dynamics, deserve special recognition. Eric Hehs, editor of Lockheed's *Code One Magazine*, was most helpful. He provided early GD documents and briefings on the Supersonic Cruise and Maneuver Prototype (SCAMP) initiative and its evolution into the F-16XL experimental prototype; much of that information was original material related to Harry J. Hillaker, the unofficial "Father of the F-16." Robert J. Wetherall, who as a young engineer with GD worked on the design and development of the F-16XL, shared a massive amount of information from the formative days of the GD development effort. Robert provided an incredibly informative set of materials, including formal presentations and background material that he developed for the 2007 celebration of the 25th anniversary of the F-16XL's first flight. He has continued to provide his insights as well as a wealth of material on the inner workings of the program as it unfolded within the company.

Another extremely valuable source of information was an Air Force Air University thesis on the F-16XL program written by Patrick K. Talty, a former Air Force flight-test engineer in the F-16XL combined test force. His superior work is repeatedly referenced in the text for its excellent insights and thoughtful assessment of F-16XL capabilities and limitations.

The Honorable Thomas P. Christie, former Director of Operational Test and Evaluation (DOT&E) within the Department of Defense and a key player in the early development of the Lightweight Fighter program, provided valuable insights into the political environment as it related to the Air Force Dual-Role Fighter decision.

Thomas "Tom" Grindle, Aircraft Maintenance Division chief at NASA Dryden Flight Research Center, furnished important insights into the structural layout and design of the F-16XL and the conduct of its flight-test program.

Joseph R. Chambers, head of the NASA Langley Dynamic Stability Branch in the 1980s and, later, division chief over the Laminar Flow Control Project Office (LFCPO) during the F-16XL supersonic laminar flow control (SLFC) research activity, provided extremely worthwhile observations and comments that clarified certain aspects of the research effort and greatly enhanced this work. A prolific author and documenter of NASA Langley aerodynamic research efforts, Joe was closely involved in the cooperative F-16XL development effort with General Dynamics and worked closely with Harry Hillaker from the birth to the death of the program.

Gregory V. Lewis, Vice President and Director of the National Test Pilot School (NTPS) in Mojave, CA, and Russ Stewart, flight-test instructor at the NTPS, very graciously furnished photographs of their unique two-seat Saab Sk 35 Draken double-delta flight-test training and research aircraft. The author and editor deeply appreciate their assistance, for the Draken's design anticipated that of the F-16XL by over a quarter century. The NTPS, a remarkable and unique civilian educational institution staffed by veteran leaders in flight-test operations, practice, and methodology, trains test pilots and flight-test engineers from around the world using the Drakens and a variety of other fixed-wing and rotary-wing aircraft.

Other former and current NASA Langley personnel who reviewed and commented on the manuscript include Marilyn E. Ogburn, Mark A. Croom, Jerry N. Hefner, Jay Brandon, and Roy V. Harris, all of whom played significant roles in the program. The contributions of many other NASA research staff members, who are too numerous to list here but are mentioned in the body of the text, were of immense importance in documenting NASA research with the F-16XL. Their formal publications produced over the years provided a rich body of technical knowledge related to every aspect of NASA F-16XL-related research. They deserve a special compliment for their dedication and technical excellence in support of U.S. aeronautical research.

Last but far from least, there are several individuals at the IDA who contributed their special talents in advising and assisting me in this endeavor. These include retired USAF Col. Warren L. "Jug" Jagodnik, Dr. John Richard Nelson, and Megan McCarty. The staff of the IDA Technical Library was of immense help in obtaining many significant reports and documents related to the F-16XL. In this regard, Amanda Talcott and Peter Droubay deserve special thanks. Carol Ruppe assisted with typing and final formatting of the appendices.

Bibliography

Books and Monographs

Andersson, Hans G. *Saab Aircraft Since 1937*. Washington, DC: Smithsonian Institution Press, 1989.

Aronstein, David C., Michael J. Hirschberg, and Albert C. Piccirillo. *Advanced Tactical Fighter to F-22 Raptor: Origins of the 21st Century Air Dominance Fighter*. Reston, VA: American Institute of Aeronautics and Astronautics (AIAA), 1998.

Aronstein, David C., and Albert C. Piccirillo. *Have Blue and the F-117A: Evolution of the Stealth Fighter*. Reston, VA: AIAA, 1997.

Aronstein, David C., and Albert C. Piccirillo. *The Lightweight Fighter Program: A Successful Approach to Fighter Technology Transition*. Reston, VA: AIAA, 1996.

Art, Robert J. *The TFX Decision: McNamara and the Military*. Boston, MA: Little, Brown and Company, 1968.

Borchers, Paul F., James A. Franklin, and Jay W. Fletcher. *Flight Research at Ames: Fifty—Seven Years of Development and Validation of Aeronautical Technology*. Washington, DC: NASA, 1998.

Bowles, Mark D. *The "Apollo" of Aeronautics: NASA's Aircraft Energy Efficiency Program (1973–1987)*. Washington, DC: NASA SP-2009-574 (2009).

Brandt, Stephen A., Randall J. Stiles, John J. Bertin, and Ray Whitford. *Introduction to Aeronautics: A Design Perspective*. Reston, VA: AIAA, 2004.

Braslow, Albert L. *A History of Suction-Type Laminar Flow Control with Emphasis on Flight Research*. Washington, DC: NASA Monograph in Aerospace History Number 13, 1999.

Chambers, Joseph R. *Innovation in Flight: Research of the NASA Langley Research Center on Revolutionary Advanced Concepts for Aeronautics.* Washington, DC: NASA Monograph in Aerospace History Number 39, SP-2005-4539 (2005).

Chambers, Joseph R. *Modeling Flight: The Role of Dynamically Scaled Free-Flight Models in Support of NASA's Aerospace Programs.* Washington, DC: NASA SP 2009-575 (2009).

Chambers, Joseph R. *Partners in Freedom: Contributions of the Langley Research Center to U.S. Military Aircraft of the 1990's.* Washington, DC: NASA Monographs in Aerospace History Number 19, SP-2000-4519 (2000).

Conway, Erik M. *High Speed Dreams: NASA and the Technopolitics of Supersonic Transportation, 1945–1999.* Baltimore, MD: Johns Hopkins University Press, 2005.

Coulam, Robert F. *Illusions of Choice: The F-111 and the Problem of Weapons Acquisition Reform.* Princeton, NJ: Princeton University Press, 1977.

Day, Richard E. *Coupling Dynamics in Aircraft: A Historical Perspective.* Washington, DC: NASA SP-532 (1997).

Drendel, Lou. *F-16 Fighting Falcon in Action—Aircraft No. 53.* Carrollton, TX: Squadron/Signal Publications, 1982.

Ethell, Jeffrey, and Alfred Price. *Air War South Atlantic.* New York: Macmillan Publishing Company, 1983.

Hallion, Richard P., ed. *NASA's Contributions to Aeronautics,* v. 1. Washington, DC: NASA SP-2010-570-Vol. 1 (2010).

Hallion, Richard P., and Michael H. Gorn. *On the Frontier: Experimental Flight at NASA Dryden.* Washington, DC: Smithsonian Books, 2003.

Hirschel, Ernst Heinrich, Horst Prem, and Gero Madelung, eds. *Aeronautical Research in Germany from Lilienthal until Today.* Berlin: Springer-Verlag, 2004.

Holder, Bill. *Lost Fighters: A History of U.S. Fighter Programs That Didn't Make It.* Warrentown, PA: SAE International, 2007.

Hutto, Walter D. *F110 Fighter Power: F-16/F110-GE-100 Pilot Awareness Program*. Cincinnati, OH: General Electric Company, 1987.

Jane's Information Group. *Jane's Aero Engines, Issue Thirty*. Alexandria, VA: Jane's Information Group, Inc., 2011.

Jane's Information Group. *Jane's All The World's Aircraft*. F-16XL entries in various annual volumes. London, UK: Jane's Information Group, Inc., 1981–82, 1982–83, 1983–84, 1985–86, 1995–96.

Jenkins, Dennis R. *McDonnell Douglas F-15 Eagle, Supreme Heavy-Weight Fighter*. Arlington, TX: Aerofax, 1998.

Knott, Eugene F., John F. Schaeffer, and Michael T. Tulley. *Radar Cross Section: Its Prediction Measurement and Reduction*. Norwood, MA: ARTECH House, Inc., 1985.

Levaux, Hugh P., and Mark A. Lorell. *The Cutting Edge: A Half Century of U.S. Fighter Aircraft R&D*. Santa Monica, CA: RAND Corp., MR-939-AF (1998).

McCormick, Barnes W. *Aerodynamics, Aeronautics, and Flight Mechanics*. New York: John Wiley & Sons, Inc., 1995.

McLean, F. Edward. *Supersonic Cruise Technology*. Washington, DC: NASA SP-472 (1985).

Miller, Jay. *The X-Planes: X-1 to X-45*. London, UK: Ian Allen Publishing, Ltd., 2005.

National Research Council. *U.S. Supersonic Commercial Aircraft: Assessing NASA's High Speed Research Program*. Washington, DC: National Academy Press, 1997.

Slife, James C. *Creech Blue: Gen Bill Creech and the Reformation of the Tactical Air Forces, 1978–1984*. Maxwell Air Force Base, AL: Air University Press, 2004.

Spick, Mike, ed. *The Great Book of Modern Warplanes*. London, UK: Salamander Books Ltd., 2000.

Thompson, Milton O. *Flight Research: Problems Encountered and What They Should Teach Us.* Washington, DC: NASA Monographs in Aerospace History no. 22, SP-2000-4522 (2000).

Wallace, Lane E. *Flights of Discovery: 50 Years at the NASA Dryden Flight Research Center.* Washington, DC: NASA SP-4309 (1996).

Wegg, John. *General Dynamics Aircraft and Their Predecessors.* Annapolis, MD: Naval Institute Press, 1990.

Whitford, Ray. *Design for Air Combat.* London: Jane's Publishing Company, Ltd., 1987.

Yenne, Bill. *Convair Deltas: From Sea Dart to Hustler.* North Branch, MN: Specialty Press, 2009.

Reports, Papers, Articles, Dissertations, and Presentations

(No author credited.) "Arrow-wing F-16 Airborne Again." *Flight International* (March 25, 1989): 7.

(No author credited.) "Dryden Readies F-16XL for Flight Test." *Aviation Week & Space Technology* (March 20, 1995).

(No author credited.) "Dual-Role F-15 to be Delivered in 1988." *Flight International* (March 10, 1984).

(No author credited.) "Evolutionary F-16XL Makes Its First Flight One Day After Its Rollout at Fort Worth." *General Dynamics World* 12, no. 7 (July 1982).

(No author credited.) "F-15 Wins US Fighter Contest." *Flight International* (March 3, 1984).

(No author credited.) "F-16XL Aircraft Fly Out of Storage to Perform Supersonic Flight Tests." *Aviation Week & Space Technology* (March 27, 1989).

(No author credited.) "F-16XL Enters Flight Test Program." *Aviation Week & Space Technology* (July 12, 1982).

(No author credited.) "F-16XL Readied for Flight Testing." *Aviation Week & Space Technology* (July 5, 1982).

(No author credited.) "F-16XL to Test SLFC Wing Design." *Aviation Week & Space Technology* (November 14, 1994).

(No author credited.) "F-16XLs Pass 100 Hours." *Flight International* (December 11, 1982).

(No author credited.) "First Flight for F-16XL." *Flight International* (July 17, 1982).

(No author credited.) "GD Loses, and Wins." *Flight International* (March 10, 1984).

(No author credited.) "General Dynamics Developing F-16XL Hardware." *Aviation Week & Space Technology* (April 6, 1981).

(No author credited.) "McDonnell Douglas Prepared to Compare F-15E and F-15ES." *Aerotech News and Review: Journal of Aerospace and Defense Industry News* 9, no. 24 (December 9, 1994).

(No author credited.) "NASA F-16XL Laminar-Flow Tests Will Aid HSCT Effort." *Flight International* (February 1, 1995).

(No author credited.) "NASA Winds Up SLFC Project." *Flight International* (October 23–29, 1996): 28.

(No author credited.) "SCAMP Cuts Drag, Increases Fuel Load." *Aviation Week & Space Technology* (August 18, 1980).

(No author credited.) "USAF Canvasses Close Air Support." *Flight International* (July 20, 1985): 10.

(No author credited.) "USAF Studies New Fighters." *Aviation Week & Space Technology* (April 27, 1981).

(No author credited.) "USAF Wants Both F-15E and F-16E." *Flight International* (November 13, 1982): 1426.

(No author credited.) "Washington Round Up: Dual Role Fighter." *Aviation Week & Space Technology* (February 23, 1984).

Adams, R.S., and J.C. Elrod. "F-16XL Ground Vibration Test No. 1 (Air-to-Air)." General Dynamics Corporation. Report 400PR066 (July 9, 1982).

Adams, R.S., and J.C. Elrod. "F-16XL Ground Vibration Test No. 2 (Air-to-Ground)." General Dynamics Corporation. Report 400PR083 (December 20, 1982).

Anders, Scott G., and Michael C. Fischer. "F-16XL-2 Supersonic Laminar Flow Control Flight Test Experiment." NASA/TP-1999-209683 (December 1999).

Anderson, Bianca T., Jolen Flores, Stephen Landers, and Eugene L. Tu. "A Parametric Study of the Leading Edge Attachment Line for the F-16XL." AIAA Paper-91-1621 (June 1991).

Anderson, Bianca T., Stephen F. Landers, and Bruce H. Rowan. "F-16XL Supersonic Laminar Flow Control Glove Initial Flight Test Results." NASA TM-104270 (1993).

Anderson, Bianca T., and Marta Bohn-Meyer. "Overview of Supersonic Laminar Flow Control Research on the F-16XL Ships 1 and 2." Society of Automotive Engineers Paper 921994 (1992).

Anderson, Bianca T., and Marta Bohn-Meyer. "Overview of Supersonic Laminar Flow Research on the F-16XL Ships 1 and 2." NASA-TM-104257 (October 1, 1992).

Anderson, John D. "NASA and the Evolution of Computational Fluid Dynamics." Case 7 in *NASA's Contributions to Aeronautics*, edited by Richard P. Hallion. Washington, DC: NASA SP-2010-570-Vol 1 (2010).

Anderson, Seth B. "A Look at the Handling Qualities of Canard Configurations." NASA-TM-88354 (September 1986).

Arnal, D., and J.P. Archambaud. "Laminar-Turbulent Transition Control: NLF, LFC, HLFC." Paper 15 in *Proceedings of the NATO Research and Technology Organization/von Karman Institute Lecture Series on Advances in Laminar-Turbulent Transition Modeling*, held in Genèse, Belgium, June 9–12, 2008. RTO-EN-AVT-151 (September 2009).

Aronstein, David C., and Albert C. Piccirillo. "The F-16 Lightweight Fighter: A Case Study in Technology Transition." In *Technology and the Air Force: A Retrospective Assessment*. Washington, DC: Air Force History and Museums Program, 1997.

Badcock, Kenneth J. "Evaluation of Results from a Reynolds Averaged Multiblock Code Against F-16XL Flight Data." Presented at the 45th AIAA Aerospace Sciences Meeting and Exhibit, Reno, NV, January 8–11, 2007. AIAA Paper 2007-0490 (2007).

Badcock, Kenneth J. "Numerical Solutions for the CAWAPI Configuration on Structured Grids at University of Glasgow/University of Liverpool, United Kingdom." Chapter 6 in *Summary Report of Task Group AVT-113*. RTO-TR-AVT-113 AC/323 (AVT-113) TP/246 (October 2009).

Badcock, Kenneth J., Oklo Boelens, Simone Crippa, Adam Jirasek, John Lamar, and Arthur Rizzi. "Lessons Learned from Numerical Simulations of the F-16XL at Flight Conditions." *Journal of Aircraft*: 46, no. 2 (February 2009): 423–444.

Badcock, Kenneth J., Oklo Boelens, Adam Jirasek, and Arthur Rizzi. "What Was Learned from Numerical Simulations of F-16XL (CAWAPI) at Flight Conditions." AIAA Paper 2007-0683 (2007).

Beard, Jonathan. "Metal Glove Speeds Supersonic Planes." *New Scientist* 132, 1798 (December 7, 1991): 27.

Behbahani, Alireza R. "Need for Robust Sensors for Inherently Fail-Safe Gas Turbine Engine Controls, Monitoring, and Prognostics." Published in *Proceedings of the 52nd International Instrumentation Symposium, held in Cleveland, Ohio, 7-11 May 2006*. AFRL-PR-WP-TP-2007-217 (November 2006).

Benoliel, Alexander M. "Aerodynamic Pitch-Up of Cranked Arrow Wings: Estimation, Trim, and Configuration Design." Thesis, Virginia Polytechnic Institute & State University, Blacksburg, VA, May 1994.

Bensinger, C.T. "F-16XL Flight Flutter Tests." General Dynamics Corporation, Report 400PR100 (July 20, 1983).

Benson, Lawrence R. "Softening the Sonic Boom: 50 Years of NASA Research." Case 4 in *NASA's Contributions to Aeronautics*, edited by Richard P. Hallion. Washington, DC: NASA SP-2010-570-Vol 1 (2010).

Berry, F. Clifton Jr. "The Revolutionary Evolution of the F-16XL." *Air Force Magazine* 66, no. 11 (November 1983).

Black, G. Thomas, and David J. Moorehouse. "Design Conference Proceedings—Technology for Supersonic Cruise Military Aircraft." U.S. Air Force Flight Dynamics Laboratory, AFFDL-TR-77-85 (1976).

Boeing Commercial Airplane Company. "Application of Laminar Flow Control to Supersonic Transport Configurations." NASA CR-181917 (July 1990).

Boelens, O.J., S.P. Spekreijse, H.A. Sytsma, and K.M.J. de Cock. "Comparison of Measured and Simulated Flow Fields for the Full Scale F-16XL Aircraft." Presented at the 45th AIAA Aerospace Sciences Meeting and Exhibit, Reno, NV, January 8–11, 2007. AIAA Paper 2007-0489, 2007.

Boelens, O.J., K.J. Badcock, A. Elmilgui, K.S. Abdol-Hamid, and Massey, S.J. "Comparison of Measured and Block Structured Simulations for the F-16XL Aircraft." *Journal of Aircraft* 46, no. 2 (March-April 2009): 377–384.

Boelens, O.J., S. Goertz, S.A. Morton, W. Fritz, and J.E. Lamar. "Description of the F-16XL Geometry and Computational Grids Used in CAWAPI." AIAA Paper 2007-0488 (2007).

Boelens, O.J., K.J. Badcock, S. Goertz, S.A. Morton, W. Fritz, S.L. Karman, Jr., T. Michal, and Lamar, J.E. "F-16XL Geometry and Computational Grids Used in Cranked-Arrow Wing Aerodynamics Project International." *Journal of Aircraft* 46, no. 2 (March–April 2009): 369–376.

Bohn-Meyer, Marta R. "Constructing Gloved Wings for Aerodynamic Studies." NASA TM 100440 (May 1988).

von Bose, D.R., P.K. Tierney, and J.W. Wilson. "F-16XL Stability and Control Data Substantiation Report." General Dynamics Report, 400PR050 (May 1982).

Bower, J.N., and S.R. Scott. "The F-16XL Flight Test Program." *15th Annual Symposium Proceedings*. Society of Flight Test Engineers, August 1984, 9-1 to 9-5.

Boyne, Walter J. "Airpower Classics: J35 Draken," *Air Force Magazine* 94, no. 12 (December 2011).

Brandon, Jay M., Glaab, J. Louis, Phillip W. Brown, and Michael R. Phillips. "Ground-to-Flight Handling Qualities Comparisons for a High Performance Airplane." Presented at the *AIAA Atmospheric Flight Mechanics Conference*, Baltimore, MD, August 7–9, 1995. NASA-TM-111925, AIAA Paper 95-3457 (August 1995).

Brandon, Jay M., and John V. Foster. "Recent Dynamic Measurements and Considerations for Aerodynamic Modeling of Fighter Airplane Configurations." AIAA Paper 98-4447 (1998).

Brandon, Jay M., Vladislav Klein, Patrick C. Murphy, and Bandu N. Pamadi. "Prediction of Unsteady Aerodynamic Coefficients at High Angles of Attack." *AIAA Atmospheric Flight Mechanics Conference and Exhibit*, Montreal, Canada (August 6–9, 2001).

Brown, Alan. "NASA Dryden Chief Engineer Marta Bohn-Meyer Dies in Airplane Crash." NASA DFRC Press Release 05-60 (September 19, 2005).

Brown, Fred A. "SR-71 Sonic Boom Disturbances." NASA DFRC Press Release 96-35 (July 11, 1996).

Browne, Malcolm W. "Device is Found to Reduce Air's Drag on Jet Wings." *New York Times*, November 21, 1991.

Buckner, J.K., D.B. Benepe, and P.W. Hill. "Aerodynamic Design Evolution of the YF-16." AIAA Paper 74-935 (1974).

Bulban, Mark J. "Mach 2.2 F-16 Development Underway." *Aviation Week & Space Technology* (July 21, 1980): 20–22.

Bushnell, Dennis M. "Scaling: Wind Tunnel to Flight." *The Annual Review of Fluid Mechanics* 38 (2006): 111–128.

Bushnell, Dennis M., and Mujeeb R. Malik. "Supersonic Laminar-Flow Control." *Research in Natural Laminar Flow and Laminar-Flow Control.* NASA CP-2487 Part 3 (1987).

Bushnell, Mart H., Lt. Col. USAF, Director F-16E Combined Test Force. "Subject: Lt General Skantze F-16XL Briefing/Flight." Memorandum to AFFTC/CCP, January 24, 1983.

Campbell, James F., and Russell F. Osborn. "Leading-Edge Vortex Research: Some Nonplanar Concepts and Current Challenges." NASA CP-2108 (November 1979).

Canaan, James W. "Acid Test for Aeronautical Technology." *Air Force Magazine* 69, no. 1 (January 1986).

Carlson, H.W., and D.S. Miller. "The Influence of Leading-Edge Thrust on Twisted and Cambered Wing Design for Supersonic Cruise." Presented at the AIAA Aircraft Systems and Technology Conference, August 11–13, 1981, Dayton, OH. AIAA Paper 81-1656 (August 1981).

Chambers, J., and S. Grafton. "Aerodynamic Characteristics of Airplanes at High Angles of Attack." NASA TM 74097 (December 1977).

Cogan, Bruce, and Seung Yoo. "Handling Qualities Prediction of an F-16XL-Based Reduced Sonic Boom Aircraft." *NASA Tech Briefs* (October 1, 2010).

Collier, F.S., W. Pfenninger, M.C. Fischer, and R.D. Wagner. "Supersonic Laminar Flow Control on Commercial Transports." In *Proceedings of the 17th Congress of the International Council of the Aeronautical Sciences.* Washington, DC: AIAA, 1990.

Conahan, Frank C. "Letter to the Honorable Caspar W. Weinberger, the Secretary of Defense, Subject: Concerns About the Air Force Approach to the Dual Role Fighter Comparison." United States General Accounting Office, GAO/NSAID-84-49 (January 19, 1984).

Conahan, Frank C. "Letter to the Honorable Joseph P. Addabbo, Chairman, Subcommittee on Defense, Committee on Appropriations, House of Representatives, Subject: Evaluation of Sole-Source Award for Ejection Unit Development." United States General Accounting Office, GAO/NSIAD-84-85 (April 6, 1984).

Congressional Budget Office Special Study. "A Review of the Department of Defense Dec 31, 1981 Selected Acquisition Report (SAR)." Congress of the United States, Congressional Budget Office, May 1982.

Congressional Budget Office Special Study. "A Review of the Department of Defense Jun 30, 1982 Selected Acquisition Report." Congress of the United States, Congressional Budget Office, September 1982.

Congressional Budget Office Special Study. "A Review of the Department of Defense Sep 30, 1982 Selected Acquisition Report." Congress of the United States, Congressional Budget Office, December 1982.

Congressional Budget Office Staff Working Paper (Preliminary Analysis). Congress of the United States, Congressional Budget Office, May 1984.

Congressional Budget Office Study. "Tactical Combat Forces of the United States Air Force: Issues and Alternatives." Congress of the United States, Congressional Budget Office, April 1985.

Croft, John. "NASA Could Put F-16XL Back in the Air." *Flight International* (October 7, 2007).

Cummings, Russell M., S.A. Morton, and S.G. Siegel. "Computational Simulation and Experimental Measurements for a Delta Wing with Periodic Suction and Blowing." *Journal of Aircraft* 40, no. 5 (May 2003): 923–931.

Cummings, Russell M., Scott A. Morton, and David R. McDaniel. "Experiences in Accurately Predicting Time-Dependent Flows." *Progress in Aerospace Sciences* 44, no. 4 (May 2008): 241–257.

Cummings, Russell M., David R. McDaniel, and Scott A. Morton. "F-16XL Unsteady Simulations for the CAWAPI Facet of RTO Task Group AVT-113." AIAA Paper 2007-0493 (2007).

Curry, Marty. "NASA F-16XL Completes Digital Flight Control System Verification." NASA DFRC News Release 98-21 (April 14, 1998).

Curry, Marty. "NASA F-16XL Makes First Flight with Digital Flight Control System." NASA DFRC News Release 97-50 (December 17, 1997).

Curry, Marty. "F-16XL Projects." Dryden Aircraft, NASA DFRC, March 5, 2008.

Curry, Marty. "F-16XL (Ship #2)." Dryden Aircraft, NASA DFRC, April 22, 2009.

Curry, Robert E. "Dynamic Ground Effect for a Cranked Arrow Wing Airplane." NASA Technical Memorandum (TM) 4799 (1997).

Davis, M. Bruce, Christopher L. Reed, and Patrick J. Yagle. "Hybrid Grid Solutions on the (CAWAPI) F-16XL Using Falcon v4." Presented at the 45th AIAA Aerospace Sciences Meeting and Exhibit, Reno, NV, January 8–11, 2007. AIAA Paper 2007-0680 (2007).

Davis, M. Bruce, Christopher L. Reed, and Patrick J. Yagle. "Numerical Solutions for the CAWAPI Configuration on Unstructured Grids at Lockheed Martin, United States." Chapter 13 in Summary Report of Task Group AVT-113. NATO RTO-TR-AVT-113 (October 2009).

Dornheim, Michael A. "F-16XL Considered as Tailless Test Platform." *Aviation Week & Space Technology* (November 11, 1996).

Ehrenberger, L.J., Edward A. Haering, Jr., and Stephen A. Whitmore. "Preliminary Airborne Measurements for the SR-71 Sonic Boom Propagation Experiment." NASA TM 104307 (September 1995).

Eidetics Corporation. "Eidetics Awarded Phase III SBIR from NASA Langley Research Center (LaRC)." Press Release, May 2001.

Elbers, W.K. "Wind Tunnel Data Report 1/9-Scale F-16E Pressure Model NASA Ames Research Center Tests 517-1-11 and 517-1-97." General Dynamics Corporation, Report 400PR037, Vol. II (December 1981).

Ellis, J.A. "Flutter Analysis of F-16XL Air-to-Air Configurations." General Dynamics Corporation, Report 400PR062 (June 28, 1982).

Elmiligui, Alaa, Khalid Abdol-Hamid, and Steven Massey. "PAB3D Simulations for the CAWAPI F-16XL." Presented at the 45th AIAA Aerospace Sciences Meeting and Exhibit, Reno, NV, January 8–11, 2007. AIAA Paper 2007-0491 (2007).

Ennis, Michael. "The Plane the Pentagon Couldn't Stop." *Texas Monthly* (June 1981): 132–251.

Ennix, Kimberly A. "Engine Exhaust Characteristics Evaluation in Support of Aircraft Acoustic Testing." NASA TM 10426 (June 1993).

Epstein, Charles. "Taking the Drag Out of Bombs." *Flight International* (August 21, 1982).

Erickson, Gary E. "High Angle-of-Attack Aerodynamics." *Annual Review of Fluid Mechanics* 27 (1995): 45–88.

Finley, Dennis B. "Final F-16XL Aerodynamic Status Report and Flight Test Results." General Dynamics Corporation, Fort Worth Division. Report 400PR139, Contract F33657-78G-0004-0009 (September 1985).

Finley, Dennis B., and W. Elliot Schoonover, Jr. "Design and Wind Tunnel Evaluation of Vortex Flaps for the F-16XL." NASA TP-3106 (1986).

Fischer, Michael C. "F-16XL Supersonic Laminar Flow Control Program Overview." In *NASA Langley Research Center First Annual High-Speed Research Workshop, Part 4*. NASA, April 1, 1992, 1811–1820.

Fisher, Bruce D., David F. Fischer, John E. Lamar, and Clifford J. Obara. "Flight, Wind-Tunnel and Computational Fluid Dynamics for Cranked Arrow Wing (F-16XL-1) at Subsonic and Transonic Speeds." NASA/TP-2001-210629 (February 2001).

Fischer, Michael C., and Chandra S. Vemuru. "Application of Laminar Flow Control to the High Speed Civil Transport—The NASA Supersonic Laminar Flow Control Program." Presented at the Aerospace Technology Conference and Exposition, Long Beach, CA, September 1991. SAE Paper 912115 (September 1, 1991).

Flanagan, William. "NASA and Supersonic Cruise." Case 10 in *NASA's Contributions to Aeronautics*, edited by Richard P. Hallion. Washington, DC: NASA SP-2010-570-Vol 2 (2010).

Flores, J., E. Tu, B. Anderson, and S. Landers. "A Parametric Study of the Leading Edge Attachment Line for the F-16XL." Presented at the 22nd AIAA Fluid Dynamics, Plasma Dynamics and Lasers Conference, Honolulu, HI, June 24–26, 1991. AIAA Paper 91-1621 (June 1991).

Flores, Jolen, Lyndell King, and Eugene Tu. "Code Validation for the Simulation of Supersonic Viscous Flow about the F-16XL." Presented at NASA Langley Research Center, First Annual High-Speed Research Workshop, Part 4, April 1, 1992, 1893–1908.

Forgey, D.H., W.C. Wilde, and N.N. Weis. "F-16XL Flight Control System Description Report." General Dynamics Corporation, Report 400PR042 (December 1982).

Fox, Mike C., and Dana K. Forrest. "Supersonic Aerodynamic Characteristics of an Advanced F-16 Derivative Aircraft Configuration." NASA Technical Paper (TP) 3355 (July 1993).

Frink, N.T. "A Concept for Designing Vortex Flap Geometries." NASA TP-2233 (December 1983).

Fritz, Willy. "Hybrid Grid RANS Solutions for the CAWAPI F-16XL." Presented at the 45th Aerospace Sciences Meeting and Exhibit, Reno, NV, January 8–11, 2007. AIAA Paper 2007-0492 (2007).

Fritz, Willy, M. Davis, Steve Karman, Todd Michal. "Reynolds-Averaged Navier-Stokes Solutions for the CAWAPI F-16XL Using Different Hybrid Grids." *Journal of Aircraft* 46, no. 2 (February 2009): 409–422.

Garino, David P. "General Dynamics to Spend $53 Million on Two Versions of Its F16 Fighter Plane." *The Wall Street Journal* (December 8, 1980).

Garrison, Peter. "The Hammer: For Every Airplane, There's a Region of the Flight Envelope Into Which It Dare Not Fly." *Air & Space Magazine* (March 2001).

General Dynamics Corporation. "F-16F (XL) Demonstration Aircraft Flight Activity." Foldout Chart, General Dynamics Corporation, Fort Worth Division (undated, circa mid-1985).

General Dynamics Corporation. "F-16XL Final Performance Flight Test Results (PHASE 1)." General Dynamics Corporation, Fort Worth Division. Report 400PR141, Contract F33657-78G-0004-0009 (July 31, 1985).

General Dynamics Corporation. "F-16XL Flight Test Program, Final Report." General Dynamics Corporation, Fort Worth Division. Report 400PR142, Contract F33657-78-G-0004/0009 (December 20, 1985).

General Dynamics Corporation. "F-16XL No. 1 Ground, Flight Test and Delivery, Revision A-1." General Dynamics Corporation, Fort Worth Division, April 1, 1982.

General Dynamics Corporation. "F-16XL Rollout and First Flight." *Division Log*, General Dynamics Corporation, Fort Worth Division. Bulletin 1098 (July 22, 1982).

General Dynamics Corporation. "General Dynamics F-16XLC/D MULTIROLE FIGHTER." General Dynamics Corporation Marketing Brochure, Fort Worth Division (undated, circa 1983).

General Dynamics Corporation. "Manufacturing/Project Planning Chart: F-16XL Production Flow (Two Place Aircraft)." General Dynamics Corporation, Fort Worth Division, January 26, 1983.

General Dynamics Corporation. "Preliminary Design Drawing: Internal Arrangement, Dual Role Fighter Aircraft." General Dynamics Corporation, Fort Worth Division. F-16 DRF Proposal, April 22, 1983.

Goertz, Stefan, and Adam Jirasek. "Numerical Solutions for the CAWAPI Configuration on Unstructured Grids at KTH/FOI, Sweden." Chapters 10 and 11 in *Summary Report of Task Group AVT-113*. NATO Research and Technology Organization, RTO-TR-AVT-113 AC/323 (AVT-113) TP/246 (2007).

Goertz, Stefan, and Adam Jirasek. "Steady and Unsteady CFD Analysis of the F-16XL Using the Unstructured Edge Code." Presented at the 45th

Aerospace Sciences Meeting and Exhibit, Reno, NV, January 8–11, 2007. AIAA Paper 2007-0678 (2007).

Goertz, Stefan, Adam Jirasek, Scott Morton, David McDaniel, Russell Cummings, John Lamar, Khaled Abdol-Hamid. "Standard Unstructured Grid Solutions for Cranked Arrow Wing Aerodynamics Project International F-16XL." *Journal of Aircraft*: 46, no. 2 (February 2009): 385–408.

Gottschalk, Mark A. "Going with the Flow: Developments in Laminar-Flow Technology May Dramatically Reduce Drag in Next Generation Aircraft." *Design News* (September 9, 1996).

Grafton, Sue B. "Low-Speed Wind-Tunnel Study of the High-Angle-of-Attack Stability and Control Characteristics of a Cranked-Arrow-Wing Fighter Configuration." NASA TM 85776 (May 1984).

Grafton, Sue B., and Nguyen, Luat T. "Wind Tunnel Free-Flight Investigation of a Model of a Cranked-Arrow Wing Fighter Configuration." NASA TP 2410 (1985).

Green, John E. "Laminar Flow Control—Back to the Future?" Presented at the 38th Fluid Dynamics Conference and Exhibit, Seattle, WA, June 2008. AIAA Paper 2008-3738 (2008).

Green, Lawrence L., Angela M. Spence, and Patrick C. Murphy. "Computational Methods for Dynamic Stability and Control Derivatives." Presented at the 42nd Aerospace Sciences Meeting and Exhibit, Reno, NV, 2003. AIAA Paper 2004-0015 (2004).

Gursul, I., and Z. Wang. "High Angle of Attack Aerodynamics." *Encyclopedia of Aerospace Engineering.* John Wiley & Sons, Ltd., 2010.

Haering, Edward A., Jr. "SR-71 Experiment on Propagation of Sonic Booms." *NASA Tech Briefs* 20, no. 1 (January 1996): 68–69.

Haering, Edward A., Jr., L.J. Ehrenberger, and Stephen A. Whitmore. "Preliminary Airborne Measurements for the SR-71 Sonic Boom Propagation Experiment." Presented at the 1995 High Speed Research Program Sonic Boom Workshop, NASA Langley Research Center, Hampton, VA, September 12–13, 1995. NASA TM 104307 (1995).

Hahne, David E. "Low-Speed Aerodynamic Data for a 0.18-Scale Model of an F-16XL with Various Leading-Edge Modifications." NASA TM 1999-209703 (1999).

Hallion, Richard P. "A Troubling Past: Air Force Fighter Acquisition since 1945." Presented at the Triangle Universities' Security Seminar on Changing Technologies and New Weapons Systems, Durham, NC, February 2–3, 1990. *Airpower Journal* (winter 1990).

Hallion, Richard P. "Sweep and Swing: Reshaping the Wing for the Jet and Rocket Age." Case 1 in *NASA's Contributions to Aeronautics*. NASA SP-2010-570-Vol 1 (2010).

Hallion, Richard P. "The Air Force and the Supersonic Breakthrough." In Neufeld et al, eds., *Technology and the Air Force: A Retrospective Assessment*. Washington, DC: Air Force History and Museums Program, 1997.

Harrington, Caitlin. "Leaner and Greener: Fuel Efficiency Takes Flight." Case 12 in *NASA's Contributions to Aeronautics*, edited by Richard P. Hallion. Washington, DC: NASA SP-2010-570-Vol 1 (2010).

Harris, Roy V., Jr., and Jerry N. Hefner. "NASA Laminar-Flow Program—Past, Present, and Future." In *Research in Natural Laminar Flow and Laminar-Flow Control*. NASA CP-2487, pt. 1 (1987).

Hart, C.E. "F-16XL Fighter Engineering Organization Assignment of Responsibilities." General Dynamics Fort Worth Division, Project Engineering Memorandum (PEM) No. 19-1.1, November 20, 1980, Revised December 30, 1980.

Hart, C.E., Chief Engineer, F-16XL Program. "Memo to F-16XL Engineering Personnel: F-16XL Weight Saving." General Dynamics, Fort Worth Division, F-16XL-ENG-48 (April 10, 1981).

Hehs, Eric. "Harry Hillaker: Father of the F-16." *Code One Magazine* (April 1991).

Hehs, Eric. "Marta-Bohn-Myer: NASA Flight Researcher." *Code One Magazine* (April 1994).

Hillaker, Harry J. "The F-16: A Technology Demonstrator, a Prototype, and a Flight Demonstrator." *Proceedings of AIAA Aircraft Prototype and Technology Demonstrator Symposium*, March 23–24, 1983, Dayton, OH, AIAA Paper 83-1063 (March 1983).

Hillaker, Harry J. "F-16XL Flight Test Program Overview," 2nd AHS, IES, SETP, SFTE, and DGLR Flight Testing Conference, Las Vegas, NV, November 16–18, 1983. AIAA Paper 83-2730 (November 1, 1983).

Hillaker, Harry J. Letter to Paul J. Kinson, publisher/editor, *Aerotech News and Review,* January 24, 1995.

Hillaker, Harry J. F-16XL Presentation to the Lone Star Aero Club, Arlington, TX, September 3, 1998.

Hillaker, Harry J. "SCAMP: Supersonic Combat and Maneuvering Prototype Program." General Dynamics Corporation, Fort Worth Division, September 1977.

Hillaker, Harry J., Vice President and Deputy Program Manager, F-16XL. Memo to D.R. Kent, December 15, 1980.

Hinman, K.R. "F-16E Point Paper." General Dynamics Corporation, July 27, 1981.

Hoffman, Sherwood. "Bibliography of the Supersonic Cruise Research (SCR) Program from 1977–Mid-1980." NASA Report 1063 (December 1980).

Holme, O. "Den Aerodynamiska Bakgrunden till Viggens Vingsystem" ("The Aerodynamic Background of the Wing System of the *Viggen*"). *Kosmos* (1968).

Holmes, Bruce J., and Clifford J. Obara. "Flight-Measured Laminar Boundary-Layer Transition Phenomena Including Stability Theory Analysis." NASA TP-2417 (1985).

Holzman, Jon K., Lannie D. Webb, and Frank W. Burcham, Jr. "Flight and Static Exhaust Flow Properties of an F110-GE-129 Engine in an F-16XL Airplane During Acoustic Tests." NASA TM 104326 (November 1996).

Huber, Mark. "Mach 1 for Millionaires: Briefcase-Toting Suits Who Travel in Bizjets—Those Will Be the Next Pioneers in Supersonic Flight." *Air & Space Magazine* (March 2006).

Humphries, John A., and Donald J. Caughlin. "F-16XL Flying Qualities with the Large Normal Shock Inlet." Air Force Flight Test Center Technical Report TR-85-34 (November 1985).

Jiang, Bin, Jian Liang Wang, and Yeng Chai Soh. "Robust Fault Diagnosis for a Class of Linear Systems with Uncertainty." In *Proceedings of the 1999 American Control Conference*, August 2002.

Johnson, J.L., S.B. Grafton, and L.P. Yip. "Exploratory Investigation of the Effects of Vortex Bursting on High-Angle-of-Attack Lateral-Directional Stability Characteristics of Highly Swept Wings." AIAA Paper 80-0463 (March 1980).

Jones, S.E., and N.S. Yakzan. "F-16XL Digital Flight Control System Handling Qualities Analysis Report." General Dynamics Corporation, Fort Worth Division. Report 72PR206 (February 1996).

Joslin, Ronald D. "Aircraft Laminar Flow Control." *Annual Review of Fluid Mechanics* 30 (1998): 1–29.

Joslin, Ronald D., Robert F. Kunz, and David R. Stinebring. "Flow Control Technology Readiness: Aerodynamic Versus Hydrodynamic." AIAA Paper 2000-4412 (2000).

Joslin, Ronald D. "Overview of Laminar Flow Control." NASA TP-1998-208705 (October 1998).

Karman, Steve, Brent Mitchell, Shane Sawyer, and Justin Whitt. "Unstructured Grid Solutions of CAWAPI F-16XL by UT SimCenter." Presented at the 45th AIAA Aerospace Sciences Meeting and Exhibit, Reno, NV, January 8–11, 2007. AIAA Paper 2007-0681 (2007).

Kehoe, Michael W. "A Historic Overview of Flight Flutter Testing." NASA TM 4720 (October 1995).

Kehoe, Michael W. "Aircraft Flight Flutter Testing at the NASA Ames-Dryden Flight Research Facility." NASA TM-100417 (May 1988).

Kelly, Jeffrey J., Mark R. Wilson, John Rawls, Jr., Thomas D. Norum, and Robert A. Golub. "F-16XL and F-18 High Speed Acoustic Flight Test Data Base." NASA CD TM-100006 (1996).

Kent, D. Randy, Vice President and Program Director, F-16XL Program. Memorandum to Richard E. Adams, Vice President and General Manager, General Dynamics Fort Worth Division, December 12, 1980.

Kent, D. Randy, Vice President and Program Director, F-16XL Program, General Dynamics Fort Worth Division. Letter to Brig. Gen. G.L. Monahan, Aeronautical Systems Division, January 7, 1981.

Kent, D. Randy, Vice President and Program Director, F-16XL Program. "F-16XL Fighting Falcon First Flight Certificate." General Dynamics Corporation, Fort Worth Division, July 3, 1982.

Kent, D. Randy. "F-16XL First Flight Anniversary Celebration: Perspectives on the F-16XL Program." Presentation to the F-16XL First Flight 25th Anniversary Celebration, Lockheed Martin Corporation, Fort Worth, TX, July 3, 2007.

Kent, D. Randy. "F-16XL Program Organization." General Dynamics Fort Worth Division, F-16XL Program Directive Memorandum No. 2, November 25, 1980.

Kim, Sungwan, Patrick Murphy, and Vladislav Klein. "Evaluation and Analysis of F-16XL Wind Tunnel Data from Dynamic Tests." Presented at the AIAA Atmospheric Flight Mechanics Conference, Austin, TX, August 11–14, 2003. AIAA Paper 2003-5396, NASA TM-2004-213234 (June 2004).

Kim, Sungwan, Patrick Murphy, and Vladislav Klein. "Evaluation and Analysis of F-16XL Wind Tunnel Data from Static and Dynamic Tests." NASA TM 213234 (June 2004).

King, David, and Donald S. Massey. "History of the F-15 Program: A Silver Anniversary Remembrance." *Air Force Journal of Logistics* 21, no. 2 (winter 1997).

Klein, Vladislav, and Patrick C. Murphy. "Aerodynamic Parameters of High Performance Aircraft Estimated from Wind Tunnel and Flight Test Data." *Proceedings of the NATO Research and Technology Organization (RTO)*

Systems Concepts and Integration (SCI) Panel Symposium, Madrid, Spain, May 5–7, 1998. NATO RTO-MP-11 AC/323 (SCI) TP-7 (1999).

Klein, V., P.C. Murphy, T.J. Curry, and J.M. Brandon. "Analysis of Wind Tunnel Longitudinal Static and Oscillatory Data of the F-16XL Aircraft." NASA TM-97-206276 (December 1997).

Klein, V., P.C. Murphy, and N.M. Szyba. "Analysis of Wind Tunnel Lateral Oscillatory Data of the F-16XL Aircraft." NASA TM-2004-213246, AIAA Paper 2004-3786 (August 2004).

Klein, Vladislav, and Patrick Murphy. "Estimation of Aircraft Nonlinear Unsteady Parameters from Wind Tunnel Data." NASA TM-1998-208969, December 1998.

Korstian, J.D. "F-16XL-1 Daily Status/Pilot Flight Report." General Dynamics Corporation, Fort Worth Division, July 6, 1982.

Kozicharow, Eugene. "USAF Selects F-15 as Dual-Role Fighter." *Aviation Week & Space Technology* (March 5, 1984).

Lake, Jon. "Fairey Deltas: FD.1, FD.2, & BAC 221." *Wings of Fame* 11 (1998).

Lamar, John E., and James M. Luckring. "The Cranked-Arrow Wing Aerodynamics Project and its Extension to the International Community as CAWAPI: Objectives and Overview." Chapter 3 in *Summary Report of Task Group AVT-113*, RTO-TR-AVT-113 AC/323 (AVT-113) TP/246 (October 2009).

Lamar, John E. "Cranked-Arrow Wing (F-16XL-1) Flight Flow Physics with CFD Predictions at Subsonic and Transonic Speeds." *Meeting Proceedings of the RTO AVT Symposium on Advanced Flow Management, Part A—Vortex Flow at High Angle of Attack*, held in Loen, Norway, May 7–11, 2001. AVT-072, RTO-MP-069(I) AC/323 (AVT-072/073) TP/47 (March 2003).

Lamar, John E., Roy T. Schemensky, and C. Subba Reddy. "Development of a Vortex-Lift-Design Method and Application to a Slender Maneuver-Wing Configuration." Presented at the AIAA 18th Aerospace Sciences Meeting, Pasadena, CA, January 14–16, 1980. AIAA Paper 80-0327 (January 1980).

Lamar, John E., R.T. Schemensky, and C.S. Reddy. "Development of a Vortex Lift Design Procedure and Application to a Slender-Maneuver-Wing Configuration." *Journal of Aircraft* 18, no. 4 (April 1981): 259–266.

Lamar, John E., Clifford J. Obara, Bruce D. Fisher, and David F. Fisher. "Flight, Wind-Tunnel and Computational Fluid Dynamics Comparison for Cranked Arrow Wing (F-16XL-1) at Subsonic and Transonic Speeds." NASA/TP-2001-210629 (February 2001).

Lamar, John E. "High Angle of Attack Aerodynamics." Paper 6 in *Special Course on Engineering Methods in Aerodynamic Analysis and Design of Aircraft*, Presented at the Middle East Technical University, Ankara, Turkey, May 6–10, 1991, at the von Karman Institute for Fluid Mechanics, Rhode-St.-Genèse, Belgium, May 13–17, 1991, and at the Universidad Politécnica, Madrid, Spain, May 20–24, 1991. AGARD Report AR-73 (January 1992).

Lamar, John E., and Khaled S. Abdol-Hamid. "Numerical Solutions for the CAWAPI Configuration on Unstructured Grids at the NASA LaRC, United States." In *Summary Report of Task Group AVT-113*. NATO Research and Technology Organization. RTO-TR-AVT-113 (AVT-113) TP/246 (October 2009).

Lamar, John E., and Clifford J. Obara. "Overview of the Cranked-Arrow Wing Aerodynamics Project International." Presented as AIAA Paper 2007-0487 at the 45th AIAA Aerospace Sciences Meeting and Exhibit, Reno, NV, January 8–11, 2007. *Journal of Aircraft*: 46, no. 2 (March–April 2009): 355–368.

Lamar, John E. "Prediction of F-16XL Flight Flow Physics." *Journal of Aircraft* 46, no. 2 (March–April 2009): 354.

Lamar, John E., and C.J. Obara. "Review of Cranked-Arrow Wing Aerodynamics Project: Its International Aeronautical Community Role." AIAA Paper 2007-0487 (January 2007).

Lamar, John E., Catherine K. Cronin, and Laura E. Scott. "A Review of Steps Taken to Create an International Virtual Laboratory at NASA Langley for Aerodynamic Prediction and Comparison." *Progress in Aerospace Sciences* 40, no. 3 (April 2004): 163–172.

Lamar, John E. "Some Vortical-Flow Flight Experiments on Slender Aircraft That Impacted the Advancement of Aeronautics." *Progress in Aerospace Sciences* 45, Issue 6-8 (August 2009): 147–168.

Lamar, John E. "Subsonic Vortex Flow Design Study for Slender Wings." Presented at the AIAA 16th Aerospace Sciences Meeting, Huntsville, AL, January 16–18, 1978. AIAA Paper 78-154 (January 1978).

Lamar, John E., and K.S. Abdol-Hamid. "USM3D Unstructured Grid Solutions for CAWAPI at NASA LaRC." AIAA Paper 2007-0682 (2007).

Lamar, John E., Catherine K. Cronin, and Laura E. Scott. "Virtual Laboratory Enabling Collaborative Research in Applied Vehicle Technologies." In *Proceedings of the NATO RTO AVT-113 Symposium on Flow Induced Unsteady Loads and the Impact on Military Application*, Budapest, Hungary, April 25–29, 2005. NATO RTO-TR-AVT-113 (October 2009).

Lamar, John E., and J.F. Campbell. "Vortex Flaps—Advanced Control Devices for Supercruise Fighters." *Aerospace America* (January 1984): 95–99.

Lambourne, N.C. "Control Surface Buzz." In *Reports and Memoranda No. 3364.* London: Aeronautical Research Council, Ministry of Aviation, 1964.

Landers, Stephen F., John A. Saltzman, and Lisa J. Bjarke. "F-16XL Wing Pressure Distributions and Shock Fence Results from Mach 1.4 to Mach 2.0." NASA TM-97-206219 (1997).

Lessard, Wendy B. "Subsonic Analysis of 0.04-Scaled F-16XL Models Using an Unstructured Euler Code." NASA TP-3597, 1996.

Lockheed Martin. "25 Years of F-16XL: Jul 3, 1982—Jul 3, 2007." Commemorative Chart distributed at 25th Anniversary F-16XL First Flight Celebration, Lockheed Martin Corporation, Fort Worth, TX, July 3, 2007.

Lockheed Martin, "25th Anniversary F-16XL Fighting Falcon First Flight Invitation." Lockheed Martin Corporation, July 3, 2007.

Lockheed Martin. "The Official F-16XL Fighting Falcon First Flight TRIVIA CONTEST." Multiple Choice Questionnaire distributed at 25th Anniversary F-16XL First Flight Celebration, Lockheed Martin Corporation, Fort Worth, TX, July 3, 2007.

Loman, R.B., J.W. Wilson, and S.D. Johnson. "F-16XL Stability and Control Flight Test Report." General Dynamics Corporation Report 400PR106, Addendum I (December 1985).

Lucking, James M. "An Overview of the RTO Symposium on Vortex Flow and High Angle of Attack Aerodynamics." In *Proceedings of the 2002 International Council of the Aeronautical Sciences (ICAS) Congress*, 2002.

Lyons, Robert F., Maj., USAF. "The Search for an Advanced Fighter: A History from the XF-108 to the Advanced Tactical Fighter." Air Command and Staff College. Report Number 86-1575 (April 1986).

Mankins, John C. "Technology Readiness Levels: A White Paper." Office of Space Access and Technology, NASA Headquarters, April 6, 1995.

Marshall, Laurie A. "Boundary-Layer Transition Results from the F-16XL-2 Supersonic Laminar Flow Control Experiment." NASA TM-1999-209013 (December 1999).

Marshall, Laurie A. "Summary of Transition Results from the F-16XL-2 Supersonic Laminar Flow Control Experiment." Presented at the AIAA Applied Aerodynamics Conference, Denver, CO, August 14–17, 2000. AIAA Paper 2000-4418 (August 2000).

Mason, W.H. "Some High Alpha Aerodynamics." Lecture Charts, Configuration Aerodynamics Class, Department of Aerospace and Ocean Engineering, Virginia Polytechnic Institute and State University, Blacksburg, VA, 2010.

McDaniel, D.R., R.M. Cummings, K. Bergeron, S.A. Morton, and J.P. Dean. "Comparisons of Computational Fluid Dynamics Solutions of Static and Maneuvering Fighter Aircraft with Flight Test Data." In *Proceedings of the Institute of Mechanical Engineering*, Vol. 223: Part G, *Journal of Aerospace Engineering* (2009): 323–340.

McKenna, James T. "Smart Supersonic Wing." *Popular Mechanics* 173, no. 2 (February 1996).

McKinney, Jim. "Memorandum to F-16XL Development Team, Subject: F-16XL First Flight." General Dynamics Corporation, Fort Worth Division, July 6, 1982.

McKinney, Jim. "F-16XL Flight No. 1 Pilot Report." General Dynamics Corporation, Fort Worth Division, July 3, 1982.

McParlin, Stephen C., and Robert W. Tramel. "Taxonomy of Flight Mechanics Issues for Aircraft, and Underlying Fluid Dynamics Phenomena." AIAA Paper 2009-744 (2009).

Meacham, M. "F-16XL Aircraft Fly Out of Storage to Perform Supersonic Flight Tests." *Aviation Week & Space Technology* (March 27, 1989): 27.

Meyer, Robert R., Jr. "Overview of the NASA Dryden Flight Research Facility Aeronautical Flight Projects." NASA TM 104254 (1992).

Michal, Todd, Derek Babcock, Matthew Oser, Mori Mani, and Frederick Roos. "BCFD Unstructured-Grid Predictions on the F-16XL (CAWAPI) Aircraft." Presented at the 45th AIAA Aerospace Sciences Meeting and Exhibit, Reno, NV, January 8–11, 2007. AIAA Paper 2007-0679 (2007).

Michel, Marshall L. III. "The Revolt of the Majors: How the Air Force Changed After Vietnam." Dissertation, Auburn University, Auburn, AL, December 15, 2006.

Miller, David S., and Roy T. Schemansky. "Design Study Results of a Supersonic Cruise Fighter Wing." Presented at the AIAA 17th Aerospace Sciences Meeting, New Orleans, LA, January 15–17, 1979. AIAA Paper 79-0062 (January 1979).

Molloy, Matthew H., Maj., USAF. "High-Speed Flight and the Military." AU/ACSC/136/1999-04, Air Command and Staff College, Air University, Maxwell AFB, AL, April 1999.

Morris, O.A. "Subsonic and Supersonic Aerodynamic Characteristics of a Supersonic Cruise Fighter with a Twisted and Cambered Wing with 74° Sweep." NASA TM X-3530 (August 1977).

Morroco, J.D. "Langley to Receive NASA F-16XL." *Aviation Week & Space Technology* (June 11, 1990): 22.

Morton, Scott A., David R. McDaniel, and Russell M. Cummings. "F-16XL Unsteady Simulations for the CAWAPI Facet of RTO Task Group AVT-113."

Presented at the 45th Aerospace Sciences Meeting and Exhibit, Reno, NV, January 8–11, 2007. AIAA Paper 2007-0493 (2007).

Murphy, Patrick C., Vladislav Klein, and Nathan M. Szyba. "Progressive Aerodynamic Model Identification from Dynamic Water Tunnel Test of the F-16XL Aircraft." Presented at the AIAA Atmospheric Flight Mechanics Conference and Exhibit, Providence, RI, August 16–19, 2004. AIAA Paper 2004-5277 (2004).

Murphy, Patrick C., and V. Klein. "Validation of Methodology for Estimating Aircraft Unsteady Aerodynamic Parameters from Dynamic Wind Tunnel Tests." Presented at the AIAA Atmospheric Flight Mechanics Conference, Austin, TX, August 11–14, 2003. AIAA Paper 2003-5397 (2003).

Nangia, R.K., and A.S. Miller. "Vortex Flow Dilemmas and Control on Wing Planforms for High Speeds." Presented at the Research and Technology (RTO) Task Group on Aeronautical Vehicle Technology (AVT) held in Loen, Norway, May 7–11, 2001. In *Symposium on Advanced Flow Management: Part A—Vortex Flows and High Angle of Attack for Military Vehicles*, NATO RTO-MP-069(I) (2002).

NASA. "Aircraft Flutter Testing—Transportation." *NASA Spinoff*, 1997, 62.

NASA Dryden Flight Research Center. "Return to Flight and Supportability Study." Solicitation Number NND07204397Q-DAC, DFRC Code A (Research and Development) (June 20, 2007).

NASA Dryden Flight Research Center Fact Sheet. "F-16XL Laminar Flow Research Aircraft." FS-023-DFRC (December 3, 2009).

NASA Dryden Flight Research Center. "F-16XL Ship #2 Supersonic Laminar Flow Control." *http://www.nasa.gov/centers/dryden/history/pastprojects/F16XL2* (undated).

NASA Dryden Flight Research Center Technology Facts. "F-16XL Supersonic Laminar Flow." TF-2004-12-DFRC (2004).

NASA Dryden Flight Research Center Fact Sheet, "F-16XL-1 Testbed Aircraft Project Summary." FS-051-DFRC (December 3, 2009).

NASA Dryden Flight Research Center News Release. "NASA Conducts Sonic Boom Tests with SR-71." NASA DFRC NR 95-02 (January 24, 1995).

NASA Dryden Flight Research Center News Release. "NASA F-16XL Completes Digital Flight Control System Verification." NASA DFRC NR 98-21 (April 14, 1998).

NASA Dryden Research Center. "X-29." Fact Sheets. December 12, 2009. *http://www.nasa.gov/centers/dryden/news/FactSheets/FS-008-DFRC.html.*

NASA. "High-Speed Research (HSR), Smoothing the Flow Over Supersonic Wings, Supersonic Laminar Flow Control." NASA Langley Research Center Fact Sheet FS-1996-09-17 (September 1996).

NASA Langley Research Center Fact Sheet. "High-Speed Research (HSR)— Smoothing the Flow Over Supersonic Wings." NASA LaRC FS-1996-09-17-LaRC (September 1996).

NASA Langley Research Center Fact Sheet. "NASA's High Speed Research (HSR) Program—Developing Tomorrow's Supersonic Passenger Jet." NASA LaRC Overview Fact Sheet (Undated).

NATO Science and Technology Organization. "Understanding and Modeling Vortical Flows to Improve the Technology Readiness Level for Military Aircraft." In *Summary Report of Task Group AVT-113*. NATO Research and Technology Organization. RTO-TR-AVT-113 AC/323 (AVT-113) TP/246 (October 2009).

Nelson, J. Richard. "F/A-22 Independent Cost Estimate." Institute for Defense Analyses. Report P-4029 (August 2005).

Norlin, Ken A. "Flight Simulation Software at NASA Dryden Flight Research Center." NASA TM-104315 (October 1995).

Norris, Guy. "The Final Frontier." *Flight International* (December 23, 1998–January 5, 1999): 29–31.

Norris, Guy. "Smooth and Supersonic." *Flight International* (May 18, 1994): 32–33.

National Transportation Safety Board (NTSB). "NTSB Accident Brief: Pilot/ Race 177, *The Galloping Ghost*, North American P-51D N79111, Reno, Nevada, Sep 16, 2001." NTSB/AAB-12/01, PB2012-916203 (August 27, 2012).

Obara, Clifford J. "Sublimating Chemical Technique for Boundary-Layer Flow Visualization in Flight Testing." *Journal of Aircraft* 25 (June 1988): 493–498.

Ogburn, Marilyn E., T. Luat, and Phillip W. Brown. "Simulation Study of a Cranked-Arrow Wing Fighter Configuration at High Angles of Attack." NASA TM 85800 (November 1984).

Owens, D. Bruce, Jay M. Brandon, Mark A. Croom, C. Michael Fremaux, Eugene H. Heim, and Dan D. Vicroy. "Overview of Dynamic Test Techniques for Flight Dynamics Research at NASA LaRC." Presented at the 25th AIAA Aerodynamic Measurement Technology and Ground Testing Conference, June 5–8, 2006, San Francisco, CA. AIAA Paper 2006-3146 (2006).

Paulk, R.A. "A Wind Tunnel Test to Determine the Separation Characteristics of Several Stores from the F-16XL Aircraft at Mach Numbers from 0.5 to 1.96." Arnold Engineering Development Center. AEDC-TSR-82-P20 (July 1982).

Pfenninger, Werner, and Chandra S. Vemuru. "Design Aspects of Long Range Supersonic LFC Airplanes with Highly Swept Wings." SAE Paper 881397 (October 1988).

Phillips, Edward H. "NASA Readies F-16XL for High-Lift Tests." *Aviation Week & Space Technology* (September 13, 1993): 50–52.

Piccirillo, Albert C. "The Advanced Tactical Fighter—Design Goals and Technical Challenges." *Aerospace America* 22, no. 11 (November 1984): 74–79.

Pike, John. "Dual Role Fighter." *GlobalSecurity.org*, updated July 7, 2011 (retrieved October 11, 2011).

Pike, John. "F-16E/F/F-16XL Fighting Falcon." *GlobalSecurity.org*, updated July 7, 2011 (retrieved October 11, 2011).

Polhamus, Edward C. "A Concept of the Vortex Lift of Sharp-Edge Delta Wings Based on a Leading-Edge-Suction Analogy." NASA TN D-3767 (December 1966).

Polhamus, Edward C. "Applying Slender Wing Benefits to Military Aircraft." Presented as AIAA Paper 83-2566 at the AIAA/AHA Aircraft Design, Systems and Technology Meeting, Fort Worth, TX, October 17–19, 1983. In *Journal of Aircraft* 21, no. 8 (August 1984): 545–559.

Polhamus, Edward C. "Vortex Lift Research: Early Contributions and Some Current Challenges." In *Vortex Flow Aerodynamics—Volume I, Proceedings of Conference held Oct 8-10, 1986 at Langley Research Center.* NASA CP-2416, Paper No. 1 (1986): 1–30.

Powell, Arthur G., S. Agrawal, and T.R. Lacey. "Feasibility and Benefits of Laminar Flow Control on Supersonic Cruise Airplanes." NASA CR 181817 (July 1989).

Powell, Arthur G. "Supersonic LFC: Challenges and Opportunities." In *Proceedings of the NASA Langley Research Center First Annual High-Speed Research Workshop, Williamsburg, Virginia, May 14-16, 1991, Part 4*, April 1, 1992: 1823–1840.

Preston, J.H. "The Determination of Turbulent Skin Friction by Means of Pitot Tubes." *Journal of the Royal Aeronautical Society* 58, no. 109 (1954).

R.L. Radkey, H.R. Welge, and R.L. Roensch. "Aerodynamic Design of a Mach 2.2 Supersonic Cruise Aircraft." *Journal of Aircraft* 15, no. 6 (June 1978): 351–357.

Rao, Dhanvada M. "Leading-Edge Vortex Flaps for Enhanced Subsonic Aerodynamics of Slender Wings." In *Proceedings of the 7th Congress of the International Council of the Aeronautical Sciences.* ICAS Paper 80-13.5 (1980).

Rao, Dhanvada M. "Low-Speed Wind Tunnel Study of Longitudinal Stability and Usable-Lift Improvement of a Cranked Wing." NASA CR-178204 (1987).

Rao, Dhanvada M. "Vortical Flow Management for Improved Configuration Aerodynamics—Recent Experiences." In *Proceedings of the AGARD*

Symposium on Aerodynamics of Vortical Type Flows in Three Dimensions. AGARD CP-342 (1983).

Reed, Wilmer H. III. "Aeroelasticity Matters: Some Reflections on Two Decades of Testing in the NASA Langley Transonic Dynamics Tunnel." NASA TM 83210 (September 1981).

Richard, Susan J., Anthony E. Washburn, Martin J. Morris, and John F. Donovan. "Pressure Sensitive Paint Studies of Vortical Flow at Low Speed." Presented at the SAE Aerotech 95 Symposium, Los Angeles, CA, September 18–21, 1995. SAE Technical Paper 951989 (1995).

Richardson, Doug. "F-16 Fighting Falcon." In *The Great Book of Modern Warplanes.* London: Salamander Books Ltd., 2000.

Ritchie, Steve. "An Eagle for All Arenas." *Air Force Magazine* 66, no. 11 (November 1983).

Rivers, Robert A. "NASA's Flight Test of the Russian Tu-144 SST." Case 15 in *NASA's Contributions to Aeronautics*, edited by Richard P. Hallion. Washington, DC: NASA SP-2010-570-Vol 2 (2010).

Rizzi, Arthur, Adam Jirasek, John Lamar, Simone Crippa, Kenneth Badcock, and Okko Boelens. "Lessons Learned from Numerical Simulations of the F-16XL Aircraft at Flight Conditions." *Journal of Aircraft* 46, no. 2 (February 2009): 423–441.

Rizzi, Arthur, K. Badcock, A. Jirasek, and O. Boelens. "What Was Learned from Numerical Simulations of F-16XL (CAWAPI) at Flight Conditions." Presented at the 45th Aerospace Sciences Meeting and Exhibit, Reno, NV, January 8–11, 2007. AIAA Paper 2007-0683 (2007).

Robinson, Clarence A. "Air Force to Develop New Fighter." *Aviation Week & Space Technology* (March 30, 1981).

Robinson, Clarence A. "USAF Pushes Production, Performance." *Aviation Week & Space Technology* (March 16, 1981).

Robinson, Clarence A. "USAF Studies Fighters for Dual-Role, All-Weather Operations." *Aviation Week & Space Technology* (January 3, 1983).

Ropelewski, Robert R. "F-16XL Shows Advances in Range, Ride and Flying Qualities." *Aviation Week & Space Technology* (September 26, 1983).

Rosenbaum, Robert. "Survey of Aircraft Subcritical Flutter Testing Methods." NASA CR-132479 (August 1974).

Russ, Robert D., Lt. Gen., USAF. "The Fighter Roadmap." *Air Force Magazine* 67, no. 6 (June 1984).

Russ, Robert D., Maj. Gen., USAF. "Tactical Fighter Development: We Have Debated Long Enough." *Air Force Magazine* 64, no. 4 (April 1981).

Saounatsos, Yorgo E. "Technology Readiness and Development Risks of the New Supersonic Transport." *Journal of Aerospace Engineering* 11, no. 3 (July 1998): 95–104.

Scofield, Jan W., Sheryl R. Scott, and Edwin A. Thomas. "F-16XL Phase I Flying Qualities Evaluation—Final Report." Air Force Flight Test Center Technical Report TR-83-26 (September 1983).

Scott, William B. "Dryden Readies F-16XL for Flight." *Aviation Week & Space Technology* (March 20, 1995).

Scott, William B. "NASA-Led Team to Study Supersonic Laminar Flow." *Aviation Week & Space Technology* (November 2, 1992).

Shrout, B.L. "Aerodynamic Characteristics at Mach Numbers from 0.6 to 2.16 of a Supersonic Cruise Fighter Configuration with a Design Mach Number of 1.8." NASA TM X-3559 (September 1977).

Skantze, Lawrence A., Lt. Gen., USAF. "Headquarters Aeronautical Systems Division (AFSC)." Letter to Mr. Richard E. Adams, Vice President and General Manager, General Dynamics Corporation, October 15, 1980.

Smith, Bruce A. "Dryden Analyses Test Section Problem." *Aviation Week & Space Technology* (November 6, 1995).

Smith, Bruce A. "F-16XL Flights Could Aid in HSCT Design." *Aviation Week & Space Technology* (October 23, 1995).

Smith, Bruce A. "Laminar Flow Data Evaluated." *Aviation Week & Space Technology* (October 7, 1996).

Smith, C.W., J.F. Campbell, and J.K. Huffman. "Experimental Results of a Leading-Edge Vortex Flap on a Highly Swept Cranked Wing." In *Tactical Aircraft Research and Technology*. NASA CP-2162 (1980): 563–580.

Smith, John W., and Terry Montgomery. "Biomechanically Induced and Controller Coupled Oscillations Experienced on the F-16XL During Rolling Maneuvers." NASA TM-4752 (1996).

Smith, Kenneth L., W. Bernie Kerr, and Gary L. Hartmann. "Design Methods for Integrated Control System, Phases I and II." Air Force Wright Aeronautical Laboratory Technical Report TR-84-2088 (April 1984).

Spearman, M. Leroy. "The Evolution of the High-Speed Civil Transport." Presented at the AIAA Aircraft Design, Systems, and Operations Meeting, Monterey, CA, August 11–13, 1993. NASA TM-109089 (February 1994).

Spellman, M.W. "Model and Test Information Report 1/9-Scale F-16E Force and Loads Model." General Dynamics Corp. Report No. 400PR026 (August 1981).

Stachowiak, Susan J., and John T. Bosworth. "Flight Test Results for the F-16XL with a Digital Flight Control System." NASA TP-2004-212046 (March 2004).

Sweetman, W. "F-16XL: GD Hatches a New Falcon." *Interavia* 38 (July 1983): 747–748.

Talty, Patrick K., and Donald J. Caughlin. "F-16XL Demonstrates New Capabilities in Flight Test at Edwards Air Force Base." *Journal of Aircraft* 25, no. 3 (March 1988): 206–215.

Talty, Patrick K., Maj., USAF. "F-16XL Demonstrates New Capabilities in its Flight Test Program at Edwards AFB, California." Air Command and Staff College. Report Number 86-2490 (April 1986).

Thompson, Mark. "F-16 Begins Scrap for Air Force Contract." *Fort Worth Star-Telegram*, August 29, 1982.

Tierney, Sheryl Scott. "F-16XL Follow-On Development Flying Qualities Evaluation." Air Force Flight Test Center Technical Report TR-85-31 (November 1985).

Tierney, Sheryl Scott. "Inflight Excitation of the F-16XL." Third AHS, CASI, DGLR, IES, ISA, ITEA, SETP, and SFTE Flight Testing Conference, Las Vegas, NV, April 2–4, 1986. AIAA Paper 86-9782 (1986).

Ulsamer, Edgar. "A Roadmap to Tomorrow's Tactical Airpower." *Air Force Magazine* 66, no. 12 (December 1983).

Ulsamer, Edgar. "In Aeronautics Affordability is King." *Air Force Magazine* 63, no. 12 (December 1980).

Ulsamer, Edgar. "In Focus: The Dual Role Eagle—USAF Chooses the F-15E as Derivative Fighter." *Air Force Magazine* 67, no. 4 (April 1984).

Ulsamer, Edgar. "Scoping the Technology Baseline." *Air Force Magazine* 65, no. 12 (December 1982).

USAF. "F-16C/D Blocks 25, 30, and 32 Flight Manual." USAF Technical Order (T.O.) 1F-16C-1, May 14 (1990).

USAF. "TACAIR Dual Role Fighter Requirement Briefing for the House Armed Services Committee Research and Development Subcommittee." USAF Tactical Air Command, March 24, 1982.

Valasek, John, and Lawrence A. Walchli. "High Speed, Low Angle-of-Attack Pneumatic Vortex Control." AIAA Papers 98-4449 and A98-37266 (1998).

Vernon, Lura. "In-Flight Investigation of a Rotating Cylinder-Based Structural Excitation System for Flutter Testing." AIAA Paper 93-1537 (1993).

Vernon, Lura. "In-Flight Investigation of a Rotating Cylinder-Based Structural Excitation System for Flutter Testing." NASA TM-4512 (January 1993).

Voracek, David F. "Ground Vibration and Flight Flutter Tests of the Single-Seat F-16XL Aircraft with a Modified Wing." NASA TM-104264 (June 1993).

Wagner, R.D., M.C. Fischer, F.S. Collier, Jr., and W. Pfenninger. "Supersonic Laminar Flow Control on Commercial Transports." In *Proceedings of the 17th Congress of the International Council of the Aeronautical Sciences*, 1990.

Wang, Zhongjun, C. Edward Lan, and Jay M. Brandon. "Unsteady Aerodynamic Effects on the Flying Characteristics of an F-16XL Configuration." Presented at the AIAA Atmospheric Flight Mechanics Conference, Denver, CO, August 14–17, 2000. AIAA Paper 2000-3910 (2000).

Warwick, Graham. "Beyond the N-Wave: Modifying NASA's Arrow-Wing F-16XL Could Help Pave the Way for Low-Boom Supersonic Transports." *Aviation Week & Space Technology* (March 23, 2009).

Warwick, Graham. "Boeing Studies F-16XL Low-Sonic-Boom Demonstrator." *Aviation Week & Space Technology* (March 23, 2009).

Warwick, Graham. "US Fighter Options." *Flight International* (July 16, 1983).

Wetherall, Robert J. "F-16XL First Flight Anniversary Celebration: The GD Years." Presentation given at the F-16XL First Flight 25th Anniversary Celebration, Lockheed Martin Corporation, Fort Worth, TX, July 3, 2007.

Wetherall, Robert J. "F-16XL First Flight Anniversary Celebration: The NASA Years." Presentation given at the F-16XL First Flight 25th Anniversary Celebration, Lockheed Martin Corporation, Fort Worth, TX, July 3, 2007.

Whipple, R.D., and W.L. White. "Spin-Tunnel Investigation of a 1/25th Scale Model of the General Dynamics F-16XL Airplane." NASA-TM-85660 (October 1, 1984).

Whitt, Justin. "Computational Modeling of Steady, Compressible, Viscous Flow for the F-16XL Fighter Aircraft." The University of Tennessee at Chattanooga, November 5, 2006.

Wilhite, Alan W., and Robert J. Shaw. "An Overview of NASA's High Speed Research Program." In *Proceedings of the 22nd International Congress of Aeronautical Sciences*. Harrowgate, United Kingdom: August 27, 2000.

Woan, C.J., P.B. Gingrich, and M.W. George. "Validation of a Supersonic Laminar Flow Concept." Presented at the AIAA 29th Aerospace Sciences Meeting, Reno, NV, January 1991. AIAA Paper 1991-0188 (1991).

Young, James O. *History of the Air Force Flight Test Center, 1 Jan 1982—31 Dec 1982, Volume I.* Edwards AFB, CA: Air Force Flight Test Center, 1983.

James O. Young. *History of the Air Force Flight Test Center, 1 Jan 1983—30 Sep 1984, Volume I.* Edwards AFB, CA: Air Force Flight Test Center, 1984.

Zhiwei, Shi, Huang Da, Wu Genxing, and Gong Zheng. "Effects of Coupled Motion Unsteady Aerodynamic Model on Flight Characteristics Simulation of Aircraft." *Acta Aeronautica et Astronautica Sinica* 29, no. 6 (November 25, 2008): 1424–1428.

About the Author

Albert C. Piccirillo is a retired Air Force colonel with 3,000 flying hours, mostly in fighters. His experience includes assignments in research and development, ground and flight test, fighter operations, and program management involving aircraft, engines, guided missiles, and avionics systems. As Advanced Tactical Fighter system program director, he headed the Air Force conceptual development effort and the subsequent source selection that resulted in the selection of Lockheed and Northrop for design and flight test of the YF-22 and YF-23 air superiority fighter prototypes. Previously, he managed several advanced weapons development programs and headed an engineering unit responsible for flight testing of uncrewed aircraft. Operational and research and development duties included combat tours in the F-4 fighter during the Vietnam War and assignments with the Naval Aircraft Engine Laboratory, the Aircraft Propulsion Division of the General Electric Company, the Air Force Flight Test Center, the USAF Aeronautical Systems Division, and Air Force Studies and Analyses. He headed the C3 Systems Department at PRC, Inc., and was a principal aerospace engineer and manager of the Joint Technology Division at ANSER, Inc. He is currently an adjunct research staff member at the Institute for Defense Analyses. The author of numerous books and professional papers, Mr. Piccirillo holds a B.S. degree in aeronautical engineering from the Pennsylvania State University and an M.S. degree in aerospace engineering from the Air Force Institute of Technology. He is an associate fellow of the American Institute of Aeronautics and Astronautics.

A wind tunnel test model of a modified F-16 fuselage fitted with a forward-swept wing mounted in the NASA Langley Unitary Plan Wind Tunnel in 1980. (NASA)

Index

Page numbers in **bold** indicate pages with illustrations.
A reference to an endnote is indicated with an "n" after an entry's page number.

C

E